THE
HERMETIC MARRIAGE
OF
ART AND ALCHEMY

"*The Hermetic Marriage of Art and Alchemy* is a sumptuous examination of where our relationship with imagination and our capacity to create intersects with the spiritual and psychic realms. Bremner provides a rich look at the historical movements that have transformed the modern artistic and esoteric landscapes while providing the reader with an in-depth exploration of creation itself. A fantastic guide for both the artist and magical practitioner alike!"

LAURA TEMPEST ZAKROFF, AUTHOR OF
SIGIL WITCHERY AND *VISUAL ALCHEMY*

"The past decade has witnessed a resurgence of interest in the art and philosophy of Hermeticism, especially among seekers searching for keys to unlock the arcana shrouding this mysterious art. Artist Marlene Seven Bremner makes a significant contribution to this study with *The Hermetic Marriage of Art and Alchemy,* a book rich in colorful illustrations, poignant imagery, and penetrating analysis. Written in a clear and easy-to-understand language that will appeal both to the specialist and the curious alike. This scholarly work is certain to please connoisseurs of the Royal Art with a useful aid to reference, time and again, on decoding the mysteries of life."

DAVID PANTANO, TRANSLATOR OF
THE HERMETIC PHYSICIAN AND AUTHOR OF
THE MAGIC DOOR: A STUDY ON THE ITALIC HERMETIC TRADITION

"When people use terms like 'magical' to describe the work of the imagination they are straying much closer than they know to some of the deepest secrets of human existence. Those secrets are the alchemical prima materia of Marlene Seven Bremner's latest book. Capably researched, vividly illustrated, and trenchantly argued, this is a treat for those who know their way around the realm of the magical imagination and a revelation for those who are just setting foot on that potent and life-affirming path."

JOHN MICHAEL GREER, AUTHOR OF
THE TWILIGHT OF PLUTO AND *THE DRUID PATH*

"In 2022 Marlene's first book, *Hermetic Philosophy and Creative Alchemy,* was one of the great discoveries of the year for me. And this new volume makes me all excited again! I would not call it a sequel but a way of going deeper into that magical realm, where alchemical thinking and practice meet the art world. And what she tells us here—again with astonishing clarity for such a complex matter—is true for the visual arts but also for the performing arts, writing, and other forms of creativity. Another gem from Marlene Seven Bremner, including the wonderful paintings that accompany the book."

RUDOLF BERGER, PERFORMING ARTS PROFESSIONAL
AND CREATOR OF THE *THOTH HERMES PODCAST*

"A remarkable work in scope and depth that explores art as alchemy, Bremner provides the ground for a much-needed discussion on the esoteric currents that have surfaced throughout various art movements such as Symbolism, Dada, and Surrealism. And in doing so, she articulates the basic premise of alchemy—that all creations arise from the same principles. Then, using these alchemical principles and processes, Bremner shows how to incorporate them into your work with clear, insightful descriptions of exercises for the artist/alchemist. *The Hermetic Marriage of Art and Alchemy* is a 'must-have' for anyone seriously working in or investigating the intersection of art and alchemy."

BRIAN COTNOIR, AUTHOR OF *PRACTICAL ALCHEMY,*
ALCHEMY: THE POETRY OF MATTER, AND *ON ALCHEMY*

"Bremner envisions the integration of the modern-day practice of creative alchemy with a deep understanding of its representations in the visual and poetic arts. By locating imagination at the center, Bremner makes evident the hidden connections between alchemy and artists whose gaze initiates psychological change and spiritual evolution. This book is both an esoteric meditation and a feminist call to reclaim personal authority over consciousness and reject hierarchical ideologies in favor of personal exploration. This book is a must-read for historians of ideas, the arts, and practitioners of the esoteric."

LESLIE KORN, PH.D., M.P.H., AUTHOR OF *RHYTHMS OF RECOVERY*

"*The Hermetic Marriage of Art and Alchemy* is an unprecedented work in decoding the opacity of alchemical allegory and charting the pervasive cultural influence of esotericism. Its rich imagery discloses the intimate mechanisms of modernism within a panoramic assimilation of occult philosophy. Bremner evokes a textured interpretation of ancient arcana through informed and embodied knowledge of their processes, imparting effectual praxis for sacred operations that impel the reader toward spiritual and creative actualization."

MICKI PELLERANO, ARTIST, ASTROLOGER,
AND HOST OF *TIME LORD TV*

THE
HERMETIC MARRIAGE
OF
ART AND ALCHEMY

IMAGINATION, CREATIVITY,
and the GREAT WORK

MARLENE SEVEN BREMNER

Inner Traditions
Rochester, Vermont

Inner Traditions
One Park Street
Rochester, Vermont 05767
www.InnerTraditions.com

Cataloging-in-Publication Data for this title is available from the Library of Congress

ISBN 978-1-64411-290-8 (print)
ISBN 978-1-64411-291-5 (ebook)

Printed and bound in China by Reliance Printing Co., Ltd.

10 9 8 7 6 5 4 3 2 1

Text design and layout by Virginia Scott Bowman
This book was typeset in Garamond Premier Pro, Gill Sans, and Legacy Sans with Harmonique used as the display typeface

To send correspondence to the author of this book, mail a first-class letter to the author c/o Inner Traditions • Bear & Company, One Park Street, Rochester, VT 05767, and we will forward the communication, or contact the author directly at **www.marlenesevenbremner.com**.

To my mother

The Mirror of Art and Nature: top level, the primal pair of the eagle and lion and the transformation of *prima materia* (nature) to *ultima materia* (art); middle level, diagrams of elemental transmutation; lower level, the alchemist performing distillation and calcination. Engraving by R. Custos, 1616.

Courtesy of Wellcome Collection

Contents

Acknowledgments

Embarking on the great work of writing this book has been a life changing experience, requiring an immense amount of focus, determination, and inner struggle, and many years of dedication. While I've spent the majority of that time alone at my desk and buried in books, I could not have done this without the many people who have believed in me and supported me in great and small ways. This book was originally conceived in conjunction with my previous book, *Hermetic Philosophy and Creative Alchemy: The Emerald Tablet, the Corpus Hermeticum, and the Journey through the Seven Spheres*. Therefore, I'd first like to extend my gratitude to all those I acknowledged in that book, and include here a few others that specifically contributed in some way to the completion of this present book.

I would like to thank the entire team at Inner Traditions for their hard work in bringing this book to its completion. In particular, VP and Editor in Chief Jeanie Levitan and Acquisitions Editor Jon Graham, for believing in me and giving me the opportunity to share this vision with the world; Assistant to Editor in Chief Patricia Rydle, for her guidance and assistance throughout the completion of both books; my Publicist Manzanita Carpenter for her hard work with marketing; and my Project Editor Renée Heitman for her invaluable editing work.

I am privileged to have many loyal patrons of my work who stuck by me as I took time to complete this work. The endless hours of research, writing, and revision would not have been possible without their continued support. It hasn't been easy to balance writing full-time with the demands of being a self-employed artist, and I'm incredibly grateful to all the wonderful people who have contributed to keeping me fed and housed over these last several years. I would especially like to thank a few dear friends and loyal supporters, who made substantial financial contributions, some who also provided invaluable feedback and reviews of the book: Rich Lilly, one of the kindest and most giving people I have ever known; Gregory Copley, a dear and wise friend who so generously supported me through the hardest months; Breeana Giesy, for her sweet friendship and continual support along the way; Bob Brzuszek, who once again offered his expert feedback regarding my chapters on Dada and Surrealism, in addition his long-standing patronage; Kelly Murphy, for her incredible friendship, financial support, and truly helpful feedback on the *Albedo* chapter; Kenzie Cagle, a wonderful friend who has made such a substantial contribution to my work for many years; Mark F. Barone, friend, teacher, contributor, and spiritual support who helped me navigate the emotional ups and downs of my long and lonely desert hermitage, as well as provided his keen eye in editorial review of the *Citrinitas* chapter; Rev. Dr. Richard William Banach, my sweet friend who has always believed in me and preserved me in the Great Work, and who provided a thoughtful review of two chapters; and my father Steve Bremner, a true inspiration to me, for his support, kind review of two chapters, and for getting me out on a great rafting adventure in the midst of my serious endeavors.

Though I have spent most of the the last two years in Hermetic seclusion, I have so many friends near and far that have been there for me, and for that I am deeply grateful. Once again I am extremely indebted to Russell Moore, a lovely human being and a true friend who has stood by me through the writing process. His peaceful ranch and the solitude it provides have been invaluable for such an all-consuming endeavor. Many thanks as well to Nathan Gay, a dear friend and fellow Hermeticist. Thank you to my beautiful friend June Kerseg-Hinson, whose brilliant light came into my life all because of a broken cup. I'd also like to give a warm thanks to Jonah Emerson Bell for his editorial assistance and for being by my side during the final weeks of completing this book. His encouragement and belief in my work have given me strength through the most difficult final stages of revision.

Finally, I would like to thank all the alchemists, artists, and scholars who have inspired and informed the writing of this book, for their dedication to their craft and the gift they have imparted to the world. We are all part of the creative energy of the universe, connected through time and space, and I hope that in some small way I am honoring their legacies while contributing to the continual evolution of Hermetic wisdom and artistic vision.

INTRODUCTION
Imaginatio Vera

In the heart of every individual slumbers an artist, a poet, which we must know how to awaken.

—Jean Delville, *The New Mission*

All things have their origin in the imagination, through which we commune with the greater story of the cosmos. Imagination is a divine faculty, the greatest gift of our human existence; however, its expression is often frustrated, and its importance grossly underestimated. Though artists, alchemists, and sages throughout the centuries have recognized the true power of imagination, it must compete with the pervading rational, materialistic, and realist paradigm. Since the Enlightenment—the Age of Reason—the subjective experiences of the imagination, dreams, and feelings have been relegated to the realm of the "unreal."

Alchemy and other occult mysteries were a significant influence upon the great art movements of the nineteenth and twentieth centuries, from Romanticism to Surrealism, as artists sought to reclaim the true power of the imagination from the grips of classicism, naturalism, rationalism, materialism, positivism, and nationalism. Alchemy was a link with the medieval past and the Renaissance, the world of myth and possibility, trodden underfoot by the heavy stampede of progress. Science and the Enlightenment heralded the end of an era of supposed naïveté and superstition. What was real, verifiable, solid, objective—this is what the new era valued. Not the subjective impressions of feelings, imaginal realms, and dreams. These repressive tendencies in the name of progress created a backlash in the arts that is still reverberating today over two hundred years

1

later. From the sentimental softening of the Romantic spirit and the dark and mythic ruminations of Symbolism to the complete revolt of Dada and the unconscious revelations of Surrealism, alchemy has played its part in both subtle and overt ways.

The conflation of the word *imaginary* with the "unreal" is why Henry Corbin, scholar of Islamic mysticism and advocate for the imagination's powers of transformation, coined the term *mundus imaginalis,* or the "imaginal world," as a means of breaking through preconceptions, for the unreality of the *imaginary* is deeply ingrained in the collective psyche. This corruption has necessitated the fight to liberate the imagination, dreams, and the unconscious from its subjugation by the "real"; to reassert the value of subjective wisdom and the inner world. Dada and Surrealist artist Jean Arp proclaims, "This tidal wave seems to be breaking now against dreams. The dream is reappearing like a miracle. It contains what it has always contained: imagination, faith, reality."[1] When we allow ourselves to not only acknowledge the power of the inner world, but to integrate it within the creative process of our life, then we become part of this tidal wave and the re-emergence of the dream.

The word *imagination* derives from the Latin *imaginationem,* meaning imagination or "fancy." It is the wondrous capability of the mind to form new ideas; to allow us to see, feel, and hear things in a way that does not require the bodily senses; to form and mold images according to our will. Yet imagination is much more than simple fancy and must be differentiated; it is the means by which the world is constituted and by which we find our self-sameness with One creative Source of all things. Equated with the image-making ability of the mind, as the root of the word *imago* implies "an image" or "a likeness," it is one of the ways we translate the symbols arising from the unconscious, and ultimately connect the conscious and unconscious parts of ourselves.

Through the imagination all things are possible, and it is with this secret and malleable substance that we continually create our lives and the world around us. Throughout the centuries the powers of the *imaginatio* have been well known and revered by alchemists who have sought to create the alchemical holy grail and central goal of alchemy, known as the philosopher's stone, or *lapis philosophorum*. The stone is a symbol of divine consciousness, liberation, wholeness, perfection, and enlightenment, having the power to transmute base metals into gold, to work as a universal panacea, and to bestow immortality. The stone represents the most ennobled expression of our very own wondrous imagination, refined and augmented through the *magnum opus*, or the "Great Work."

In my previous book, *Hermetic Philosophy and Creative Alchemy*, I explored how the Hermetic tradition underlying alchemy posits a view of the cosmos as a unified field of energy, in which all things are connected. The stars are not so far away as they appear, but rather live within us as forces of destiny. By understanding how the stars influence us through polarization, we can learn how to enter a creative state of being in which we become masters of our own fate—what is referred to as *gnosis*, or true self-knowledge. I showed how the Royal Art of alchemy has its deepest roots in ancient Egypt and is much more than the vain pursuit of transmuting lead into gold, associated with charlatans and snake-oil salesmen and with mercury-poisoned madmen obsessed by their pursuits in their laboratories. Much work has been done to retrieve the rich tradition of alchemy out of the dung heap of ignorance, and to show not only the validity of its technical aims, but to reveal its profound spiritual wisdom. The knowledge of alchemy can be traced back to the ibis-headed god of the Egyptians, known as Thoth, who brought humanity the wisdom of the Sun, the Moon, and the stars. Thoth's worship goes back to the earliest times in Egypt, and in the Hellenistic era (331–323 BCE) Thoth was syncretized with the Greek god Hermes, becoming *Hermes Trismegistus*, or Hermes "Thrice-Greatest."

My previous book examined in depth one of the most renowned texts of the Hermetic and alchemical tradition, known as the *Tabula Smaragdina*, or the *Emerald Tablet of Hermes*, a short treatise that provides a doctrine of unity and a concise poetic conception of creation. Its most essential precept is that "all things were from one,"[2] also referred to as the "One Thing." In alchemical theory, great importance is placed upon microcosmic and macrocosmic relationships—the human and earthly realm below, and the celestial realm of the gods and heaven above. All things are considered as emanating from a unified source, variously called God, the One, the Good, the Supreme, the Absolute, Consciousness, Truth, and many other names. From this ineffable unity the primal forces of the opposites emerge, moving by involution and increasing levels of density into matter, eventually returning by a process of evolution back to Source. This endless cycle of regeneration is depicted alchemically by the ouroboros, the snake in the form of a circle consuming its own tail.

The One Thing is the imagination, which connects the Above and Below in a continual creation, the *creatio continua*. In its original state the One Thing is known as the *prima materia,* or "primal matter," the first matter, mother, and source of all things. Within this undifferentiated consciousness exist all the elements of matter in a state of latent potential. It is a *massa confusa,* the confused mass of chaos that precedes creation. Our great work is to break this open and transform its latent potentiality into the *ultima materia,* or final matter of the stone. Born out of the primal matter, the *lapis philosophorum* also contains within it the powers of the four elements from which all things are formed— Earth, Water, Fire, and Air. When brought to perfection, the *lapis* is true imagination, the *imaginatio vera,* wielding the powers of the elements to transmute consciousness and matter. In this book I will take you through a practical approach to creative alchemy to discover the secret of the philosopher's stone and to unlock the full potential of your personal and unique creative genius. This is a process of self-discovery, healing, self-transformation, and mystical union with the Eternal Self.

True imagination is not fantasy, but imagination in its most exalted form. It is a divine gift, the same image-making power of the Creator by which the world is formed. Through harnessing the *imaginatio vera* we come to know ourselves as co-creators with the universe itself. In fact, the *imaginatio* is defined as "the Star in Man, the Celestial or Supercelestial Body," by Rulandus the Elder in his *Lexicon of Alchemy*.[3] The fifteenth-century Swiss alchemist, naturalist, physician, theologian, and philosopher, Paracelsus, or Theophrastus Bombastus von Hohenheim (1493–1541), proposed that every person has an interior aspect that he called the "invisible man," hidden from the visible aspects of the senses and thoughts and superior to them, and accessible only through the imagination.[4] It is invisible because it is only known through its effects, relating to the veiled aspect of the unconscious, which can only be indirectly accessed. Corresponding to the astral body, this invisible man is the subtle body where the stars exert their celestial influence, and through which the human being has the great power to affect the stars in turn. Through various psycho-spiritual processes of purification and refinement upon this invisible body, the alchemist activates the "true imagination" by which the marvelous reveals itself in every aspect of life.

Paracelsus had a great many things to say about the imagination, including how the imagination of a pregnant woman could affect the development of the child within her; how imagination can be directed at others for good or for bad; and further, that one can use imagination and a pious attitude to divert the negative effects of a bad imagination.[5] This is possible because, as he says, "Imagination acts through magnetic attraction on an object in the outside world."[6] He explains how "the intention of imagination kindles the vegetative faculty as the fire kindles wood," acting as the motive power of the body.[7] The imagination is the most powerful instrument at our disposal, having influence over health and sickness, success and failure, life and death.[8] The great occultist Éliphas Lévi echoed this sentiment:

> Imagination, in effect, is like the soul's eye; therein forms are outlined and preserved; thereby we behold the reflections of the invisible world; it is the glass of visions and the apparatus of magical life. By its intervention we heal diseases, modify the seasons, warn off death from the living and raise the dead to life, because it is the imagination which exalts will and gives it power over the Universal Agent. Imagination determines the shape of the child in its mother's womb and decides the destiny of men; it lends wings to contagion and directs the arms of warfare.[9]

It is not just the alchemists and occultists that extoll the virtues and powers of the properly directed imagination. We also find this view in the teachings of Lao Tzu, who advises, "Have in your hold the great image and the empire will come to you."[10] In the esoteric Christian mysticism of Neville Goddard, he interprets scripture as a divine initiation into the powers of imagination. For example, regarding the sixty-fourth chapter of the book of Isaiah, which reads, "O Lord, Thou art our Father. We are the clay. Thou art our Potter. We are the work of Thy hand," Goddard says:

> The word translated the "lord" is "I AM." That is our Father; and you can't put "I AM" away from yourself. Now, the word translated "potter" is "imagination." He didn't say, "the potter,"—"our Potter." . . . So here, my own wonderful human imagination is now identified with the Lord. It's the word "Jehovah." And this is called the "father." So, I am Self-begotten. We are self-begotten. We're not the product of something other than ourselves. These terms are interchangeable: "the Lord," "Father," "Potter," "Imagination;" For "potter" is defined in the Concordance as "imagination; that which forms or molds into form; that which makes a resolution; that which determines."*[11]

According to Goddard, God is "our own wonderful human imagination."[12] The Christian apologist and author C. S. Lewis asserts that "human will becomes truly creative and truly our own when it is wholly God's, and this is one of the many senses in which he that loses his soul shall find it. . . . When we act from ourselves alone—that is, from God in ourselves—we are collaborators in, or live instruments of, creation."[13] This notion that our true creative power and imagination unifies us with God as formative co-creators of the universe is reflected in a message received by Gitta Mallasz. A survivor of the Nazi Holocaust in Hungary, Gitta and her friends had the transcendant experience of receiving angelic communications regarding the role of the human being in uniting the above and below.[14] The following is a transcription of one of her communications, beginning with the angel's words

---

*Underline present in the original.

in capital letters, her response as "G," and a description of the medium's bodily reaction to the transmission:

YOU ARE THE ONE WHO FORMS—
NOT THE FORMED.
G. What must I do to become *the one who forms?*

Now Hanna's body seems to lose its usual qualities and transform into an instrument serving totally, with nothing held back: her movements are simple, meaningful, and dignified. Even her arm seems different to me. It radiates concentrated force, the muscles tense, and I am strongly reminded of Michelangelo's sculptures. An abrupt gesture strikes like lightning.
—BURN![15]

As this passage implies, it is by enduring the fire that we awaken our true creative, formative powers. With its purifying and transformational effects, fire is the essential element for the completion of the Great Work. As the Polish alchemist and philosopher Michael Sendivogius (1566–1636) advises, "the whole process, from beginning to end, is the work of fire."[16] True imagination is the *secret fire* by which all miraculous transmutations are made possible. As it is written by Paracelsus, "His art should be baptized in the fire; he must have himself been born from the fire, and tested in it seven times and more."[17] At its essence, the fire that transforms us is the fire of love.

THE ROYAL MARRIAGE AND ESSENTIALS OF THE ALCHEMICAL ART

At the heart of alchemy is the search for divine love and unity. As it is asked in the alchemical text *Tractatus Aureus,* "When was there placed before your eyes the idea of most fervent love, the male and the female embracing each other so closely that they could no more be torn asunder, but through unsearchable love became one?"[18] This divine love is an inner mystical union and reconciliation of the polarized forces of the mind: active/passive or conscious/unconscious. These two primary states of energy, active and passive, are sometimes called the celestial niter and celestial salt, or "volatile" and "fixed," relating to the male and female sexual forces that work together in the act of creation. In alchemical imagery they are often depicted as a King and Queen, *Rex* and *Regina,* or the Sun and Moon, given the Latin names *Sol* and *Luna*. "Its father is the Sun and its mother the Moon," as it says in the *Emerald Tablet*. These primal progenitors are the philosopher's gold and the philosopher's silver, together conceiving the philosopher's stone. They are related to the two principles present in all things, Sulfur—red, male; and Mercury—white, female. Thus the colors red and white are emblematic of the alchemical art, and the union of the Red King and White Queen, known as the sacred marriage or *hieros gamos,* is one of the primary goals of the *magnum opus*. With alchemy's roots in ancient Egypt, the symbolic conjunction of the red and white may be related to the Red Crown of Lower (northern) Egypt and the White Crown of Upper (southern) Egypt, which were united in one double crown known as the *pschent* or *sekhemty,* "the Two Powerful Ones." It symbolized the unification of the Upper and Lower kingdoms under a single ruler. The Red and White Crowns were also correlated with the solar and lunar eyes.

Salt was introduced by Paracelsus as a third principle, corresponding to the *corpus,* or body. Together these three form the alchemical trinity of Body (Salt), Mind (Mercury, or Spirit), and Soul (Sulfur), also called the three essentials. In psychological terms, these correlate with the cognitive functions of sensation, intellect, and imagination, and they all must work together for the wholeness of the individual to be realized. The body, or *corpus,* is that which holds things together in the way that salt forms a solid structure. Within the matrix of the body are the two primal forces born of one blood—Sulfur and Mercury. Mercury, or the *spiritus,* is like the breath or *pneuma* that enlivens the body and infuses it with spiritual and philosophical consciousness. Spirit is closely aligned with *Logos*. Sulfur, or the *soul,* also called *anima,* is that which *animates* the body—it is fiery, propulsive, and expansive. Soul is closely aligned with *Eros*.

Also essential to alchemy is an understanding of the four elements: Earth, Water, Fire, and Air, all of which are present in the *prima materia* in an undifferentiated state. In the world of matter—energy in various states of vibration—the four elements are present in varying proportions. Earth and Water represent the fixed aspect, while Fire and Air relate to the volatile. The three essentials—Salt, Mercury, and Sulfur—evolve out of the four elements. Salt corresponds to the fixed elements Earth and Water; Sulfur to the volatile Air and Fire; and Mercury, being of a neutral quality that can be both fixed and volatile, corresponds to Water and Air.

Mercury and Sulfur form their own polarity as the primal pair held within the structured Salt of the body. Yet Sulfur, being equated with the active/volatile principle of life, is also the polar opposite of Salt, equated with passive/fixed qualities of matter. Mercury, sharing in the nature of both, forms a link between Sulfur and Salt. Think of this as consciousness and matter. Consciousness correlates with the heavenly realms. Within the material body, the unconscious or "invisible" part of us resides, yet it makes itself known to the conscious mind in subtle ways. It is like the underworld, and Mercury, as the messenger of the gods, is endowed with the power to traverse both the heavens and the underworld. The conscious and unconscious mind are often in conflict; the ego tends to suppress the irrational upwellings of the unconscious, which evades understanding by the conscious mind. Yet as it is written in the *Emerald Tablet,* "that which is above is from that which is below, and that which is below is from that which is above, working the miracles of one."[19] Therefore these opposites are ultimately of the same unified nature, and the Great Work of alchemy guides us in their reconciliation.

The unconscious is like the *prima materia,* the primal source of all creative potential. In alchemy, it is the secret matter from which the work begins, the mother of the *lapis philosophorum,* and its opening signifies the beginning of the Great Work. How do we go about breaking open this vast storehouse of our innate creative potential? Often depicted as an egg, the *prima materia* can be cracked open in different ways. Sometimes it is with a sword, a symbol of the conscious mind that breaks it open and releases its contents into awareness. Sometimes it is through alchemical digestion that the *prima materia* is softened and opened, through a slow breakdown of its component parts into an assimilable form. In other cases, it is by fire, and in others by water, or by the serpent who coils around it and breaks it open by its embrace of desire. In any case the *lapis,* the secret matter of alchemy, is to be found within, as the "Old Hermit of Jerusalem" Morienus (fifth century) tells us that "this matter comes from you, who are yourself its source, where it is found and whence it is taken."[20] It is an inner journey that takes us to the depths of the soul.

There are worlds within the unconscious, elemental chaos and forces of which may be expressed in both creative and destructive ways. The more we can shine the light of consciousness into the dark waters, uniting the above and below, the more creative control we have over how these forces shape our lives. However, as long as we remain disconnected from the unconscious, we are at the mercy of the seven principal rulers that govern fate. These are the seven traditional planets, or wandering stars, visible to the naked eye, each of which corresponds to a different metal: the Sun—*gold;* the Moon—*silver;* Mercury—*quicksilver;* Venus—*copper;* Mars—*iron;* Jupiter—*tin;* and Saturn—*lead.* Of these the Sun and gold are the most noble of them all, correlating with the majesty of the King and the Crown, with divine authority and consciousness. Silver is also a noble metal, correlating with the Moon and the exalted Queen of the unconscious. Within all of the metals the three principles are present; their proportions determine the relative purity or corruption of the metals. Through the royal art the three principles can be brought to balance, transmuting the corrupted metals into the noble silver and gold. As we will explore in part II of this book, these seven metals exist within the subtle body as seven energetic centers. They are like gateways between the conscious and unconscious and can be accessed through the imagination.

ART, ALCHEMY, AND THE UNCONSCIOUS

Sigmund Freud developed a vertical model of the mind that has been compared to an iceberg; we are only able to see directly that small portion of the iceberg that lies above the surface, "the tip of the iceberg," which represents the conscious mind and the subjective ego, while the bulk of the iceberg lies below the surface of the water. Just below the surface lies the preconscious mind, which is visible through the water and contains contents that can potentially rise into conscious awareness, for example with "Freudian slips" of the tongue when we say something unintended, or when we behave in irrational or compulsive ways. Further down is the unconscious, that which is not visible to conscious awareness and which functions automatically. The unconscious is a reservoir of hidden or repressed memories, feelings, urges, and thoughts, as well as the source of unconscious behaviors, reactions, phobias, and neuroses. While we may be unaware of these hidden aspects within ourselves, the unconscious none-theless influences consciousness and can be accessed through techniques like hypnosis, free association, and dreamwork. The ways that it manifests itself in our consciousness can be quite dangerous, like the iceberg that sank the *Titanic.*

The Swiss psychoanalyst Carl Jung differentiated between two pri-mary levels of the unconscious—the personal unconscious, realm of the shadow, and the collective unconscious, source of archetypal and mythi-cal symbols that are common to all. The personal unconscious is formed from our lived experiences, like our memories and subconscious material that seeps out into consciousness, and is fed by conscious material trick-ling down into it. The collective unconscious exists at the deepest level of the unconscious. It is the source of ancestral material outside of our per-sonal experience, the inherited collection of deep-seated beliefs, spiritual-ity, instincts, and sexuality. We access the collective unconscious through the personal, and the collective in turn influences the development of the personal unconscious.

The commonality and shared quality of the collective unconscious implies that it is *one,* and out of this collective Oneness each individual and subjective consciousness is constellated.[21] "Such a point of view," writes Jung, "was inaccessible to the alchemist, and having no idea of the theory of knowledge, he had to exteriorize his archetype in the traditional way and lodge it in matter, even though he felt . . . that the centre was paradoxically in man and yet at the same time outside him."[22] Building on the work of Jung, Marie-Louise von Franz asserts that alchemy was "*the* Western way of dealing with what we call today the collective uncon-scious or the objective psyche," projecting their imaginations into their alchemical retorts much like it is projected inward to the subtle body in Indian and Chinese Taoist yoga.[23] The creative works in a similar manner, projecting the unconscious via the imagination into their creations, and thereby externalizing it in a form through which its numinous messages can be understood.

The unconscious speaks in correspondence, symbols, signs, metaphor, synchronicity, and subtle ineffable impressions. It is vague, mysterious, suggestive, and impressionable. Its nature is soft and receptive, awaiting suggestions from the conscious mind and other inputs which it then absorbs into itself, dissolves, and recombines into something new. The more the unconscious is engaged with, the more it will speak and make itself known. It speaks through the body, through aches, pains, and disease to the sweetness of health and subtle energetic tingles and pleasures. It speaks through dreams in the night and longs to reach the conscious mind, leaving little fragments to grasp upon waking or full-on memories of strange and haunting imagery. In our dreams, reveries, and inner visions we become liberated from the constraints of the body, capable of flying or becoming another person or animal. Dreams communicate to us that which is otherwise hidden in the unconscious. Our dream life is fluid and defiant of the laws of physics, logic, and cause and effect that we experience in the waking world, and we are likewise not consciously in control (except in the case of lucid dreaming). This makes for some fascinating material to be investigated by those curious enough to take the time; indeed, dreams were one of the defining inspirations of the Surrealists and their predecessors.

It is not just the imaginary realm that is relegated to the "unreal," but the unconscious itself has been considered relatively inferior or subordinate to the conscious in the field of psychological science. In the article "The Unconscious Mind," John Bargh and Ezequiel Morsella explain that there tends to be a "conscious-centric" bias in the field of psychological science, where the conscious is considered real and the unconscious is a shadow thereof.[24] This is partially due to a conflation of *unconscious* with *subliminal,* rooted in early conceptions of the word that relate it to unintentional behavior. The original meaning of *unconscious* appeared in the early 1800s in relation to hypnotism, as the hypnotized subject was "unconscious," or unaware of the hypnotically induced causes of their own behavior. The word was also used in relation to Darwin's *On the Origin of Species* (1859) to describe "unconscious selection" in nature. Yet the unconscious is an intelligence of nature that allows it to transform and adapt, a quality that research shows extends to humans. As the authors aptly note, "In nature, the 'unconscious mind' is the rule, not the exception."[25]

Freud's theories regarding the unconscious and the dream were a major influence upon the Surrealists. Their aim of fusing together the conscious and unconscious into a new unified state was closely aligned with the goal of the *magnum opus*. They valued irrationality, primitivism, childhood, and insanity; in its primitive state and even up until the Enlightenment (and even in some cultures today), humanity inhabited a surreal world in which dream and "reality" were not so clearly defined. Like within the mind of a child who has not yet been indoctrinated into the world of the rational, symbols are still living entities. In alchemical terms, it is a state of *solutio,* or solution, in which the consciousness is immersed and unified within the greater body of the *prima materia,* the first mother. As the occult artist Austin Osman Spare aptly notes, "Out of the flesh of our mothers come dreams and memories of the Gods."[26] The further we are from this state, the more polarity pulls at us and thrusts us into all kinds of energetic tugs-of-war, perceived to be with the world or with the "other," and yet in truth they are occurring with various "separated" aspects of the self.

To return to a unified conception of the world requires a process of deconditioning. We must dissolve the rigid bonds we have constructed to give order to the world and reconnect with our original nature, and then integrate our subjective experience with the objective by a process of *coagulatio,* or coagulation. Thus the old alchemical axiom *solve et coagula:* to dissolve and coagulate as a process of purification and refinement. Through the projection of the unconscious world of dreams and feelings into the alchemical retort, the alchemist engages in a *participation mystique,* a term coined by Lucien Lévy-Bruhl and used by Jung that refers to the mystical participation, or identification between a subject and object—a blending of the inner world of fantasies, personal associations, symbols, dreams, and mythological motifs with the external world of people, places, and objects. By reconnecting with this unified vision of reality, the alchemist can observe the close relationship between consciousness and matter.

This has been considered by some to be an alchemical form of meditation and was compared by Jung with his process of "active imagination," which involves confronting the fantasies of the unconscious through visualization.[27] In much the same way, the artist projects the contents of their inner world into their creation, and a dialogue unfolds. To be *inspired* is to be filled with the spirit that dissolves the boundaries between the inner and the outer world, for the *spirit* is the universal solvent—philosophical Mercury, the waters of the wise. The messenger of the gods, Mercury is the link between soul and body, consciousness and matter, and the method he uses to communicate is through the language of symbols and poetry. In this way, the artist is submersed and dissolved in the imaginal realm, the *prima materia;* the other part of the formula, coagulation, is the ability to create, to bring *idea* into *form* in the material world. As Hermes teaches, "Coming to be is nothing but imagination."[28] The philosopher's stone is like a key that unlocks the gateway to the imaginal world, allowing us to inhabit a state of uninhibited flow between within and without, above and below, the higher Self and Ego.

Through the union of art and alchemy, an artist of any medium can come to reach the goal of the *magnum opus.* Both the artist and the alchemist are continually purifying and refining their work, separating the pure from the impure, and bringing it to its ultimate perfection. Like the creative process, the alchemical *opus* moves through various stages through which both the alchemist and artist, and their "matter," are transformed. As Paracelsus defines it, "Alchemy is the art that separates what is useful from what is not by transforming it into its ultimate matter and essence."[29] Because the outer reflects the inner, this is also an inner process of spiritual transformation and the realization of inner mystical union, *unio mystica,* equivalent to the Hermetic concept of gnosis, true self-knowledge, or to Jung's concept of individuation, a life-long process resulting in the individual's self-actualization and attainment of spiritual completion. This work takes place creatively, spiritually, psychologically, and energetically. Alchemy is the Royal Art of transforming the Self into its very own masterpiece, to realize that the Self is the Supreme

Being, the One Thing, the *ultima materia,* or "ultimate matter."

Visual art, poetry, and allegory have played an important role in illustrating alchemical operations and philosophies in the alchemical tradition. With symbolism and correspondence, alchemical art speaks directly to the unconscious, working in tandem with alchemical discourse to reach deeply into the Mind, Body, and Soul. The art of the alchemists was as much literary and poetic as it was pictorial. We think of Ripley's enigmatic poetry in the *Twelve Gates* and Michael Maier's epigrams, fugues, and discourses wed with images in *Atalanta Fugiens,* or *The Twelve Keys of Basil Valentine,* the *Splendor Solis* series, the haunting imagery of the *Aurora consurgens,* the *Rosarium Philosophorum, The Book of Pictures* of Zosimos, and the allegorical story of the great work as told in *The Chemical Wedding by Christian Rosencreutz.* In both writing and imagery, alchemy is notoriously enigmatic, partially due to a traditional precedent of concealing the secret art from the profane, and partially to induce in earnest initiates a state of alchemical meditation in which the symbols activate hidden aspects of the psyche.

Alchemy provides a rich tapestry of symbolism from which to draw inspiration. This in and of itself can be a transformative process—to simply study alchemical art and reproduce one's own versions of its themes. However, another layer to the Royal Art is the dialogue that takes place between one's own unconscious world of personal symbology and the external image that is produced. Without the *participation mystique* of the unconscious, nothing significantly new will be born within the artist. From this participatory relationship with reality, the artist and their art are not two separate entities, but one unfolding process, just as the Creator and Created are one and the same. Transformation that occurs within one is reflected in the other.

As previously mentioned, the *hieros gamos,* or sacred marriage of the King and Queen, is one of the primary aims of the alchemical work. This can be understood as the union of the male, fertilizing spirit with the receptive, female body of nature. The conscious and unconscious aspects of Mind, while conceptualized as two different things, one above and one below the surface, are in truth one unified Mind that appears to be separated by duality. Entering into the *participation mystique* is a way of remembering their initial unity, which, through consummation, produces a third aspect of Mind, like Corbin's *mundus imaginalis,* neither conscious nor unconscious but existing as the child of the imagination, otherwise known as the Divine Androgyne: a perfect union of male and female aspects integrated in one body.

The Mercurial child exists in continual creative flow between the conscious and unconscious, finding the neutral center between desire and aversion, attraction and repulsion. It is a childlike curiosity, openness, and imaginative faculty of the Mind that takes over, carefree and uncondi-tioned by the world of set assumptions and limitations. What is external is no longer seen as separate from the individual, but a reflection and/or projection of what is held within. Reality becomes a fluid medium with which to work, and a greater perspective of the one encompassing energy of life mediates reactionary states of mind. To be "in the flow," to be *inspired,* is to be filled with the *spirit* that dissolves obstructions to creative expression, to find the "solution" and receive the visions of unmediated consciousness. As the Symbolist painter and Theosophist Jean Delville writes, "Occult cosmogony teaches that the physical universe is the mate-rialization of the fluid universe. In fact all forms of Nature pre-exist in a fluid state before existing in a state of objective matter."[30]

To undertake the Great Work is to set out on a journey toward self-mastery and merge with the infinite, taking on the responsibility of First Cause and realizing that the beginning and end of all things lies within. Successful mastery of the Self is mirrored in the mastery of one's life and creative endeavors, as the internal processes of transmutation are reflected and projected externally into physical reality. Following the alchemical path attunes the Self to the rhythms of the spheres, so that one is naturally creating in time with the seasons, the spinning of the zodiac, planetary influences, and the environment. Becoming one with the All, the Self exists in effortless flow. This is the essence of creative alchemy, a psycho-spiritual art that purifies the individual self of accumulated unconscious or energetic patterns that inhibit self-expression, vitality, and success in the world, and is a formula for transforming energy into its most ennobled expression.

Energy follows attention. When we focus our attention on a goal, energy begins to move in the direction of its completion. In this work, we bring our attention to the goal of Self-liberation, using alchemical operations to transform, transmute, and transfigure the Self. The energy released in this process then becomes available for the act of creation, our innate gift. In the words of the great Dada and Surrealist artist Marcel Duchamp, "You don't define electricity; you see see electricity as a result, but you can't define it. . . . You see, that is the same thing with art: you know what art does but you don't know what it is. It is a sort of inner current in man, or something which you don't have to define."[31] Creative alchemy is for everyone, because everyone, by the mere fact of being human, is the artistic creator of their own mythic life. As the Supreme Being, the Self is infinitely creative. Whether or not the Self is creating works of art to be experienced with the senses, the Self is nevertheless creating the world around it with imagination, in *creatio continua,* a process that knows no end. Bringing our own creative imagination into alignment with that of the Creator requires a process of purification and exaltation of our primal matter, and the discovery of the *lapis philosophorum.*

Before we approach the *magnum opus,* I would like to take you on a historical journey through four influential art movements of the nineteenth and twentieth centuries: Romanticism, Symbolism, Dada, and Surrealism. In these chapters I will show how the relationship with the unconscious, the subjective, and the imaginal realm has been conceptualized in the past, and how it has evolved; how alchemy and the occult influenced these movements; and how artists of these periods integrated alchemical principles in their work. Their artistry in life, and the potency of the creations that emerged from their struggles against convention and their triumphs, can help us understand our role as artists today. Awakening true imagination and the quest for creative freedom remains a quintessential aspiration of the individual today, as it has been in centuries past. As we move through the *magnum opus* in part II of this book, I will draw upon art and literature from these momentous art movements to illustrate the stages and processes by which we can find the sources of our inner blockages, transmuting them into the *lapis philosophorum,* our creative genius.

PART I

Alchemy and Imagination

❋ ❋ ❋

Beloved imagination, what I most like in you is your unsparing quality.

—ANDRÉ BRETON,
MANIFESTO OF SURREALISM (1924)

1
Romanticism
Irrational Freedom

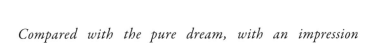

Compared with the pure dream, with an impression unanalyzed, definite art, positive art, is a blasphemy.

—CHARLES BAUDELAIRE

In reaction to religious dogma, traditional authority, superstition, and persecution, the Enlightenment was a necessary swing of the pendulum, seeking to wrest collective consciousness from the grips of religious control, to understand nature outside of the bounds of the church, turning to science and reason. However, science has been no less guilty than the church in the suppression of the unconscious and the collective human shadow, relegating the irrational, imaginative, chimeric, and mythical to arrant insignificance or pathology. The revolutionary movement of Romanticism demanded a rebalancing of the scales, asserting the right of the irrationality of nature, the unseen and the unspoken realities, the world of dreams and subtle impressions, of subjective feelings, and the life principle itself, to stand upon equal ground with what science considers to be verifiable truth. Charles Baudelaire (1821–1867), the French poet and art critic, describes Romanticism as "situated neither in choice of subject nor in exact truth, but in a mode of feeling."[1] It is "intimacy, spirituality, colour, aspiration towards the infinite, expressed by every means available to the arts."[2] Value was placed on intuition, inspiration, and the power of the imagination; on the originality and authenticity of the artist, in reaction against the restraint and sober qualities of Neoclassicism. As Hugh Honour writes, "Romantics were claiming the right to go their own way unhelped and unhindered—in order to develop their individual sensibilities and to express their innermost feelings without regard to, and often in defiance of, theoretical rules and social conventions."[3] This revolutionary current carried on and gained further traction with Symbolism and Surrealism, and the romantic "mode of feeling" has influenced art, literature, and philosophy to the present day.

Surrealism and its aims of realizing the union of dream and reality has its roots in the Romantic movement, beginning at the end of the eighteenth century and flourishing into the middle of the nineteenth century. Though the art and literature of this period was diverse, a common theme was to liberate the imagination and to ignite the emotional world of the artist—also the aim of creative alchemy. Romantic-era artists rebelled against Enlightenment values of reason, order, and rationality, instead favoring sensibility, or strong and violent emotionality that was removed from rational thought. It was a reaction and rebellion against social mores and conventions, against the ugliness of industrialism and the unfeeling world of commerce. What the romantic spirit sought above all was the uninhibited expression of strong, passionate emotionality. For the Romantics, the destructive consequences of such unrestrained passion were of little concern. As Bertrand Russell explicates, those who cast off the social restraints of prudence and surrender to their passions "acquire a new energy and sense of power from the cessation of inner conflict, and, though they may come to disaster in the end, enjoy meanwhile a sense of godlike exaltation which, though known to the great mystics, can never be experienced by a merely pedestrian virtue."[4] Giving free rein to the irrational drives of the unconscious is indeed a way to reconcile the inner conflict that arises when these impulses are suppressed. As such, the Romantic spirit was aligned with the alchemical work of reconciling the opposites, the conscious and unconscious, which rests upon the initial recognition of the shadow, one's inner darkness. It was a return to the self over the collective, the inner over the outer, at first appearing as self-interest, but with time and further exploration emerging as the key to wisdom, transforming through the work into a selfless fountain.

We can see why occult and alchemical influences played a part in forming the worldview of the Romantics, who were enamored by all things exotic, strange, ancient, and faraway: mesmerism, ghosts, Gothic architecture, the Middle Ages, the art of the Orient. Many of these inspirations and the ideas surrounding them were not novel to the Romantic era, but can be traced back to Hermetic philosophy and to Vico and Böhme; the fascination with nature's immense power, esotericism, the supernatural, medieval art and literature, and exoticism were all present in the preceding century and extend back much further.[5] Still, the explosion of new ideas pertaining to art and literature that took the form of Romanticism were of a new and revolutionary nature that continued to evolve.

In contrast to Classical ideals of human sensibility and a mild, harmonious nature, Romanticism emphasized the wild, uncharted, and dangerous aspects of nature, reflecting the intensity of their inner emotional world. They rejected the mechanistic conceptions of nature held in the eighteenth century, emphasizing instead the individual's subjective connection with it. Thus nature was depicted in all of her many moods, from a source of illumination to a destructive and unpredictable force. In the descriptive poetry of John Keats (1795–1821) one finds a tender reverence for nature that is elevated by his transcendent imagination:

> *For what has made the sage or poet write*
> *But the fair paradise of Nature's light?*[6]

Keats was particularly inspired by William Wordsworth (1770–1850), whose poetry so vulnerably reveals the deep reflections of a soul in communion with the natural world and its purifying powers. Wordsworth's autobiographical poem "The Prelude" is considered to be the pinnacle of English Romantic poetry. Yet there was more than a mere reverence for nature in the poetry of the Romantics. Nature was the gateway to an experience of expanded consciousness and unification with the Divine. As James Twitchell asserts in his article "Romanticism and Cosmic Consciousness," the Romantic fascination with cosmic consciousness, present on both sides of the Atlantic, was largely rooted in the poetry of Wordsworth.[7] Indeed, we find such aspirations in the lines of "The Prelude":

> *Not with the mean and vulgar works of man,*
> *But with high objects, with enduring things—*
> *With life and nature—purifying thus*
> *The elements of feeling and of thought,*
> *And sanctifying, by such discipline,*
> *Both pain and fear, until we recognise*
> *A grandeur in the beatings of the heart.*[8]

Wordsworth identifies the eternal wisdom and spirit of the universe with nature, which he attributes with an enduring and purifying quality. By placing the source of the passions of the human soul within those "high objects" and "enduring things," the lowest of these passions are absolved and made holy. In this way Wordsworth exalts the human condition to the divine and heavenly realms through our indelible interconnection with life and nature. As Twitchell elucidates, the Romantics saw nature as a gateway to heightened experiences, but the ultimate goal of the Romantics was "a movement beyond nature to higher levels of awareness, to cosmic consciousness."[9] In this light, Nature is not an end in itself, but that which must be transcended in order to come into contact with the pure awareness of the Self. Twitchell contends that what the Romantics succeeded in doing was to bring experiences that had hitherto been restricted to religious and mystical domain into the literary mainstream.[10] Perhaps the best example of this transcendent experience from Wordsworth is to be found in "Tintern Abbey" (1798), in which he writes of "that blessed mood,"

> *In which the burthen of the mystery,*
> *In which the heavy and the weary weight*
> *Of all this unintelligible world,*
> *Is lightened:—that serene and blessed mood,*
> *In which the affections gently lead us on,—*
> *Until, the breath of this corporeal frame*
> *And even the motion of our human blood*

Almost suspended, we are laid asleep
In body, and become a living soul:
While with an eye made quiet by the power
Of harmony, and the deep power of joy,
We see into the life of things.[11]

This passage, particularly the "eye made quiet" that sees "into the life of things," brings to mind the alchemical notion of the *lumen naturæ,* the light of Nature, spoken of by Paracelsus as that which is imparted to humanity from the stars, the source of all truth and knowledge. It is the hidden, invisible life permeating nature and that which composes it, simultaneously existing within the Self. Sendivogius proclaims that "Nature has her own light, which is not visible to the outward eye." He continues: "[W]here the light of Nature irradiates the mind, this mist is cleared away from the eyes, all difficulties are overcome, and things are seen in their very essence."[12] Paracelsus asserts that the chief study of a philosopher "is the investigation of the operations of Nature," which is "one and indivisible" and whose end and beginning is God.[13] Those who wish to examine Nature ought to be "like unto Nature herself . . . truthful, simple, patient, and persevering."[14] Like the Romantics who perceived the infinite and eternal light abiding in Nature, the alchemists conceived of the *lumen naturæ* as a guiding light that never ceases to shine "before the eyes of every man, but which is seen by few mortals."[15] Perhaps this is the light guiding the poet who figures in Percy Bysshe Shelley's poem "Alastor, or The Spirit of Solitude," for whom

By solemn vision, and bright silver dream,
His infancy was nurtured. Every sight
And sound from the vast earth and ambient air,
Sent to his heart its choicest impulses.[16]

While the Romantic temperament was inspired by nature's simple, eternal, and purifying allure in a rapidly changing world, it was more enraptured by its wildness, unpredictability, and violence. Paintings of shipwrecks became popular during this time, most famously represented by the horrifically hopeless *The Raft of the Medusa* (1819) by Géricault.[17] The fascination with destructive powers also translated into portrayals of human dramas: tragedy, passion, anger, horror, grief, and battle. The pre-eminent French Romantic painter, Eugène Delacroix, depicted such scenes in paintings like *The Massacre at Chios* (1824) and *Combat of the Giaour and the Pasha* (1835). In Delacroix's lithographs the animal passions are given raw and powerful expression, as in paintings like *Lion Hunt* (1854) and *Jaguar Attacking a Horseman* (ca. 1855, see figure 1.1), demonstrating his own depth of Romantic feeling and expression of the irrational realms. In his journal he describes the fevered state that gave birth to such powerful works:

> There is an old leaven working in me, some black depth that must be appeased. Unless I am writhing like a serpent in the coils of a pythoness I am cold. I must recognize this and accept it, and to do so is the greatest happiness. Everything good that I have ever done has come about in this way.[18]

On another level the Romantic exploration of nature had to do with humanity's relationship with—and desire to control—the irrational, unpredictable forces of creation. Mary Shelley's (1797–1851) Gothic novel, *Frankenstein; or, The Modern Prometheus* (1818), is a clear example of this, drawing upon the alchemical themes of the search for the philosopher's stone and the elixir of life, said to bestow immortality and expel all diseases.[19] Victor Frankenstein, influenced by such natural philosophers as Agrippa, Paracelsus, and Albertus Magnus, developed a fascination with these grandiose alchemical notions and determined to harness the powers of creation to make a human form, like the alchemical concept of the *homunculus,* or "little man." To his horror he succeeds in creating an enormous monstrosity that he then spends his life trying to destroy. This creature represents a misuse of imagination, with no sense of divine purpose or goodness motivating Frankenstein's artificially created life, and no connection to his own unconscious. He rejects his creation as one rejects their own darkness, avoiding responsibility for its destructive expressions. Yet these repressed parts long to be known; they are only dangerous when not under-

Fig. 1.1. *Jaguar Attacking a Horseman,* by Eugène Delacroix (ca. 1855).
Courtesy of Wikimedia Commons

stood. Frankenstein's "monster" is in fact quite tenderhearted, absorbed in wonder at the majesty of the world, desiring above all else to be known and loved by humanity. His rejection by these "amiable creatures" and by his own creator elicits his violence and vengeful murders, just as the unconscious, if not accepted and integrated, is the bitter root of collective ills.[20]

It was during the Romantic era that the myth of the misunderstood genius and tortured artist came into being, epitomized by works like

Fig. 1.2. *Le Désespéré* (*Desperation* or *the Desperate Man*),
by Gustave Courbet.
Courtesy of Wikimedia Commons

Gustave Courbet's self-portrait, *Le Désespéré* (*Desperation* or *the Desperate Man*) (1843–1845, see figure 1.2).[21] Romantic artists sympathized with the mentally ill, as in Delacroix's *A Mad Woman* (1822), and were fascinated by nonrational experiences, idealizing the persona of the melancholic artist. As Craig Stephenson explains, "the revolutionary force of Romanticism resided not in its rejection of Reason, but rather in relocating the life principle in the depths, in the irrational underworld of the dead"—a shift in consciousness that coincided with reforms in the treatment of the insane.[22] These dark irrational forces are clearly depicted in the painting that came to be an icon of Romanticism, *The Nightmare* by Henry Fuseli, in which a woman lies draped over a bed in what appears to be a horrific sleep paralysis, tormented by an impish demon (see figure 1.3).[23] Perhaps even more haunting are the Black Paintings of Francisco de Goya (1746–1828), a Spanish painter of great import and a herald of Romanticism. Painted at the end of his life on the interior walls of his own home, the Black Paintings are filled with nightmarish scenes of ghoulish figures and witches. These paintings and other macabre works of the Romantic era reveal the contrast between light and dark, between the "real" and the unconscious world of dreams.

Baudelaire, who considered himself Delacroix's equivalent in the world of poetry, reached into the depths of the passions in his writing in the same spirit that Delacroix did with painting, exploring taboo subjects like death, sex, homosexuality, depression, and addiction. Delacroix's Romantic fervor and imagination, balanced with classical purity and order, earned him Baudelaire's undying admiration.[24] Delacroix held that imagination is

Fig. 1.3. *The Nightmare,* by Henry Fuseli (1781).
Courtesy of Wikimedia Commons

the most significant quality of the artist, yet equal to it is technical ability and control, and the two ought to be merged in a spirited self-possession.[25] These qualities are also often observed in Baudelaire's poetry.

Nothing was more vital to the Romantic spirit than the unbridled imagination, birthed from the inner depths of the artist. Delacroix writes, "In some people this inner power seems almost non-existent, but with me it is greater than my physical strength. Without it I should die, but in the end it will burn me up—I suppose I mean my imagination, that dominates me and drives me on."[26] Baudelaire considered imagination to be the root of innovation and the "*Queen* of the faculties," without which all of the faculties are useless, and even virtue becomes a "hard, cold, sterilizing thing."[27] Yet Baudelaire emphasized that imagination grows more powerful when it is helped in its work, and made all the more formidable when combined with factual observation.[28] In "Romanticism and the Esoteric Tradition," Wouter J. Hanegraaff writes that the romantic perspective "implied a close *participation* of the perceiving subject in the perceived object, which means that the object (the world) is *constituted* in the very act of perception."[29] This identification, or union, between the subject and object, like the alchemical *hieros gamos* (sacred marriage), engenders an understanding of imagination's true function, which is the continual creation of the world through the body of nature. To be able to lose oneself in inexplicable depths and then return with the technical skill to interpret the unknown through form, color, sound, and words is the highest achievement of the artist, who plays the role of both shaman and alchemist. Keats's doctrine of *Negative Capability* comes to mind: to be "capable of being in uncertainties, mysteries, doubts, without any irritable reaching after fact and reason."[30] In order to retrieve anything from the dark, unfathomable sea, we must be willing to dive in. This doctrine, recognizable in the Surrealist vision, was in direct opposition to realism's negation of the imagination. In a letter, dated August 23, 1799, to a displeased Rev. Dr. Trusler regarding commissioned work that Trusler felt was too imaginative, the English poet and artist William Blake (1757–1827) asserts that "to the Eyes of the Man of Imagination, Nature is Imagination itself. As a man is, so he sees."[31] In the irrational realm of nature and the feminine, the subject is immersed and dissolved, a transcendent surrender to the imagination without grasping for explanation. For Blake, human imagination was the Divine Body in which all things exist, the eternal world of possibilities: "The Imagination is not a State: it is the Human Existence itself."[32]

The Romantics also held a fascination with myth and symbol, and an affection for the past, for myths, for the eternal and unchanging beauty and marvel of the world. Yet symbols, for the Romantics, were not static and easily defined, as the direct relationship between emblems and ideas employed in Renaissance and Baroque art. The Romantic ideal held symbols to be dynamic and rooted in individual experience, which they freely used to express their own personal sentiments, either according to tradition or in completely new ways.[33] Essentially, the Romantics held a nondualistic view of the world, where the inner and outer are experienced as one. Indeed, a symbol's power is potentiated by our personal connection with it. Likewise, myths are significantly more meaningful when we find within them our own story. Myths contain within them the solution to transforming "the problem," and because symbols and myths function on both personal and universal levels, the artist who accesses both aspects is capable of transmuting the inner and the outer worlds. As Edmund Wilson writes in *Axel's Castle,* "The Romantic poet, then, with his turbid or opalescent language, his sympathies and passions which cause him to seem to merge with his surroundings, is the prophet of a new insight into nature: he is describing things as they really are; and a revolution in the imagery of poetry is in reality a revolution in metaphysics."[34]

The attraction of the eternal imagination in an era marked by the "gloomy beacon" of progress, as Baudelaire described it, was reflected in the concomitant occult revival occurring through this period, by which many artists and writers were influenced.[35,36] Baudelaire had a personal relationship with the great esotericist and poet Eliphas Lévi (1810–1875), whose occult writings would be a significant influence on the Symbolists to come. The search for the unknown and for the marvelous so central to the Romantic spirit made for an easy assimilation of the occult ideas of the time, including Mesmerism, Illuminism, Spiritualism, and magic.[37] The theosophical writings of Emanuel Swedenborg (1688–1772), the Swedish scientist, philosopher, Christian mystic, and theologian, influenced such notable poets and writers as Blake, Goethe, Nerval, Coleridge, Dostoevsky, Yeats, Emerson, and Whitman.[38] Swedenborg is credited with originating the term "correspondence" to explain the relationship between the spiritual and material worlds, which of course has its much more ancient origins in the *Emerald Tablet* ("as above, so below"). Correspondence, for Swedenborg, was "angelic knowledge," through which humankind could communicate with heaven; everything in the body, as well as all things of the world, have their origin and cause in the spiritual world.[39] This extends to the dynamic relationship between the inner and outer worlds, in clear contrast with the Cartesian separation of mind and matter in which mind is an abstraction and matter is "real." Swedenborg had his own notion of the macrocosm and microcosm, referring to the heavens as a "universal human," or *Maximus homo,* with each part of the individual human corresponding to some part of this larger, heavenly body.[40]

Swedenborgism seemed to be of particular interest to Blake, though he wavered in his opinions on the subject; Swedenborg's influence on Blake's *The Marriage of Heaven and Hell* is evident.[41] In a passage deprecating Swedenborg's lack of originality and imagination, accusing him of repeating "all the old falsehoods," Blake writes that Paracelsus and Böhme are much more apt to arouse inspiration; however, even they pale in comparison to Dante and Shakespeare.[42] As Anna Balakian writes in *The Symbolist Movement,* Blake was conveying that "it was not the originality of Swedenborg's theories that made it such an attractive cult, but rather Swedenborg's ability to sum up and popularize so many parallel mystical notions that were inherent in the cabalistic and hermetic cults."[43] Nonetheless, the way Swedenborg transmitted these mystical ideas, whether "old falsehoods" or not, held a great appeal for the Romantics.

In his *Biographia Literaria,* Samuel Taylor Coleridge (1772–1834), also influenced by Swedenborg as well as Kant and Schelling, writes that he considers the imagination in a primary and secondary aspect. The primary imagination is the "living Power and prime Agent of all human Perception," linked directly with the continual creation of the universe, united with Divine Mind, whereas the secondary imagination co-exists with "conscious will," "differing only in *degree*" from the primary. It is that which "dissolves, diffuses, dissipates, in order to re-create."[44] Like the alchemists, Coleridge emphasizes that imagination is not to be confused with fancy, which he relates to a kind of memory and the choice of the poet in their application of the law of association, namely in terms of aesthetics, or the "drapery" of poetic genius. On the other hand, imagination he considers to be an "esemplastic" power, meaning "to shape into one," endowing this faculty with a unifying power and deeming it the "soul" of poetic genius.[45] This is clearly reminiscent of the "One Thing" spoken of in the *Emerald Tablet,* or the imagination that unifies reality.

Swedenborg's mark is apparent in the works of the eccentric literary Romantic Gérard de Nerval (1808–1855), whose poetry and other writings explore the fine line between imagination and fantasy, or creative genius and madness. Alchemical and occult references are scattered throughout his work, which is imbued with a syncretism weaving together various mythologies, religions, and philosophies epitomizing the boundlessness of his psyche. Nerval, whom Breton considered a forerunner of Surrealism, was greatly inspired by dreams and the supremacy of the "spirit world" over the material, in large part due to his own bouts of madness, which began at age thirty-three. In his stirring Hermetic sonnet "Golden Sayings," quoting Pythagoras, he writes that "Everything is sentient!," then extrapolates that "everything has power over your being," and "even matter is imbued with a word."[46] Nerval is well known for the time he walked his lobster, on a leash of blue ribbon, through the Palais-Royal gardens—a poetically absurd act suggesting this all-pervading sentience. Reality and imagination were closely bound together for Nerval, and through his own mental instability he remained lucid enough to continue writing. *Aurélia, or Dreams and Life* (1855) was a short novel written, upon the suggestion of his physician, Dr. Émile Blanche, as a way out of his own lunacy. Written while in and out of institutions, *Aurélia* merges dream and life as the protagonist, considered to be Nerval himself, descends into madness. The first installment of *Aurélia* was published in the distinguished *Revue de Paris* in 1855; Nerval took his own life before the second installment was released later that year.

Wilson names Nerval as one of the first precursors of Symbolism, but gives more importance to Poe in this regard. Feeling an affinity with Poe, Baudelaire developed a passionate interest in his work. Through his publication and translation of Poe's tales in 1852, Poe became influential in French literature and succeeded in transforming Romanticism into a new form, emphasizing a "suggestive indefiniteness of vague and therefore spiritual *effect*" as an element of true musical (poetic) expression, a central element of Symbolist poetry.[47] While the Romantic artists were primarily concerned with liberating the imagination from civilized sterility, the transition to Symbolism marked the shift to symbolic thought and a deeper dive into the dark waters of the unconscious.

2
Symbolism
Dark Dreams and Ideals of the Other World

When materialism is rotten-ripe magic takes root.

—Joris Karl Huysmans, *Là-Bas*

Symbolism began in France in the later decades of the nineteenth century as a literary movement, seeking to represent absolute truths symbolically through metaphor, mainly as a reaction to realism. It would become the primary link between the Romantic era and Surrealism, particularly through Baudelaire. His book of poetry, *Les Fleurs du Mal* (The Flowers of Evil, 1857), is considered the first literary work in the Symbolist style. Perceived as obscene and a threat to public decency, this book incited a public uproar; as a result, Baudelaire was fined and the book was censored by the French authorities. Like Romanticism, Symbolism had a predilection for the exotic and mythical, for subjectivity and irrationality, for freedom of expression, and for an illusory and symbolic world. Yet the Symbolists descended much deeper into the dark abyss of the dream. If we can liken Romanticism to the opening of the Great Work and initial confrontation with inner darkness, then Symbolism was the conflict arising from the opposites, the conscious and unconscious. It was a complete rejection of realism and a full immersion in the unconscious world of symbols, creating a stark separation between the inner and outer world.

Swedenborgism became a unifying source for the Symbolists, in particular his ideas concerning correspondence, which served as a means of translating the ineffable impressions of their inner peregrinations. In the

"Exposition Universelle," Baudelaire writes of "the immense keyboard of the universal *correspondences,*" which are understood and brought into consciousness through the imagination, or as he says in his sonnet "Correspondences," man passes through a "*forêts de symboles,*" a forest of symbols that look upon him with familiar eyes.[1] For Baudelaire correspondence is equivalent to analogy, sometimes expressed in his writing as a Swedenborgian duality between the natural and the divine, at other times between the inner experience and the outer world of nature. He emphasizes the scientific element of the imagination; the poet, who is "intelligence itself," applies imagination through the mind and through the senses, linking the subjective and objective worlds.[2] "That which is created by the mind lives more truly than matter," writes Baudelaire.[3] As Balakian elucidates, it was this dualism between the inner feeling world of the poet and the external world of nature that distinguished it from Romanticism.[4]

For the Romantics, correspondence spoke of the precedence of the inner world and the divine over the sensual world of nature, and, as noted by Balakian, "it was the withdrawal as much as possible from outside stimuli that brought the visionary into the purest forms of the poetic state."[5] Any deeper appreciation and union with the irrational, with the beauty of nature, and with dreams was simply a symbol of the ascendancy of the spirit, a "preview" of what's to come in the hereafter, rather than an end in itself. Dreams for the Symbolist, on the other hand, were much more personal, Delphic, and deviant. In his book *Symbolism,* Michael Gibson writes that Symbolism stands opposed to the "limited 'reality' of the age, to the given, to the profane. A symbol, by its very nature, refers to an absent reality."[6] As he explains, the industrial revolution created a split in the Western world between dream and reality, particularly in places where Catholicism, a richly symbolic religion, predominated. Dissonance resounded in the clash between worlds and could only be alleviated by either moving with the tide, or against it. The Symbolists and Decadents chose the latter, spurning progress and vapid materialism and retreating into solipsistic self-absorption, seeking allusion over reality and indulging in melancholic nostalgia.

Whereas Romanticism was a rebellion against the constriction of Neoclassicism and Enlightenment values, Symbolism was a reaction to a second wave of the trend toward realism that emerged as Naturalism, a literary return to the mechanistic worldview as seen through biology. This was, in part, related to the publication of Darwin's *On the Origin of Species* and the theory of evolution, which brought humanity back down to earth from its Romantic exaltation. Naturalism was also a general rejection of Romanticism's saccharine emotionality.[7] The French author Émile Zola (1840–1902) was the vanguard of literary Naturalism, and in England the movement's ideas were propounded by the theories of the eminent writer and art critic John Ruskin (1819–1900). Ruskin advocated for the Pre-Raphaelite Brotherhood of England, a small group of artists that formed from a shared desire to piously imitate the Creator's work in nature while also harking back to the purity of the Middle Ages. Naturalism was mimetic of nature, its adherents lauding objective realism as the quintessence of fine art, in addition to being socially responsible by dealing with "real-world" issues. Where the Symbolist found immense value in unseen realms, the Naturalist found only illusion and folly. As the industrial age churned forward, the Symbolists and Decadents chose to linger in the other world of dark dreams, lunar fantasies, myths and legends, and the symbolic realm where the subjective and the transcendent still reigned. The whirling hum of the industrial revolution offered no consolation for the meaningful world that the Symbolists felt themselves to have lost in the span of a few decades, and the deterministic realism and technical precision of poetic Naturalism failed to satisfy the inner drives of the soul.[8]

Symbolist aspirations for absolute freedom found ardent expression through the poetry and life of Arthur Rimbaud (1854–1891). Greatly inspired by Baudelaire, whom he called "the first visionary, the king of poets, *a real God*," Rimbaud sought to make himself a visionary, depriving himself and submitting to suffering to attain the unknown:

A Poet makes himself a visionary through a long, boundless, and systematized *disorganization* of *all the senses*. All forms of love, of suffering, of madness; he searches himself, he exhausts within himself all poisons, and preserves their quintessences. Unspeakable torment, where he will need the greatest faith, a superhuman strength, where he becomes among all men the great invalid, the great criminal, the great accursed—and the Supreme Scientist! For he attains the *unknown!* Because he has cultivated his soul, already rich, more than anyone![9]

This conviction, written when Rimbaud was just sixteen, emerged from his own adolescent rebellion and was accompanied by a torrent of acerbic poetry that spared no victims: verses pervaded by scatological references, derogatory remarks, licentiousness, whores, goiters, polyps, pox, and all manner of human depravity in vivid detail. His life as a young adult was full of excesses. In 1871 he left the French provincial town of his childhood for Paris, where his love affair with the poet Paul Verlaine (1844–1896)—and the disorganization of the senses—ensued. They lived together in sordid rooms on the Left Bank, sleeping all day then immersing themselves in absinthe and hashish visions by night. It was a life of scandals, drama, and a shooting incident that put Verlaine in prison and sent Rimbaud back to his mother with a bandaged hand, where he composed *Une Saison en Enfer* (A Season in Hell). As the Surrealist David Gascoyne writes, "it was not only against old literary forms that Rimbaud revolted, it was against old stupidities, conventions, morality—the whole life of the epoch of capitalist prosperity in which he lived."[10] Likely through Baudelaire, Rimbaud was familiar with occult teachings, particularly the writings of Eliphas Lévi (1810–1875) and Jules Michelet's *La Sorcière* (Satanism and Witchcraft, 1862), contributing to his desire to express unconscious truths and beauty as he found them in the mundane appurtenances of daily life.[11]

Despite the dramatic and intimate relationship between Rimbaud and Verlaine, their poetry is quite different. Balakian makes a good case that Rimbaud is not a true Symbolist, but rather a proto-Surrealist ahead of his time. Without his close relationship to Verlaine and their scandalous escapades, he would have been quite inconsequential to Symbolism.[12] Verlaine had a much greater influence over the Symbolists.[13] His poetry is intimate, nostalgic, bearing the Symbolist marks of a lunar melancholy and attention to the musicality of the words, and his tempered ambiguity remains accessible on account of his poetry's simple humanity. Rimbaud, while certainly cryptic and personal in his writing, was drawn to life and adventure. He was the eternal vagabond, who eventually turned his back on poetry altogether, wandering the world and living the life—albeit brief—of freedom to which he had always been called. His form of escapism was, for the most part, one of outward expansion, compared to the Symbolist flight into the inner sanctum of dark dreams and self-absorption. Verlaine, on the other hand, sought escape through involutionary illusions, and thus we find in his poetry the doleful vocabulary of the Symbolist ambience: weariness, sadness, ennui, night, the moon, shade, dream, snow, owls; even the sun, when it is mentioned, is described in terms of its "languor" or "monotonous glare," or referenced in the "quiet death of the sun."[14]

The Symbolist proclivity for enigmatic and musical verse found its highest realization in the poetry and prose of Stéphane Mallarmé (1842–1898). Along with Baudelaire, Rimbaud, and Verlaine, Mallarmé was one of the most important poets in France in the second half of the nineteenth century, essential to the emergence of Symbolism. Mallarmé was the master of allusion and felt that "to name an object is to do away with the three-quarters of the enjoyment of the poem which is derived from the satisfaction of guessing little by little: to suggest it, to evoke it— that is what charms the imagination."[15] The avoidance of plainspoken and direct verse became a defining hallmark of the Symbolists, replacing blunt reality with a personal web of symbols and correspondences. For Mallarmé, this was an alchemical process of purification and transmutation, or as A. R. Chisholm puts it, "He strips the object of its materiality by transmuting it into a psychological experience, into a nexus of sensations and ideas."[16] This effectively does away with the portrayal of the thing itself and evokes the effect that it produces through sound and rhythm. In his essay "Magie," Mallarmé writes about a new approach to the Great Work of the alchemists and the philosopher's stone, to be accomplished "without a forge, the manipulations and poisons cooled into something other than precious stones, in order to continue by intelligence alone."[17] Mallarmé's *Grand Œuvre* (Great Work), which was never completed, was, in the words of Chisholm, his ongoing attempt "to transmute everyday realities into their higher correspondences, just as the alchemists had sought the Philosopher's Stone which would enable them to transmute base metals into gold."[18] Familiar with Lévi's writings, Mallarmé suggests a congruity between poet and magician, and the magical transmutations that each are endeavoring to produce:

> I claim that, between the old procedures and the magic spell that poetry will always be, a secret parity exists. . . . To evoke, with intentional vagueness, the mute object, using allusive words, never direct, reducing everything to an equivalent of silence, is an endeavor very close to creating: it is realistic within the limits of the idea uniquely put in play by the literary sorcerer, until an illusion equal to a look shines out. Verse is an incantation! And one cannot deny the similarity between the circle perpetually opening and closing with rhymes and the circles in the grass left by a fairy or magician.[19]

The musicality of Symbolist poetry was indeed much like an incantation, more attuned to the *inner music* of the poem and its ability to affect the listener or reader in a particular way. As elucidated by Marcel Raymond in *From Baudelaire to Surrealism*:

> [T]he "musical" poet must be capable of feeling the affinities existing between the world of sound and the world of thought . . . the problem is to bring out mysterious "correspondences"; certain syllables, thanks to an infinitely subtle accord with the meaning of the word which they compose, by virtue of the confused memories evoked by this word even more than by its sonorous charm, actually "move" the mind, magnetize it in a specific direction.[20]

Mallarmé believed in the possibility of poetry imbuing the poet with the same capacity as the Creator, not as individual artists but rather through the collective efforts of all poets and artists across the centuries.[21] Chisholm asserts that this is the denouement of Mallarmé's *Un Coup de Dès* (A Dice Throw at Any Time Never Will Abolish Chance, 1897), a lengthy poem in which his style and unorthodox syntax would find its apogee of ambiguity and originality, distinguished by long spaces, varied capitalizations, abstruse narrative, and even a preface by the author explaining the musical intonations to be employed in its reading.

The writer Joris-Karl Huysmans (1848–1907) was quite fond of Mallarmé, making him one of the favorite writers of his protagonist in *À Rebours* (Against Nature, 1884), the Duc Jean Floressas des Esseintes. An eccentric *fin-de-siècle* aesthete who grows disillusioned by the materialism, politics, and judgmental intellectualism of contemporary life, des Esseintes escapes outward aestheticism and "puerile displays of eccentricity" to a life of self-indulgent solitude and hermitage.[22] The individual crisis of des Esseintes and his escape into a world of his own artistic making—filled with books, art, decadent furnishings, flowers, and perfumes—leading to an implosion of neurotic ailments, mirrors the sentiments of Mallarmé in his essay "Crisis of Verse," in which he describes the nineteenth-century fin-de-siècle as distinct from the eighteenth as being not a revolution, but a "trembling of the veil in the temple, with significant folds, and, a little, its rending."[23] Like des Esseintes isolating himself from the world in a Hermetic separation and purification, Mallarmé dreamed of a "pure work," implying "the disappearance of the poet speaking."[24]

In "Prose (For des Esseintes)," considered to be his most Hermetic poem and a return tribute to Huysmans, Mallarmé walks with his "Sister," like the alchemical *soror mystica,* to a secret garden upon an isle filled with irises, gladiolas, and lilies.[25] It is a garden of "ideas, glory of long desire," yet his mystical sister allays his exuberance with a glance, and the two of them become silent. Like the "disappearance of the poet speaking," in silence ideas and desires are transmuted—distilled—into something much greater than the rational mind can elucidate through impulsive words. He writes, "the manifold lilies' stem would grow / to a size far beyond our reason." This pure Hermetic restraint, discipline, and ascetic response to his "initial wonderment" is in clear contrast to des Esseintes's plunge into the indulgence and fulfillment of every desire, which leads him to the abyss, spiritual death, and rebirth. Yet Mallarmé concludes "Prose" with a triumphant resurrection and a sepulcher inscribed with the word *Pulcharia,* meaning "beauty," suggesting that death may be met with a childlike humor when one acts with a "patient will."

Des Esseintes was also enraptured by the Symbolist-Decadent works of Gustave Moreau and Odilon Redon, surrounding himself in his sequestration with evocative artworks that would "transport him to some unfamiliar world, point the way to new possibilities, and shake up his nervous system by means of erudite fancies, complicated nightmares, suave and sinister visions."[26] Redon's nightmarish visions left him in a malaise, which he would remedy by then turning to the tranquil figure in Redon's *Melancholy,* whereby his gloom was replaced by a "languorous sorrow."[27] His descriptions of Moreau's *Salome Dancing before Herod* (see figure 2.1) and *The Apparition* are remarkably insightful and moving, painting a picture with his words that rivals the works themselves. He calls Moreau a "mystical pagan," an "illuminee who could shut out the modern world so completely as to behold, in the heart of present-day Paris, the awful visions and magical apotheoses of other ages."[28] Des Esseintes compares Moreau's paintings to Baudelaire's poetry, an author for whom he held boundless admiration. Baudelaire's "Correspondences" is a palpable influence throughout the novel, with des Esseintes's excess of synesthetic pleasures, most notably in his collection of liqueur caskets he calls a "mouth organ," "providing his palate with sensations analogous to those which music dispenses to the ear."[29]

Imagination and correspondence are each as central to the magician as they are to the artist and poet. Magic and creativity aspire to the same transcendent aims, whether that is a divine elevation or a union between the internal and external worlds. Recall Lévi's statement that the imagination "is the glass of visions and the apparatus of magical life."[30] Imagination is responsible for destiny; how we imagine ourselves and the world to be is what shapes reality. Or as Baudelaire writes, "As [imagination] has created the world . . . it is proper that it should govern it."[31] Baudelaire also calls painting "an evocation, a magical Operation," a union between the artist and the external world; the specific formulae of such an operation would be the "acme of imbecility" to probe.[32] Huysmans comes quite close to the magical power of the imagination through des Esseintes, who considered artifice to be "the distinctive mark of human genius," and believed in the imagination's ability, by focusing all of one's attention upon a single detail, to provide a surrogate experience in place of the "vulgar reality of actual experience."[33]

Naturally the Symbolists were fascinated by alchemy and often employed its processes metaphorically. While physical alchemy experienced a period of

Fig. 2.1. *Salome Dancing before Herod,* by Gustav Moreau, 1876.
Courtesy of Wikimedia Commons

ignominy following the Enlightenment, it was carried on in a spiritual form through nineteenth-century occultism and given new life through the words and visions of a disillusioned age. Much of the occult tradition was transmitted through Lévi, but there was also the founding of Madame Blavatsky's Theosophical Society, the resurrection of the Rosicrucian Brotherhood by Joséphin Péladan, as well as Edward Schuré's book *The Great Initiates* (1889). Each of these figures played a significant role in disseminating Hermetic and

Fig. 2.2. *Des Esseintes,* by Odilon Redon, frontispiece for
À Rebours by J. K. Huysmans, 1888. The Stickney Collection.
Courtesy of Art Institute Chicago

Indian teachings in the later decades of the nineteenth century and were impactful in the esoteric beliefs underlying Symbolist art.

The unification of the opposites, so central to alchemical initiation, is related by Schuré to the roots of religious tradition. He writes of the "two geniuses" that we all bear within us, one related to the Semitic current rooted in Egypt and transmitted by Moses that "contains absolute and superior principles: the idea of unity and universality in the name of a supreme Principle which . . . leads to the unification of the human family." The other Aryan current, sourced in India, "contains the idea of ascending evolution in all terrestrial and supra-terrestrial kingdoms," leading to "an infinite diversity of developments in the richness of nature and the many aspirations of the soul."[34] The reconciliation of these two currents of genius—the Semitic descending from God to humanity, and the Aryan ascending from humanity to God, "would be truth itself." In fact Schuré writes that humanity's salvation, and our progress as a species, depends unequivocally upon the reconciliation of these two geniuses, which he compares to the terms *spirituality* and *naturalism*.[35] These might also be termed *evolution* and *involution*. This duality was expressed by Carl du Prel's concept of the human mind being "Janus-faced," with one face turned to the sensory world and the other—the "transcendental subject"—the face of the mind that is active in the unseen world of the unconscious, particularly in states of trance, dream, hypnotism, somnambulism, and clairvoyance.[36]

Whether the opposites are conceived of in a religious, mystical, philosophical, or psychological light makes little difference; the alchemical promise of the great work is that their successful *coniunctio* produces the philosopher's stone. Yet this reconciliation was out of reach for many of the Symbolists. William Godwin's novel *Saint-Léon* (1799), about an impoverished French aristocrat who obtains the elixir of immortality and the secret of making gold—the philosopher's stone—was mentioned by Delacroix in his journal: "These fatal secrets are the cause of every imaginable disaster, but in the midst of his afflictions he finds a hidden pleasure in the strange powers that set him apart from the rest of mankind. Alas! I have not been able to discover the secret, and am reduced to regretting in myself the powers that were this man's only consolation."[37] A similar remorse is felt in Baudelaire's "Alchimie de la douleur," where he writes of Hermes, who both assists and frightens him, and makes him a peer of Midas, the saddest of all alchemists.[38] Transmutation is reversed; gold becomes iron, and the poem ultimately ends with a sepulcher, intimating Hermes's role as a psychopomp. Rimbaud, too, in *Une Saison en Enfer,* wrote a combination of prose and poetry called the "Second Delirium: The Alchemy of the Word." Remorseful for youthful naïveté when he believed in "every kind of magic," he thus begins an investigation into the unknown: "I turned silences and nights into words. What was unutterable, I wrote down. I made the whirling world stand still."[39] Yet even upon seeing gold, he "could not drink."[40]

Hidden within the Symbolist representations of alchemy lies the essence of the movement's perplexity, namely a confusion between the male and female that led to the depiction of Woman as the unknowable and sinister temptress, a *femme fatale* and chimera of irrational fancies, or on the other hand, the virgin, mother, or unattainable ideal. Woman's dangerous sexuality and exotic allure is depicted in Franz von Stuck's shadowy painting *Sin* (1893, figure 2.3), as well as in *The Kiss of the Sphinx* (ca. 1895). The castrating woman was a repeating theme, in Moreau's depiction of Salome and in the nightmarish works of Alfred Kubin (1877–1959) and Edward Munch (1863–1944). One thinks of Kubin's *Death Leap* or *The Egg* (1901–1902), in which a tiny man makes a headlong dive between two mountainous thighs and into the dark abyss of a devouring vulva. These portrayals evince a fear of the feminine, as *femme fatale* or devouring mother, in the male Symbolists that speaks to a much deeper reorientation in their collective psyche. In the fin-de-siècle melancholy resulting from a rapidly changing world, the Symbolists were grappling with the link between birth and death, intimately tied up in their conception of Woman. Balakian writes, "at the core of symbolism . . . was man's struggle against the void, as he visualized the power of death over consciousness."[41] There was just as much despair in birth as there was in death, as conveyed by Munch when he said, "My art is rooted in a single reflection: why am I not as others are? Why was there a curse on my cradle? Why did I come into the world without any choice?"[42] Gustav Klimt's *Hope I* (1903), a haunting portrait of a pregnant woman overshadowed by deathly skulls and menacing faces, suggests the relationship between the primordial womb, birth, and death.

Fig. 2.3 *Die Sünde* (Sin), by Franz von Stuck, 1893.
Courtesy of Wikimedia Commons

Symbolism's struggle with the void is well captured in Mallarmé's "Un Coup de Dès,"[43] a poem so hermetic and private that it transcends the personal altogether and exists as an irrational world all its own, and yet contained within its unconventional, sprawling lines is an alchemical process of purification. The void is confronted as humanity's relationship with the primordial sea of the unconscious, and the relationship between thought, will, destiny, chance, and creation. The imagery suggests a recognition of "the shadow buried in the deep" that causes one's ship to waver, and an impotency and senescent passivity in the face of chaos—a shipwreck, the abandoned helm, a fallen quill. It is the journey of the Hermit, or the old wise man, who turns away from the world to follow his inner light, and in the process must acknowledge his own shadow. In the poem the "united horizon" evokes the merging of the Above and Below, and the "ultimate conjunction with probability." Here, in submission to something far greater than the personal self, the shadow is purified:

> . . . *caressed and polished and restored and washed*
> *softened by the waves and set free*[44]

Mallarmé uses the word *Nuptials* that, in the context of other words like *united* and *conjunction,* suggests the alchemical royal marriage and unification of opposites, of conscious and unconscious. The limits imposed upon the infinite—a "false mansion" of thought—dissolve in the mist, along with reality itself. In "these indefinite regions," the only hope for the lost helmsman to hold onto any sense of meaning is to follow their cynosure toward the fixation of purified thought—the steadiness that sanctifies. In the final line, Mallarmé concludes that "Every Thought emits a Dice Throw," a casting of energy directed into the unknown, the spermatic masculine creative force thrown into the "primordial spray," where it is united in sacred marriage with the receptive, feminine body of the unconscious, to be birthed into manifestation.

The polarization of the opposites, such as that depicted in von Stuck's *Water and Fire* (1913), was a source of anxiety, but it was also an aspect of Symbolist idealism, as portrayed in Delville's *The Love of Souls* (1900). Woman, whether virgin or *femme fatale,* was the quintessential subject, and Symbolist imagery was often portrayed with a lunar and nocturnal ambience, aligning with their fearful veneration of the feminine. In both Woman and the night, they were confronting the abyss within themselves. Whatever evil they felt lurking in these depths was projected onto Woman as the mostly male artists made an initial, fearful, and hesitant flirtation with the unconscious that would later explode into consummation in Surrealism, when artists sought to remove all barriers to the unconscious realm.

Correlating to the Moon's gravitational pull upon the Symbolist psyche, the relationship between good and evil was also a source of fascination and inspiration. Comte de Lautréamont (1846–1870), under the pen name of Isidore Lucien Ducasse, wrote *Les Chants de Maldoror* (1869), a prosaic novel that Gascoyne calls "a debauch of imagination," and that the Surrealists and Dadaists would later come to acclaim as a masterpiece.[45] The book charts the persistently evil wanderings of Maldoror and is filled with surreal and terrifying imagery, a nightmare in which "the sleeper cries out like one condemned to die, until he awakens and discovers that reality is three times worse than dream."[46] Ferdinand Hodler (1853–1918) portrayed such a scene in *Night* (1890), in which a man appears to be in the midst of a night terror, suffering the oppressive weight of an ominous form veiled beneath a black robe. In both cases what is being represented is like the terrifying and devouring aspect of the unconscious.

The Symbolist fascination with evil extended to a fixation with Satan, whom they tended to view as either a Saturnian figure or in the positive role of Lucifer, the "light-bringer" who guides souls into the darkness as a form of initiation. Jean Delville's painting *Les Trésors de Satan* (Satan's Treasures, 1895), places Satan in an underwater dream world, with swirling octopus tentacles instead of wings amidst a scape of æthereal coral and blue depths. At his feet an orgiastic array of men and women—his treasured souls— appear to be in a state of ecstasy as opposed to eternal damnation, entranced by their sensual desires and the array of pearls and coins around them. This painting suggests an *enantiodromia* of the fires of hell and torment into a watery realm of dreamy reverie, the abysmal depths of the soul, that ultimately leads to initiation when Satan's spell of materialistic desire is broken. As Maximillian Rudwin explains in "The Satanism of Huysmans," it was in this light that Huysmans went from Purgatory to Paradise, placing his faith in diabolism over the constricting boredom of life and the insipidity of humanity.[47] Huysmans's *Là-Bas* (Down There, or The Damned, 1891) was a controversial book replete with demonism, supernaturalism, astrology, theology, sorcery, necromancy, alchemy, Qabalism, and Satanism, with influences of Baudelaire, Barbey d'Aurevilly's stories in *Les diaboliques* (1874), and Felicien Rops's series of etchings *Les Sataniques* (1884).[48] Yet it was Huysmans's decadence that underscored his obsession with diabolism. "The taste of Huysmans for all that is artificial and high in flavor," writes Rudwin, "as seen in *À Rebours,* inclines him toward demonism. Decadentism passes almost imperceptibly into diabolism." In this work Huysmans highlights the trends of Satanism and Luciferianism in contemporary France, the former associated with evil and the latter with good. The two main characters of *Là-Bas* are both bachelors: Durtal, a Paris-based writer approaching forty years of age, and his erudite friend, Des Hermies, who acts as Durtal's initiator into contemporary Satanism. The name Des Hermies evokes Hermes Trismegistus, the psychopomp, at times a Devilish trickster and the legendary father of alchemy. Indeed, Huysmans's conception of Satanism was tied up in the Hermetic, alchemical, Rosicrucian, Illuminist, Masonic, and other occult trends of his time, and the close relationship between Satanism and alchemy is a recurring theme of the book.[49] Baudelaire, too, made use of this correlation in his poem "Au Lecteur," in which he invokes "Satan Trismegist:"

> *Pillowed on evil, Satan Trismegist*
> *Ceaselessly cradles our enchanted mind,*
> *The flawless metal of our will we find*
> *Volatilized by this rare alchemist.*[50]

Throughout *Là-Bas,* Durtal is engaged in writing a biography of Gilles de Rais, a fifteenth-century confessed serial child killer thought to be the inspiration for Bluebeard ("Barbe bleue"). His interest in de Rais draws him to explore the nobleman's passion for alchemy and demonism and his pursuit of the "great work." In one passage he writes,

[I]f Satan pleased, they should finally find this powder which would load them with riches and even render them almost immortal—for at that epoch the philosopher's stone passed not only for an agent in the transmutation of base metals, such as tin, lead, copper, into noble metals like silver and gold, but also for a panacea curing all ailments and prolonging life, without infirmities, beyond the limits formerly assigned to the patriarchs.[51]

In relating this to his present day, he touches on a naturalistic shift in attitude concerning the stone, its "medical and divine virtues" being relegated to "a molecular transformation" of an organic nature.[52] In *Là-Bas* Huysmans clearly breaks away from the naturalists, striving for a new principle, a "spiritual naturalism" in line with Schuré, or as Rudwin puts it, "a synthesis of body and spirit, of matter and mind, of the seen and the unseen," which gave to the spiritual dimension its own reality and validity.[53]

The saturnine proclivity of the Symbolists was tempered by their striving for the Ideal. In the article "The Symbolist Aesthetic and the Impact of Occult and Esoteric Ideologies on Modern Art," Marja Lahelma illustrates how the Symbolist ideals of inward vision, intuition, and dematerialization were rooted in a religious exploration that found meaning in esoteric and occult beliefs.[54] Lahelma links the "inner vision" of the artist, which became so important to the Romantic and Symbolist artists—iconically captured by Redon's painting *Closed Eyes* and in Jean Delville's *Orphée*—with Neoplatonism, through which this concept found its way into occult philosophy. Neither Plotinus nor Plato held imitative art in high esteem, valuing instead the connection to the higher, divine realms that could be accessed by turning inward, thus perceiving the eternal truths hidden behind appearances.[55]

Aesthetically defined by the critic Albert Aurier, the anti-naturalist pictorial symbolism emphasized allusion and subjective artistic vision expressed in simplified forms.[56] Symbolism found its way into visual art beginning with the work of Paul Gauguin (1848–1903), lauded as the movement's leader by Aurier in his 1891 article, "Symbolism in Painting: Paul Gauguin." However, Symbolism was given its name and definition in *The Manifesto of Symbolism* by Jean Moréas on September 18, 1886. While mainly directed at poetry, Moréas gives an apt description of the Symbolist ethos that true art is a union of the ideal and subjective expression:

The enemy of didacticism, declamation, false sensibility and objective description, symbolic poetry seeks to clothe the Idea with a sensory form which, nevertheless, should not exist as an end-in-itself but as a form which, though serving at all times to express the Idea, must remain subjective. The Idea, in its turn, must not be allowed to be deprived of the sumptuous robes of external analogy; for the essential character of symbolic art consists in its never leading to the concentration of the Idea in itself. Thus, in this art, scenes of nature, the actions of human beings, all concrete phenomena are not there to manifest themselves; they are sensory appearances intended to represent an esoteric affinity with primordial Ideas.[57]

The work of Gustave Moreau (1826–1898), considered to be the "founding father of French Symbolism," preceded Moréas's manifesto by about twenty years, and there were many others whose work is considered precursory to Symbolism.[58] Thus Moréas was really just giving a name to an artistic phenomenon that had been in existence for some time. Visual artists felt Moréas's words gave a voice to their sentiment that art is about ideas, and thus identified themselves as Symbolists. Moreau was the quintessential model for the expression of Idealism. His ornately decorated and spellbinding mythical dreamscapes, with their ghostly outlines and coruscating adornments, convey an unbound imagination prone to excess, reeled in by the transcendent influence of the Ideal. His paintings portray Hermetic themes, the material of myth, legend, and scripture, but as Gibson elucidates, this alone did not make him a Symbolist. It was in his choice of subject that his style was definitively Symbolist, for in depicting androgynous male figures and castrating females like Salome, he was giving form to the "psychodrama" of his age, in which sexual roles and identities were undergoing a collective transformation.[59]

Moreau was among the artists that the Belgian painter, writer, and Idealist Jean Delville (1867–1953) considered to be part of the "living tradition" of art, along with Michaelangelo, Da Vinci, Raphael, George Frederick Watts, and others. The living tradition, he writes, "is in eternal accord with the evolution of art in general and with the evolution of personality in particular," as opposed to the "dead tradition" that relied on formulaic and conventional approaches.[60] Delville strove to express higher spiritual messages in an initiatory fashion through his art, rejecting realism and materialism in favor of the Ideal, which he conceived as a trinity of spiritual beauty (Idea), plastic beauty (Form), and technical beauty (Execution). He believed that the end of materialism was drawing near and

Fig. 2.4. *Jupiter et Sémélé,* by Gustave Moreau, 1895.

Courtesy of Wikimedia Commons

that a new spiritual age was dawning in which science, religion, and philosophy would be synthesized into the "Science of the Ideal": "Above the overthrow of materialism, so fatally crushing to the soul and spirit, already soars, in the redeeming light, the mysterious transformation of thought."[61]

Greatly interested in the occult, Delville sought to illuminate and edify through artistic harmony informed by a synergistic relationship between magic, Hermeticism, and Qabalah. He believed these three traditions were the key to attaining perfect human knowledge. Theosophy and the great occultists of the day, including Schuré, Lévi, Péladan, St. Yves D'Alveydre, and Blavatsky, influenced much of his thought. He also subscribed to Rosicrucianism, and his work was shown at Péladan's *Salon de la Rose+Croix,* Rosicrucian art and music salons that Péladan opened with the vision of uniting the arts through occultism and aestheticism, spurning impressionist, realist, and naturalist art. In 1896, Delville modeled his own salon after the *Rose+Croix,* called *Salon d'Art Idéaliste,* to break into the avant-garde and create his own artistic movement fueled and inspired by Hermetic and occult ideologies, charged with a spiritual servitude to humankind through the expression of the Ideal. In the Hermetic-alchemical approach this is achieved through refinement and purification of the self, through initiation and, ultimately, gnosis, true self-knowledge. As Delville asserts,

> The artist is a kind of alchemist. Art is a species of occult chemistry. Lead can be turned into gold, but the laws which bring about this wonderful transmutation must be understood. Just as the magician by the radiation of his will brings under his sway the wanderings and formless forces of astral space, so the artist, guided by his genius, brings into order the imperfect images of life by infusing into them the system of his thought.[62]

Only through purifying the self—and idealizing or spiritualizing one's being—can the artist gain access to the higher realms and become aware of the Ideal.[63] Yet Idealism, in Delville's lofty conception, is obliged to create "Moral Beauty," antithetical to what he considered "the black magic of art, which consists in spiritualising what is evil," no doubt tied to the "fatal scourge of materialism."[64] He was ardently opposed to naturalism, Impressionism, landscapes, still-lifes, positivism, and realism because they lacked the *Ideal*—that which elevates the soul—calling them "a false conception of Nature, a false conception of Life, a false conception of Art."[65] In kind he felt that religious art had become utterly depraved and disconnected from the true source of spiritual wisdom and truth.

Like Delacroix and Baudelaire before him, Delville maintained that the imagination must be joined by technical acuity to reach perfection in art. Yet just as important as *technique* are *idea* and *form:* "Without *idea,* the work fails in its intellectual mission; without *form,* it fails in its mission towards nature; without *technique,* it fails to reach perfection."[66] The attention to the Idea was a defining element of Symbolism, expanding art beyond the level of appearances. Yet this Idealism also resulted in the shift away from Symbolism.[67] With World War I came a disillusionment that demanded something entirely revolutionary from art, something that the "other world" and solipsistic Decadence had no answer for. There was a new and pressing need to recreate the world from the state of depravity into which it had fallen. From the influence of Freud's unraveling of the unconscious and investigation of dreams arose a true curiosity about those veiled aspects of the psyche that nonetheless exert a powerful influence over consciousness. While not disappearing entirely, Symbolism was overshadowed by a preference for primitivism over decadence, by the need for art to address social concerns, and the growth of the new twentieth-century movements, including Dada and Surrealism. Whereas the Symbolists were content to live in the world of dark dreams and ideals, Dada and Surrealism sought to dive into the sea of the unconscious and retrieve its hidden contents, no matter how absurd and hideous they might be, and bring them into the light of consciousness.

3
Dada
Cutting to the Chance

Freedom: Dada Dada Dada, a roaring of tense colors, and interlacing of opposites and of all contradictions, grotesques, inconsistencies:
LIFE

—TZARA, *DADA MANIFESTO*, 1918

Dada was an absurdist protest to the senselessness of war; a negation of nationalism, industry, media, art, literature, and society in general; a shocking and rebellious destructivism; a protest against complacency and ennui; and an awakening of the imagination to new possibilities. The alchemists repeatedly point to the necessity of decay in the great work, and this is what Dada did for art. Dada broke art down to its most basic components and stripped it of its egoism, ultimately paving the way for something new to be born. Dada was a new kind of descent into irrationality and journey into the unknown, demanding a re-evaluation of everything that art had ever stood for. Beginning in Zurich during World War I, Dada was manifestly anti-nationalist, anti-cultural, anti-establishment, anti-art, and, ultimately, "anti-Dada." In a retrospective talk given in 1970, German writer Richard Huelsenbeck (1892–1974), one of Dada's founders, described Dada as "a protest without a program, without a political program" that arose from a "deep creative doubt."[1] It offered no alternatives or solutions, and had no ties to politics or systems of any kind because its driving motivation was freedom, particularly of the individual. Huelsenbeck asserts, "To protest what is wrong is a creative act. It becomes a power in itself."[2]

The word *Dada* means "hobby-horse," among many other things. It was purportedly chosen at random in February 1916 from the dictionary by Tristan Tzara (1896–1963), one of the founding members of the movement and editor for the publication *Dada*.[3] Tzara was a Romanian emigrant who arrived in Zurich during the war, where he soon befriended the poets Hans (Jean) Arp, Hugo Ball, and Huelsenbeck. Around the same time the *Cabaret Voltaire* was opened by Ball and Emmy Hennings, a café that held riotous poetry readings, exhibitions, and concerts, and that would be a focal point for the movement. After the closing of the Cabaret Voltaire, a Dada Gallery opened and began exhibiting paintings by Kandinsky, Paul Klee, Arp, Max Ernst, Giorgio de Chirico, Modigliani, and Prampolini.

On July 14, 1916, Hugo Ball (1886–1927) recited his *Dada Manifesto* at the first Dada soirée, which aptly conveys the irrational spirit of Dada:

> How does one achieve eternal bliss? By saying dada. How does one become famous? By saying dada. With a noble gesture and delicate propriety. Till one goes crazy. Till one loses consciousness. How can one get rid of everything that smacks of journalism, worms, everything nice and right, blinkered, moralistic, europeanised, enervated? By saying dada.[4]

It also declares Ball's poetic inclinations toward mysticism, magic, and the spiritual quality of words: "A line of poetry is a chance to get rid of all the filth that clings to this accursed language, as if put there by stockbrokers' hands, hands worn smooth by coins. I want the word where it ends and begins. Dada is the heart of words."[5] Ball was interested in a "return to the innermost alchemy of the word."[6] His sound poetry, or *Verse ohne Worte* (Poems without words), expressed the vibrational potency of sounds combined with ritual movements, much like a magical incantation. As John Elderfield explains, his sound poems were inspired by the concept of Wassily Kandinsky's "inner sound" (*innerer Klang*) of words.[7] Ball strove to express the inner vibrational essence of the word in the same manner the alchemist aims to extract the hidden essence of matter. Thus the "word," when seen as energy, was equated with the *Logos* as a "magical complex image."[8] His sound poems were composed of "magically inspired" vocables, sounds without meaning, engendering "a new sentence that was not limited and confined by any conventional meaning." From this arose the possibility of hearing the inner sound, or "the innately playful, but hidden, irrational character of the listener."[9] For Ball, magic in all its forms was the resulting effect of art as well as of individualism.[10] He saw artistic creation as "a process of conjuring," and he expressed the conviction that understanding the laws of magic was a prerequisite of being a visionary.[11]

A longtime friend of Ball, Huelsenbeck was a novelist, journalist, poet, as well as a physician and psychiatrist, and a leader of German Dada.[12] He also authored various historical accounts of the Dada movement throughout his life. Like Ball, Huelsenbeck recited sound poems, conjuring African dialects in the spirit of primitivism, the Dada trend of seeking the irrational and uncontrolled within their preconceived notions of what they considered to be "primitive" cultures. In his own "Dada Manifesto," Huelsenbeck proclaims, "By tearing to pieces all the platitudes of ethics, culture, and inwardness, which are merely cloaks for weak muscles, Dadaism has for the first time ceased to take an aesthetic position toward life."[13] Throughout his life Huelsenbeck expressed a passion for creative irrationality and the aspects of our experience that are beyond reason.[14]

It was after Huelsenbeck and Ball left Dada, disconcerted with the direction in which it was headed, that Tzara announced the official beginning of Dada as a movement in 1917.[15] Tzara's 1918 "Manifeste Dada" was a radical declaration against morals, philosophy, art, systems, logic, social hierarchies and values, and even against manifestos and principles; proclaiming the "great negative work of destruction . . . indomitable madness, decomposition," and the "interlacing of opposites and all contradictions."[16] The Dada poets and artists relied on chance to access the unconscious, as Tzara explains in "To Make a Poem," describing a process of cutting out words from newspaper articles, placing them in a bag, and shaking them up to create a randomly ordered poem.[17]

Collage also functioned to elicit the element of chance, with a wealth of photographic images in media publications that could be drawn upon to evoke unconscious expression and limiting rational control in the creation of art. Like Huelsenbeck, Hans, or Jean, Arp (1886–1966), was interested in irrational creativity as a means of self-revelation, seeking to channel the unconscious through his collages, poetry, paintings, and sculptures. He created collages in a divinatory fashion by dropping squares of paper at random. Huelsenbeck considered Arp "the greatest artist in the dada group. Precisely because he glanced neither to the left nor to the right, he wanted to change art more than anything; and he believed that it was only through art that one could change human life."[18] As a child Arp was deeply interested in dreams, later writing that "the world of dream and memory is the real world."[19] This fascination would find its external reflection in Sophie Taeuber, who he described as living "endlessly linked to the reality of dream."[20] Taeuber was a painter and artist of many mediums who Arp eventually married, and the two of them often worked collaboratively.

Photomontage, composed of images cut out of mass media publications, allowed German Dadaists to make acute visual commentaries of a political nature criticizing the Weimar Republic.[21] Hannah Höch (1889–1978), one of the originators of photomontage, made a stunning critique of the Weimar Republic in her most famous work, *Cut with the Kitchen Knife Dada through the Last Weimar Beer-Belly Cultural Epoch of Germany* (1919–1920). This richly detailed assortment of seemingly chaotic images amidst machinery and gears places male figures of the former Empire and the new regime, as well as the military, in the upper right, or "anti-Dada" section; in the lower right are the Dadaists and communists. This piece speaks to the alchemical idea of separating and reuniting the opposites. Interspersed throughout are the active women of Dada that Höch envisioned as cutting through the "excess fat" of the Weimar epoch with their political empowerment, a point emphasized by her placement of a newspaper clipping in the lower right showing the European countries where women could vote or would soon be able to, including Germany.[22] As Karen Barber points out, the use of a "kitchen knife" implies "women's work," thus intimating the relationship and importance of women in the Dada revolution.[23] This also points to the unconscious, irrational aspects that must be allowed expression. A variety of women appear, some bearing the heads of her male Dada peers, mocking their "flamboyant bravura," while at the same time evoking the alchemical hermaphrodite and the union of opposites.[24]

For Höch, photomontage was a "journey of discovery," a gateway to a "new magical territory, for the discovery of which freedom is the first prerequisite."[25] Yet she asserts that it is still necessary to have a disciplined approach, mindful of color and form, to achieve integration. This attitude separated her from the Dadaist ethos. As Peter Boswell comments in his essay "Hannah Höch: Through the Looking Glass," Höch had always been more attuned to her own inner voice, approaching her work subjectively and maintaining a respect for "Art," tradition, and aesthetic concerns, which was a source of ridicule from her male peers in Dada.[26] Höch went on to create paintings exhibiting a clear Surrealist influence, often combining imagery of mechanics and nature and exploring her own unconscious expressions through highly emotional and disproportionate figures and portraits.

Like the alchemists, Dada artists saw destruction as a means to creation. Marcel Duchamp (1887–1968), who had more of an influence on Dada and Surrealism than nearly anyone else and yet managed to remain detached from both movements, worked from a desire to "break up forms—to 'decompose' them much along the lines the cubists had done," but he "wanted to go further—much further—in fact in quite another direction altogether."[27] Such was the spirit that created *Nude Descending a Staircase, No. 2* (1912) and *The Bride Stripped Bare by her Bachelors, Even* (or *The Large Glass,* 1915–1923). This latter work, standing at over nine feet tall, is a painting on glass with a distinct separation between the above and below, giving the painting a Hermetic composition conjuring the *Emerald Tablet*. In the upper panel is a series of connected geometrical shapes consisting of a mechanical and abstract "bride," and in the bottom is "La Machine Célibataire" (The Bachelor Machine), as Duchamp calls it. Their equal spacing denotes the balance of the opposites. As Jack Burnham explains, a Hermetic message is encoded in the title. Found on the reverse side of the "chocolate grinder" in the center of the bottom panel, the title has specific divisions between the male and female (*La Mariée Mise À Nu Par / Ses Célibataires, Même*), and ends with the word *Même,* meaning "Even," denoting balance. Numerologically, the first division, referring to the bride, has eighteen letters and aligns with the number of the Moon card of the tarot and the principle of decay. The second division of the bachelors adds up to nineteen, which is the male Sun card and the principle of regeneration.[28] Burnham suggests that the seven funnel shapes in the bottom panel refer to the seven lower Sephiroth of the Tree of Life.[29]

Duchamp was interested in reduction and turning inward, away from external influence, feeling that "an artist might use anything—a dot, a line, the most conventional or unconventional symbol—to say what he wanted to say."[30] He strove to escape the physical approach to painting and creation of visual products, instead focusing on the expression of ideas, placing importance on the title, and drawing inspiration from literature. In this way painting was "once again at the service of the mind."[31] Dada, which Duchamp called "a metaphysical attitude," represented a radical break from a materialistic and physical style of painting, and a means to free oneself from a limited state of mind susceptible to influence by the environment or the past. Duchamp's *Bride Stripped Bare* was inspired by the French writer Raymond Roussel, whom he admired for having produced "something completely independent—nothing to do with the great names or influences."[32]

Duchamp originated the Dada art form he called *Ready-Made,* in which the artist simply chooses a prefabricated object as their art piece. One of his famous Ready-Made pieces, called *Fountain,* was a marble lavatory bowl, which he signed "R. Mutt"; unsurprisingly it was rejected by the New York *Salon des Indépendants* as a submission in 1917.[33] That a premade object could be considered art is categorically "anti-art," forcing us to reflect upon what art actually is and how the role of the artist transcends the physical act of creation to reach the level of mind, where ideas and concepts are expressed through choice of object. What inspired the artist about this object, and why we should care, becomes the object of contemplation. Nadia Choucha, author of *Surrealism & the Occult,* documents Duchamp's interest in alchemy and Hermeticism and how these currents influenced his work. She writes that "placing a 'profane' object, such as a urinal, into a 'sacred' space, such as an art gallery" is an "act of aesthetic alchemy" that subverts the hierarchy of value in the art world and exhibits the Hermetic doctrine of correspondence: "as above, so below."[34] Duchamp's Ready-Made sculpture, *Bicycle Wheel* (1913), consisting of a stool with an inverted bicycle wheel inserted into the top of it, similarly reflects an alchemical *coniunctio oppositorum* between the ever cycling and volatile *opus circulatorum* of the "above" and the fixed four legs of the stool as the material world "below."

Marcel Duchamp had a close relationship with his younger sister, Suzanne Duchamp-Crotti (1889–1963), also a Dadaist painter, collagist, sculptor, and draughtsman. With both Marcel and her other older brother Jacques Villon having acquired fame as painters, and the fact that she was a woman, it was difficult for her to receive recognition as an artist in her own right. Much of her work, in Dada fashion, combined painting, collage, and language, such as her well-known piece titled *Broken and Restored Multiplication* (1918–1919; see figure 3.1). This painting suggests an alchemical influence. Its title evokes the process of multiplication involved in perfecting the philosopher's stone. Yet elements in its composition also suggest an alchemical and occult theme. Its series of overlapping spheres is redolent of a universal diagram in a state of disorder. This chaotic arrangement is exacerbated by the inverted Eiffel Tower, reminiscent of a compass and perhaps an allusion to the sixteenth arcanum of the tarot, the Tower, representative of destruction that leads to new perceptions. Hence the words placed topsy-turvy around the painting read: "The mirror would shatter, the scaffolding would totter, the balloons would fly away, the stars would dim."[35] Interestingly we find two bright stars at the top of the painting: a mercurial white star corresponding with the female, superimposed on the gold, male sun; and a sulphuric red star, the male principle, touching the upper right point of a female lunar crescent. Within the separation and disarray of the painting, these stars and their placement denoting opposing principles suggests the alchemical *hieros gamos,* sacred marriage. This painting seems to use Hermetic symbolism to express a personal experience of the chaos caused by war and the hope of reconciliation; hence the implication of the title, which is "broken" and "restored," alluding to the alchemical axiom *solve et coagula.*

Duchamp's early Ready-Mades like the *Bicycle Wheel,* from 1913, presaged the Dada movement, and along with his friends Francis Picabia (1879–1953) and Man Ray (1890–1976) he was part of the initial Dada stirrings that co-occurred in New York in 1915.[36] As a painter Picabia had worked in a great variety of styles, including Impressionism, Abstract art,

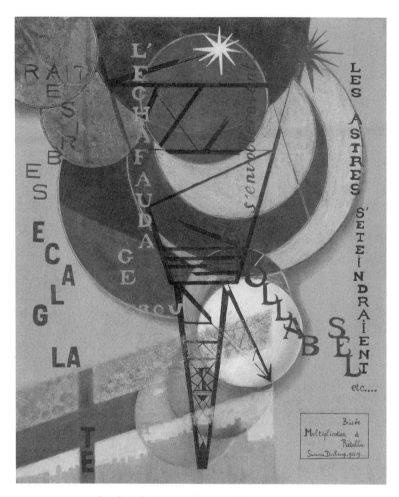

Fig. 3.1. *Broken and Restored Multiplication,*
by Suzanne Duchamp-Crotti, 1918–1919.
Courtesy of WikiArt

and Cubism, and often shifted between different styles, breaking convention without remorse. He became increasingly inspired by mechanical imagery and geometry, and this theme was present in his early Dada work in which he used color sparingly and included other materials like wood and metallic powders. He also gave poetic titles to his work within the composition that seem to bear no correlation to the image itself—one finds a similar disparity between certain alchemical texts where the illustrations and accompanying discourses seem unrelated. His first wife, Gabrielle Buffet-Picabia, explains that "these titles are exceedingly mysterious for anyone who hopes to find in them any key to reality. The whole develops in an imaginary realm, where the relations between words and forms have no objective, representational intent, but recreate among themselves their own intrinsic relations."[37]

Picabia's Dada paintings were particularly influential for Max Ernst (1891–1976), a key figure in both Dada and Surrealism. Ernst's early work was both Cubist and Expressionist, however in 1919 he became fully involved with Dada in Cologne, an epicenter of the German Dada movement. Ernst, along with the communist poet and artist Johannes Theodor Baargeld, released the incendiary Dada publication *Der Ventilator,* and in the same year Ernst produced *Fiat Modes pereat ars* (Let there be fashion, down with art), an incredible portfolio of highly irrational and dreamlike lithographs. Ernst was influenced by the work of Italian artist Giogio de Chirico, considered to be the chief precursor of Surrealism with his *Scuola Metafisica* (Metaphysical Art) style.[38] This influence is evidenced in Ernst's 1919 painting *Aquis Submersus* (Submerged in Water). The painting depicts a pool beneath a dark sky, surrounded by a disjunctive assortment of small buildings. Aloft in the sky is a clock, which appears as a moon reflected upon the water's surface. In the water is a half-submerged diver, and in the foreground is a mysterious and statuesque figure. Within this dreamy scene we are reminded of the necessity for the artist to submerge themselves in the watery world of the unconscious to retrieve inspiration.

Cologne Dada, according to Ernst, was not concerned with shocking the bourgeoisie; it was a cathartic release of "vital energy and rage" in response to the war.[39] In 1920 a scandalous Dada exhibition was held in Cologne, called *Dada-Vorfrühling* (Dada Early Spring). Attendees were forced to enter through a lavatory and then led to the bloody aquarium of Baargeld's *Fluidoskeptik.* Ernst also included a wooden object with an ax tied to it by a rope, which the participants were invited to use destructively to express their own rage, a pervasive feeling throughout post-war Germany. As Gascoyne relates, "Dada expressed nothing but revolt: it was delirium, the public could never understand it unless they felt the same way themselves."[40] The exhibition was so shocking that the police shut it down, only reopening it after a pornographic reproduction of Dürer's engraving *Adam and Eve* was removed.[41] The Dada movement in Cologne continued to have exhibitions for the next couple of years. Ernst relocated to Paris in 1923, where he would join the likes of Picabia, Tzara, Breton, and Paul Éluard, the latter of whom became his close friend and colleague.

The Dada movement inevitably fractured from within, beginning as early as 1924, due to conflicts within the group. Despite its brevity, Dada continued to exist even as other movements took the center stage of the world's attention, and it was an important influence in the development of Surrealism, as well as certain aspects of modern, abstract, and contemporary art. From the ashes of Dada's destructive flames the spirit of the movement was resurrected in Surrealism in an evolved form, a transition that Gascoyne describes as "dialectic," and initiated by the nonconforming Dadaists.[42] Where Dada was defined by negation, destruction, dissolution, and nihilism, Surrealism was "negation of negation; a new affirmation," seeking to unify the rational and irrational realms in a new coagulated form.[43]

4
Surrealism
The Automatic Solution

Surrealism's achievement is to have proclaimed that all normal humans are completely equal in relation to the subliminal message, and to have maintained constantly that this message is a common heritage of which we each have only to claim our share, and which must at all costs soon cease to be seen as the preserve of the few. Every man and every woman deserves the personal conviction that they themselves can, by right, have resource at will to this language which is not in any way supernatural, and is the vehicle, for each and every one of us, of revelation.

—ANDRÉ BRETON, "THE AUTOMATIC MESSAGE"

A century has now passed since the birth of Surrealism in 1920, the year of the first technically Surrealist text and the same year that Dada began to flourish in Paris. Like Dada, Surrealism was a revolutionary movement, a reaction to the absurdity of the war and a disdain for the bourgeois values that catalyzed it. Initially a literary movement, it didn't take long for it to affect the other arts, including collage, sculpture, painting, theater, and cinema. Dada was like an alchemical destruction and dismemberment of art; a reduction of the artistic ego to its most basic elements and a necessary step leading to its regeneration, which the Surrealists realized in their creative drive to unify the inner and outer world, the irrational and rational. Through the techniques they developed in automatism, surprising juxtapositions, and the element of chance, they aspired to liberate the imagination and unconscious from their subjugation by the "real." Alchemy, magic, and the occult played a significant role in the way that the Surrealists came to understand the unconscious, evident in their creative expressions and theoretical writings.

The inception of Surrealism is generally considered to be the year that André Breton wrote the first *Manifeste du surréalisme*—1924—but the first true surrealist text was *Les Champs magnétiques,* or *The Magnetic Fields* (1920), a collaborative collection of automatic writings by André Breton (1896–1966) and Philippe Soupault (1897–1990). Breton and Soupault were introduced by the poet and playwright Guillaume Apollinaire (1880–1918), who coined the term *surréalisme* in 1917. Apollinaire used it as the subtitle for his play, *Les mamelles de Tiresias: Drame surrealiste* (*The Breasts of Tiresias*), which became the model for avant-garde theater and a key influence of Dada, while the subtitle was taken on by the artists and writers, who called themselves Surrealists.

The Renaissance and Baroque eras were of great influence on many Surrealists, most notably the extraordinarily bizarre tableaus of Hieronymus Bosch and his follower Pieter Bruegel the Elder, as well as the juxtaposition in Giuseppe Arcimboldo's portraits composed of fruits. We've already noted many Surrealist precursors from the nineteenth century in the preceding chapters. Also of great import were the essential writings of Lautréamont, whose phrase "beautiful as the chance meeting on a dissecting table of a sewing machine and an umbrella" epitomized both the Surrealist tenet of objective chance and the meeting of the opposites;[1] Apollinaire and his friend Pierre Reverdy, a poet who wrote of "the bringing together of two remote realities" in 1918;[2] Duchamp with his Ready-Mades; Picasso, one of the first to exemplify Surrealism in painting; Giorgio de Chirico; and the early work of Ernst.

Hegel, Neitzsche, Husserl, and Revel played a role in contributing to Surrealist philosophy, and we mustn't exclude the importance of the anti-capitalist doctrine of Marx, which spoke to the Surrealist desire to liberate the imagination from the dulling effects of the working world, as well as their "tenet of total revolt," shockingly asserted by Breton in his *Second Manifesto*. Also pivotal was the psychological component found in Freud's theory of the unconscious and dreams, the crux of the Surrealist

Fig. 4.1. *The Disquieting Muses,*
by Giorgio de Chirico, 1916–1918.
Courtesy of WikiArt

outlook, as well as the spiritism and psychological studies of mediumship
of Flournoy, Charcot's studies on female hysteria, and Janet's theories concerning psychological automatism.[3]

Occult and alchemical influences of the nineteenth and early twentieth
centuries, like Lévi and Schuré, in large part filtered through Symbolism

and the Romantics, joined with many contemporary Hermetic works emerging in the 1920s, leading to an increased use of alchemical imagery by the Surrealists in the later part of the decade and onward, particularly after World War II.[4] There were also the works of the medieval alchemists, like Flamel, Lully, and Agrippa that provided source material to inspire and inform the Surrealists. Important contemporary influences included Herbert Silberer's psychoanalytic interpretations in *Hidden Symbolism of Alchemy and the Occult Arts* (1917). François Jollivet-Castelot published three novels in the 1920s that were likely part of the Surrealists' fascination.[5] Fulcanelli's *Le Mystère des Cathédrales* (1926) explored the alchemical secrets hidden in the Gothic cathedrals of Paris, inspiring the Surrealists who spent time exploring the famed alchemical sites of the city.[6] Fulcanelli's student, Eugène Léon Canseliet, also produced consequential works, as did Albert Poisson.

Other aspects of Hermeticism, like magic, Qabalah, and tarot, were part of many of the Surrealists' repertoire of occult influences that they combined with their artistic methods for accessing the unconscious, evident in the work of Duchamp, Matta, Seligman, Victor Brauner, Ernst, Leonora Carrington, Remedios Varo, and Salvador Dalí. Surrealism itself is a magical art, as Breton implies in "Secrets of the Magical Surrealist Art," found in the first *Manifesto,* and in his references to Agrippa's Third and Fourth Books of Magic in his *Second Manifesto.*[7] Salvador Dalí (1904–1989) wrote a magical book about painting called *50 Secrets of Magical Craftsmanship,* while Kurt Seligman (1900–1962), an American Surrealist, wrote books and articles on the occult. Because of his wealth of knowledge Seligman became the magic authority of the Surrealist group. Patrick Waldberg notes in his book *Surrealism:* "The surrealists asked their poets and their painters to know how to enchant, which, properly speaking, is a magical process. There must be between the work and the spectator a 'clicking,' a shock, a current, which acts and transforms. 'Beauty,' stated Breton, 'will be convulsive or it will not be.'"[8] One likely source of inspiration was E. A. Grillot de Givry's occult book *Le Musée des sorciers, mages et alchimistes* (1929), rich with Hermetic and alchemical imagery from old manuscripts and paintings, as well as works by artists like Dürer and Goya.[9] Other magicians and initiates that served as alchemical and

Hermetic sources of inspiration included René Alleau, Pierre Mabille, Kurt Seligman, Malcolm de Chazal, and Maurice Baskine.[10]

Leading up to Surrealism's official inception with the first *Manifesto* was a period of experimentation in automatism, trance, and dreams, beginning with *Les Champs magnétiques* and lasting from about 1920 to 1923, frequently referred to as "*La période des sommeils* (the period of sleeping fits)."[11] During these induced trance states, the early Surrealists initiated dialogues resulting in what they considered to be true poetry. The transition from Dada to Surrealism in its final year, 1922–1923, was described by Louis Aragon (1897–1982) as a *mouvement flou,* a vague or flux movement.[12] In his essay "Une Vague de rêves" (A Wave of Dreams, 1924), he provides an essential exposition of the *mouvement flou* and the pivotal role of chance, illusion, dreams, and the fantastic in the Surrealist view of a unified reality.[13] "The first surrealists," he writes, "having reached an extreme of fatigue by the abuse of what still seemed to them a mere game, saw rise up before them the wonders, the great hallucinations that accompany the drunkenness of religions and physical narcotics."[14] Aragon proposes the "existence of a mental substance," of which thought was only a component, and which was capable of undergoing transmutations and becoming concrete, evoking the One Thing. Also reminiscent of Rimbaud's "alchemy of the word," he describes how they experienced the written word becoming tangible to sensation and, reciprocally, how sensations and thoughts could be reduced into a single word. The poet, director, actor, and theorist Antonin Artaud (1896–1948) related this to theater: "We watch mental alchemy creating a gesture out of a state of mind, the dry, naked, linear gestures our acts might have if they sought the absolute."[15] This mental substance, Aragon declares, is "nothing other than vocabulary."[16] The importance of language to the Surrealists can be summed up in the words of Breton: "Language has been given to man so that he may make Surrealist use of it."[17]

As for Breton and Soupault, with their peregrinations through the *Magnetic Fields,* Aragon writes that they had no sense of authorship, and that it was "an Energy" that made the greatest impression upon them in their experiments, "a sense of no longer being themselves, an incomparable feeling of well-being, a liberation of the mind, an unprecedented ability to produce images and the supernatural tone of their writings," and a perception of "a great poetic unity which runs from the prophetic works of all peoples to *Les Illuminations* and *Les Chants de Maldoror*."[18] This poetic unity was something that could be accessed through trance states, and alludes to the many literary and visual precursors to Surrealism in ages past. The Surrealist fascination with trance extended to their use of automatism to induce the *dissolution of all the senses,* by which they enacted a crucial part of the alchemical work.

AUTOMATISM: A UNIVERSAL SOLVENT

Normally associated with Surrealism, automatic drawing was already in practice by late nineteenth-century spiritualists, including a group of women known as "The Five." By as early as 1896 this group was using automatism in the form of mediumistic drawings and writings created during séances contacting "high masters." Among their members was the Swedish artist Hilma af Klint (1862–1944), who in 1906 began channeling, through a spirit guide, extremely innovative abstract paintings, called *The Paintings for the Temple,* and copious notebooks of writings that would convey a crucial message for humankind. Though her work had no connection with or influence upon Surrealism, af Klint shared in the Surrealists' desire to portray the unseen and to make the unknown known. She perceived her work as coming from an externalized spirit, differing from how the Surrealists employed automatism to access their own subconscious. In either case it is something unknown, not directly available to the conscious mind, that must be invited through mediumship or automatism to express itself verbally and visually. However, Breton asserts, the spiritualist aim is to dissociate the personality of the medium, while "the Surrealists' aim is nothing less than to unify that personality."[19]

The term "automatic drawing" was first coined by the English artist and occultist Austin Osman Spare (1886–1956), who despite being considered a precursor to the Surrealists was unknown to them.[20] His work is highly sexual, rich with dark lines and mysterious, indeterminate, morphing figures, in some cases resembling art nouveau and in others, demons from magical grimoires. Spare describes inducing a hypnotic state in himself by staring into a mirror, and then drawing as though in trance for hours. Not unlike af Klint, during the automatic spell he felt "obsessed or possessed by the spirit of some artist, perhaps a dead artist."[21] Yet he also considered automatism to be a way of directly contacting the subconscious.

In his seminal work, *The Book of Pleasure (Self-Love): The Psychology of Ecstasy* (1913), Spare elucidates his mystical ideas concerning self-love and duality, sigil magic, and the subconscious.[22] He presents a union of opposites like the Surrealists' in his conception of a unified universal mind, which he calls *Kia*. In the chapter titled "Automatic Drawing as Means to Art," he asserts, "the one law of Art is its own spontaneity. Its pleasure and freedom."[23] The lack of spontaneity is, in fact, the cause of bad art, as when some learned mannerism obstructs the freeflow of creative energy from the subconscious. For Spare, art is "the sub-conscious love of all things," as well as the expression of the unrealized wisdom of the subconscious. Thus, he defines automatic drawing as "a vital means of expressing what is at the back of your mind,"[24] resulting in imagery that is both original and filled with symbolic meaning.

Spare considers automatism to be the "manifestation of latent desires," though it must be practiced with courage and honesty, with no cognitive conception or guidance, in order that the subconscious might express itself. The technique may be improved with practice in allowing the complete free movement of the hand, drawing simple scribbles without regard for the outcome and with the mind "in a state of oblivion."[25] In time certain forms begin to emerge from the chaos—suggestive to the imagination, personal, and surprising—and the process becomes a form of illumination and "ecstatic power." Spare attributes the genius of Shakespeare's *Hamlet* to a state of revelatory automatism, and asserts that "all significant art . . . comes from that source."[26] Thereby the objects of repression are brought to the surface of awareness, and through the spontaneous expression one may be relieved of the weight of the unknown causes of restlessness, obsession, and ennui.

Breton and Soupault's collaboration in the automatic writing of *Les Champs magnétiques* was inspired by Breton's experiences during the war. Breton was a medical student with a keen interest in mental illness before his conscription. He explored his interests by employing Freudian methods of psychiatric examination on shell-shocked patients, trying to obtain from them swiftly spoken monologues free from self-criticism and inhibition, in what he likened to "spoken thought."[27] He was also influenced by psychologist Pierre Janet's book *Psychological Automatism,* the product of his psychological research at Le Havre from 1882 to 1888.[28] Janet differentiates between total automatism on the one hand—catalepsy, artificial somnambulism (hypnotism), and "successive existences" (alternating personalities)—and partial automatism on the other, including states of absent-mindedness prone to suggestion by means of certain types of distractions, like automatic writing, which could be employed to evoke the subconscious.[29] Breton confided to Soupault his sentiment that the technique of automatic writing could be applied to himself to obtain spontaneous automatic material, and the pair decided to "blacken some paper," producing some fifty pages by the end of the day. They opposed revision of any kind, and the results were much the same for both of them: a tendency toward over-construction, but altogether passionate and rich with surprising imagery as well as humor.[30] This new method of self-discovery and pure expression they called "Surrealism," paying homage to the recently passed Apollinaire for the word, but giving more credit to Nerval as exhibiting the spirit they were invoking with their automatic experiments.[31] Breton's definition of Surrealism and its philosophy emphasizes the nature of thought and also directly describes automatism:

> SURREALISM, *n.* Psychic automatism in its pure state, by which one proposes to express—verbally, by means of the written word, or in any other manner—the actual functioning of thought. Dictated by thought, in the absence of any control exercised by reason, exempt from any aesthetic or moral concern.[32]

After listing a great many writers as intermittent Surrealists—"Sade is surrealist in sadism; Hugo is surrealist when he isn't stupid; Mallarmé is surrealist when he is confiding"—Breton criticizes them for their pride and for wanting more than to "serve simply to orchestrate the marvelous score."[33] The following passage from the 1924 *Manifesto* elucidates his stance:

But we, who have made no effort whatsoever to filter, who in our works have made ourselves into simple receptacles of so many echoes, modest recording instruments who are not mesmerized by the drawings we are making, perhaps we serve an even nobler cause. Thus do we render with integrity the "talent" which has been lent to us. You might as well speak of the talent of this platinum ruler, this mirror, this door, and of the sky, if you like.[34]

One of the first Surrealist painters to experiment with automatic drawing, André Masson (1896–1987), describes it as a two-part process: in the first, "pure scrawl" manifests on paper, consisting of gesture, rhythm, and incantation as a result of entering the void and allowing the unconscious to manifest spontaneously. In the second phase, "the image that was latent reclaims its rights."[35] Masson also supported the Surrealist concept of unifying the opposites, stating, "The unconscious and the conscious, intuition and understanding must operate their transmutation on the mind in radiant unity."[36] Masson would often induce states of delirium, working under duress without eating or drinking, as a means to awaken the unconscious mind.[37] Also adept at automatic drawing was Joan Miró (1893–1983), who along with Man Ray and Yves Tanguy produced collaborative *Exquisite Corpses*. Miró described his painting method as entirely unpremeditated, as though in a dream.[38] Like Masson, Miró conducted his automatic drawings in two stages: first, pure automatism, and second, adjustment and refinement.[39] He also relied on fasting for long periods to facilitate altered states and was inspired by the world of dreams and hallucinations.[40]

Max Ernst experimented with a wide array of techniques; however, automatism was central to his methods. There were many events in Ernst's childhood affecting his development as an artist, including a hallucination of strange organic forms emerging from the lines of a false mahogany panel.[41] For a time Ernst diverged from painting and developed several innovative collage techniques. He compares collage to Rimbaud's "simple hallucination," or like "the alchemy of the visual image."[42] It was "a chance meeting of two distant realities on an unfamiliar plane," a sort of alchemical union akin to the pure act of love, which promulgates their complete transfiguration.[43] His most famous Surrealist technique for arresting the critical mind was what he called *frottage,* which involves placing paper over textured surfaces and rubbing pencil or pigment over them, creating abstract and surreal compositions. Ernst was inspired by Leonardo da Vinci's *Treatise on Painting,* in which he discusses the painter's ability to observe indistinct visual stimulus, such as spots on the wall, clouds, or ashes upon a hearth, and to use their artistic genius of invention to create fantastical compositions. However, he stressed, the technical acuity to depict convincingly that which is suggested is crucial to making proper use of such an imaginative technique. *Frottage* became a quintessential Surrealist technique, along with *grattage,* a similar method executed with paint on canvas.

Breton compared automatism to hypnotism, removing the obstacles blocking hidden creative potential; that it would, if followed to its natural end, lead the writer to visual hallucinations.[44] Thus automatism acts like the mythical alkahest sought by the alchemists, a universal solvent capable of dissolving all other substances, including gold, into their elemental parts. Like the alkahest, automatism dissolves the barriers between the "real" and the "unreal," and reduces the ego to its original matter, revealing the hidden aspects of the unconscious. In the process its component parts are not destroyed but are made available to the conscious mind so they may be acknowledged and integrated on a higher level of awareness. Ultimately the task is to extract the primal pair of Sol and Luna, the soul and spirit, from the unconscious so that they may be purified and reunited into one. The alkahest is Mercury, which we can relate to the Will, and to the spirit and messenger capable of moving between heaven and earth, or as a psychopomp who guides the initiate into the underworld of the unconscious.

Breton cautioned that in both visual and written automatism "there is a great risk of departing from Surrealism if the automatism ceases to flow *underground.* A work cannot be considered Surrealist unless the artist strains to reach the total psychological scope of which consciousness is only a small part."[45] This led Breton to criticize Dalí who, despite having developed the method of "paranoiac-critical activity" used to induce hallucinatory states (for example by gazing into the grains of wood and allowing the imagination to produce fantastic imagery—pareidolia) as well as methods similar to *frottage,* still relied too heavily on classical techniques and academicism.[46] On the other hand, Yves Tanguy's often bleak and highly imaginative landscapes, filled with indeterminate biomorphic forms and often evoking the underwater world of the unconscious, adhered to pure Surrealist form, relying on nothing outside of his internal world.

There were, in fact, two primary approaches used by the Surrealists that demonstrate divergent philosophies within the movement, as explained by Waldberg. On one side, which Waldberg calls the "emblematics," artists like Ernst, Masson, Miró, Matta, Hérold, and Lam were less concerned with exact representation of the idea than they were with its suggestion. On the other side were the "descriptives," or "naturalists of the imaginary," as Waldberg puts it, who were inspired by De Chirico and painted unreal compositions in which the depicted objects adhered to the standards of realism. Dalí, Magritte, Delvaux, and Toyen fall into this latter category.[47] Magritte often represented objects out of context and in exaggerated sizes to draw attention to the inherent mystery present in everyday life. Dalí was steadfastly deliberate in his methods, contrary to the spirit of automatism, but was admired by the Surrealists for his ability to enter hallucinatory states with a measure of composure, allowing him to render his visions with scrupulous detail. He is well known for proclaiming "I don't do drugs. I am drugs." This type of art is sometimes referred to as Magical Realism, exemplified by De Chirico, Dalí, Delvaux, Alexander Kanoldt, Adolf Ziegler, and Frida Kahlo. Emerging in the 1920s, Magical Realism shares many commonalities with Surrealism: strange juxtapositions, fantasy, invented objects, and dreamlike imagery. Yet the Magical Realists focused on the strangeness of reality as opposed to the mysteries of the unconscious.

Dalí came upon the Surrealist scene in 1929, and in many ways has come to represent Surrealism. He developed his method of "paranoiac-critical activity" to exploit the natural state of paranoia through controlled methods, tapping into the powerful associations between divergent objects accessible in such states, and transmuting the subjective into verifiable reality. His use of double images illustrates this objective, in which two images are combined in such a way that both are apparent to the viewer at once. This could theoretically be multiplied from two images to a greater number depending on the artist's breadth of associative imagination and paranoiac aptitude. In his own work Dalí demonstrated "the representation of six simultaneous images without any one of them undergoing the least figurative deformation. . . . Different viewers see different images in this picture; it goes without saying that the treatment is scrupulously realistic."[48] Notable examples of this method are his paintings from 1929, including *The Great Masturbator, The Memory of the Woman Child,* and *The Invisible Man.* Sometimes the various conjoined objects are defined in the title, as in the case of *Sleeping Woman, Horse, Lion* (1930), *Swans Reflecting Elephants* (1937), and *Apparition of Face and Fruit-dish on a Beach* (1938). Nadia Choucha calls the paranoiac-critical method Dalí's philosopher's stone, effectively unifying the opposites in a method that "united frenzy and lucidity and transformed his aberrant perceptions into art."[49]

FEMME-ENFANTS
AND THE UNCONSCIOUS

With their interest in hallucinations, madness, mediums, and seers—and in the dream, the unconscious, and unfiltered self-expression—the Surrealists were also fascinated and inspired by their conception of women. Between the two movements of Symbolism and Surrealism, women's suffrage took hold in many European countries. Women were becoming more empowered, and the concept of the "New Woman" provided a model for women to stand on equal footing with men. Hence Surrealism naturally had an evolved relationship to the feminine. Indeed, far more female Surrealists were recognized than female artists in earlier art movements. Yet the male Surrealists still tended to have a patronizing attitude toward their female counterparts; the *femme-fatale* of the Symbolists had become the Surrealist *femme-enfant,* the woman-child, as portrayed in Breton's Surrealist novel *Nadja.* This conception of the female was essentially inferior, for though the woman-child was the Surrealist muse, inspiring their imaginations in the creation of marvelous works of art, they never expected her own creative capabilities to be equal to theirs.

Part of the allure of the *femme-enfant* was the Surrealist fascination with the primitive, childlike mind that still inhabited a unified reality in which conscious and unconscious—or as Breton says, perception and representation—are not dissociated from one another, as they are in the typical adult.[50] In the 1924 *Manifesto* he writes that "the mind which plunges into Surrealism relives with glowing excitement the best part of its childhood . . . where everything nevertheless conspires to bring about the effective, risk-free purgatory of oneself."[51] He felt that Surrealism offered a second opportunity to revisit one's childhood state and to affect the "dissolution" of the senses, returning to the *single original faculty* that had split in the normal adult.[52] Thus the *femme-enfant* embodied the qualities of intuition, irrationality, innocence, loyalty, submissiveness, and spontaneity. However, it wasn't just the male Surrealists for whom the woman-child was a muse; female Surrealists drew upon this image in an empowered way that asserted their place as equals amongst their male peers. Take for instance the many young girls pictured in the paintings of Dorothea Tanning, such as *Children's Games, Eine Kleine Nachtmusik,* and *The Magic Flower,* or Leonor Fini's paintings *La Leçon D'anatomie* and *Bathers.* Many of Fini's paintings depict empowered women, often in the form of a sphinx, and sometimes androgynous figures in a way that defied the patriarchal mores of Surrealism, placing men in a more submissive position.

The theme of the idealized woman, or *anima,* takes many forms: the virgin, whore, medusa, mermaid, angel, goddess, witch, soror mystica, maiden, mother, crone. Breton portrayed the idea of woman as a savior who could lead the way to the occultation of Surrealism, along with mediums and hysterics, "those who are not afraid to conceive of love as the site of ideal occultation of all thought."[53] The liberation of the feminine and women's independence were vital to changing society. Thus in his "Letter to Seers" (1925) he entreats the women mediums to "give up this passivity."[54] In another essay Breton asserts that "Surrealism has never been tempted to hide from itself the element of glittering fascination in man's love for woman . . . in Surrealism, woman is to be loved and honored as the great promise," holding the key to the realization of the *primordial Androgyne* and the nullification of soul-body dualism.[55]

Automatism, gateway to the unconscious, was a way of accessing the repressed powers of the feminine through which the transformation of the world would be realized. Drawing upon Freud, the Surrealists were interested in the exposition of the unconscious to purify humanity from the dark, repressed undercurrents and corruption, which they saw as the cause of war. Ernst was the example *par excellence* according to Paul Éluard, who writes that "around 1919, when the imagination sought to rule and subdue the dismal monsters strengthened by war, Max Ernst resolved to bury old Reason, which had caused so many discords and disasters, not under its own ruins—from which it makes monuments—but under the free representation of a freed universe."[56] Artaud called it a "corruption of Reason," and declared, "We reject progress . . . come and tear down our houses."[57] Salvador Dalí's *The Burning Giraffe* (1937) illustrated this desire to reduce to ashes the "old Reason" by a tiny giraffe burning in the distance, which he considered prophetic of war and called "the masculine cosmic apocalyptic monster." In the foreground are two looming feminine forms propped up by sticks, the main figure's body affixed with many open drawers—a reference to Freud's notion that the unconscious is like a drawer to be opened and its contents investigated (a repeating theme in Dalí's work). Interestingly the giraffe also appears in the 1930 Surrealist satirical film, *L'Age D'Or* (The Age of Gold), written collaboratively by Dalí and Luis Buñuel. This masterpiece of Surrealist cinema, in which the sexually repressive mores of family, society, and the Catholic Church are comically criticized, opens with a nature documentary on scorpions and their aggressive behavior, venomous tails, anti-social behavior, and love of darkness. Their tendency to burrow under stones and hide from the glaring sun metaphorically speaks to the dominant theme of the film. Society's repressed aggression and sexuality is like a venomous and dangerous creature lurking beneath the unturned stones of the unconscious, leading to irrational aggression, bourgeois hypocrisy, and ultimately war. The film follows the arc of a man and woman thwarted in consummating their passionate love, undergoing an alchemical separation that causes the man to act out his repressed sexuality in several irrational violent acts. Upon their reunion, the man could care less that their passionate affair has cost the lives of countless innocent women and children. When she falls into the arms of another man, however, he violently destroys her boudoir and throws everything out the window, including a burning fir tree, an archbishop and his staff, machinery, white pillow feathers, and a statue of a giraffe. Here again, the giraffe likely reflects Dalí's later use of it as a harbinger of war.

The essential difference between Freud and the Surrealists, as Balakian notes, is that the Surrealists intentionally sought out the absurdity of dreams and hallucinations in their writing to create a new reality. Freud, on the other hand, used dreams in clinical analysis to illustrate disturbances of the personality, maintaining a strict separation between the outer world and the interior world of dream. He held a dogmatic conviction in his sexual theory of the unconscious, eschewing any mysterious conception of it. In fact, he was adamant that it must be defended "against the black tide of mud . . . of occultism," a view that catalyzed the definitive split between Jung and Freud.[58] In comparison, Balakian states that the Surrealist approach "was not an observation or interpretation of the subconscious world but a colonization."[59] Transformation, rather than interpretation of the world, became the goal of the Surrealists. Breton's concluding words in "Speech to the Congress of Writers" encapsulate this objective: "'Transform the world,' Marx said; 'change life,' Rimbaud said. These two watchwords are one for us."[60] It was through the subconscious that the Surrealists sought to enact this revolutionary transformation.

Drawing on the material in dreams allowed the Surrealist to work with the unknown aspects of the self, thereby getting closer to a complete picture of the internal self in relation to the external. Breton described Freud as a sort of savior of the unconscious and irrational dimension of the human experience, which had been lost to rationalism, logic, materialism, and common sense. "I have always been amazed at the way an ordinary observer lends so much more credence and attaches so much more importance to waking events than to those occurring in dreams."[61] The waking state, in Breton's summation, is a "phenomenon of interference," whereas the mind of the dreamer is marked by freedom from such interference, capable of flying uninhibited through all contradictory states, expressing both good and evil, dying only to be reborn— "reawaking among the dead."[62]

Surrealism gives equal ground to the absurd, the unexpected, the perverse, the mundane and aesthetically ambivalent, discarding the notion that art necessarily be created with the end result of beauty as its aim.

The sexually explicit, violent, and dark writings of the Marquis de Sade (1740–1814) greatly influenced Breton and other Surrealists on account of his "desire for moral and social independence."[63] This fascination is memorialized in Man Ray's painting, *Portrait of the Marquis de Sade* (1938), in which he appears in profile with the Bastille burning to the ground. Outsider art and the art of the mentally ill, of children and untrained artists, was also greatly valued.[64] And as the quote of Breton at the beginning of this chapter expresses, the gift of the "subliminal message" and of Surrealism is available to everyone; it is not the sole domain of self-proclaimed artists and seers, but rather something that we can all tap into if we can let loose the imagination.[65]

When creativity is not subject to prescribed rules and not attached to any specific outcome, it allows for a spontaneous outflowing from the unconscious that carries within it an authentic expression of the Soul, free from contrivances. This is what the Surrealist movement sought to move the focus away from aesthetic and technically skilled creations to reveal the value of authentic acts of creation, unfiltered by the desire to please an audience. While this is certainly possible at any skill level, from novice to master, the master differs in having developed the muscle memory that liberates the imagination by allowing effortless expression of the body without mental interference. It is the feeling that one's hand is being moved, not by directives of the mind, but by Spirit. The trained artist, however, runs the risk of becoming trapped in technique and chained by the rules of their training. Like a shy lover, the unconscious needs to be given the space to emerge, but if the conscious, rational mind is dominant and exerting control, it will remain hidden from our view. One of the shared aims of alchemy and Surrealism is to break down the rational ego that inhibits, with its conditioned rejection of absurdity, the freeflow of unconscious and imaginal elements. The imagination, subjugated by the "reign of logic," as Breton writes, "is perhaps on the point of reasserting itself, of reclaiming its rights."[66]

The clash of the opposites within the human experience, and the suffering wrought by dualism, is the driving impetus for the Surrealist, who by their art seeks reconciliation. It is the unconscious and subjective experience that has been repressed, denied, and invalidated by the domination of the conscious, objective experience, and thus reconciliation has its beginnings in the liberation of the unconscious. As the unconscious corresponds with the feminine, we see that this movement is intimately connected with feminism and the fight for equal rights for LGBTQIA+ and marginalized communities. It is in essence a movement away from patriarchal, masculine, conscious domination to attain an equanimous existence wherein the two polarities are united in one. The Surrealists aimed to affect this change in the mass consciousness; however, it can't be said that they succeeded, for this is a state that humanity has not yet attained—the complete merging of the "real" and the "imaginary." Until enough individuals undergo the alchemical *solve et coagula* to reveal the underlying resolution of waking life with its mysterious mistress of the night, to realize, as Breton asserted, that it is "the imagination which alone *causes* real things," a goal toward which only the few are inspired, then the completion of the Surrealist vision will remain a distant fantasy.[67]

ALCHEMY AND
THE SURREALIST'S STONE

The investigative spirit of Surrealism is on par with the motive of the alchemist, who seeks to understand the relationship between consciousness and matter; likewise, both are synonymous with the Hermetic search for gnosis. Breton believed in "the future resolution of these two states, dream and reality, which are seemingly so contradictory, into a sort of absolute reality, a *surreality*."[68] This resolution of the conscious and unconscious minds is nothing other than the alchemical unification of Sol and Luna, the two primal principles of Sulfur and Mercury; the interaction between these two primary aspects of the human experience is itself an act of creation.

More than resolving the conflict, however, Surrealism seeks to find that place where the opposites already exist in unity. On another plane altogether, this superreality or surreality could be discovered, resulting in the "annihilation of the being into a diamond, all blind and interior, which is no more the soul of ice than that of fire."[69] This jewel evokes the self-perfecting motivation of the *opus* and the creation of the *lapis philosophorum.* Breton also directly compares the goals of the Surrealist with the alchemist, calling the philosopher's stone "that which was to enable man's imagination to take a stunning revenge on all things, which brings us once again, after centuries of the mind's domestication and insane resignation, to the attempt to liberate once and for all the imagination by the 'long, immense, reasoned derangement of the senses' and all the rest."[70] In his first *Manifesto* (1924) there is a passage with a clear alchemical parallel to the dangers of opening the *prima materia,* or the unconscious. He remarks that in this shadowy region there is the "soluble fish," and then compares himself with it: "am I not the soluble fish, I was born under the sign of Pisces, and man is soluble in his thought!"[71] This solubility speaks to Mercury as the solvent breaking down barriers to the unconscious, as well as a certain level of mercurial illusion. Artaud noted this in relation to the illusion of theater, writing, "All true alchemists know that the alchemical symbol is a mirage as the theater is a mirage."[72] Alchemical symbols "start the mind on its way toward that fiery purification, that unification and that emancipation," leading the way to the unconscious mind, which is ultimately unknowable, save for by the illusory nature of dreams and those subtle impressions we can never fully grasp.[73] "Our brains are dulled by the incurable mania of wanting to make the unknown known, classifiable," writes Breton.[74]

Soluble Fish (1924) is also the name of a surrealist work of Breton's, replete with Hermetic and alchemical imagery, conveying themes of sexuality, inner exploration, death, and metamorphosis.[75] He mentions the zodiac and associated archetypes (lion, bull, virgin, twins) as well as the date March 21, which he calls "the first day of the feminine season of flame," which is the first day of Aries, the traditional time to begin the alchemical *magnum opus.* There are also many other alchemical references, including lines like "the dew of evening and the sweat of stars," "the road to immortality," "I closed my eyes to spy or purify myself," and "What saint with an apron of roses has caused this divine extract to flow in veins of stone?"[76] References to Mercury and to the colors red and white appear throughout, and he writes of alchemical imagery like bones and blood, milk, circles and triangles, snakes, verdigris, the lodestone, and a central furnace. Birds and "underwater elevators" evoke the up and down movement of a circular distillation and the levels of the unconscious. The number eight is mentioned several times, conjuring the Hermetic doctrine of the eighth sphere and the transcendence of fate. One can find each of the four elements, Earth, Water, Fire, and Air, represented in *Soluble Fish,* as well as allusions to the four stages of the alchemical *opus,* as we will return to in the chapters to follow.[77]

Like many alchemical texts, the disarray in which it is presented obscures the meaning of Breton's *Soluble Fish*. Indeed, this inherent disorderly quality of Surrealist automatic writing is reminiscent of the alchemical tradition of veiling the secrets in allegories, intentional misspellings, endless and mixed metaphors, riddles, parables, and by jumbling the order of operations to confuse the unworthy. However, this is also a method of awakening the collective unconscious within the reader, so long as they don't exert too much effort in analysis. The cryptic presentation reaches beyond the rational, critical faculties of the mind, touching something much deeper. While we can appreciate them and certainly interpret them to a certain degree, we must respect the mystery of the unknowable that exists between the lines and allow the words and images to penetrate the unconscious.

This quality of occultation appears in one particularly alchemical book by Ernst, who was also greatly influenced by alchemical imagery and philosophies. It was around 1920 that alchemical imagery started to make itself apparent in his work, likely influenced by Silberer's psychoanalytic interpretations of alchemy in *Hidden Symbolism*.[78] His third book of collages, *Une Semaine de Bonté* (A Week of Kindness, 1934), a series of 182 collages with no accompanying text other than the title pages, is really a kind of anti-novel, defying simple interpretation and rational sequencing.[79] The lack of a linear story is part of the disorder that allows the viewer to make their own subjective meaning from the images. However, the book is Hermetically organized into seven chapters after the days of the week, which as we know correspond to the seven planets; to each chapter Ernst assigns one of "Seven Deadly Elements." Created from found illustrations in nineteenth-century novels and scientific journals, reorganized and printed photomechanically, the collages appear as seamless images.[80] Like many alchemical engravings they are replete with suggestions of sexual aggression, animal-headed humans reminiscent of ancient Egyptian gods, various stages of meta-morphosis, and elemental themes (see figures 4.2 and 4.3). The first four books (Sunday through Wednesday) represent the four elements of Earth, Water, Fire, and Air, or, as Ernst defines them, mud, water, fire, and blood. Adhering to the occultation of the art, each of the covers is of a different color that doesn't correspond with the traditional colors for the elements or with the stages of the Great Work: burgundy for mud, green for water, red for fire, and blue for blood. Volume five, with a yellow cover, represents the quintessence, the fifth element, and contains within it the chapters Thursday through Saturday.

Fig. 4.2. Collage by Max Ernst, from "The Lion of Belfort,"
vol. I in *Une Semaine de Bonté* (A Week of Kindness, 1934).
Digital Image © The Museum of Modern Art/Licensed by SCALA / Art Resource, NY
© 2022 Artists Rights Society (ARS), New York / ADAGP, Paris

Fig. 4.3. Collage by Max Ernst, from "The Rooster's Laugh,"
vol. 5 in *Une Semaine de Bonté* (A Week of Kindness, 1934).
Digital Image © The Museum of Modern Art/Licensed by SCALA / Art Resource, NY
© 2022 Artists Rights Society (ARS), New York / ADAGP, Paris

In her article "Max Ernst's Alchemical Novel: '*Une Semaine de Bonté*,'" M. E. Warlick relates the first three chapters (Sunday through Tuesday) to the three primary stages of the *magnum opus,* as well as the three in volume 5 (Thursday through Saturday) as a further stage of refinement leading to the production of gold, while Wednesday, in the middle, serves as a transition.[81] However it also makes sense to divide the seven days into four and three, numbers symbolic of earth and heaven, or the fourfold model of the alchemical *opus* combined with the alchemical trinity. In this format the first four chapters (Sunday through Wednesday) correspond to the four stages: mud is the earthy quality of the first stage (*nigredo*), water the purification of the second (*albedo*), fire the application of heat to the vessel (*citrinitas*), and blood the reddening in the last stage (*rubedo*). The final three chapters in volume 5 (Thursday, Friday, and Saturday) then relate to the birth of the stone and its further refinement and augmentation. As we move through the four stages of the *opus* we will see in more detail how Ernst's chapters relate to them.*

Like the collages of *Une Semaine,* animal imagery featured prominently in Ernst's paintings, but it was the bird with which he personally identified. Birds also feature extensively in alchemical illustrations, often used to demonstrate the various stages of the work—a crow for putrefaction, a dove for ablution, and a phoenix for the red conjunction. They are also sometimes shown flying up or down inside the alchemical vessel, representing the movement of volatile gasses. Birds and eggs are a common symbol for many of the Surrealists, including the Czech painter Toyen and Remedios Varo. Inspired by alchemy, magic, science, mysticism, and the occult, Varo depicted clear alchemical symbolism in her painting *Creation of the Birds* (1957), in which a hybrid human-owl woman refracts the light of a star through a prism onto her canvas, from which two small birds emerge. Meanwhile an alchemical vessel receives cosmic effluence from the stars, transmuting it into a trinity of pigments as the three primary colors deposited on her palette.

Ernst's preoccupation with birds began at fifteen when a fusion between birth and death, and between birds and humans, was traumatically inculcated in his mind. To his horror he discovered the corpse of his beloved pink cockatoo; it was at this same moment his father announced the birth of his sister Loni. The impact of these two coinciding events was so disturbing that Ernst fainted, and the event catalyzed a period of crises involving fits of hysteria, depression, and exalted mystical states. Throughout his life Ernst drew upon such periods of emotional crises as crucial sources of creative inspiration.[82] The conflation of birds and humans, impressed upon his imagination, evolved into a totemistic character in his paintings known as Loplop, a birdlike shamanistic or mythical representation of himself that he referred to as the *Bird Superior,*

---

*All of the images from Max Ernst's *Une Semaine de Bonté* (A Week of Kindness) referred to throughout this book are visible on the Museum of Modern Art website (MoMA.org).

"an extraordinary phantom of model fidelity who attached himself" to Ernst.[83] This alter ego became a sort of personal psychopomp and mouthpiece, standing at the gateway between the conscious and unconscious and acting as his messenger. Following a profusion of bird imagery in his work through the 1920s, Loplop appears in Ernst's collage novel *The Hundred Headless Woman* (1929), taking on various forms including a swallow and playing the hero alongside the "Hundred-Headless" woman, whom he also names "Perterbation," his sister who, like the unconscious, "keeps her secret."[84] From there Loplop appears in numerous works in which he is "presenting" various personas within frames. However, it is in Ernst's paintings using the technique of decalcomania that the true character of Loplop comes to life, such as *The Barbarians* (1937), or the owls and other birds appearing in *The Robing of the Bride* (1940) and *Marlene* (*Mother and son*) (1940–41).

Decalcomania, a technique of pressing paint against canvas, often with a flat sheet of paper or glass, creates unexpected results that can be refined. Originated by Oscar Dominguez, the technique was further developed by Ernst and other Surrealists. *The Robing of the Bride* was painted with this technique during the upheaval of World War II, when Ernst was separated from his lover, Leonora Carrington, and involved with Peggy Guggenheim, a lover and patron. As Joanna Moorhead describes, the central imposing figure of the painting is Guggenheim, who is pushing Leonora out of the picture, while a helpless and disempowered Max, or Loplop, stands by with a broken spear.[85] Interpreted alchemically, the red robe of the central form is evocative of the *rubedo* and the Red King, yet it adorns a woman's pale body, placing this figure as the androgynous union of the red and white primal pair. The owl-like face alludes to Athena's bird of wisdom, as well as the messenger of the night and the unconscious. Meanwhile, a strange green hermaphrodite occupies the lower right corner of the painting—crying, pregnant, and ready to give birth to the philosopher's stone. Similar themes are present in one of Ernst's most remarkable paintings, *The Antipope* (1941), painted after his move to New York with Guggenheim when Ernst was still hoping to rekindle his relationship with Carrington. Again, a female form robed in red appears, this time with the head of a horse, with an owl-like face in its crowning adornments. Like

Max's totem Loplop, Leonora often painted the figure of a horse as an animal totem symbolic of herself, and thus Max's use of horse-headed figures in *The Antipope* is suggestive of his ongoing involvement with her.[86]

Born in the year of Apollinaire's first use of the term *Surrealism,* Carrington (1917–2011) was a British artist who immigrated to Mexico after World War II. Interested in alchemy, Tibetan Buddhism, and Celtic mythology, her paintings and stories abound in magical and alchemical imagery. Her relationship with Ernst, which began a year after seeing Ernst's work at London's first International Surrealist Exhibition in 1936, was no doubt an influence in this regard.[87] Ernst became her teacher, showing her his *frottage* technique and opening her up to a world of new intellectual ideas, and she quickly became part of the Surrealist group in Paris. Later in her life, Carrington defined Surrealism as "a state of the spirit and no more; a state that can't be explained."[88] Her paintings became increasingly more extraordinary as time went on, especially after her heroic journey through mental illness, documented in her short story "Down Below." The political upheaval of World War II brought the idyllic honeymoon phase of Ernst and Leonora's relationship to an end, precipitating her mental decline. In 1939, Ernst, a German citizen, was interned by French authorities; in 1940 he was placed in a concentration camp, having been declared by Hitler a "degenerate artist." In "Down Below," Leonora describes eating sparingly and drinking wine during their separation, working at her vines and having to spray them with sulfur, and working up a sweat that she felt was purifying her.[89] Meanwhile Belgium was collapsing, the Germans had arrived in France, and eventually Carrington was convinced to leave Saint-Martin and flee to Spain before the arrival of the encroaching Germans.

During her journey Leonora experienced a dissociative separation of mind and body, feeling that her mind, in manifesting itself, would have an immediate effect on her body and upon other objects. This was the beginning of Leonora's *dissolution of all the senses,* brought on by the stress of her separation from Ernst and the looming threat of war. After two failed attempts at crossing the border to Spain she finally made it to Madrid, where Leonora became convinced that Madrid was "the world's stomach" and that she was the chosen one who must restore it to health, explaining her own dysentery as the "illness of Madrid" manifesting itself in her intestinal tract.[90]

Leonora's deteriorating mental health led to her involuntary admittance to the Santander Mental Asylum in Spain. Her account of her experiences at the sanatorium is harrowing, but reveals a consistent awareness of her own Hermetic transmutation and a deep understanding of her body as the alchemical vessel. At one point she attempted to use an egg as though it were a crystal ball, calling it "the macrocosm and the microcosm." She found "Hermetic answers" to her queries in street posters and experienced a sense of inner completion: "I was all, all was in me." When she stopped menstruating for three months, she "was transforming [her] blood into comprehensive energy—masculine and feminine, microcosmic and macrocosmic—and also into a wine which was drunk by the moon and the sun." The tortures she endured in the sanitarium were purifying her so she could attain Absolute Knowledge: "I felt that, through the agency of the Sun, I was an androgyne, the Moon, the Holy Ghost, a gypsy, an acrobat, Leonora Carrington and a woman."[91] She gave an "alchemistic life" to her personal objects, and in the final stages of her illness she recognized the necessity of extracting the various personalities that had come to inhabit her mind, constructing a physical representation of one of the characters from a three-legged table and a chair, topped by a decanter for a head, in order to externalize the imposing consciousness and rid herself of it.[92] These various personalities are given visual representation in her unnerving painting *Down Below* (1941), populated by five unique women in a nocturnal garden, evidently a depiction of the grounds at Santander.

Carrington's descent into the underworld and her recovery, as difficult as it must have been, was also transcendent, revealing to her in a visceral way the unity of the macrocosm and microcosm. This experience undoubtedly deepened her relationship to painting, and it was after this time that some of her most profound work was created. She immigrated to Mexico, where she created a new life among a small artist's community, including Varo and her husband, Benjamin Péret, Diego Rivera, and Frida Kahlo. Here she devoted herself to her creative work.

Carrington often employed the colors of the alchemical *opus* in her work: red, white, and black, in addition to depicting obvious alchemical symbols. In *Green Tea* (1942), we see a red dog with full breasts and a white horse, each chained to a tree growing from their own tails, evoking the ouroboros. The underworld appears at the bottom of the painting in a cavern of bats and mummies. To the left, a purple vessel with a unicorn's horn holds four stags. The central figure of the painting is wrapped like a mummy in what appears to be a black-and-white cow's hide, unifying the opposites. *The Giantess* (1947) features a Bosch-like monumental character in a red dress and white cloak holding a tiny egg, a symbol of the alchemical vessel. Birds emerge from the figure's cloak and flutter around, while in the background we see an ocean-like sky filled with spectral sea creatures and sailing ships, mysterious forms of the unconscious. Alchemical vessels appear in her painting *Nigromante* (The Conjurer, 1960), in which the main figure is an androgyne robed in black and white. Nearby an alchemical vessel, redolent of a flower bud, contains a white doglike creature enfolded by white wings. The entire painting, situated in an enclosed room—again suggestive of the vessel— is dominated by black, white, and gray, except for six blue eggs and a red wall. *Operation Wednesday,* painted in 1969, features an enigmatic figure veiled in black next to an alchemical vessel and other laboratory apparatus. The tiled ground beneath them is covered in magical scribblings and populated by demonic creatures, as well as a dead dove whose blood is spilling out, evoking the alchemical transition from the white to the red. The transition from the initial blackening (*nigredo*) work of the *magnum opus* to the stage of purification is portrayed in *Bird Bath* (1974). Here a red and white dodo-like bird is being washed by two figures in black, one of them whose head is a crow, a common symbol for the *nigredo*. *The Burning of Giordano Bruno* (1964) conveys the alchemical *hieros gamos,* the red conjunction of the opposites (*rubedo*), by a strikingly overall red coloring and the inclusion of the reddish-gold lion (Sulfur) and white unicorn (Mercury) crowned by Mercury's symbol.

Dalí also had an interest in alchemy, claiming to be a descendent of the Catalan alchemist and philosopher Raymond Lully.[93] "My whole life is an alchemy that transmutes everything into gold," he writes in his *Unspeakable Confessions,* a view that extended to his understanding of the human body as akin to the alchemical vessel:

I have an alchemist's view of the human being. I do not believe in an abstract notion of man—his genitals, his odors, his excreta, the genes of his blood, his Eros, his dreams, and his death are an integral part of existence. I believe on the contrary that the "substance being sought is the same as that from which it must be derived," which is the basic principle of alchemy. Every element of matter has a treasure within it. And man to me is alchemical matter par excellence: the well from which wealth must flow, the gold mine of the absolute, provided you know how to transcend it. Gold is the true proof of knowledge, of God, of the laws of life, and the deeper morality.[94]

In another passage Dalí writes, "Every morning I need to have the golden diarrhea rain down on my head, and for each of my drawings to turn into legal tender, so my gold can go and multiply incessantly in the bank," intimating the magical relationship between his art and the golden fertilizing rains spoken of in alchemy, and the multiplying powers of the stone.[95] He was aware of the shared correlation between gold, excrement, and the subconscious, and saw his paranoiac-critical method as a way to "perform a phenomenal transmutation."[96] This correlation formed a primary theme in *L'Age D'Or*. Near the beginning images of churning feces and a flushing toilet reveal the substrate upon which the "Age of Gold" is founded. Throughout the film bourgeois society is criticized, as they remain oblivious to the "shit" that none of them want to see unfolding around them as they enjoy their privileged existence.

In one of Dalí's particularly striking paintings, *Project for "Bacchanale"* (1939), a giant white eyeless swan occupies the foreground, its breast in the shape of a cracked egg with a gaping black void. A golden pyramid rests behind it, showing only its outer bases with steps leading up, suggestive of the stairs that are climbed by the initiate or hero setting out on the journey. The swan, like the philosophical egg, has been opened, and it appears as though the void is the only way to the path leading up the treacherous mountain, the peak of which bears a hole echoing that in the swan. Visible through the opening, a beautiful golden palace awaits. In the sky are clouds of flame, the fires of transformation, and all around are skeletal fragments, suggesting the figurative death of the hero on their journey to the golden palace. The whiteness of the swan signifies the purifying effect of stepping into the abyss, for in the darkness is where the inner light, the *lumen naturæ,* is born by necessity, just as the stone—the true imagination—is birthed from the *prima materia.* "All great art is born of alchemy and going beyond death," writes Dalí, "but I make gold by transcending my innards through hyperconsciousness."[97]

Alchemy, with its goal of unifying opposing principles and its wisdom concerning various stages of transmutation, provided a wealth of inspiration to the Surrealists, aligning with their search for the "marvelous" in all things.[98] Where Romanticism was a liberation of the imagination and subjective feeling of the artist; Symbolism an exploration of the unconscious waters and the dark, decadent dreams below; and Dada a destructive reorientation to art; Surrealism is the royal marriage, extracting the treasures from the bottom of the unconscious sea, reducing the primacy of aesthetic quality in favor of personal revelation and the unified authenticity of the artist, and transmuting lead into gold through automatism. Like the alchemists in their laboratories, the Surrealists gazed into their creations while simultaneously turning inward to give birth to works that have multiplied through time in the imaginations of all who see them. Although they certainly recognized the dangers and the risks involved in such a venture, they were willing to descend into the unknown. Thus Breton asks in the *Second Manifesto,*

> Does one or does one not want to risk everything for the mere pleasure of perceiving in the distance, at the bottom of the crucible into which we propose to cast our slim resources, what is still left of our good reputation and our doubts, together pell-mell with the pretty, "sensitive" glassware, the radical notion of impotence and the foolishness of our so-called duties, *the light that will cease to fail?*[99]

What the Surrealists understood was the power of the *mundus imaginalis* in accessing the unconscious *prima materia,* the first matter of the stone, and bringing it to perfection through their magical art. In some cases, like with Ernst, the stages of the *opus* and the goal of the *coniunctio oppositorum* seem well represented and clearly acknowledged. His painting

Men Shall Know Nothing of This (1923) depicts the union of the Sun and Moon, and is inscribed on the back with the words, "The picture is curious because of its symmetry. The two sexes balance one another." Ernst himself admitted that this painting was imbued with alchemical significance.[100] In others alchemy appears as a persistent metaphor and inspiration yet remains occulted. Then there are those for whom the Great Work manifests in the events and dramas of their lives, as in the case of Leonora Carrington and her journey into and out of alchemical dissolution. Automatism provides an artistic means of delving deep into the uncharted territory of our own dark imaginings and transmuting our hidden obsessions into eternal artforms. Through reconciliation we find our way to gnosis and the attainment of the philosopher's stone. By integrating one's own creative process with the *magnum opus*, one engages on the path of creative alchemy, leading to inner and outer transformation and a full liberation of the true imagination.

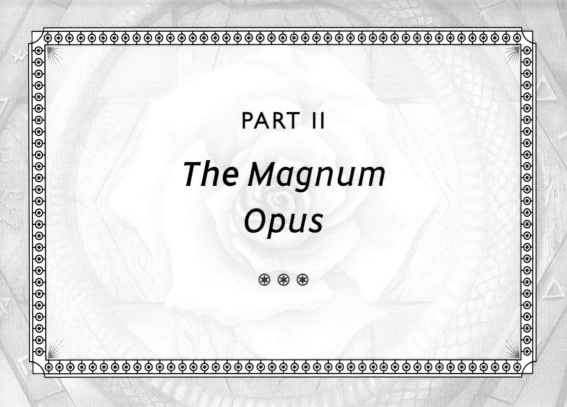

PART II

The Magnum Opus

✦ ✦ ✦

The twofold fiery male must be fed with a snowy swan, and then they must mutually slay each other and restore each other to life. The air of the imprisoned fiery male will occupy three of the four quarters of the world, and make up three parts of the imprisoned fiery male, that the death-song of the swans may be distinctly heard. Then the swan roasted will become food for the King, and the fiery King will be seized with great love towards the Queen, and will take his fill of delight in embracing her, until they both vanish and coalesce into one body.

—Basil Valentine, the Sixth Key

5
Creative Alchemy
Essentials of the Great Work

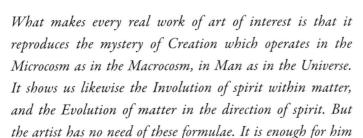

What makes every real work of art of interest is that it reproduces the mystery of Creation which operates in the Microcosm as in the Macrocosm, in Man as in the Universe. It shows us likewise the Involution of spirit within matter, and the Evolution of matter in the direction of spirit. But the artist has no need of these formulae. It is enough for him to recognize by intuition and experience the hierarchy of the generating Principles of Beauty. For so the great ones worked and ever will work.

—Edward Schuré

The quote above by Edward Schuré posits that we have, as artists, the ability to replicate in our own art the very processes of Creation itself, without the need of understanding the formulas involved. However he is speaking of the "great ones" that have liberated their imagination and realized their creative expression to its fullest potential. How do we become these great artists, producing great works of timeless beauty, when we are limited by opposing energies and thoughts, by social and familial conditioning, and other unconscious factors inhibiting our authentic creative voice? Alchemy teaches us the formulas by which latent potentialities can be accessed and liberated, so that we may become fully self-actualized, not only in our artistic abilities, but in the creation of our lives.

Following the arc of artistic expression from Romanticism, Symbolism, and Dada, to Surrealism, we see how the hidden world of the artist and their unbounded imagination has slowly been wrested from its subjugation, first as an assertion by the Romantic artists to express the freedom of their emotional subjectivity and spiritual relationship with nature as the created world of God; then as a deeper dive into the world of dreams and a shadowy exploration of sexuality, the feminine, and an initial submersion into the unconscious that came through Symbolism; to realms of complete abstraction and nihilism and even a rejection of art in the Dada movement; and finally, to the unifying drive of the Surrealists to bring together the real and unreal into a new reality altogether. All of these artistic movements set the stage for modern and contemporary art and the diversity and freedom we see in art today. Like waves in a vast sea, these historical movements in art have not dissipated, but remain part of the whole, finding their expression in various ways and continuing to inspire and inform new work.

For the Symbolists it was the idea that became more important than the image; this was taken to an extreme by the Dadaists, with protest itself becoming the creative act. The Surrealists have come the closest to the ideal that the inner and outer worlds may be wed in an alchemical sacred marriage, in which the limitations of the conscious mind are mitigated to allow for complete freedom of imagination. In all cases, it was the *infinite* that was the unifying source of inspiration for all these movements, yet the word carried a different meaning for each, as Balakian concludes: "The Romanticist aspired to the infinite, the symbolist thought he could discover it, the surrealist believed he could create it."[1]

In the chapters to follow, we will explore creative alchemy, a method in which the artist—as *artifex,* the master of their art—approaches their work as the *magnum opus* that it really is. This goes beyond the creation of fantastic forms and expressions to an intimate relationship between consciousness and matter, presupposing inner transmutation through the creative process and, in turn, a spiritization of art that multiplies in the external world. If we are not being transformed—if our art is not itself transforming as much as it is transformative—then we run the risk of art becoming a vapid and hollow expression of some perverted obsession, or distorted by our desire for fame or fortune, repeating formulas that promise external success at the expense of true inner liberation and authenticity. We must abolish the expectation for consistency and predictability, not allowing ourselves to fall into material entrapments and the quest for fool's gold—the reduction of art to a commodity that strips it of its true divine purpose. We must resist comparing ourselves with the culturally conditioned notions of success and dedicate ourselves to the marvelous power of creation in everything that we do. When these aims rob us of our authentic imagination and ability to continually transform ourselves through our work, then we have lost the essence of our creative power.

In the words of Delville, "Materialism is the artist's foe, because it wastes or destroys in him the ideal and creative powers of his being. The genius of art is not to be reconciled to the ignoble attitude of materialism."[2] Innovation necessarily breaks through formulaic conventions and offers a means to ascend to new levels of imaginative potential. True wealth for the artist is not material compensation, but a union between right livelihood and unhindered authenticity, which contributes to spiritual evolution. When success and riches become the driving force behind the creative act, we trade our soul in the process, lost in the quest for fool's gold.

A true union of the conscious and unconscious realms necessitates not just the Surrealist techniques that remove, as much as possible, the influence of the rational mind in the creative act, but also an ability to be consciously involved in the transmutations we experience through creation. As we will explore shortly, these transmutations involve a *disintegration of all the senses* and a merging with the unconscious, as well as a conscious integration of all the strange treasures retrieved from the abyss. As a result, the art that we create, in harmony with our subjective experience, is both surreal and ideal, depending on where we find ourselves in our personal creative evolution. In any case, the beginning is certain death, and this is the process of liberating the imagination from conscious control through a complete debasement of the artistic ego. We must make the journey inward, as Nicolas Flamel advises: "If you would know how metals are transmuted, you must understand from what matter they are generated, and how they are formed in the mines; and that you may not err, you must see and observe, how those transmutations are performed in the bowels or veins of the earth."[3]

Effectively, the royal marriage of art and alchemy brings the transformative alchemical process into the creative process, to the extent that art transforms its creator as it is being created. This distinguishes it from realism and mimetic art that simply reproduces what is externally observed. With every creation some part of the artist is changed; the more substantial the inner transmutation, the more the completed creation will transmute the world. This is akin to the alchemical *proiectio,* the projection of the alchemist's exalted state of consciousness into the external world, thereby transmitting spiritual truth in the process. Yet the only way this is accomplished is if the artist can access the deeper reaches of their being, to succumb to the terrors of the unknown—the *prima materia*—and to face the dragons that lie therein.

Art created for mere aesthetic quality, imitation, monetary gain, or from a place of compulsive escapism will not suffice. When art is created in a way that simultaneously transmutes the soul of its creator, it is imbued with a subtle and sublime quality and will naturally have a powerful effect on others. It is evident when an artist is working from the *prima materia* because their work is inarguably authentic, unique, and continually changing. It is all too easy as an artist to get comfortable with a particular style and then proceed to produce countless repetitions of the same thing. Sure, this may lead to capitalistic success in a world where everyone is striving to create their own brand, to produce predictable results, and to please their audience. And certainly, there are times when we become possessed with a certain theme in our work that compels us to continue exploring the same concept, whether this leads to economic success or not. We can become haunted by an archetype, an idea, taking years or a lifetime to understand and integrate it through the creative process. The alchemists believed that Nature will, in its own time, transmute lead and the other ignoble metals to silver and gold; however this can take inordinate lengths of time. Yet through the royal art, the alchemist comes to understand these natural processes and facilitates them to transpire at a much faster pace. There is nothing wrong with taking the slow road and allowing things to unfold in their own time. Yet the appeal of alchemy is powerful, undeniable, inner and outer transmutation. While it may not always be fast, alchemical transmutation is undoubtedly a quickening of natural processes. And when it does happen swiftly, when we find ourselves in the heat of the crucible, our ego and limiting beliefs burning and transmuting into wafts of smoke, it can be downright frightening. However, if we wish to engage on the alchemical path as an artist, we must relinquish all fears—the fear of failure, of the darkness within, of the vulnerability of authentic expression regardless of aesthetics, and of our creative evolution as an artist.

Creative alchemy is concerned not only with the Idea, but the *inner realization of the Idea*. What is the result of the work? Is it just another picture in our repertoire? Or has something fundamental changed within us as a result? Through the various alchemical processes of the *magnum opus,* we come to discover a more fantastic existence in which the waking and dream worlds are no longer seen as separate, but are intimately interwoven and share in one another continuously, in what Breton called "a state of grace."[4] They are different, but the same; two, but one. A unity of the conscious and unconscious is not created, but realized within the artist through the unfolding evolution of their own personal *magnum opus.* We learn the language of our own dreams by opening a dialogue between conscious curiosity and unconscious mystery, the head and the tail of the ouroboros that unites the beginning and the end, the will and the desire both unified in a shared transcendent factor. Art created from the transcendent Idea wed to its personal experience, and ultimate realization within the artist, will be inherently spiritualized.

Delville believed that only through purifying the self could the artist gain access to the higher realms and become aware of the Ideal.[5] This is the essence of creative alchemy: to develop techniques to access the unconscious, as well as conscious and deliberate, rational work that integrates the higher order of the treasures retrieved from the unconscious. Through the deconstructive methods of Dada and the irrational approach of Surrealism, we break down the structures of the ego and release the dragons of the unconscious. Creative alchemy then teaches us how to purify and refine with the powers of water and fire, dissolving in the unconscious and coagulating through conscious effort, all the while engaging with our art in the material realm as a plastic response to the processes unfolding within our vessel. Then we process through digestion, spiritize through fermentation, integrate through coagulation and fixation, so that we can achieve the power of multiplication and projection through the sublime, unobstructed imagination—the *lapis philosophorum*.

We aspire to the perfection of the soul so that our creations are of a pure, truthful, and spiritual nature, refined by many repeated ablutions of the mind through which imagination is liberated of its restrictions. In our own authentic voice, by the grace of Tahuti, Thoth, Mercury, Hermes, by any name and in all forms—east, south, west, and north; above and below; without and within; in the belly of the wind and nursed by the earth; child of the Sun and Moon; the one who sheds their skin, who is both air and water, lion and unicorn, dragon and hero—we realize our shared being with the supreme, never-ending, miraculous creative power of the Cosmos.

✦ ✦ ✦

Traditional alchemical artwork of the Middle Ages exists as a testament to a time when the demarcation between the conscious and unconscious was not yet so clearly defined. Allegories, parables, irrational imagery, symbols, vagueness, labyrinthine and coded recipes, and endless variations on a single theme are hallmarks of the alchemical art because the alchemists knew that, ultimately, the secret matter is unknowable and unquantifiable, and that all these variations are *one*. So affirms Merculinus, as quoted in the *Rosarium*, that although these orders "be diverse in reason, yet they are all one in matter."[6] The stark separation between the real and unreal, the rational and irrational, was most clearly asserted by the Enlightenment and Scientific Age, after which anything that wasn't verifiable, objective, concrete, factual, and solid was thrown away into the dung heap of the "imaginary." Little did the rationalists realize, however, that all great discoveries and inventions have their origins in that very dung heap, which is the first matter and the last where "this one Stone [that] hath all names" is hidden.[7] Never will the enigma give way to complete penetration, for the deeper we may thrust our sword into the heart of the rose, the more it will shed its petals and continue unfolding from its ever-receding center located in the Self.

Certainly, alchemical artists worked within a range of symbols familiar to the tradition. However, it is evident from the fact that nearly every alchemical manuscript claims to be the sole true and dependable account of the Work that alchemy is inherently unique and different for each artist. According to Morienus,

> [T]he wise varied their maxims and compositions only because they wished them to be understood by men of wisdom and prudence, while the ignorant should remain blind to them; clearly it was for this reason that the wise wrote variously in their books of the stages of the operation. . . . Although all the authorities used different names and maxims, they meant to refer to but one thing, one path and one stage.[8]

That the generation of the stone proceeds through the changing colors of black, white, and red is agreed, yet sometimes there is the yellow stage between the white and red, and some say the work ends in violet as the red becomes perfected. Regardless of the discrepancies, we must make the Work our own and be transformed in the process, for that is the only way to generate the *lapis philosophorum* and bring it to perfection. That is the one path of which Morienus speaks—the path inward. As each of us is absolutely unique in our being, so our alchemical art will vary accordingly.

While we can look to the alchemical processes and ordering of the stages as guides, we must realize the individual, personal, and unique nature of our own artistic approach, allowing ourselves to be flexible, creative, innovative, and adaptable. Further, we must remember that at the core of the work and of utmost importance is the transmutation of the egoic self into the transpersonal Self. In the words of Carl Jung,

> He who does not understand how to free the "truth" in his own soul from its fetters will never make a success of the physical opus, and he who knows how to make the stone can only do so on the basis of right doctrine, through which he himself is transformed, or which he creates through his own transformation.[9]

The alchemical marriage between the spirit and soul, white and red, is a marriage of spirituality and creativity; one without the other will not bring you to the goal. The *magnum opus* begins by separating this pair from their bonded state in the *prima materia* into the opposites and the four elements, de-robing them from the energies of the spheres, dissolving and putrefying them, then purifying them for their divine union, which is the realization of Oneness within the adept and from which flows forth the wellspring of true imagination. While we must come to know ourselves as a bodiless eternity, we must also inhabit the endlessly changing fluidity of being, in which we are co-creating with the wholeness that orchestrates the symphony of life. Through the spirit we receive inspiration; through the soul we give in the form of our creations.

An artist's evolution progresses through various stages of development leading to increased levels of refinement of both the art and the Self. With each successive stage, new discoveries are made and deeper truths about the Self, truths beyond the level of ego, are accessed. Increasing levels of subtlety are achieved to create a sublime malleability and adaptiveness to the trials and tribulations of life. The philosopher's stone is both the beginning material for this unfolding process and its final product. It is found within the alchemist in its raw state and brought to perfection, just as the seed of a creative idea is born in the darkness of the unknown, and brought to fruition through vision, imagination, and dedication. No matter what form of art we are engaged with, the process involves the relationship between consciousness and matter, through which we develop an authentic and transcendent creativity. We turn again to the words of Delville: "Before understanding or attaining to the purification of form, the artist ought to endeavour to purify his soul."[10]

In the following chapters we will rely on the fourfold process in which the *magnum opus* progresses through four distinct color changes as the fire's intensity increases. These colors provide the names of the four stages: *nigredo*—"blackness," *albedo*—"whiteness," *citrinitas*—"yellowness," and *rubedo*—"redness." Alternatively, they are referred to as *melanosis, leucosis, xanthosis,* and *iosis.* Before we begin our journey into the first stage of the *nigredo,* let us review the essential components of alchemical theory (see also *Hermetic Philosophy and Creative Alchemy*).

THE TWO POLARITIES

Balancing the polarities is as fundamental on the magical path as it is in the alchemical *opus,* and the *caduceus,* the staff of Hermes, is quintessential to both traditions. This balance requires the initiate to assess the active and passive principles of *Sulfur* and *Mercury,* as they express themselves in life and the creative process. These we understand as the alchemical Sol and Luna, or the Chinese concepts of *yang/yin*; as light/dark, positive/negative, expansive/contractive, hot/cold, dry/moist, masculine/feminine, volatile (gaseous)/fixed (solid), *spiritus* (spirit)/*anima* (soul), good/evil, *coelum* (heaven)/*terra* (earth), life/death, and all opposites.

Understanding both extremes and their union in the third principle, which is the neutral field in which the opposites interact, we learn to find the balance, not swinging like a pendulum between extremes, but flowing effortlessly between opposing principles like the lemniscate, with no resistance. There is a time to create and a time to await inspiration, just as there is a time for waking and a time for dreaming. As we learn to listen to our own inner voice, we accept the ebb and flow of creativity.

THE THREE PRINCIPLES IN PHYSICAL EXPRESSION AND CREATIVITY

PRINCIPLE	PLANET	SELF	POLARITY	CREATIVE PROCESS
Sulfur 🜍	Sun ☉	Soul/ Consciousness	Active	Creative Impulse
Mercury ☿	Mercury ☿	Spirit/Thought	Neutral	Inspiration
Salt 🜔	Moon ☾	Body/ Unconscious	Passive	Materialization

CORRESPONDENCE

Correspondence is another quintessential aspect of engaging with alchemy, for it provides a symbolic language of communication between the conscious and the unconscious, the macrocosm and the microcosm, the outer and the inner. There are many wonderful sources for learning about correspondences and I highly recommend Aleister Crowley's *Liber 777* and Stephen Skinner's *The Complete Magician's Tables,* which served as references for many of the correspondences listed below and in the appendices. The principle of correspondence, elucidated in the Hermetic axiom "As Above, So Below," may be thought of as an aspect of the collective unconscious, accessible to all and serving as a bridge between symbols of myths and traditions around the world. Yet our work is not simply to memorize correspondence and follow it by rote, but to integrate it with our own personal symbolic world, much like the Symbolists sought to do.

THE FOUR ELEMENTS
AND MAGICAL CORRESPONDENCES

	EARTH	WATER	FIRE	AIR
Symbol	▽	▽	△	△
Tetragrammaton	ה	ה	י	ו
Tarot	Pentacles (Disks)	Cups	Wands	Swords
Zodiac	Taurus, Virgo, Capricorn	Cancer, Scorpio, Pisces	Aries, Leo, Sagittarius	Gemini, Libra, Aquarius
Archangel	Auriel	Gabriel	Michael	Raphael
Season	Winter	Autumn	Summer	Spring
Direction	North	West	South	East
Kerub	Taurus—Bull	Scorpio— Eagle	Leo—Lion	Aquarius— Man
Implement	Pentacle	Cup	Wand	Dagger
Spirit	Gnomes	Undines	Salamanders	Sylphs
Animals	Hooved and horned creatures	Creatures of the water	Pawed, clawed, or scaly	Winged creatures

THE FOUR STAGES OF THE *MAGNUM OPUS*

Nigredo	*Albedo*	*Citrinitas*	*Rubedo*
Black	White	Yellow	Red
Death	Conception	Gestation	Birth
Emanation	Creation	Formation	Manifestation

The Seven Stars

When combined together, the four elements and the three principles correspond to the seven traditional planets. These in turn relate to the seven chakras of the subtle body, from the base of the spine to the crown of the head. Understanding these relationships lies at the heart of creative alchemy, for the chakras bridge the inner and outer experience of the artist, helping us to see the connections between our bodies and the celestial bodies above. Extended correspondence charts of the chakras and planets are included in appendices A and B.

The four stages of the *magnum opus* correspond with the work of the lower chakras:

Nigredo:	Root	Earth	Saturn ♄
Albedo:	Sacral	Water	Jupiter ♃
Citrinitas:	Solar Plexus	Fire	Mars ♂
Rubedo:	Heart	Air	Venus ♀

The *rubedo* represents the successful attainment of harmonious relationship between the elements, serving as a foundation for the work of opening the upper chakras and experiencing the union of Sol and Luna in the *hieros gamos:*

Fixation:	Throat	Mind/Spirit	Mercury ☿
Multiplication:	Third Eye	Body/Salt	Moon ☽
Projection:	Crown	Soul/Sulfur	Sun ☉

PLANETARY QUALITIES

PLANET	METAL	QUALITIES AND ALCHEMICAL THEMES
Sun ☉	Gold	Illumination, Consciousness, Passion, Activity, Truth, Self-knowledge, Expression; Fiery, Active, Strong; Masculine*; King; Father; Eagle, Lion, Phoenix, Cock
Moon ☽	Silver	Dreams, Visions, Unconscious, Imagination, Rest, Purification; Watery, Receptive; Feminine; Queen; Mother; Dove, Unicorn, Dog, Hen
Mercury ☿	Quicksilver/ Mercury	Mind, Thought, Neutrality, Communication, Inspiration, Movement, Spontaneity; Airy and Watery; Changeable, Swift, Active, Fluid; Androgynous; Virgin; Dragon, Snake
Venus ♀	Copper	Love, Desire, Beauty, Sensuality, Compassion; Earthy and Airy; Unifying, Compassionate, Softening; Feminine; Sister; Dove, Swan
Mars ♂	Iron	Will, Action, Impulse, Aggression, Ambition, Power; Fiery and Watery; Separating, Discerning, Passionate, Active; Masculine; Brother; Dragon, Wolf, Cock
Jupiter ♃	Tin	Creativity, Expansion, Power, Wisdom, Justice, Travel, Visionary; Fiery and Watery; Philosophical, Benevolent, Fertilizing, Active; Masculine; Golden Rain; Eagle, Swan
Saturn ♄	Lead	Work, Discipline, Structure *or* Rest, Release, Letting Go; Earthy and Airy; Contractive, Putrefying, Restrictive; Masculine; Skeleton, Death; Wolf, Raven, Dragon

*The terms masculine and feminine in this table are not to be taken as absolute, but simply represent the predominant energy of each planet. In truth all of the planets may be understood in a nonbinary way, exhibiting both masculine and feminine qualities.

Dancing with the Stars

One of the ways that we can begin to attune ourselves to planetary energies is to align ourselves creatively with celestial timing. When we do this it not only deepens our relationship with the archetypes, but it facilitates communication between the conscious and unconscious while also stimulating the imagination. This is like dancing to the music of the spheres, moving in harmony with the flow of cosmic forces. Traditionally, the seven planets each rule over a different day of the week.

PLANETS AND DAYS OF THE WEEK

PLANET	DAY
Sun	Sunday
Moon	Monday
Mars	Tuesday
Mercury	Wednesday
Jupiter	Thursday
Venus	Friday
Saturn	Saturday

Planetary Hours

We can further attune ourselves to the planetary energies by timing our activities with the planetary hours. Like the twenty-four-hour day, there are twenty-four planetary hours in the day; however these are calculated from sunrise to sunset, and from sunset to sunrise. Each of these periods is divided by twelve to create twelve planetary hours in the day and twelve in the night. The first hour of each day, beginning at sunrise, aligns with the planetary ruler of that day. For instance, Saturday begins with the hour of Saturn. From there the planets progress in the Chaldean order of the planets (♄ Saturn, ♃ Jupiter, ♂ Mars, ☉ Sun, ♀ Venus, ☿ Mercury, ☽ Moon) and then repeat. Since the length of the day and night varies throughout the year, the length of the planetary hours varies throughout the year.*

---

*Apps and websites exist that calculate planetary hours.

PLANETARY HOURS SUNRISE TO SUNSET

	(Sunrise) 1	2	3	4	5	6	7	8	9	10	11	12
Saturday	♄	♃	♂	☉	♀	☿	☾	♄	♃	♂	☉	♀
Sunday	☉	♀	☿	☾	♄	♃	♂	☉	♀	☿	☾	♄
Monday	☾	♄	♃	♂	☉	♀	☿	☾	♄	♃	♂	☉
Tuesday	♂	☉	♀	☿	☾	♄	♃	♂	☉	♀	☿	☾
Wednesday	☿	☾	♄	♃	♂	☉	♀	☿	☾	♄	♃	♂
Thursday	♃	♂	☉	♀	☿	☾	♄	♃	♂	☉	♀	☿
Friday	♀	☿	☾	♄	♃	♂	☉	♀	☿	☾	♄	♃

PLANETARY HOURS SUNSET TO SUNRISE

	(Sunset) 13	14	15	16	17	18	19	20	21	22	23	24
Saturday	☿	☾	♄	♃	♂	☉	♀	☿	☾	♄	♃	♂
Sunday	♃	♂	☉	♀	☿	☾	♄	♃	♂	☉	♀	☿
Monday	♀	☿	☾	♄	♃	♂	☉	♀	☿	☾	♄	♃
Tuesday	♄	♃	♂	☉	♀	☿	☾	♄	♃	♂	☉	♀
Wednesday	☉	♀	☿	☾	♄	♃	♂	☉	♀	☿	☾	♄
Thursday	☾	♄	♃	♂	☉	♀	☿	☾	♄	♃	♂	☉
Friday	♂	☉	♀	☿	☾	♄	♃	♂	☉	♀	☿	☾

Planetary Magic

One way of connecting with the planetary energies is to begin a daily ritual of some kind that acknowledges and honors the planets, and to make petitions to them for their divine aid and wisdom. This can be an extremely helpful practice as one goes through the *magnum opus.*

First we want to create a dedicated space for our ritual work, like an altar in a quiet area of our home that we can decorate with items that correspond to the planets we wish to work with (see appendix B). Invoking the planets in their hour and on their day can be facilitated by reciting invocations to them from the *Orphic Hymns,* or those found in *Picatrix,* or writing one's own invocation.[11] The planetary gods are enticed by the offerings we make to them, like burning an incense specific to them and lighting a candle in a corresponding color. We may also gather stones, plants, food and drink offerings, or animal figures or other totem objects that bear either a traditional correspondence or a personal correspondence to the planet one desires to work with and place these upon our altar.

Dressing in a way that reflects the planets' colors and qualities can help to deepen our connection with them and signify our earnestness. For instance, while invoking Jupiter one might wear an outfit that is deep blue or purple—royal colors and vestments that make you feel like royalty. Whereas for Mars we might wear something red or yellow, a bright active color and active clothing in which we are ready to spring into action. We can work with the metals associated with the planets in terms of the jewelry we wear or other objects that we can incorporate into our rituals.

Be creative with this and allow your inspiration and intuition to guide you. After invoking the desired planet, we can then petition them, or say a prayer, for their aid and blessings as we go about our lives and our work. Take some time after the invocation and petition to simply meditate in their energy, allowing space for their wisdom to come through in the form of spontaneous thoughts, visions, and sensations.

LUNAR MAGIC

As the closest celestial body to Earth, the Moon has a powerful influence over the tides and the cycles of animal and vegetable life on Earth, affecting us all physically, emotionally, and psychically. The Moon also holds sway over our dreams and visions, nurturing creativity and fertilizing the imagination. We might think of aligning our creative flow with the planets and circle of the fixed stars as conscious or *yang,* while aligning with lunar cycles is a way to get in touch with the more *yin* or unconscious side of our creativity while also helping us to tap into the collective unconscious. During the Moon's 29.5-day lunation cycle there are phases that are also differentiated as being more *yang* and active or more *yin* and receptive, to which we can attune our own creative flow for increased potency.

> *Dark Moon:* Deep receptivity, *yin*, seeds planted in darkness, dreaming, shadow work, prophecy
>
> *New Moon:* New beginnings, initiating new projects, *yang*, setting intentions, birth
>
> *Waxing Moon:* Growth, increase, development, *yang*, inspiration, constructive work, trust
>
> *Full Moon:* Culmination of energies from the New Moon, *yang*, manifestation, power, passion
>
> *Waning Moon:* Decreasing energy, *yin*, reflection, processing, letting go, purification

In addition to the lunar phases, the swift moving Moon transitions through the zodiac, spending about 2.5 days in each sign, taking on the powers and influences of those signs and their ruling planets. Lunar calendars are helpful tools for keeping track of the Moon's movements through the heavens. Pay attention to what sign the new and full moons fall in and significant events like lunar and solar eclipses.

THE ZODIAC

While the planetary hours and days serve as more immediate means of aligning our creative alchemy operations, the Sun's movement through the twelve signs of the zodiac has a great bearing on the cosmic energies at play around us. We can time our creative rhythms accordingly, choosing the most conducive time to engage with different parts of our process and gaining inspiration from the energetic fluctuations occurring throughout the year. Traditionally the *magnum opus* begins with the initiating fire of Aries.

ZODIAC SIGNS AND THEIR QUALITIES

ZODIAC SIGN	RULING PLANET (POLARITY)	MODALITY	ELEMENT	ARCHETYPE	QUALITIES
♈ Aries	Mars (+)	Cardinal	Fire	Ram	Leader, Initiating, Impulsive, Active
♉ Taurus	Venus (-)	Fixed	Earth	Bull	Stable, Dependable, Hardworking, Sensuous, Romantic
♊ Gemini	Mercury (+)	Mutable	Air	Twins	Swift, Changeable, Intellectual, Impulsive, Energized
♋ Cancer	Moon (-)	Cardinal	Water	Crab	Nurturing, Receptive, Loyal, Emotional
♌ Leo	Sun (+)	Fixed	Fire	Lion	Strong, Willful, Leader, Ambitious, Active
♍ Virgo	Mercury (-)	Mutable	Earth	Virgin	Practical, Organized, Logical, Reliable
♎ Libra	Venus (+)	Cardinal	Air	Scales	Balanced, Honest, Compassionate, Agreeable
♏ Scorpio	Mars (-)	Fixed	Water	Scorpion	Emotional, Passionate, Intense, Loyal
♐ Sagittarius	Jupiter (+)	Mutable	Fire	Archer	Independent, Philosophical, Idealistic, Driven
♑ Capricorn	Saturn (-)	Cardinal	Earth	Sea Goat	Determined, Hardworking, Ambitious, Practical
♒ Aquarius	Saturn (+)	Fixed	Air	Water Bearer	Idealistic, Intellectual, Rebellious, Active
♓ Pisces	Jupiter (-)	Mutable	Water	Two Fishes	Dreamy, Creative, Empathic, Intuitive

Essential Dignities of the Planets

Essential Dignity refers to the condition of a planet as it moves through the different zodiac signs. If the zodiac were a play with each of the signs representing a role, then the planets would be the actors. Some of the roles would be more comfortable for them, and others would not fit well. Thus the planets are either strengthened or weakened depending on their position. The four major dignities are domicile, exaltation, detriment, and fall. While there are other dignities—triplicity, terms/bounds, and Decans/faces—the four major dignities are a good starting point for beginning to work with zodiacal and planetary timing.

ESSENTIAL DIGNITIES OF THE PLANETS

ZODIAC SIGN	DOMICILE	EXALTATION	DETRIMENT	FALL
Aries	Mars ♂	Sun ☉	Venus ♀	Saturn ♄
Taurus	Venus ♀	Moon ☾	Mars ♂	–
Gemini	Mercury ☿	–	Jupiter ♃	–
Cancer	Moon ☾	Jupiter ♃	Saturn ♄	Mars ♂
Leo	Sun ☉	–	Saturn ♄	–
Virgo	Mercury ☿	Mercury ☿	Jupiter ♃	Venus ♀
Libra	Venus ♀	Saturn ♄	Mars ♂	Sun ☉
Scorpio	Mars ♂	–	Venus ♀	Moon ☾
Sagittarius	Jupiter ♃	–	Mercury ☿	–
Capricorn	Saturn ♄	Mars ♂	Moon ☾	Jupiter ♃
Aquarius	Saturn ♄	–	Sun ☉	–
Pisces	Jupiter ♃	Venus ♀	Mercury ☿	Mercury ☿

Domicile: A planet is said to be in its domicile, or "at home," in the sign that it rules. A planet in its domicile, called "domal dignity," is in the strongest position it can have. Here it is the most auspiciously placed and has the most power.

Detriment: Also known as the planet's "exile" or "adversity," detriment refers to when a planet is positioned in the opposite zodiac sign from its domicile. Planets are in their weakest position, or debilitated, when in detriment and are unable to express themselves as freely.

Exaltation: Each of the planets has one sign that is a particularly good position for it, known as its exaltation. Here the planet is stronger than if it is in its detriment or fall, but it is not quite as strong as when positioned in its domicile.

Fall: A planet is in its fall, or "depression," when it is positioned in the sign opposite its exaltation. This is a weak position, though not as debilitating as being in detriment.

Decans

Each of the zodiac signs is further divided into the Decans (also called Decanates or Faces), from the Greek *deka,* meaning "ten." These add increased significance to where a planet resides within a sign according to its degree and are considered sub-rulers of a sign. Since there are twelve zodiac signs, each one occupies 30° of the 360° circle. Each 30° is composed of three Decans of 10° each. According to the Chaldaean model, these begin with the first Decan of Aries (1°–10°), which is assigned to Mars. Then the Decans proceed in the Chaldaean order of the planets (Saturn, Jupiter, Mars, Sun, Venus, Mercury, Moon) so that the second Decan of Aries (11°–20°) is ruled by the Sun, and the third Decan is ruled by Venus. The first Decan of Taurus is then ruled by Mercury, and so on. Thus if Venus appears in the twelfth degree of Scorpio, it is within the second Decan, or Face, of Scorpio, which is ruled by the Sun.

Chaldaean Decans

SIGN	1ST DECAN RULER	2ND DECAN RULER	3RD DECAN RULER
Aries	Mars	Sun	Venus
Taurus	Mercury	Moon	Saturn
Gemini	Jupiter	Mars	Sun
Cancer	Venus	Mercury	Moon
Leo	Saturn	Jupiter	Mars
Virgo	Sun	Venus	Mercury
Libra	Moon	Saturn	Jupiter

(continued on next page)

(continued from previous page)

SIGN	IST DECAN RULER	2ND DECAN RULER	3RD DECAN RULER
Scorpio	Mars	Sun	Venus
Sagittarius	Mercury	Moon	Saturn
Capricorn	Jupiter	Mars	Sun
Aquarius	Venus	Mercury	Moon
Pisces	Saturn	Jupiter	Mars

It is common nowadays to group the Decans according to "triplicity," referring to the elemental triads of the zodiac. Thus the rulers of the three decans are the rulers of the same elemental signs. For instance, Aries corresponds to the fire element, so its Decans are ruled by the rulers of the three fire signs: Aries, Leo, Sagittarius. Thus the first Decan of Aries is ruled by Mars, the second by the Sun, and the third by Jupiter.

Decans According to Triplicity

SIGN	IST DECAN RULER	2ND DECAN RULER	3RD DECAN RULER
Aries	Mars	Sun	Jupiter
Taurus	Venus	Mercury	Saturn
Gemini	Mercury	Venus	Uranus/Saturn
Cancer	Moon	Pluto/Mars	Neptune/Jupiter
Leo	Sun	Jupiter	Mars
Virgo	Mercury	Saturn	Venus
Libra	Venus	Uranus/Saturn	Mercury
Scorpio	Pluto/Mars	Neptune/Jupiter	Moon
Sagittarius	Jupiter	Mars	Sun
Capricorn	Saturn	Venus	Mercury
Aquarius	Uranus/Saturn	Mercury	Venus
Pisces	Neptune/Jupiter	Moon	Pluto/Mars

Plate 1. Submit the black toad to a gentle gestation, and await
the carbuncle's illumination of the darkness.
Bufo in Utero, Marlene Seven Bremner, 2018,
oil on panel, 14 x 14 in.

Plate 2. The winged youth emerges from its prison and ascends the cinnabar mountain. Here lies the bridal chamber of the King and Queen.
Roasting Cinnabar (Dragon's Blood), Marlene Seven Bremner, 2017, oil and casein on panel, 11 x 14 in.

Plate 3. In the warm belly of a swamp lantern, a gentle coction prepares
and purifies the matter to receive the golden ferment of the Soul.
The Golden Pill, Marlene Seven Bremner, 2015,
oil on canvas, 30 x 40 in.

Plate 4. The quickthorn pierces through the mortified body, embraced by the serpent of endless transformation.
Nigredo: The Black Haw (1/4), Marlene Seven Bremner, 2018, oil on panel, 6 x 6 in.

Plate 5. Hermaphroditic holy flowers, redolent o' death, bring us hope for the fruits to come.
Albedo: Flor-Aphrodite and the Whitehorn's Embrace (2/4), Marlene Seven Bremner, 2018, oil on panel, 6 x 6 in.

Plate 6. Solar inspiration tinges the white stone yellow, as the imagination is spiritually ripened.
Citrinitas: To Yellow the Wings, Await the Swelling Haws (3/4), Marlene Seven Bremner, 2018, oil on panel, 6 x 6 in.

Plate 7. The red stone of true imagination is borr within the vessel when the primal pair are brought t union and transmuted by the power of love.
Rubedo: Forever Fixed in the Heart of the Sun (4/4), Marlene Seven Bremner, 2018, oil on panel, 6 x 6 in

Plate 8. Withdraw from the senses in the temple of the Moon,
where flows the elixir of immortality.
The Elixir of Salt, Marlene Seven Bremner, 2019,
oil on canvas, 11 x 14 in.

Plate 9. Joy enters the body of Luna as the red tincture tinges all the world.
The Rule of Submission,
Marlene Seven Bremner, 2017,
oil on panel, 8 x 8 in.

Plate 10. Of solar fire and lunar water, of life and death, make one. Thus you will have the philosopher's stone, opening to daylight, and folding into dreams.
Quintessence of a Day's Dream,
Marlene Seven Bremner,
2021, oil on panel, 8 x 10 in.

Plate 11. Join the rose and cross, the above and below, the end and beginning, and the window of authentic inspiration will open to thee.
Harmonia Elementorum, Marlene Seven Bremner, 2017,
oil on panel, 11 x 14 in.

Plate 12. Extract the lovers from the depths of the sea. Purify and reunite
the red and white, and thus you will reach the golden gate of infinite imagination.
The Lovers of Temperance at Eden's Gate, Marlene Seven Bremner, 2017,
oil on panel, 18 x 18 in.

The Chaldaean and triplicity systems of assigning the planets to the Decans need not conflict with one another, and both planetary sub-rulers can be considered when working with the Decans. Understanding the Decans helps us to fine-tune our planetary timing. Whereas a planet is in a beneficial aspect in its domicile or exaltation, it may be challenged by an inimical relationship with the sub-ruler of the Decan within that sign.

ALCHEMICAL PROCESSES: PRACTICAL AND CREATIVE ALCHEMY

Each of the zodiac signs corresponds to a different alchemical process, illustrated in figure 5.1 on page 118 and described below. Creative alchemy is a conceptual art of transmuting energy on multiple levels, and the twelve alchemical operations are techniques to be used accordingly. As such it is best not to think of any of these processes too dogmatically, but to see them as fluid ideas to facilitate our personal process of transmutation, which may not be linear and neatly divided. Further, multiple processes may be co-occurring at different levels of one's experience. (These processes are listed in order of their appearance in the *magnum opus* to follow.)

Calcination: Reduction to ashes by application of intense heat; the reduction of the ego in order to access authentic creativity and destroy limiting self-beliefs.

Putrefaction: Purification by decomposition; breaking down fixed beliefs that inhibit creative expression and imagination, resulting in the generation of ideas.

Dissolution: Dissolving a substance with chemical solvents or water; submersion in the feminine world of dreams and symbols (automatism as exploratory process).

Distillation: Extracting the liquor (spirit) or oil (soul) from a substance through heating, cooling, and condensation; isolating the essence of a creative idea or separating the subtle from the gross.

Sublimation: Conversion of a solid directly to a gas and back to solid without passing through the liquid state; spiritualizing the work and channeling sexual energy into creative passion.

Fig. 5.1. The four and the three multiply as the twelve—zodiac signs shown with corresponding planetary rulers, elements, and alchemical processes.

Digestion: Gentle heat applied to a substance over a long period of time; rest period allowing things to unfold in their own time as ideas and inspirations are processed, or the gestation period.

Fermentation: The process by which a substance is transformed and given new life through a fermenting agent; activating authentic inspiration and true imagination.

Congelation/Coagulation: Conversion of a fluid to a solid through cooling (water to ice), evaporation, or crystallization; ideas coalescing and the solidification of creative projects.

Fixation: The removal of volatility from a substance such that it endures the fire; the work takes on its final form, creative energies and spiritual lessons are integrated, and the conscious and unconscious are wed within the artist.

Inceration: The completed stone is fused into a waxy malleable substance; final creative/healing crisis as the work is reaching perfection and the pressure is high, ultimately providing an opportunity to step into true creative freedom.

Multiplication: Augmentation of the stone's tincturing powers and the multiplication of gold; complete liberation of the imagination and increased sphere of influence in one's creative work.

Projection: The stone (tincture) is used to transmute base metals into gold; complete union of spiritual and creative processes (gnosis, *creatio continua*) and the ability to creatively transmute reality.

THE HERMETIC PATH

As we move through the stages of the *magnum opus* in the chapters to follow, let us remember to keep our work Hermetically sealed to protect our creative process. As we are advised in the *Rosarium Philosophorum,*

> Remember that your door be well and firmly shut, that he which is within fly not out and thus by the help of God you shall obtain a wished effect. Nature makes her operation by little and little, therefore, I would also that you should do so, yea rather let your imagination be according to nature, and see according to nature, of which bodies are regenerated according to nature in the bowels of the earth. Imagine this by true imagination and not phantastically and likewise see in what colour the decoction of them is made, in whether it be violent or pleasant.[12]

Or as Hermes counsels, "Avoid converse with the many [on these things]; not that I would that thou shouldst keep them selfishly unto thyself, but rather that thou shouldst not seem ridiculous unto the multitude."[13] A Hermetic approach to creativity implies a certain level of discretion when it comes to sharing the details of our process, which helps us to prevent energy leakages and potential interference. We must also become comfortable with solitude, for this is where our deepest and most profound inner work takes place. The Romantic painter Delacroix recognized this calling in his own creative process, reflecting in his journal from March 31, 1824:

> How can one keep one's enthusiasm concentrated on a subject when one is always at the mercy of other people and in constant need of their society? . . . [T]he things we experience for ourselves when we are alone are much stronger and fresher.[14]

As we balance the polarities, we recognize that there are times for solitude and times for society, just as there are times for creating and times for resting.

Also of prime importance in beginning the creative *magnum opus* are the *intention* and *attention* of the artist. Intention implies our resolve to engage in our own personal transformation and awaken hidden potentials within ourselves, to approach our work piously and with devotion, and to hold in our hearts a pure purpose and goal in mind that is oriented toward the greater good. Attention is like the fire beneath our alchemical vessel. It is the inner preparedness and ability to focus our energies toward the completion of the work, the commitment to ourselves on the journey of true self-discovery, and our ability to perceive the sympathetic relationships between the inner and outer world. Creating alchemically requires of the artist an inner transmutation; a familiarity with correspondence; an intrepid dedication to inner truth; and a Hermetic approach to life that involves study, alignment between the microcosm and macrocosm, and application of Hermetic principles. In this art it is paramount that one be dedicated to continual learning. Edward Schuré, quoting the ancient sages, writes, "Through profound study and constant application, man can put himself in conscious touch with the hidden forces in the universe."[15] In this self-education, intuitively approached, we may turn to nature or to books, making connections from as many sources as we can to receive inspiration. Then we work creatively and apply what we have learned, allowing our inner transmutation to awaken our true imagination and cultivate an uninhibited creative expression.

I conclude this introductory chapter to the *magnum opus* with a passage from Basil Valentine's "Twelve Keys":

> Give yourself wholly to study, and be not flighty or double-minded. Let your mind be like a firm Rock, in which all the various sayings of the Sages are reduced to the unity of their common meaning. For a man who is easily influenced in different directions is not likely to find the right path.[16]

6
Nigredo
Putrefaction and the
Generation of the Idea

*In the shadow we again see a precious terror. Thank God,
it's still only Purgatory. With a shudder, we cross what
the occultists call dangerous territory. In my wake I raise
up monsters that are lying in wait; they are not yet too ill-
disposed toward me, and I am not lost, since I fear them.*

—André Breton, *Manifesto of Surrealism* (1924)

The creative work of the *magnum opus* begins in the *nigredo,* otherwise
known as *melanosis,* or "blackening." It is a return to the chaos preceding creation, described by the Egyptians as an impenetrable darkness and
ocean of utter stillness; by the Sumerians as a primeval sea; and in the
Hermetic teachings as a boundless watery darkness. From the abyss, the
void, the gaping maws of vast emptiness, all life emerges. Hence we are
advised in the *Rosarium,* "When you see your matter going black, rejoice,
you are at the beginning of the work."[1] This is a Saturnian dark night of
the soul in which we come face to face with our shadow—those parts of
ourselves that we do not want to see, or cannot see. Shadow work pertains to the personal unconscious, through which we must pass in order
to access the greater depths of the collective unconscious. While we are
all likely familiar with the concept of the shadow, let us refer to Jung's
definition of the shadow as being the negative, dark, and inferior parts of
the personality, met with great resistance.[2] Confronting it is key to deeper
knowledge of the self.

The unacknowledged shadow becomes projected onto others and onto the world to the extent that it is perceived as entirely external to the ego-personality. It is of utmost importance to the artist who seeks to create authentically that the organs of receptivity are not obscured by their own shade. Jung explains that when the shadow becomes conscious, a split is caused between the opposites and a conflict arises that can "strain our psyche to the breaking point, if we take them seriously, or if they take us seriously."[3] While there appears to be no logical solution, the process has its own way of providing a solution that comes with a feeling of grace. Here is where the next phase of the opus begins, the *albedo,* the stage of purification. Until then, however, it is necessary to undergo an initiation into the dark night of the soul.

One finds a prime example of the conflict between the opposites in the first volume of Ernst's *Une Semaine de Bonté.*[4] In this chapter, called "Sunday," is related by Ernst to the element "mud" and as an example, the "Lion of Belfort." Mud, correlated with the first matter of creation in the Phoenician and Orphic cosmogonies, is found within the caverns of the earth where the alchemist must search for the primal matter, a journey inward to retrieve the two principles from their primal undifferentiated state within the raw metals, to be separated and purified.[5] The lion—correlated with the Sun, Sunday's ruler—symbolizes consciousness, gold, the King, Sulfur, and earth. Also a symbol of primal matter, the lion must be conquered at the beginning of the work. Silberer's *Hidden Symbolism* begins with an alchemical parable in which the initiate is required to overcome a lion. In doing so, he dissects (separates) him and finds the red blood and white bones, just as the red and white, or male and female "children" are separated from their undifferentiated primal state.[6] In one of the first collages, Ernst portrays a lion-headed man whose entire torso is composed of a large globe and sunflower. Following is a collage of a woman with a white lily crowning her head, symbolic of the lunar principle and philosophical Mercury; as Silberer notes, red lions and white lilies are alternate names for the red man and white woman.[7] The opposing primal forces represent the incestuous relationship of brother and sister, or male/active and female/passive aspects battling within, equivalent to the *spiritus* (*Logos*) and *anima* (*Eros*).[8] Two lions in the fourth plate of *The Book of Lambspring* demonstrate this, accompanied by the text "It is the greatest prodigy that of two lions is made one" (see figure 6.1).[9] The implicit eroticism and aggression in Ernst's first chapter demonstrate the initial conflict and union of the two primal forces, merged together in one of the collages in a single figure with two heads—one of a woman and one of a male lion, symbolic of the Divine Androgyne (see figure 4.2 on page 85).

Becoming aware of the shadow precipitates a confrontation between the conscious and unconscious, and with it a journey into the dark night. The grimness of the situation is well-captured by Hesiod, who tells us

Spiritus & Anima funt conjungendi & redigendi ad corpus fuum.

Fig. 6.1. The male and female lion as the spirit and soul within the forest of the body. From *The Alchemical Book of Lambspring.* In *Musaeum Hermeticum Reformatum Et Amplificatum,* 1678.

Courtesy of Science History Institute

that Night emerges from Chaos along with "hateful Doom and dark Fate and Death," with Sleep and the "tribe of Dreams." Night also gives birth to Cavil, Misery, Resentment, Deceit and Intimacy, Old Age, Strife, the Hesperides, the Fates, "and the mercilessly punishing Furies who prosecute the transgressions of men and gods."[10] The Hesperides, intimating the fruit to be harvested from enduring the dark passage, balances these difficulties of the *nigredo*. This is the quintessential underworld journey, an experience of purgatory. The punishment received, while it may feel like being burned alive or rotting away, has a purifying effect, as the word *purgatory,* from the Latin *purgatoria,* a "means of cleansing," implies. Such an experience can occur unwillingly, catalyzed by the trials and tribulations of life, or willingly when one courageously chooses to descend into the underworld, like the Sumerian goddess Inanna. We may be shocked at some point by our own reactivity to a situation, realizing that there is something unconscious underlying it that we have been hitherto unaware of. Whatever mental construct or negative impulse is in control must die, and this death wish of the ego is the call of the Great Below. We must temporarily relinquish our power to sink into the depths of our being and confront our hidden and neglected shadow, represented in the Sumerian myth as Inanna's sister Ereshkigal, dark queen of the underworld. Integration of our dark side demands that the ego be humbled and broken down, just as Inanna is turned into a rotting piece of meat and hung upon the wall by her sister. This metaphorical death is an opportunity to release whatever is no longer truly serving our authentic creative expression. In the midst of our suffering, we can acknowledge and validate the pain of our dark side, sorely neglected up to now, giving it love and accepting it as an integral part of us. In this process we recognize how our unconscious has been secretly holding the reins of our conscious behavior, and we begin the work of bringing our conscious and unconscious into collaborative harmony.

The dim light of Saturn, the "star of melancholy," who is both sower and reaper, guides our journey into the night. His cold and gloomy emanation ushers us into decay, and yet within the weak, tawny, distant light of this star we can perceive an exalted beacon of redemption. Creatively, the *nigredo* is a dance with death, what has been called the *melencolia artificialis,* or "artist's melancholy," experienced as a painful and frustrating disconnection from the soul that animates and from the spirit that inspires. We are relegated to the earth realm, stuck in the mud, beset with heaviness and inertia, brought to a crawling pace alongside the slow-moving Saturn. This journey takes us "down the strange lanes of hell, more and more intensely alone," to borrow the words of D. H. Lawrence.[11] Yet through the narrow passage of despair the soul and spirit can be liberated from their earthly prison in order to remember their divine perfection and eternal nature, from which artistic authenticity and the augmentation of imagination is made possible.

Saturn rules over the root chakra and the Earth element, corresponding to the bones. It is common in alchemical engravings to see depictions of corpses, skeletons, bones, tombstones, a black sun, graves, and ravens as references to the *nigredo* and to Saturn. Breton's *Soluble Fish* conjures the *nigredo* with corpses, lead pellets, an underground cave, a gravestone, black rain, and ashes.[12] As we work with the heaviness of lead, the root chakra, and the Earth element, we are getting in touch with the base aspects of our being—exposing the shadow, acknowledging our vulnerability, and developing courage through facing our fears, particularly the fear of death. The root chakra connects the physical body (*corpus*) and first level of the auric body, called the Ætheric Body. Through facing the fear of death and acknowledging the shadow, we make contact with the æthereal part of ourselves that is beyond the physical plane. The result is a realization that we are more than the body, and that there is an enduring and eternal quality of our awareness even as the matter of our physical form is constantly transforming. Recall the words of Sendivogius quoted in part earlier:

> For in regard to our Holy and Blessed Art he for whom the sun shines not, walks in thick darkness, and he who does not see the light of the moon, is involved in the shades of night. Nature has her own light, which is not visible to the outward eye. The shadow of Nature upon our eyes is the body. But where the light of Nature irradiates the mind, this mist is cleared away from the eyes, all difficulties are overcome, and things are seen in their very essence, namely, the inmost heart of our Magnesia, which corresponds to the respective centres of the Sun and Earth. The bodily nature of things is a concealing outward vesture.[13]

Before we can see the *lumen naturæ* and awaken to the beyond, we must turn inward, allowing ourselves to be humbled, reduced, and returned to earth. As Valentinus writes,

> All flesh that is derived from the earth, must be decomposed and again reduced to earth; then the earthy salt produces a new generation by celestial resuscitation. For where there was not first earth, there can be no resurrection in our Magistery. For in earth is the balm of Nature, and the salt of the Sages.[14]

Let us compare this passage to the words of Huelsenbeck in his article "Der neue Mensch" (The New Man, 1917): "We must become very humble before the power of our soul if we wish to experience the imponderable exalted moment, which gives us an answer to most complicated questions, an answer superior to the most precise calculations."[15] Essentially, bodies, metals, or egos must be broken down into their most basic components in order for them to be resurrected and exalted in their transmutation. In our work, we must break down the accumulated "body" of ideas about others, the world, our creative capacities, and ourselves, to be resurrected into a new form and to generate new, truly creative ideas illuminated by the light of Nature.

The first step on the path to self-mastery, and creative mastery, is to become self-aware. As long as we have not confronted our own shadow, our vision will be obscured by its unconscious manifestation in our lives. The body can be broken down by fire or by water, generally accomplished by the alchemical processes of *calcinatio* and *putrefactio,* respectively.

CALCINATIO:
BURNING THE EGO TO ASH

The phoenix renews her youth
only when she is burnt, burnt alive, burnt down
to hot and flocculent ash.

—D. H. LAWRENCE, *PHOENIX*

Calcination, or *calcinatio,* is associated with the zodiacal sign of Aries (March 21–April 19), the Ram, the cardinal fire sign of spring. After the long dark winter, the fire of Aries represents the first degree of fire for the alchemical work. Silberer asserts that "the first step is purification, releasing, that is, otherwise also conceived as calcination, etc.; it takes place through conscience, under whose influence the hard man is made tender and brought to fluidity."[16] The time it takes for spiritual calcination to unfold is in proportion to the density of our lead. In the lab calcination is done within a crucible that can withstand the intense heat required to bring matter to a fine ash, like we see in figure 6.2. An alchemist holds a pair of tongs in his left hand for stoking the fire of calcination. With his right hand he points to a plant split into two roses, symbol of the divergent motions of the two inner forces that must be united through the work by the unifying Mercury. A lion (Sulfur) devours the serpent (Mercury), like the calcining flames, or as the corrosive fire of a solvent, such as sulphuric acid, dissolves a metal.

While the fires burn, the soul may be either manically driven, perhaps to the point of exhaustion, or simply beset with self-doubt, anxiety, compulsive behavior, lack of focus, or an imbalance leading to an excess of ideas over disciplined or inspired creative output. Whatever the case may be, it is an *active* state of transformation. The nature of this transformation is determined by the daimons, the spiritual powers of the planets whose essence is activity, and who drive the lower part of the human soul, for better or worse. Calcination may be experienced in both positive/expansive and negative/contractive ways. It can't be rushed, but may be facilitated by study, contemplation, divination, rituals and invocations, dreamwork, and shadow work—anything that helps to decondition the mind and provide new inspiration. The creative alchemical approach shifts the focus from the *passive* experience of the very *active* assaults of the *nigredo,* to *active* engagement with the daimons, by which one assumes the roles of the gods and begins directing the process, thereby flipping the poles and ascending into the rational part of the soul.

The heat that we apply to our crucible during this time, which is the intensity of our attention, intention, and desire for transformation, has several effects upon the matter. To begin with, impurities within the *body*

Fig. 6.2. Calcining fires in the crucible. Basil Valentine, "Clavis XII." In *Musaeum Hermeticum Reformatum Et Amplificatum,* Frankfurt am Main, Germany, 1678.
Courtesy of Science History Institute

are driven out by the power of the heat, rising in the vapors as smoky shadows that we may not have been aware of hitherto. Like creatures inside a burning house, they flee the fire and are exposed in a way that allows us to recognize the shapes and forms that our earthly desires have sheltered within the walls of our psyche, unnoticed until now. As we move through calcination, paying attention to dreams can help to provide extra insight into the nature of these shadow aspects.

Another aspect of calcination is breaking down mental structures, like walls that have held us within a space that we are ready to expand outward from. The ego can become identified with both positive and negative expressions, which will affect our ability to authentically express ourselves in the world. For example, we might stifle our creative energy out of an assumed humility, masking the fear of failure or rejection. Sometimes we are afraid of outshining others, or of the responsibility required to take our work to the next level. In a negative ego fixation, we might be stuck on thoughts of unworthiness and self-hatred, or a core belief that we don't deserve the things we desire most. Perhaps we have convinced ourselves that we are too busy to create, when truthfully we would rather be busy with other tasks than to engage creatively. In such a way we blame external circumstances for the limitations that we are choosing for ourselves unconsciously. For the transpersonal creative spirit to come through, it is necessary to break down our conditioned responses and return to our original state (*prima materia*). We must "discard the Ego like a coat full of holes," as Hugo Ball puts it, and "drop whatever cannot be sustained." Ball continues:

> There are people who simply cannot bear to give up their Ego. They imagine that they have only one specimen of it. But man has many Egos, just as the onion has many skins. It is not a matter of one Ego more or less. The center is still made of skins. It is astonishing to see how tenaciously man holds on to his prejudices. He endures the harshest torture merely to avoid surrendering himself. The most tender, innermost being of man must be very sensitive; but it is without doubt also very wonderful. Few people attain this insight and notion; because they fear for the vulnerability of their soul. Fear precludes reverence.[17]

Breaking down the "false mansion" is a process of deconstructing egoic fixations, requiring a steady, intensely concentrated fire of attention and willpower to face up to our own illusions.[18] Mars, as the planetary ruler of Aries, provides us with the fighting spirit to conquer our inner dragons. The intensity of the calcining fire will break down our conditioning, burn away base instincts and ego, and reduce us to ash, a "perfectly purified salt of absolute transparence," the *sal sapientiae* or salt of wisdom.[19]

PUTREFACTIO:
DECOMPOSITION AND SEPARATION
OF THE ELEMENTS

. . . out of the Speculum [glass] when you are working see that in the beginning you obtain a black colour, for then you will be certain that you cause putrefaction and proceed in the right method. And again, that blacknesse is cold Earth which is made by a light decoction and is often reiterated till blacknesse be most eminent.

—MICHAEL MAIER, FROM *ATALANTA FUGIENS*

The blackness of the *nigredo* is the *putrefactio* (putrefaction) that occurs with death; it is the decaying matter that also gives rise to new life. It is repeatedly emphasized in alchemical texts that nothing is generated without putrefaction, which is the way that energy (matter) is broken down to its first principles so that something new can be born. Thus, conception and putrefaction are intimately connected. Submerged in the muck, the emotional waters become a putrefying swamp and thoughts take on a negative, stagnant quality as the ego decays. One could hardly capture this mood more clearly than Percy Bysshe Shelley does in *The Spirit of Solitude*:

> *A restless impulse urged him to embark*
> *And meet lone Death on the drear ocean's waste;*
> *For well he knew that mighty Shadow loves*
> *The slimy caverns of the populous deep.*[20]

Yet from this slimy decay arise the rich nutrients required for transformation. It is in the most vile places that we find the philosopher's stone, in dung heaps and filth, or buried deep within the earth's womb. Purported to heal all manner of illnesses and provide the alchemist with eternal life, the stone is also the key to authentic creative expression because it is the very source of creativity itself.

Submitting to the transformation of putrefaction allows for the renewal of the alchemist and for a new creation to emerge. In effect, the "body" of our accumulated conditioned responses to life undergoes a process of decomposition, emitting a putrid odor as we release the emotional, mental, and physical toxicities that have been stored within us. Morienus tells us that the alchemical operation "avails nothing until after decay," and that "this matter must putrefy before it can be poured or made fluid, without which nothing will be attained."[21] Within this festering chaos, we find the *prima materia,* the original matter from which everything was formed. All the elements are involved in the process of putrefaction, just as they are all present within the *prima materia,* albeit in a disorganized state. In the words of Basil Valentine:

> For if anything is to be generated by putrefaction, the process must be as follows: The earth is first decomposed by the moisture which it contains; for without moisture, or water, there can be no true decay; thereupon the decomposed substance is kindled and quickened by the natural heat of fire: for without natural heat no generation can take place. Again, if that which has received the spark of life, is to be stirred up to motion and growth, it must be acted upon by air. For without air, the quickened substance would be choked and stifled in the germ. Hence it manifestly appears that no one element can work effectually without the aid of the others, and that all must contribute towards the generation of anything. Thus their quickening cooperation takes the form of putrefaction, without which there can be neither generation, life, nor growth.[22]

Here the Earth element is the accumulation of these hardened beliefs and ideas we hold about ourselves and the world; the Water element represents the emotional attachment and emotional reaction we have to these beliefs; with the Fire element we activate their transmutation by placing our focused attention upon the matter and remaining steadfast; and finally, through the element of Air we breathe through the transmutation and observe the changes in our thoughts.

Creatively, putrefaction represents a process of allowing ourselves to sit within the unknown, to be present with those aspects of ourselves that we want to release, and with all that is yet unborn within us. This is what stimulates the generation of new ideas and quickens the evolution of our creative capacities, and it is the first step to becoming an authentic creator in alignment with the universal truth, both in art and in living a creatively inspired and artful existence.

Death and the Inner Journey

Just as generation is rooted in putrefaction, life and death are inextricably linked, two aspects of the same cyclical process—one cannot be without the other. Heraclitus describes it as simply a change of states: "Life and death, and waking and sleeping, and youth and old age, are the same; for the latter change and are the former, and the former change back to the latter."[23] For Apollonius things are either filled with matter and visible, or rid of matter and invisible; birth and death are simply illusions.[24] Socrates asks in the *Phaedo*, "Is it not a universal law . . . that opposites are generated always from one another, and that there is a process of generation from one to the other?" He continues, "If life and death are opposites, they are generated the one from the other: they are two, and between them there are two generations."[25] As philosophers "study only dying and death," to love wisdom is a "practice of death."[26] Becoming intimately familiar with death and dying was also a primary aim of Surrealism, as Breton says in the *Manifestoes*: "Surrealism will usher you into death, which is a secret society."[27] We become members of this secret society by dying to the past and to the future, by taking our own tail in our mouth like the ouroboros and realizing that we are being continuously reborn from the death of each moment.

So long as we hold the fear of death in our hearts, we are not truly free. It looms over us like a dark cloud blocking our view of the Sun and the truth that this existence has been and always will be complete, whole, and unmoving, though the world of appearances remains in constant flux. There is no true beginning of anything, for ever do things arise from that which is, and transform in their seeming end to something else, never gone in the final way that death implies. In the words of the pre-Socratic philosopher Parmenides of Elea, "what is is uncreated, and indestructible;

for it is complete, immovable, and without end. Nor was it ever, nor will it be; for now *it is,* all at once, a continuous one."[28] And just as the end and beginning exist in continuity, in every time and place the chaos of undifferentiated consciousness is ever present, just outside the bounds of ordered experience. That we do not see or sense this is both a blessing and a curse, for the separation that occurs in chaos is a torment to the Soul that in its essence seeks order and harmony. Yet without a confrontation with this chaos, and with what we know of as death, we lack the felt experience (gnosis) of how illusory this reality is, an experience that opens the gateway of eternity.

Order emerges from chaos through the power of self-love, as in the Egyptian cosmogenesis in which Atum, "The Completed One," exists in undifferentiated unity and creates the world by masturbation; or the Greek conception of universal creation from the love of Chaos and Spirit, united as one being desiring itself within the Dark Mist. The ordering of the elements follows this act of self-love, as all things are separated out in Nature. We see this reflected in the Hermopolitan cosmogony that describes the primordial darkness composed of a group of eight deities known as the Ogdoad, representing four male-female pairs of opposites like the four elements. Yet the universe is a seamless whole, a continuous and unbroken existence without beginning or end, and thus the implication of any creation myth, whatever it may be, is less an explanation of how things *came to be,* and more an indication of how things are *coming to be* in each moment—the *creatio continua,* or continual creation whose essence is love. Love is the Spirit or Æther, the neutral field that holds polarity together. In every moment, "The Completed One" is engaged in an act of self-love that generates the world of sensory perception and the play of opposites through the elements that we experience as life. Anaxagoras and Empedocles both conceived of the cosmos as being ungenerated and indestructible, and that the only principles at work were mixture and separation of the four elements. Much like the alchemical axiom *solve et coagula,* there is a continual flux between these states of mixture and separation, which are two aspects of the One Thing. For Empedocles it was the forces of Love and Strife that maintained this cosmic balance, love engendering union and strife separation. We could compare these to *Eros* and *Logos,* or the alchemical Sulfur and Mercury, the opposing principles of attraction and repulsion, life and death, endlessly coagulating and dissolving the elemental components of the One Thing.

The key to living fully is held within the intimate and vulnerable acceptance of and communion with death. "You cannot live if you do not die psychologically every minute," writes the Indian philosopher Krishnamurti; "If you die to everything you know, including your family, your memory, everything you have felt, then death is a purification, a rejuvenating process; then death brings innocence and it is only the innocent who are passionate, not the people who believe or who want to find out what happens after death."[29] To be born anew each moment is the ultimate state of illumination, requiring that we endure the flames and putrefaction that reduce us to our most basic components, and all the pain this causes. Alchemy engenders consciousness within the individual, so that one is no longer afraid of death. Through repeated dissolutions the psyche is deconstructed and purified, separated and immolated, and then coagulated into a new solidity so that the eternal consciousness, which was always hidden within, becomes fixed. The psyche integrates on a higher level of understanding that encompasses life and death simultaneously. "To know how to suffer," we are advised by Lévi, "to forbear and to die—such are the first secrets which place us beyond reach of affliction, the desires of the flesh and the fear of annihilation. The man who seeks and finds a glorious death has faith in immortality and universal humanity believes in it with him and for him, raising altars and statues to his memory in token of eternal life."[30]

The inward journey requires a willingness to be in dark, uncomfortable places within. As instructed by the alchemical axiom *visita interiora terra rectificando invenies occultum lapidem* (VITRIOL), we must visit the interior of the earth and rectify what we find to reveal the hidden stone. Within the body we find the seven metals in their raw state, the source of our greatest power when they are brought to light, transmuted, and purified. The embodiment of eternal consciousness demands that we separate the subtle from the gross, uncovering the truth of our existence from beneath layers of false constructs. Trauma, from childhood and other life events, causes scars and contractions in the body due to unexpressed emotions, inhibiting physical, emotional, and creative expression and vitality. In the *nigredo* we are acutely aware of these chthonic forces, confronted with karmic energy patterns inherited from our families and culture. These manifest in a multitude of dysfunctional characteristics and neuroses that are not representative of who we truly are, but with which we have become identified. If left in the womb of the earth, these metals will naturally mature and push out to the surface; however nature works slowly over long spans of time—in our case, over lifetimes. Rather than waiting for nature to perfect these metals, the alchemist seeks them out, extracts them from the mines and brings them to perfection through the Royal Art. Death, as the act of letting go and transformation, is a necessary part of this process.

Beginning the Great Work means enduring—without resistance—the suffering brought on by shifting the attention to the self, rather than the external world. Doing this with honesty and responsibility can be an immensely challenging task, requiring an enormous amount of determination and courage. It is much easier to place the responsibility on others and to blame circumstances that seem beyond our control. In the words of Swedenborg,

> Anyone who imagines that the outer self can be brought into correspondence without inward struggle is mistaken. Times of trial are the means for getting rid of evil and falsity and replacing them with goodness and truth. They are also the means for reducing the attributes of the outer self to obedience, so that the outer self can serve the intermediate self (the rational self) and through this the inner self (or rather the Lord working through the inner self).[31]

By the outer self Swedenborg means the sensory being, "the part of us that thinks on the basis of sense impressions," while the inner self is "our heavenly and spiritual being." In between these is the rational being that acts as a link for communication between the inner and the outer self.[32] What we experience in the *nigredo* is a separation of these inner and outer aspects of our being, the tension of the opposites. Recognizing and feeling this tension is the first step to their reconciliation. "The repression of one of the opposites," writes Jung, "leads only to a prolongation and extension of the conflict, in other words, to a neurosis."[33] He explains that our conscious thinking mind, which seeks to make rational sense of reality and place things into concrete terms, is at odds with the unconscious and irrational tendencies that contradict it, and when these tendencies are especially contradictory they are pushed further down into the unconscious and neglected.[34] Silberer compares these irrational aspects to the repression of the Titans, the "mischief makers" locked up in the depths of Tartarus:

> The earth trembles at their attempts to free themselves. Thus the titanic forces of the soul strive powerfully upward. And as they may not live in the light of consciousness they rave in darkness. They take the main part in the procreation of dreams, produce in some cases hysterical symptoms, compulsion ideas and acts, anxiety neuroses, etc.[35]

Our work begins with exploring these conflicting aspects of ourselves, calling forth what has been ignored and pulling them out of the dark caverns into our awareness.

The *nigredo's* dark night of the soul is depicted in figure 6.3 as a melancholic alchemist dying in their vessel, heavy with saturnine lead, enduring the fury of the winds and fire. His encasement in the circle signifies his entry into the inner world, the circle of the *prima materia,* and the confrontation with the unknown. As Jung puts it, "he must be enclosed in the *vas Hermeticum* and heated until the 'moistness' that still clings to him has departed, i.e., the *humidum radicale* (radical moisture), the *prima materia,* which is the original chaos and the sea (the unconscious)."[36] Elevated above the alchemical vessel are the seven stars, or metals, including the Sun (gold) and Moon (silver), having been released from their earthly tomb in the unconscious so that they can be purified and integrated as a unity. Two winged angels—the opposites of soul (*anima*) and spirit (*spiritus*)—have been separated from the body and will later be rejoined with it in the *coniunctio*—the conjunction of the opposites. A raven rests upon his hands, placed over his sexual organs symbolizing the turn away from the generative principle of life to journey inward into the Self.

Fig. 6.3. The alchemist is enclosed in the vessel during the *nigredo*,
experiencing the separation of *anima* (soul) and *spiritus* (spirit) from
the *corpus* (body). From *Viatorium Spagyricum*,
by Herbrandt Jamsthaler, 1625.
Courtesy of Wellcome Collection

Creative and intellectual types seem to be particularly susceptible to saturnine tendencies, as Marsilio Ficino writes extensively about in the first two of his *Three Books on Life,* and as Delacroix so aptly describes in a journal entry from April 26, 1824:

All my days lead to the same conclusion; an infinite longing for something which I can never have, a void which I cannot fill, an intense desire to create by every means and to struggle as far as possible against the flight of time and the distractions that deaden my soul; then, almost always, there comes a kind of philosophical calm that resigns me to suffering and raises me above petty trifles. But here, perhaps, imagination is again leading me astray, for at the slightest mishap it is goodbye to philosophy. I wish I could identify my soul with that of another person.[37]

Delacroix captures the intensity of creative desire and the struggle against distraction; the submission to suffering and the elevated consciousness that comes from it; and the desire to escape the self, which has become utterly separated from the world. However strong the impulse may be to escape into another person or another world, we must fight it and allow ourselves to face the unknown.

The Symbolist inclination toward decadence and solipsism was a glimpse into the void; some translated what they found into great works of art, literature, and poetry that had a distinctly melancholic quality. Like the shipwrecked old man in the void of Mallarmé's "Dice Throw," we surrender:

> *in some imminent   swirl of hilarity and horror*
> *hovers   on the brink of the abyss*
> *without sprinkling it*
> *or escaping*
> *and draws from it the soothing virgin sign . . .*[38]

Mallarmé seems to suggest that the abyss is both horrifying and hilarious, the sort of maddening experience that one can confront with a certain level of humor. When we do so without sugar-coating it and without attempting to escape, the grace of the Virgin appears and bears us through the dark night. As the alchemist Thomas Vaughan (pseud. Eugenius Philalethes) writes in *Coelum Terrae, or The Magician's Heavenly Chaos,* "the Virgin's sign returns, comes Saturn's reign." In a personification of the Stone in its *nigredo,* he says:

I am not dead, although my spirit's gone,
For it returns, and is both off and on:
Now I have life enough, now I have none.

I suffer'd more than one could justly do;
Three souls I had and all my own, but two
Are fled: the third had almost left me too.[39]

The intensity of the *nigredo* may or may not inhibit creative expression because we are in the process of getting in touch with our true source of inspiration by removing impurities. Yet there is much to be gained from periods of darkness. These times may be marked by a dearth of creative energy, which for an artist can be an excruciating experience. Identification of the creator with their creation is natural, but when the creative juices dry up and the fiery passion goes cold, then what remains of the artist? They are brought back to their primal material and confronted with a loss of self and purpose. Who is the artist without their art? Where do they find a sense of self-worth if not through their chosen mode of expression? Self-doubt and self-questioning are a crucial aspect of developing authentic creativity, a way by which we probe deeper into the depths of the soul and the truth of who we are. Allowing our previously held notions of identity to "die" is painful, but rather than running from it or succumbing to escapism, when we embrace this death we are undergoing a powerful transmutation of the soul. Like the Dutch artist Jan Toorop's drawing, *Loss of Faith* (see figure 6.4), we find ourselves drowning in a sea of uncertainty. However, following the crucifixion is the resurrection, symbolized by Psyche, the Soul, who floats into the scene upon two white swans, a common symbol for the next phase of the *opus,* the *albedo,* and a sign that the dark night of the soul is coming to an end. In the top left corner of the drawing are the seven stars of the planets. A small feminine figure places her right hand upon a bright circle in Psyche's left palm and bears a sword in her left hand, while standing victoriously upon the serpentine dragon of chaos.

Fig. 6.4. The *Loss of Faith,* by Jan Toorop, 1894.
Courtesy of Rijksmuseum

The Artist's Melancholy

There is perhaps no better illustration of the *Melancholia artificialis,* or "artist's melancholy," than Albrecht Dürer's (1471–1528) *Melencolia I* (see figure 6.5), a well-known copper engraving from 1514. A winged androgynous figure—remniscent of the alchemical winged hermaphrodite—sits in a state of melancholy and creative frustration. Above their head the sands of time are falling through an hourglass, symbolic of Saturn, and a bell is ready to be tolled for the death of inspiration. Erwin Panofsky, in his book *The Life and Art of Albrecht Dürer,* puts forth that the engraving's title *Melencolia I* refers to the theory of the four humors of Classical Antiquity, as opposed to what we consider to be the definition of melancholy today, for which he quotes the *Oxford Dictionary:* "mental depression, lack of cheerfulness; tendency to low spirits and brooding; depressing influence of a place, etc."[40] These four humors—Sanguine, Choleric, Melancholic, and Phlegmatic—correspond with four different fluids within the body, as well as the four seasons, elements, winds, directions, phases of life, and the quarters of the day. Of these, the melancholic refers to autumn, the Earth element, the Boreas wind of the north, the mature age of around sixty, and the evening hours. A melancholic disposition is associated with an excess of black bile produced in the spleen, as *melancholia* derives from the Greek μέλας (*melas*), "dark, black," and χολή (*kholé*), "gall, bile."[41] Traditionally corresponding with Saturn, the melancholic was the most reviled and feared of all humors, and the black bile or gall was thought to cause insanity.[42] All this being considered, we must remember that Saturn is associated with earth and therefore both generation and putrefaction. As Panofsky articulates, "As the highest of the planets, as the oldest of the Olympians, and as the former ruler of the Golden Age, he could give power and riches. But as a dry and icy star, and as a cruel father-god dethroned, castrated and imprisoned in the bowels of the earth, he was associated with old age, disablement, sorrow, all kinds of misery, and death."[43] Saturn teaches us that life and death, generation and decay, are indivisible, both in the physical sense and in the small deaths we undergo in our personal transformation.

The main figure of Dürer's engraving holds a compass and an open book, their gaze drifting off into the distance. They seem to be frustrated by some mathematical or creative problem, unable to focus on the work at hand. Over the sea of discontent in the background, a bat flies across the sky bearing the banner inscribed with the drawing's title, *Melencolia I.* It has been put forth that the capital *I* refers to the first stage of a process, like the *nigredo.*[44] However Panofsky suggests the *I* refers rather to the first

Fig. 6.5. *Melencolia I,* by Albrecht Dürer, 1514.
Provided by the Metropolitan Museum of Art

of three types of melancholy as expounded by Henry Cornelius Agrippa in *De Occulta Philosophia,* the original version of which, from 1509–10, was a significant influence upon Dürer's composition.[45] Agrippa proposes that there are three types of geniuses that are each, in their own way, affected and influenced by the *furor melancholicus* associated with Saturn's celestial inspiration. These three geniuses are the imaginative, rational, and mental. In those for whom the imagination is the predominant faculty, the *furor melancholicus* of Saturnian inspiration engenders a *melancholia imaginativa,* closely corresponding with the *melancholia artificialis,* and especially affecting painters, artisans, and architects. When the Saturnian influence comes upon those in whom the rational faculty predominates, it produces great physicians, scientists, philosophers, and orators. Those for whom the mental faculty is strongest are apt to be theologically inspired by the Saturnian *furor.*[46]

Agrippa's ideas concerning melancholy likely influenced Shelley's *Frankenstein,* a fictional example of how the *furor melancholicus* might affect a rational mind, in this case Frankenstein, who was fascinated by the natural philosophies of alchemy.[47] Frankenstein is repeatedly drawn down into the depths of melancholic torture and despair in reaction to having created a monstrous subhuman creature, which on one level is an outward expression of his own shadow. In this sense it is melancholy itself, rooted in early childhood grief for the death of his mother, that is the monster that torments him.* It follows him relentlessly, taking away all the things he loves and holds dear, relegating him to despair, ill health, and the unbearable mental anguish of guilt for the horrible truth that he could not deny in the depths of his soul—that he created this monster by his own will and desire. In the end, Frankenstein concedes to creating a mate for his wretched creation, but then destroys her before completion, inciting the wrath of the daemon. In turn the creature takes the life of Frankenstein's bride on his wedding day, stealing from the poor melancholic man the one happiness remaining to him, his very bride, or on another level, his union with his own soul. In denying the creative impulse in his creature by destroying his female counterpart, Frankenstein also

---

*See Freud, "Mourning and Melancholia."

loses his connection to the divine feminine within himself. His internal torment and endless melancholy are a result of his own enslavement to his creative imagination, disconnected from its divine source.

The inspiration for Agrippa's notion of melancholy derived from *Libri de Vita Triplici* by Marsilio Ficino, the Neoplatonic philosopher of the Renaissance who translated the *Corpus Hermeticum.* Ficino was himself of a saturnine and melancholic disposition, reflected in his own horoscope with Saturn in Aquarius on the Ascendant—a fact that Ficino was quite preoccupied with in his writings and letters.[48] However, Ficino's overall positive view of Saturn and melancholy represented a shift from the melancholic humor's disreputable standing in the Middle Ages to an exalted state as the temperament belonging to intellectuals—poets, philosophers, and theologians—thereby ascribing to Saturn a beneficent influence associated with a contemplative life.[49] Thus the *furor melancholicus* was correlated with the *furor divinis,* Plato's "divine frenzy," which elevated melancholia to an expression of creative genius. In this way Ficino saw melancholy as a gift, reviving Aristotle's perspective on melancholia, or the "atrabilious humor" as described in his *Problemata,* where he correlates the black bile with eminent poets, philosophers, politicians, and artists.[50] As Aristotle explains it, the black bile is both hot and cold, but when heated it stimulates the passions and the intellect, giving rise to prophetic powers and inspiration.[51] He acknowledges that though melancholy's effects are variable, they may be tempered and refined to transmute it into a more ennobled expression.[52]

Ficino describes three causes of melancholy in the learned personality: the first celestial; the second natural; and the third related to human causes. The celestial cause is determined by Saturn's placement in the birth chart. Melancholy is caused naturally when pursuing difficult sciences and studies; the soul draws itself inward in contemplation, removing itself from the external world and becoming fixed in the center, which Ficino equates with Earth and black bile.[53] Finally, the human cause has to do with mental agitation causing the brain to become dry and cold (like Saturn); poor digestion resulting from a diversion of energy away from the stomach and liver to the brain and heart, causing the blood to become cold, thick, and black; and a lack of exercise; all of which darken the spirit and incite within it sadness and fear.[54] "The more difficult the work," he writes, "the greater concentration of mind it requires; and second, that the more they apply their mind to incorporeal truth, the more they are compelled to disjoin it from the body. Hence their body is often rendered as if it were half-alive and often melancholic."[55]

Ficino tempered his own melancholy disposition through physical exercise, music, and keeping regular hours.[56] Exercise increases internal fire, providing an active, heating influence to the cold and dry Saturnian black bile, helping to release superfluities through exhalations and bodily excretions. On the other hand, music nourishes and tempers the spirit, which is the "airy vapour, of our blood and the link between body and soul," providing a remedy for the separation of the soul and the body, as is so compellingly illustrated in Dürer's *Melencolia I*.[57] Finally, following a routine and keeping regular hours in one's work and daily life provides an earthy structure and a source of consistent fuel for the fire. Delacroix expresses this well: "Even one task fulfilled at regular intervals in a man's life can bring order into his life as a whole; everything else hinges upon it."[58] Consistency provides the gentle coction necessary to raise the black bile into the upper regions of the mind, stimulating the intellect and imagination—the process whereby we transform a dull torpor into a state of *furor divinis,* and putrefaction gives way to generation. Valentinus describes this process in his eleventh key:

> Saturn, who is called the greatest of the planets, is the least useful in our Magistery. Nevertheless, it is the chief Key of the whole Art, howbeit set in the lowest and meanest place. Although by its swift flight it has risen to the loftiest height, far above all other luminaries, its feathers must be clipped, and itself brought down to the lowest place, from whence it may once more be raised by putrefaction, and the quickening caused by putrefaction, by which the black is changed to white, and the white to red, until the glorious colour of the triumphant King has been attained.[59]

Yet just as Saturn must be brought down to the lowest place and raised through putrefaction, Saturn bears the scythe and the sickle, farm instruments that cut down the harvest and bring all the stalks down to the same level; in effect, cutting down illusions, analogous to the devouring quality of Saturn. The sickle's curved shape also elicits the crescent moon and feminine principle.[60] Hence Saturn is sometimes known as *Mercurius senex* to the alchemists, or Mercury as an old man, bearing an androgynous quality like the winged hermaphrodite in Dürer's engraving, who has been brought down to the lowest place.[61] The means of ascending to heaven appears as a seven-runged ladder connecting heaven and earth, while the numbers three (heaven) and four (earth) appear as indications of the angel's fixation. We find these numbers above the hermaphrodite's head in the magic square of Jupiter, ruler of the heavens and the one who can overthrow the Saturnian oppressor. Each row, column, and diagonal of the square add up to thirty-four (3 + 4 = 7). Again, in the sundial, its hand stuck between three and four o'clock. And finally, in the strange polyhedron form. This eight-faced polyhedron, now known as Dürer's solid, is composed of six polygons and two triangle faces. It may be viewed as a stretched cube balanced upon a vertex, which has been sliced at the top and bottom vertices, creating the triangle faces—the heavenly triangle meeting the Saturnian, earthy cube. The melancholy angel has fallen and is stuck somewhere between heaven and earth, not in one realm or the other, in a state of limbo.

Another important element of Dürer's engraving is the winged child, or *putto,* an infantile version of the primary figure busy at work, intently focused on writing in a ledger. Together the hermaphrodite and putto demonstrate the passive and active states of the *nigredo* in a state of separation. As Panofsky articulates, this is a separation of theoretical insight and practical skill (we might also say of *Logos* and *Eros*), resulting in "impotence and gloom" for the artist.[62] The putto sits atop a chipped millstone used for grinding grains, evoking the grinding down of the ego. Scattered around the scene are many discarded and unused carpentry and craft tools: nails, a hand plane, a claw hammer, an inkpot, and a saw. A round ball suggests the philosophical egg, or *prima materia,* the sphere of undifferentiated consciousness that must be broken open if there is any hope of reunion between the two separated parts.

Redemption for the winged hermaphrodite is held in a set of keys and a purse dangling from its belted skirt, which according to Dürer's notes, symbolize power and wealth, respectively.[63] Perhaps this suggests the power and inner wealth discovered in the confrontation with melancholy, if we are willing to submit ourselves to the transformative process. From beneath the folds of the hermaphrodite's skirt emerges the mouth of a pair of bellows, and in the crucible behind the polyhedron the flames of transmutation heat the putrefying matter.[64] Over the dark sea, a rainbow encircles a comet, signifying the *cauda pavonis,* or peacock's tail, the heavenly bridge of all colors that leads out of melancholy, merging once again into a uniform white light. The whole scene appears to be illuminated by moonlight, speaking to the lunar quality of the incoming *albedo.* Yet the sullen hermaphrodite seems completely immersed in their saturnine state, unaware of these faint glimmers of hope.

Despite the sad ending of the life of Gérard de Nerval, he managed to transmute his own darkness into an immensely powerful work in *Aurélia.* In this novel Nerval compares the figure in *Melencolia I* with a terrifying dream in which an immense androgynous being, winged and fluttering about, plummets into a dark courtyard.[65] This daemonic figure—the Self—has a rosy hue and wings that shimmer with "countless changing reflections," which Jung relates to the *cauda pavonis,* or peacock's tail.[66] Thus the dreamer on some level recognizes that the fall of the Self holds within it the possibility of redemption and return to wholeness. We are reminded also of a dream of the holocaust survivor and angelic communicator Gitta Mallasz, in which she sees a "human figure in glowing colors, radiating harmony, strength, and peace."[67] The dream indicates a new Individual formed from her image, the "one who forms." To become this radiant being she must "BURN!"[68] Going back to *Aurélia,* the dream is considered by the protagonist to confirm a premonition of his own death. Nerval also refers to *Melencolia I* in his somber hermetic sonnet *El Desdichado,* correlating it with a *black sun.*[69] This sonnet is exemplary of the *nigredo,* for he is "the man of gloom" whose tower is in ruins, and whose "*sole* star is dead." In *Aurélia,* this star shines brightly as a beacon of what the protagonist thinks is his imminent death. The black sun, or *sol niger,* represents an internal and morose Saturnian darkness, yet within its destructive fire is a hidden light.

Fig. 6.6. *Devant le noir Soleil de la MÉLANCOLIE, Lenore apparait*
(*Before the Black Sun of Melancholy, Lenore Appears*), by Odilon Redon, 1882.
Courtesy of Los Angeles County Museum of Art

A particular passage from Ficino's *Letters* about "divine frenzy" gives more context to the winged figure in *Melencolia I.* He praises his friend, Peregrino Agli, to whom the letter is addressed, as being possessed by this divine frenzy and exhibiting the hallmarks of greatness through his writing: "Without this, say Democritus and Plato, no man has ever been great. The powerful emotion and burning desire which your writings express prove, as I have said, that you are inspired and inwardly possessed by that frenzy; and this power, which is manifested in external movements, the ancient philosophers maintained was the most potent proof that the divine force dwelt in our souls."[70] Ficino tells of how souls, through their thoughts and desires, are drawn toward earthly things and depressed into bodies, drinking of the River Lethe and succumbing to forgetfulness, losing their connection with the Divine. The weight that they take on with their earthly thoughts prevents them from flying back to heaven—that is, until they can begin again to contemplate divinity. The heavenly flight is achieved through the two virtues of justice and wisdom, corresponding to moral conduct and contemplation:

> For this reason, he says, souls fly back to heaven on two wings, meaning, as I understand it, these virtues; and likewise Socrates teaches in *Phaedo* that we acquire these by the two parts of philosophy; namely the active and contemplative. Hence, he says again in *Phaedrus* that only the mind of a philosopher regains wings. On recovery of these wings, the soul is separated from the body by their power. Filled with God, it strives with all its might to reach the heavens, and thither it is drawn. Plato calls this drawing away and striving "divine frenzy," and he divides it into four parts. He thinks that men never remember the divine unless they are stirred by its shadows or images, as they may be described, which are perceived by the bodily senses.[71]

In order to fly back to heaven, two wings are required, the reunion of the active and passive aspects of the soul. Being separate, they cannot fly to the heights of heaven to experience "divine frenzy," but by inhabiting the "mind of the philosopher" they may regain these wings, which are the active and contemplative parts of philosophy. "Justice" (activity) and "wisdom" (contemplation), in Dürer's etching, are represented not only by the two main figures of putto and hermaphrodite, but by the scales of justice, relating to Jupiter, and the hourglass, relating to time and Saturn. The hourglass evokes a contemplation of the upper and lower, or heaven and earth, separated by a narrow channel, as well as the necessity of flipping the poles from time to time. In the words of Chevalier and Gheerbrandt concerning the symbolism of the hourglass, "unless we completely reverse

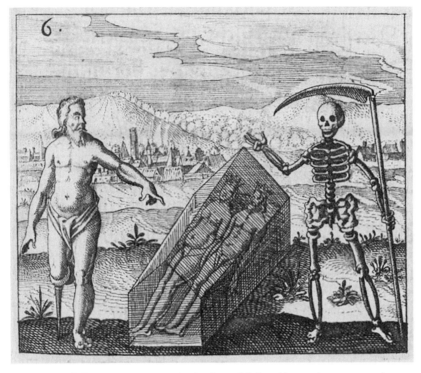

Fig. 6.7. Saturn pointing to the bodies of Sol and Luna, the active and
passive principles, united in death and *putrefactio.* From *Viatorium spagyricum,*
by Herbrandt Jamsthaler, 1625.
Courtesy of Wellcome Collection

our attitudes and activities, we shall always be drawn towards the base."[72]
Whether or not our melancholy is our primary disposition or simply an
emotional state that we endure for a given time, if we choose to see this as
the beginning of a process, as it is in alchemy, rather than an end, then we
are effectively turning the hourglass of Saturnian limitation upon its head,
opening ourselves up to a generative process.

Sometimes the justice that is required is a cathartic release that stimulates the *furor melancholicus,* a disturbingly vivid example of which is provided by the Black Paintings of Goya, so named for their heavy use of
black pigment and nightmarish scenes of witches, evil spirits, demons, and
goblins. Between the years of 1820 and 1823, Goya executed the Black
Paintings feverishly and in Hermetic seclusion, using oil paint directly
applied to the inner plaster walls of his house. This house was called the
Quinta del Sordo (House of the Deaf Man) after its previous owner who

had been deaf. In a strange synchronicity, when Goya bought this house at age seventy-two he too was completely deaf as a result of a neurological illness he had suffered at age forty-six. Goya bought the house in 1819, and between the years 1819–1820 he suffered from a completely different and nearly fatal illness. His work, which had changed following the first illness, changed dramatically again, and the terrifying Black Paintings seem to reflect his own fear of insanity, his brush with death, and his dim, Saturnian imaginings of the grotesque and evil aspects of humanity.

While Saturn's doleful signature is to be found throughout the Black Paintings, one in particular is most relevant to our discourse on Saturn as the dark star of the *nigredo*. In Goya's *Saturn Devouring His Son* (see figure 6.8), a crazed Saturn emerges from an impenetrable dark void, clutching the half-eaten body of his son in his bloody hands. His eyes burn with both surprise and horror, as though realizing his own monstrous insanity. In response to the prophecy that he would be overthrown by one of his children, Saturn devoured each one upon birth. When we act from a place of fear in relation to our creative process, the impulse is to prevent our creations from seeing the light of day for fear of them being the source of our own downfall. Bringing our creations into the world leaves us vulnerable to criticism, threatening to dethrone us from our own Saturnian rulership, a rule of limitation. We limit ourselves within the confines of our own comfort, and there we stay until something comes along to liberate (or obliterate) us. Yet these vulnerabilities provide the matter of our stone. In a sense, Saturn devouring his children represents the desire to break free of limitations, for in consuming something it transforms you. The stone disguised as baby Jupiter is taken over by the blackness of Saturn, "the Key of the Work," without which there is no generation.[73]

In states of Saturnian melancholy the mind may turn against itself in contractive negativity, believing it better to limit one's vulnerabilities than to let others prey upon them. It is also natural in a contractive phase that one desires to disappear—to go dark—and allow the *putrefactio* to take over. This may well have been an aspect to Goya's reclusivity and secrecy in creating the Black Paintings, which differed so drastically from his existing *oeuvre* of enchanting portraits and commissions for Spanish

Fig. 6.8. *Saturn Devouring His Son,* by Francisco de Goya, 1820–1823.
Courtesy of Wikimedia Commons

nobility that earned him such acclaim. In contrast, Goya didn't sign, date, or title the Black Paintings. As far as we know, he never spoke or wrote a word about them, nor did he ever show them to anyone.

Many art historians have proposed a psychological interpretation to the Black Paintings relating to his mental and physical illness; others argue it was his disillusionment due to the atrocities of war that inspired the series, having witnessed the bloody French invasion and Ferdinand's Inquisition. The Black Paintings were a further evolution of a theme running through his earlier paintings, criticizing this political upheaval and senseless inhumanity; the works were unpublished until thirty-five years after his death at a time when it was more acceptable to criticize the warring regimes. Likely the Black Paintings were an expression of his illness and fear of losing his own sanity, and of witnessing the horrors of war, famine, and poverty. These experiences were placed within the vessel of his house, sealed off from prying eyes and external influences that might contaminate their development. The paintings that resulted from this alchemical digestion, like Saturn's unlucky children, were hidden away, perhaps because Goya knew that sharing them with the world would indeed be his own ruin.

Saturn's wife, Ops, whose name means substance, treasure, and power, is a goddess of the earth and fertility.[74] She is the part of us that loves our creations and seeks to protect them. When she gave birth to Jupiter in secret and hid him away, she was committing an act of power to retain the treasured creation of her womb. Her feeding the stone to Saturn is analogous to the way that we must trick the chthonic forces within us and silence the devouring, self-critical mind. It is a different thing altogether to keep one's creation a secret, Hermetically sealed, in order to protect its power than to devour it and stifle it out of fear. Our hidden creation emerges when it has reached maturity, commanding its own liberty and the release (regurgitation) of creative potential. Allowing a creative idea to develop covertly liberates the mind from the debilitating effects of an overly Saturnian self-criticism, projected outward as the threat of a critical audience. Jupiter's return, our liberation, is the purification of mind that is the quintessence of the *albedo,* the result of our work to trick Saturn. The regurgitated stone later becomes the *omphalos* in the Temple at Delphi, a word that denotes the center of one's being.

To outwit the Old Man we have to create *our* stone in order to avoid being devoured by the negativity that can arise with the *nigredo*. Without the stone, we do not have the awareness to escape Saturn's jaws, and in effect, the darkness consumes us. Sometimes it is easier to proceed into the extreme polarity of the dark feminine contraction than to allow ourselves to be vulnerable, which is a quality of balanced feminine receptivity that comes from the dark womb. In Egyptian mythology, the *nigredo* correlates with the death and dismemberment of Osiris while the *albedo,* and dissolution, is the mourning of Isis. It is the feminine quality that softens us and allows us to be immersed in our most vulnerable feelings. It is the wisdom of Athena born from the forehead of Jupiter. It is surrender.

Separating the Black Dragon of Putrefaction

Putrefaction is assigned to the fixed water sign, Scorpio (October 23–November 21). This sign merges death and conception into one watery abyss, corresponding to the sexual and reproductive organs. Its intensity is reflected in the ability of the scorpion to sting itself with its own tail, poisoning itself for the sake of redemption. Yet the scorpion only represents the beginning of Scorpio's journey, for this is a sign of transformation. The scorpion evolves into a serpent and then an eagle, the sign's highest expression. The serpent can be equated with the black dragon of putrefaction, which still carries the venom of the scorpion and must be purged of its poisons before the final evolution of Scorpio can occur.

The Book of Lambspring portrays putrefaction as a black and venomous dragon or beast (see figure 6.9 on page 156) that must be found and beheaded, and as such it is called the head of the raven. This is the magical quest of the hero to slay the dragon, a mythical representative of all the limiting beliefs about ourselves and the world, fears and anxieties, negative and self-deprecating thoughts, imaginary and fantasy constructs, and the stories that imprison us. Essentially, we are deactivating the venomous quality of the "dragon" by our observation and awareness. To behead the dragon is to place it into our vessel and to seal it tightly so that nothing can escape as we ever so gently heat it up with the fire of our attention. Putrefaction results from the break down of "venomous" beliefs preventing us from transmuting our base aspects into their noble counterparts. Beliefs about what we as individuals are capable of and what is possible for all of humanity. Beliefs that keep us below a certain level of development and dampen our creative fire. In order to liberate our full potential as co-creators of not only our own lives but of the entire universe, we must recognize and transmute these limiting beliefs. We must become the author of our own story

PUTREFACTIO.

Fig. 6.9. Confrontation with the vicious black dragon of putrefaction.
From *The Alchemical Book of Lambspring,* in *Musaeum Hermeticum
Reformatum Et Amplificatum,* 1678.
Courtesy of Science History Institute

and make it one that we would want to experience. The old stories must be decomposed, sacrificed for new creative potentials to emerge.

Confronting the venomous and volatile parts of ourselves leads to a deeper understanding of who and what we are. Because all the elements are present in this process, one way to approach it is to take an inventory of each element as we relate to it in our lives. Ideally, all the elements would be in balance and work synergistically in a creative life that moves with the ebb and flow of action and receptivity. However, often one of the elements will be dominant while one or more will be deficient. Thus we can take some time to understand our own elemental composition and in what ways we can bring it into harmony (see appendix C). As Valentinus asserts, "the great change which takes place in these and other substances is due to putrefaction, which separates and transmutes the constituent elements."[75] The process is explained by Thomas Vaughan in the *Coelum Terrae*:

> All those influences of the elements being united in one mass make our sperm or our earth—which is earth and no earth. Take it, if thou doest know it, and divide the essences thereof, not by violence but by natural putrefaction, such as may occasion a genuine dissolution of the compound. Here thou shalt find a miraculous White Water, an influence of the moon, which is the mother of our chaos. It rules in two elements—earth and water.[76]

Before actively trying to transform what we've discovered in the putrid mire, we observe it, feel it, acknowledge its existence, and accept it. Then we can set about transmutation, by which the blackness of putrefaction gives way to a luminous white, marking the beginning of the *albedo* and the birth of our lunar consciousness. In essence, as we break things down, sitting within the miasma of our own rotting thoughts and conditioned beliefs, immersed for a time in a difficult and internally focused decomposition of the ego, eventually we see our consciousness begin to shift into a more reflective space.

The generation and return to life, which is to say creation, follows putrefaction through the reordering of the elements. First, however, separation of the elements must take place. "Separate the earth from the fire, the subtle from the gross, acting prudently and with judgment," as we are advised in the *Emerald Tablet*.[77] To the sign of Scorpio is assigned both the process of *putrefactio* and of *separatio*. As I explored in depth in the chapter on Mars in *Hermetic Philosophy and Creative Alchemy*, separation is an action of the iron of Mars and the inner strength required to behead the dragon. As we've been observing the putrefying mass of the elements, we can begin to identify those things that are the source of the "stinking water": toxic relationships, addictions, limiting self-beliefs, mental fixations, perceived obstacles such as time or resources, or anything that we see as a barrier to our creative expression. On a psycho-emotional level, separation may be experienced as the intense pain of shamanic dismemberment, flaying, mutilation, and torture. It may feel like we are being torn apart from within, or that we are being tortured by the circumstances of life, or we may feel particularly delicate and prone to "shattering." The separation of the soul from the body, mirrored by the separation of the head from the body, leaves us disconnected for a time from our divine source. However, we can harness the power of Mars to gain control of the process by beginning to separate the subtle from the gross—in other words, discerning what we want to cultivate for the betterment of ourselves and our creative expression from what is inhibiting the free flow of creative energy and limiting our potential.

After identifying the obstacles, we can begin finding solutions by actively applying the will. The expression "iron will" relates to this energy as it helps us to strengthen our intentions, correlating with the iron of Mars and the solar plexus chakra. There are many different words we use for willpower, including determination, strength, resolution, self-control, self-discipline, restraint, moderation, drive, purposefulness, commitment, dedication, tenacity, and temperance. Basically we are referring to the ability to refrain from a behavior or compulsion in the short term to obtain a long-term benefit. Whatever we want to call it, it is a function of the Fire element: the strength to sit within discomfort and not turn away, to keep our attention upon the matter as it becomes increasingly black and hold fast to our goal amidst the rising fetid vapors of negative thoughts and emotions. On another level, willpower can help us move through the putrefaction when we apply it to some positive change that we make, in turn imbuing us with the strength we need to continue the work.

In a comprehensive review of evidence on self-control (willpower) consuming a limited resource, Mark Muraven and Roy F. Baumeister found that self-control is depleted in the short term, yet is strengthened in the long term, just like a muscle.[78] Since the muscular system as a whole relates to Mars, the comparison is fittingly rooted in correspondence. What Muraven and Baumeister found, in summary, is that following the exertion of self-control in one situation, self-control in subsequent situations will suffer because the "muscle" of self-control has been depleted and only has so much strength. Self-control is also depleted when an individual is exposed to stress or when experiencing negative moods. However, they also found that regular exercise of self-control, along with periods of rest, will strengthen the "muscle" of self-control, though they caution that this last conclusion requires more evidence.[79] As with anything, developing the will takes practice. So as we observe the putrefaction occurring within our retort, we can begin to separate out the things that we want to change, whether those are thoughts and stories, behaviors, or anything else that is emitting an unpleasant odor in our lives. Through practice and strengthening of the will, we come to transmute these false and injurious aspects of the self into their nobler manifestations.

Fasting is a way that separation can be practiced. We can fast from whatever is creating interference in our body, mind, and soul, whether that is food or some other substance, behavior, activity, relationship, or any other pattern we are stuck in. To begin strengthening the will we can pick one thing that we feel a compulsion toward and take space from it through fasting, either indefinitely or for a set period of time. It needn't be the most difficult thing to abstain from, for the point is to begin strengthening our willpower. Once we exert the will in one area, over time and with practice it will become easier to exert it in other, more challenging areas of our life. Essentially this is a training technique for willpower and can be approached in the same way one might approach a fitness program.

Willpower is weakened and obscured by an excess of external influences, or perhaps it was never given the space to develop. Separation can be employed as an act of sequestration, or temporarily taking space from outside influences, which allows us to reconnect with our own true will.

This is where employing the "Hermetic seal" comes into play—creating a sacred and contained space in which to commune with our work without interruption and external influences that might contaminate a delicate process, comparable to creating a ritual circle. In our creative work this might entail setting aside dedicated time and making a dedicated space in which to work, which may help us hone our focus. Just as having an altar helps to focus our spiritual energies, the space we create holds the energy that we bring to it; each time we return it becomes easier to enter back into our creative flow.

Separation as sequestration is also what many artists are doing when they join a residency program, going away for a specified amount of time to a place where the sole focus will be their creative project. While an official residency is a wonderful opportunity, this can also be done within the context of your current life and living situation. All it takes is the decision to create a separation for yourself and enter into a creative hermitage in order to minimize distractions and focus on creating. Delacroix often remarks on his own desire to minimize the distractions of society and spend more time in solitude:

> My mind is continually occupied in useless scheming. Countless valuable ideas miscarry because there is no continuity in my thoughts. They burn me up and lay my mind to waste. The enemy is within my gates, in my very heart; I feel his hand everywhere. Think of the blessings that await you, not of the emptiness that drives you to seek constant distraction. Think of having peace of mind and a reliable memory, of the self-control that a well-ordered life will bring, of health not undermined by endless concessions to the passing excesses which other people's society entails, of uninterrupted work, and plenty of it.[80]

The work will reward us if we create the space and the time for it, whether that is one night a week within our busy schedules or a full-on residency for an extended period of time.

Separation is also a very simple and practical tool that we all use in our everyday lives. Making lists helps us separate necessary steps, keep track of supplies that we need, and gain clarity about our goals. In later stages of our work, separation comes into play as we take our Mars sword to our work in the process of revision and refinement that brings it to completion. Just as the alchemist separates the subtle from the gross in the laboratory, the artist must separate extraneous material to reveal the essence of a creation. This can be a difficult process of deciding what to keep and what must be released for the greater benefit of the creative vision, as a sculptor chisels away the excess stone or a writer edits and cuts out excessive or unnecessary material. When we have spent time and energy creating something, it can feel like we are cutting away a part of the self in this process, but ultimately we will arrive at a more refined and sublime final result.

NAVIGATING THE *NIGREDO*

Sometimes the *nigredo* is overwhelming and just requires patience and valiant endurance. We may not be ready to translate the unknown into creative expression, and this uncertainty is an uncomfortable feeling. Too often we tend to view creative blocks and depression in a negative light without realizing that this is a natural and necessary part of the process. We cannot be expected to constantly produce new work, any more than we can be expected to be awake 24/7 without sleeping. Periods of inactivity are necessary and allow us to get in touch with our deepest truth while we rest, recover, and allow everything to putrefy in order to be reborn. It is the job of the artist to reach into the inner depths and bring forth something new that the world has never seen before—to give it form. We cannot do this if we aren't willing to make the journey into the dark caverns of the unknown and be with the discomfort that arises.

The *nigredo* may also be a time of cathartic creativity that can alleviate the pressure, like the release valve on an alchemical vessel. Art created during this time may have a dark or morose quality, reflecting the pain being experienced and the struggle to overcome it. This is healing work, and art created from this place should be free of judgment and control. The result is not important; it's the expression itself that will aid in the successful transmutation of colors through the alchemical stages as the stone becomes more refined and purified.

The *magnum opus* is not a one-time event. The alchemical axiom *solve et coagula* points to the cyclical nature of the work in which we continuously dissolve and break down our metals and bring them back together in a more harmonious, authentic expression. Sometimes the death of the *nigredo* is experienced following the birth of a creation and the completion of the last stage of the *opus,* the *rubedo.* All of the excitement and energy that was required to bring this creation into form is suddenly no longer necessary, and we enter a period of rest. Like a new mother experiencing postpartum depression or a parent going through "empty nest" syndrome, there may be feelings of emptiness and sadness, and a disconnection from the clear sense of purpose that characterized the preceding phase. The liberation of completion can leave one feeling like life has suddenly lost its meaning. Grief and mourning surround completion in a similar way, though certainly to a lesser degree, to how we grieve the completion and end of a life. We must allow ourselves to feel this, to rest and regenerate as we await the inspiration for the next creation. When inspiration comes, that is the beginning of the *albedo,* a purification of washing away the dark putrefying thoughts of inadequacy, irrelevance, emptiness, voidness, and barrenness.

With practice it becomes easier to allow the *nigredo* to occur without resistance, and as such the time it takes to move through it seems to decrease as the soul becomes less and less attached to outmoded patterns of being, trusting in the process of letting go. In our journey through the underworld we retrieve our *prima materia,* our true imagination, from where it has been hidden. Like Breton's assertion that "Surrealism will usher you into death," the merging of the inner and outer world necessitates a death and rebirth process.[81] This is also how we prepare for the greatest letting go, our own physical death. As a psychopomp, Hermes guides souls as they descend into the underworld. We can call upon him as we proceed into the darkness, moving consciously into it as if we were entering a mine. It is also of immense benefit in these periods of trial to attend to the balance of the elements, and to call upon the planets for their aid and guidance. Having a daily planetary ritual will help you connect with these archetypes within yourself.

7
Albedo
Purification and the Lunar Stone

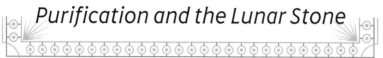

I watched the lightning tear the sky apart,
Watched waterspouts, and streaming undertow,
And Dawn like Dove-People rising on wings—
I've seen what men have only dreamed they saw!

—Arthur Rimbaud, "The Drunken Boat"

Emerging from the confusion and darkness of the *nigredo,* we now find ourselves in the *albedo,* or "whitening," a stage of increased purification in which we take a deep dive into the waters of the unconscious. The dark night of the soul gives way to the first light of day, illuminating the shadows that haunted us in the darkness and drawing us out of the *nigredo's* putrefaction and death. Heavenly dew falls upon the putrefied body and slowly brings it back to life, and in our vessel the white stone appears. This stone represents our ability to create spontaneously from the imagination, to dissolve the barriers between the conscious and unconscious mind, and to see the world in a symbolic way. In a text ascribed to Marsilio Ficino, he elaborates on the many names of "that whiteness we call the white stone, the white sun, the full moon, and calcined Lune, white silver, the white earth, fruitful, cleansed and calcined, the white Calx, and the Salt of the metals, and the calcined body, and we call it by many other names. It is moreover called the living earth, and the living and white Sulphur, when the soul has been reduced into the body, and the Impediment removed."[1] The watery and purifying qualities of the *albedo* are also symbolized as the White Queen, and in Breton's

Soluble Fish we read of virgins, mirrors, water, countless women sliding to the bottom of the sea, pearls, white hair, white rain, a white bowl, a unicorn, swans, and "an eagle as white as the philosopher's stone."[2]

Often described as the work of washing linens and "women's work," this stage leads to a whitening of the Stone as it undergoes repeated "washings" and takes on a lunar quality. As archaic and sexist as the term "women's work" is, it nonetheless alludes to the fact that water is a feminine symbol, and the *albedo* is thus a *yin* or receptive aspect of our creative process. The number of times that this washing must take place varies depending on the alchemical authors, anywhere from nine times to ten years. We have been soiled, so to speak, by the dark subterranean caverns of the *nigredo,* and must now put in the hard work of purifying the garments received from each of the seven stars until we obtain the perfect whiteness. In other words, through painful self-reflection we have recognized our own unconscious projections as originating within us, and now the feminine waters of wisdom must properly rectify them. Through developing a relationship with our own eternal spring of wisdom, we help wash away the deeply held beliefs and societal conditioning that we confronted in the previous stage. This is a quintessential aspect of developing creative authenticity and liberating the imagination, affecting us psychologically, energetically, and spiritually.

> The psychological analogy is obviously to the first hard part of an analysis where Venus, the love problem, must be washed, as well as Mars, the problem of aggression, and so on. All the different instinctive drives and their archetypal background generally appear first in a disturbed form in the earth, that is in the form of a projection—people love or hate somebody or they have a boss who depresses them and they do not know how to defend themselves.[3]

As this quote by Marie-Louise von Franz elucidates, there is a purification at this stage of the various levels of our being. In effect, we are doing our own dirty work. This washing represents the arduous task of assessing and purifying the seven metals, corresponding with the chakras. This work can take years, but for our purposes we shall consider that each of the seven

Fig. 7.1. The "women's work" of whitening the sheets in the stream
of the unconscious. From *Splendor Solis,* Germany, 1582.
British Library, Harley 3469, folio 32v.

metals/chakras should be washed seven times, for a total of forty-nine. Of course, this is just a metaphorical number, for our internal process of rectifying what we found within the bowels of the earth is not so linear that we would be able to keep track of each washing. Simply consider it a number for meditation, for each of the seven chakras resonates with each of the others for a total of forty-nine combinations. Thus the imagination and mental powers of the Moon may be blocked and depressed by the heaviness of Saturn's lead, or the pure love and copper of Venus and the heart chakra may be corrupted by the water of Jupiter's tin and the untempered desires of the lower emotional body. Through our many repeated washings, we not only address specific chakra imbalances, but the relationships between the chakras.

The *albedo's* reflective, watery quality is significant of a nascent spirituality that spontaneously emerges after the depressive *nigredo* has run its course. The brightness of the dawn, in contrast to the dark night, may blind us into thinking that this is the end of the work, but the full daybreak of the *rubedo* is yet to come. We have yet to fully integrate and solidify this new awareness. Like the swan, we float upon the surface of the water, capable of being in two worlds. Our volatile, winged nature yearns to escape into the air, while we are drawn downward to find nourishment and inspiration in the dark waters of the unconscious below. There is much work to be done before the body is made light enough and strong enough to sustain itself in flight without being scorched by the Sun's penetrating rays. It requires a deep level of integrity to bring our external experience into harmony with the inner realizations we've had thus far. We begin the process of purifying our bodies and minds to make space for the Soul, and for true inspiration. The operations of *dissolutio, distillatio,* and *sublimatio* provide different aspects of this purification and how it relates to the creative process.

DISSOLUTIO:
SUBMERSION IN THE LUNAR SEA

Dream is a second life.

—Gérard de Nerval

Dissolution, or *dissolutio,* is assigned to the Moon-ruled sign of Cancer (June 21–July 22), the cardinal water sign of summer in the northern hemisphere. It is an emotional process that brings us into contact with the *anima,* the feminine part of the soul, as the watery nature of the unconscious is directed in its rising and ebbing tides by the Moon's gravitational pull. Jung equated the *anima* with the feminine aspect of a man's unconscious, while the masculine aspect of a woman's consciousness he called the *animus.* Considering the fluidity of gender and sexuality, I find it difficult to accept such a heteronormative distinction. Historically the *anima* simply meant the soul, but more specifically the irrational tendencies of the soul in contrast to its rational part. In that sense the *anima* is the irrational, or unconscious, feminine aspect of the soul. It is receptive, impressionable, and passive, relating to Luna, to softness and moisture, to Nature, the body, and the goddess. On the other hand the *animus* is masculine, or active, representing the rational part of the soul. This is true whether we are a man or woman, transgender, or nonbinary; we all have both within us regardless of how we identify. However, we are unconsciously driven by the opposite of the dominant polarity of egoic consciousness, for the *anima* and *animus* serve a compensatory function. They beckon us into the inner world so we can develop those qualities that are most foreign and unknown to us, so we can integrate them and regain the wholeness of the Soul. For a transfemme, it's likely that the more powerful aspect of her unconscious will be the *animus.* In the case of someone who identifies as nonbinary, it could go either way, or perhaps both the *anima* and *animus* are equally matched.

Alchemically the *anima* relates to the Moon, ruler of the brow chakra, which is called *ajna* in the Hindu tradition. This is the center of the third eye, the pituitary gland, the brain, our dreams, and intuition. At this point in the work we begin to make the connection between our sensations, emotions, and thoughts and how to objectively allow these to exist without resisting them or grasping at them. As the Surrealists realized, automatism is a path to creatively access the unconscious and to facilitate the dialogue between the internal and external worlds. By subduing the rational mind and allowing for the unconscious to make itself known, we purify ourselves at the deepest level and begin the process of accessing our true imagination. Yet when we interfere with this free flow of creative energy with our conscious mind, we lose touch with the spontaneous communication of the unconscious.

Aligning with the second stage of the *opus,* Ernst represented the Water element and the Moon in the second chapter of his collage book, *Une Semaine de Bonté.*[4] This chapter, named "Lundi," or Monday, overflows with water in diverse settings—flooded parlors, stormy seas, and baths. The primarily nocturnal settings and appearance of the full moon bring this chapter into correspondence with Monday's ruling planet. Here the book transitions from the masculine lion imagery that we touched upon in the *nigredo,* and the conflict of the opposites that results from our confrontation with the shadow, to a predominance of feminine imagery. As Warlick notes, this indicates that the two principles have been successfully separated.[5] Male and female figures appear in various states of drowning or rising above the water, symbolic of the alchemical dissolution and purification. The women, mostly clad in white gowns, sometimes appear dead or sleeping, indicating a dreamy quality and the encounter with the unconscious, or *anima.*

In the prose poem "The White Water Lily," by Stephane Mallarmé, the meeting with the *anima* is well illustrated.[6] The scene takes place on a July morning, the Moon-ruled season of Cancer, as he rows his skiff aground in a clump of reeds and has a dreamlike encounter with a mysterious feminine figure. He imagines her to be like himself, and, projecting his fantasies upon the mirror of her yet veiled presence, she becomes the "feminine possibility" that will liberate him. He hears her footsteps, but cannot see her through the trees. Rather than "penetrate the mystery," he decides he'd rather not see her actual form at all, for his own projection—his inner *anima*—is the true source of his passion: "Apart, we are together: I merge into her obscure intimacy, in this moment suspended on the water where my dream is delaying the indecisive creature, better than any visit (followed by others) could do." He recognizes the disillusion that awaits him if the unknown becomes known in the reality of the woman, rather than existing in the imaginative realm of possibilities as an integral part of himself.

It isn't difficult to make a comparison between Mallarmé's scene and the *albedo,* with his use of watery imagery and reference to a swan's egg, hollow and white water lilies, an internal mirror made of crystal, dreams and illusion, solitude, and silvery mist. The title itself implies a connection

Fig. 7.2. *Dream*, by Odilon Redon 1878–1882.
Public Domain Review

with the "white woman" of alchemy, the feminine aspect of the primal matter, sometimes referred to as "white lilies."[7] Yet the episode also illuminates a quintessential choice arising from the encounter with the *anima,* the feminine passion, desire, and mysterious aspect of the unconscious—namely, that we must choose between integrating the *anima* internally,

Fig. 7.3. The linens are washed of earthy corruption and made
white by the water. From Michael Maier, *Atalanta Fugiens*,
Oppenheim, Germany: Johann-Theodor de Bry, 1618.
Courtesy of Science History Institute

and projecting her into external form. When we are too eager to dispel the
mystery, we lose touch with the essential truth that the eternal spring of
imagination is the source of our outward desires. The moment we ascribe
to this hidden power a definite face and form, it is immediately corrupted.
Losing ourselves for a time in the mysterious encounter, we must not grasp
at it, for in doing so we risk losing the immediate, intuitive, and unspoken
bond we have with the Soul.

When we submerge ourselves in the waters of the unconscious, there is also the risk of being overwhelmed by forces of our inner fantasies and losing our grip on reality. Artists walk the fine line between dream and reality and must become adept at exploring the unknown, while maintaining a connection to shore so that they are able to fixate their visions into corporeal form. This is necessary for the artist to translate the ineffable into the material so that it has the potential to positively affect the world. There is a great amount of faith—in ourselves and the Divine—required to navigate the lunar sea, and the *lunacy,* that is the hidden danger and also the blessing of the *albedo.*

Let us recall the case of Leonora Carrington, whose journey through mental illness we explored in chapter 4. In the early phase, she induced herself to purge by drinking orange blossom water to cleanse herself of society's "brutal ineptitude" and the "thick layers of filth" in order to properly reflect the "earth," by which she meant the bodies of both the macrocosm and microcosm. Prior to her admittance to the sanatorium and during her mental dissolution, in which she identified with the external world, Leonora was locked up in a hotel room where she spent time washing her clothes and making ceremonial garments from the hotel bath towels in what corresponds to an alchemical ablution and whitening phase.[8]

In contrast to Leonora's journey into the lunar sea, we want to enter these watery realms in a conscious and directed manner through alchemical meditation and creative alchemy. The fires of calcination left us in a pile of white ashes, our *prima materia* for the *albedo,* which we now dissolve in the *aqua vitae,* the waters of the unconscious, the divine feminine moisture of the Moon. Ashes are salts held in the body—crystallized emotions—that we've become aware of by burning away the dross material of our egos. Calcination was a fiery form of purification marked by intense suffering, breaking down egoic and mental fixations and confronting our deepest fears. The result is Salt, which is the wisdom attained from such trials. Dissolution is a softer, though still intense, process of breaking down false ego constructs within the celestial waters that fill us with a deeper understanding and the hope of renewal. The truth of our eternal being penetrates us all the way through, cleansing the mind of superfluous impurities hindering our progress. This conditioning, built up over a lifetime, like Mallarmé's "false mansion," dissolves in the universal solvent;

the philosophical water that "does not wet the hands."[9] Here we experience the "*solve*" part of *solve et coagula*. During this breakdown we may feel an emotional release that calls us to journey inward, to tune into our hearts and clarify what we are releasing, just as we are beginning to envision the new, more expansive structures we want to build in our imaginations. This complete submersion releases the hardened salts from the body in salty tears of grief and the sweat of the Great Work. In Shelley's *Frankenstein,* the monstrous creature's birth story can be read as an allegory for the transition from the *nigredo* to the *albedo*. He begins in darkness, in a cold and fearful state, "a poor, helpless, miserable wretch" in a state of undifferentiated anguish. Yet when he weeps and allows the suffering to penetrate him, "a gentle light" appears in the heavens, the light of the rising Moon, which enlightens his path.[10] In the soft, reflective light of the Moon, we feel a sense of relief as we allow ourselves to feel long withheld emotions. This has an extremely transformative effect on the psyche, and will create a subsequent lightness of being, though it mustn't be forced. We simply let it happen as a natural result of enduring our passage through the underworld, which releases us when we surrender.

As we rebuild the mansion of our imagination with integrity, we clarify and refine our creative expression. Imagery to meditate upon in this time period includes caves, the womb, deep wells, or the intimate, personal space within a crab or a turtle's shell. We tend to this internal space and get in touch with the profound depths that lie within, cultivating our dreams and believing in the marvelous possibilities that our liberated creativity may engender. What is it that we truly want to bring to life for ourselves? For the world? By allowing the body to be penetrated by the mercurial waters of life and imbued with the soul's wisdom, we can see more clearly the impurities that have been weighing us down and limiting our imagination. Some of these are instantly dissolved upon acknowledgment; others take more work to cleanse. We wash away impurities of the mind, just as we would do laundry or clean our house. In fact, cleaning our home or creative space, washing dishes, and doing laundry can become externalized rituals to deepen and reflect the inner cleansing that is happening. This can be quite literal, or also metaphorical in the sense that we tend to "cleaning" our relationships, behavior, and diet.

The softening effects of the dissolution help us to be vulnerable within our relationship to others, to ourselves, and to our responsibilities, coming to a place of honest expression. Cancer's archetype is the Crab, an arthropod with a rigid exoskeleton. There are times in its life that the crab outgrows its shell and, in a process similar to molting, it sheds its exoskeleton and grows a new one. This begins with a *dissolution* and weakening of the existing shell, while a new, soft shell is formed underneath. When it is ready to shed the old shell, it pulls in water, which expands and splits the old shell, allowing it to wriggle its way out. Its newly formed soft shell then begins to rapidly swell. Likewise, we use the lubricating water of the unconscious to dissolve old structures and loosen ourselves from spaces we've outgrown. Likely we've already been growing the new "shell" and all we really need to do is allow the old one to be released. As we continue growing and strengthening our new exoskeleton, we are establishing the life structures that will be our new framework for encountering reality, bigger to allow for how much we have grown in our experience of life and to encompass the vast potential of a liberated imagination. Dissolution implies vulnerability, surrender, a willingness to be absolved, which requires complete humility and self-responsibility. No longer clinging to others for comfort or to preconceived ideas of how we should express our creativity, we have begun to recognize our inherent wholeness and unique gifts. With this enveloping safety, we are softly guided further into the work, releasing those places where we are yet clinging to control, and freeing us to be our authentic selves.

As the *nigredo* was primarily a Saturnian journey relating to the root chakra and the Earth element, the *albedo* is like the return of Jupiter to overthrow Saturn and make him vomit up the rest of his children—and the stone he swallowed. Those children are the creative potentials that were locked up in the body and have now been freed for further development. There is a strong correlation between Jupiter and the Moon, and both are in different respects associated with the sacral chakra (*svadhisthana*), our creative center located in the lower belly, corresponding to the metal tin. As Democritus advises, "Mundify Tin with the choicest washing, and extract his blackness out of it, and also his darkness, and then his brightness will appear."[11]

Here we transition from earth to water, from our physicality to our emotionality, from personal survival to relationship, from within to without, from survival to creation. Jupiter's exaltation in Cancer and the planet's beneficent, expansive qualities all act to support and amplify the nurturing qualities of the water element—compassion, love, understanding, intuition, receptivity, empathy—supporting us in our emotional release. As the ruler of the heavens, Jupiter is responsible for what is created upon the Earth. We must protect this newborn king and keep him secret from Saturnian constraints. The rational, paternalistic narrative dominating the world paradigm, which dictates the impossibility of dreaming beyond our current experience, must not deter the naturally expansive creative spirit. Jupiter's symbol is the crescent of mind/spirit over the cross of matter, a combination of Luna and Earth, whose waters form the hydrolyth produced in the *albedo,* the water-stone. This stone is our strengthened and purified awareness of our true spiritual power that we will carry into the next phase of the work. It is the first solidified understanding of our role in creating our reality through our thoughts and feelings, reminding us of our inherent power as creators within the realm of matter, and elevating our creativity from simple self-expression to a mystical, magical, and alchemical love affair. Morienus advises: "Our Mercury is not had but out of melted bodies, not with common liquefaction but only with that which endureth till the man and wife be associated and united in true matrimony and this even unto whiteness."[12] Mercury, the messenger between the conscious and unconscious, requires that the bodies—the constructs of one's reality—be melted, and the liquefaction dissolves the barriers between the "real" and "imaginary."

Gérard de Nerval's novel *Aurélia, or Dream and Life* (1855), provides a compelling example of the transition from the melancholy of the *nigredo* to the dissolution of the *albedo.* In facing his metaphorical death (foreseen in the dream vision previously likened to Dürer's *Melancholia I*), the character experiences "the overflow of dream into real life," in which reality takes on a double aspect.[13] Nerval preceded Rimbaud as a representative of the visionary who succumbs to his own madness and "disorganization of all the senses," charting the underworld journey with exquisite detail and clarity.[14] While he feels lucid through this dissolving of the veil, to all

Fig. 7.4. The royal pair in a purifying bath facilitated by
the descending dove of Spirit. From *Rosarium Philosophorum,* 1550.
Courtesy of Wikimedia Commons

outward appearances his actions seem insane. In this new reality, spirits
from the world of death and dreams at times occupy the bodies of the living, acting through them without their memory and thereby gaining the
ability to physically affect the world. He follows the expanding light of his
cynosure, seemingly "ever upwards" as he sheds his "earthly garments" in
preparation for the separation of his soul and body, "flooded with electri-
cal forces," and then is promptly collected by soldiers and confined. Then
proceeds a series of visions beginning with a magnificent scene he can
only relate to the Soul's fate beyond death, but which again reminds us of
alchemical dissolution:

> Immense circles traced their way through infinity, like the rings
> touched off in water by a falling body; peopled with radiant figures,
> each region in its turn took on colour and movement and then dis-
> solved; a divinity, always the same, smiled as she cast off the fleeting
> masks of her various incarnations, and then took refuge, out of grasp,
> in the mystical splendours of the sky of Asia.[15]

Here he identifies feminine divinity of the unconscious with the East, speaking to the motherly quality of the unconscious as it reveals itself and its wisdom in the dissolution. He is aware at this point of certain events unfolding in waking reality, perceiving himself to be dividing in two—the *separatio* of vision and reality, and the creation of his double. Let us refer to the description of the dissolution given by von Franz in her analysis of an alchemical text by the Arabic alchemist Muḥammad ibn Umail (Senior):

> [T]he dissolution of the stone takes place when we interpret all symbols from within on the subjective level as an inner psychic reality, thus separating it from the material outer world. After this separation we reconnect the inner process with the facts of outer life. That is the first marriage, the first *unificatio* of the outer and inner world. The mediating element our text calls moisture . . . the divine water of alchemy which is the absolute reality of the symbolic world. Every dream we dream is a drop of the "divine water."[16]

Nerval's protagonist experiences this separation of the vision of the inner psychic reality from the outer world; however, their reconciliation is intercepted by his double, who plays a competitive role, taking his place in the royal marriage with his *anima,* Aurélia, his unrequited love. At one point in his visions he is brought back in time while conversing with a bird, symbolic of the Air element and of the spirit, and feels himself to be carried along in a "current of molten metals," in colorful streams that he perceives to be "living beings in a molecular state." Their channels are suffused with white light, whereupon he finds himself upon a shore. Here the bird has transformed into an old man—a Saturnian figure—who is cultivating the earth. As his visions continue, he finds himself in a great hall filled with familiar faces, one of whom is his uncle, who reveals to him the nature of the void, the immortality of matter, and the links between past and future.[17] He feels the boundaries of time and space dissolve and merges with the lives of countless men and women. Recall Carrington's experience of this macrocosmic unity: "I was all, all was in me."[18] In response to his uncle, Nerval's protagonist says, "We are seven," alluding to a biblical or Hermetic wholeness and harmony contained in that familial number, as well as the seven planetary archetypes. It is both a unity and a plurality, finite and limitless, which he compares to a collective "anima figure."[19]

It is then that he finds himself led by his guide, a spirit that Jung equates to Hermes *Juvenis* (youth), to a lofty mountainous city whose inhabitants are a world apart, a place of solitude where he can take in the city from above in its entirety.[20] He sees this city as a sanctuary, its inhabitants having remained "pure" and uncorrupted by outside influences and invasion. Some of these people appear dressed in white, but this is apparently an illusion dispelled by his guide, who reveals their vestments to be brightly colored. Here we recognize the purifying effects of the *albedo* and the sequestration required for this to occur, and the white color unifying all colors in one. The joy he feels within this setting brings him to tears—the emotional release of the *albedo*—realizing at once that he cannot remain here in this "lost paradise," but must at some point return to the world of the living, to connect the inner and the outer worlds. These visions, which he had while in a cataleptic state lasting several days, left him with a firm conviction of the immortality of the soul. Often the spirit that pervades a certain time or culture lives again in another time and place, brought back to life through the imagination of the artist; Nerval lived this on an extremely personal level. There was no separation between the past, present, and future. Yet despite this timeless experience, he was able to maintain enough lucidity to document the process through his writing.

Instead of reconciling the inner and outer realities, however, the protagonist descends again into madness, to a chaotic confusion of the elements, the *prima materia,* brought down once again to the first matter. This is precipitated by a prescient dream of Aurélia's death, his externalized *anima.* In his descent he witnesses an evolutionary unfolding of humanity, "strange mysteries" transpiring in Africa near the "Mountains of the Moon,"* pointing to a lunar whitening; however this is a place of suffering and decay, for the purifying effects of the *albedo* do not penetrate the illusions under which he is held captive. His underworld journey, heralded by the constellation Orion, associated with the Egyptian king of

---

*Where the legendary unicorn has often been said to hide. See *Hermetic Philosophy and Creative Alchemy,* 289.

the underworld, Osiris, releases a mighty flood. Three Elohim, like the three principles and the trinity, fight upon a mountaintop, as the Eternal Mother is abandoned and ravaged by the storm. Yet even this hopeless scene is imbued with the hope of the Evening Star—Venus, the guiding light through the underworld journey—shining above the Mother's crown. A battle of good and evil ensues as the Eternal Mother weeps and dies, and the world endures endless suffering.

"Man is double," Nerval writes, a "concurrence of two souls," a "spectator and an actor, someone who speaks and someone who replies . . . the good genius and the evil genius."[21] We are reminded of the two geniuses identified by Schuré on the collective scale as *spirituality* and *naturalism,* or du Prel's concept of the Janus-faced nature of the mind. We are reminded as well of the words of Rimbaud: "*I* is an *other.*"[22] The missed marriage is indicative of Nerval's own inability to fully emerge from the abysmal depths. This double aspect of the Self is reflected also in his friends, whom he perceives as speaking in double meanings and being split into two separate attitudes toward him—one of compassion, one of horror.[23] When one is immersed in a state of dissolution, these double aspects to reality are apparent, and become the lifeblood of the poet and the artist who works through correspondence, metaphor, and subtle impressions.

In the second part of *Aurélia,* which was published posthumously, Nerval's protagonist becomes preoccupied with religious concerns as he finds himself in limbo between dream and life.[24] He comes to understand the human soul as being both human and God, but does not feel God is with him any longer, that he is no longer worthy of his bride, whom his *doppelganger* stole from him. Immersed in the guilt he feels for having failed to fully live his life, for misinterpreting the secret of life, he wavers back and forth between suicidal ideation and morbidity and brief moments of hope. At the end of his 1945 lecture on *Aurélia,* Jung writes that the author's suicide marked "the end of a personality who had never understood how to prize open the narrow circle of the personal 'I' and grant admission to the shadow, the ambiguous herald of yet another order of things."[25] *Aurélia* ends with a tone of resolution, in which Nerval compares his experience with the "descent into Hell."[26] Read as autobiography, *Aurélia* is a cautionary tale, for Nerval did not survive his own descent into Hell, despite his positive conclusions at the end of the novel. The derangement of the senses (*dissolutio*) is, like any worthwhile pursuit, accompanied by potential dangers. While a certain level of risk is vital for deeper self-knowledge and growth, proper preparation and support are advised, particularly if one finds it difficult to keep one foot on dry land, so to speak.

There are ample ways to access a state of dissolution, from psychoactive substances to alcohol (*spirits*), in addition to involuntary unconscious breakthroughs that overwhelm the conscious mind. However dissolution may also be cultivated in natural and gentle ways that allow us to partake of this world without becoming overwhelmed or strung out, always maintaining a connection with the solid earth. Automatism, creative alchemy, and other techniques for accessing the unconscious entrain the artist to the rhythmic, symbolic language of the inner life, and through honesty and alchemical meditation this is brought into harmony with the outer world. Spending time with Mother Nature can also support connecting with our inner feminine and receptive nature. We see this urge to connect with Nature in the poetry and art of the Romantics, for whom Nature was a means of entry to experiences of cosmic consciousness.[27] Time spent within Nature, in reflective solitude, awakens a transcendent quality within us, particularly when we unite the external appearance of the natural world with our own internal being through our imaginations, through art and poetry.

Nature Walk Meditation

This meditation is for the development of intuition.

Take a walk outside, briskly or slowly, whatever helps you to clear your mind. If walking is not possible then use whatever means you have to access the outside world. A natural setting is ideal but a residential neighborhood or even a city is fine, so long as you are out in the elements. Pay attention to what you feel inside your body—bring your awareness to your hands, your arms, and your feet. Listen to the wind upon your ears, and feel the movement of your hair.

Turn your attention outward. Look at the plants, the stones, the buildings, the wildlife, the sky. Observe your environment with open curiosity and without judgment or categorization. Keep your thoughts focused on the present moment.

Pay attention to things that grab your attention. If a feeling of curiosity arises, allow this to guide you. Let yourself be drawn to a place where you feel inclined to rest for a moment. Perhaps it's a tree or a special rock, or a viewpoint. It could be a path or a road. Maybe it's a bench that you feel the desire to sit on. Listen to these impulses and, to the extent possible, follow them. Take your time to explore what has drawn your attention, if it is not intruding on anyone or anything. Be present, still, and practice the art of listening deeply to all of the elements alive within and around you.

Absorb the experience until you feel complete, and either continue your journey or make your way home. Take some time to journal about the experience or write a poem based on things that you saw and felt. If certain trees, objects, animals, or natural elements felt significant, think about what associations these bring up for you. Your own personal associations and feelings are the most relevant, but if you need some help you can research these symbols. Allow the words that you write to tap into a deeper symbolic meaning. Alternatively, you can draw or paint a picture; if you're in the midst of a creative project, see if there is a way to integrate some aspect of your nature meditation into it.

Dreamwork

The inner world of dreams is where the unconscious truly reveals itself. In our strange, irrational, nonlinear, and numinous dreamscapes we encounter the multiplicity of personalities that reside within us. They take the form of people we know, of strangers and mysterious unknown personages who beckon us to look deeply into the mirror of the Moon, to see by reflected light the visions that will guide us to gnosis, if we take the time to understand them. Landscapes, architecture, objects, animals, people, colors, and sounds—every part of a dream has a specific symbolic meaning that is intimately ours. I am reminded of a passage from American author Henry Miller in his memoir *Big Sur and the Oranges of Hieronymus Bosch:*

> [W]orlds, objects, creatures, places, all have this in common: they are ever in a state of transmutation. The supreme delight of dream lies in this transformative power. When the personality liquefies, so to speak, as it does so deliciously in dream, and the very nature of one's being is

alchemized, when form and substance, time and space, become yielding and elastic, responsive and obedient to one's slightest wish, he who awakens from his dream knows beyond all doubt that the imperishable soul which he calls his own is but a vehicle of this eternal element of change.[28]

Immensely powerful, dreams are one of the primary ways that the unconscious communicates with us, and yet they demand that we approach them with respect and patience if we wish to know their meaning. This begins, first and foremost, with the ability to remember our dreams, for all too often they slip away like shimmering fish beneath the surface of the water as we awaken into consciousness each morning. If we aren't in the habit of recalling our dreams, it may take some time to begin cultivating this faculty. The first step is to set the intention, before we fall asleep, that we wish to recall our dreams. Alejandro Jodorowsky, artist and filmmaker who made the legendary surreal films *El Topo* and *Holy Mountain,* was particularly interested in lucid dreaming. He describes his own process of replaying all of the events of his day in reverse before falling asleep, writing that "to review my day at night compares to remembering my dreams in the morning,"[29] which is done in a selective way, because we can neither remember every detail of the day or dream.

We also want to have a means of recording the dream at the ready when we awake. Writing down our dreams is key, but it can be helpful to use a recording device to capture the dream while its memory is fresh, then transcribe it later. Before getting out of bed and beginning our day, we must give ourselves time to glimpse those fish beneath the water, to recall any glimmer of imagery or feelings that might remain to us, and to give them our full attention. Often, with patience and quietude, we will remember more. Paracelsus tells us that:

Artists and students have often received instructions in their dreams in regard to things which they desired to know . . . but it very often occurs that on awakening to consciousness in the outer world all or a part of what has been learned during the dream is forgotten. If this happens and we wish to remember such dreams, we should not leave the room after rising, and speak to nobody, but remain alone and undisturbed, and eat nothing until after a while we remember the dream.[30]

No matter how little we may recall, even if it is just a faint and foggy memory of a feeling, we must write it down immediately so as not to let it escape into the shadow of the Sun. In this way we communicate to our unconscious that we wish to be in dialogue with it. Doing this with consistency, we will remember more and more of our dreams. Nurturing our dream life also requires proper sleep hygiene and mitigation of habits that inhibit deep sleep. Alcohol and marijuana both reduce the quality of REM sleep and can prevent or greatly reduce dream recall. If we're in the habit of escaping from our regular waking consciousness throughout the day or close to bedtime, we rob ourselves of the wondrous messages of our dreams. Other factors include stress, diet, sleep disorders, certain medications, and trauma.

Alternatively, we can feed our dreams by exposing ourselves to new environments, changing our daily routine, and trying new things, which provides our unconscious with more material to work with when it composes its symbolic nighttime stories.

Dream Interpretation

In order to understand what a dream is trying to convey, we can apply certain techniques of interpretation. While a complete explanation of how to do this is beyond the scope of this book, the reader is referred to Robert A. Johnson's book *Inner Work,* in which he explains in depth a four-step process, based in Jungian dream analysis.[31] These steps are (1) association, (2) dynamics, (3) interpretation, and (4) ritual, summarized briefly below. I have found this technique to be quite effective.

1. *Associations.* Record your dream in a journal dedicated to your dreamwork. Underline each of the primary dream symbols—people, places, objects, animals, colors, sounds, words, feelings, moods—nothing is insignificant when it comes to dream language. Then list these on a separate page; next to each one, write your personal associations. List all the direct associations that come to you for each

dream symbol. While personal associations take precedence, if you are at a loss, you can research symbols and see how they relate to you personally.

2. *Dynamics.* Review your associations and reflect on things occurring in your life, both inwardly and outwardly. Look for the associations that feel energized, that lead to personal revelations, and that you can connect with dynamics in your waking life. Remember: the dream speaks symbolically; each individual part of a dream is a symbol for something else, including people, who almost always indicate an aspect of the self.

3. *Interpretation.* Bring together your associations and dynamics into a clear, unified statement of personal meaning derived from the dream.

4. *Ritual.* Now it's time to bridge the unconscious and conscious worlds by performing a symbolic act or making some change in your life that helps you integrate the dream in the physical realm. It can be as simple as writing in your journal, creating a piece of art, making little adjustments in your habits and behaviors, or saying a prayer. You can make it a bit more involved so long as you are not harming others or yourself in the process. For instance, if you dream about being near water, and it is possible for you to do so, you can visit a body of water and contemplate your dream.[32]

Jungian Dream Interpretation

Another Jungian dream technique breaks down the dream into a linear sequence from beginning to end.

1. *Exposition of place*: This is usually determined in the first sentence of a dream. It is the setting, the situation, or the problem to be encountered.

2. *Development*: The problem becomes evident as the dream progresses.

3. *Culmination or peripeteia:* This is the turning point in the dream.

4. *Lysis:* Here is the ending of the dream and often the solution or result of the drama. Sometimes it is a peaceful resolution and sometimes it is a catastrophe. And sometimes there is no real lysis or conclusion at all,

which is an invitation to do active imagination in order to continue the dream (to be discussed in the next chapter).[33]

The unconscious can be a real trickster and we mustn't be too hasty in our dream interpretations. If it comes too easily or points to something we already know then we are likely not accurately interpreting the dream. The interpretation should surprise us.

Surrealist Techniques for Liberating the Unconscious

Automatic drawing and frottage provide two methods that can be employed to good effect in freeing oneself from the control of the conscious mind.

Automatic Drawing

The main idea behind automatism is to relinquish conscious control of the creative process, thereby freeing the imagination. Doing so in a swift manner, whether one is speaking, writing, drawing, or painting, is the key, for there should be no forethought involved in the process. Thus automatism requires a completely unfiltered, pure, and honest creative expression in which the rational mind is relinquished in favor of the irrational, the unexpected, and the unconscious part of the artist. A spontaneously created image may be further refined and brought to harmony through the reconciling function of the conscious mind, which begins to perceive within the chaotic expression forms and images rich with symbolic and personal meaning.

1. Allow yourself to be in a completely relaxed state. Meditating beforehand can be helpful to get out of your thinking mind. When you're ready, set the mood—burn some incense and light a candle, dim the lights, put on some music that helps you to feel in your body, perhaps something with a fast pace that helps you to move quickly as you draw.
2. Decide on a minimum amount of time that you're going to draw. It could be as little as five minutes or as long as you feel compelled.
3. I find it helpful to begin in pencil and add ink later. With a blank sheet of paper and your preferred drawing implement, begin scribbling

lightly on the paper. It can even be helpful to close your eyes at first or to unfocus your eyes. This technique can also be done with colored pencil, crayon, or even with paint.

4. As you scribble, move swiftly and try to allow your hand to move as freely as possible. Pay no attention to what is happening and simply focus on your breathing.

5. Experiment with the amount of pressure you're using and the angle of your drawing tool, and how loosely you hold your hand.

6. Experiment with shading in different areas, adding definition, or erasing.

7. As you work, pay attention to emotions that arise, and notice any forms that begin to present themselves. These can be elaborated upon, and ink may be applied over the lines. Then the pencil can be erased as the ink image becomes more distinct. Try to remain in a state of open uninhibited expression throughout the process.

8. Spend some time contemplating the image and write down any associations and ideas that arise from it. How does it make you feel? Does it remind you of anything? Can you connect it with things occurring in your internal and external experience?

Frottage

1. Take a clean sheet of paper and a piece of graphite or a soft crayon, and begin walking around your home or outside to find textured surfaces—wood paneling, the veins in leaves, fabric, gravel, cement, screens, fences, metal siding, string, mesh.

2. Press the paper against them. Hold the graphite or crayon at an angle and begin rubbing it over the texture so that it begins to transfer onto the paper.

3. Experiment with the amount of pressure you apply with the graphite.

4. Experiment with as many different textured surfaces and materials as you can find.

5. Look at your frottage drawing and see if any shapes, figures, symbols, or other patterns are apparent. If you feel called, elaborate on this imagery by adding intentional shading and outlines, or by erasing areas that feel extraneous. You can also continue to add more layers of frottage.

6. Spend some time contemplating the completed image and write down any associations and ideas that arise from it. How does it make you feel? Does it remind you of anything? Can you connect it with things occurring in your internal and external experience?

Additional Techniques for Unconscious Communication

Reverie is yet another way that we may come to receive insights from the unconscious: simply allowing ourselves to get lost in fantasy and day-dreams. When we return to consciousness after such an imaginative excursion, we can begin reflecting on the fantasies to find their hidden essence in much the same way we would look at a dream. Look at the places and the people you encountered. Follow the path of your associations, and connect these with your inner experiences to derive an understanding of what they may mean to you. The same can be applied to the experience of hypnagogia, that liminal state that occurs on the brink of sleep in which our consciousness remains lucid while we receive an influx of visual, sensory, or auditory stimulus.

Our body also speaks the language of the unconscious. Illnesses, nervous tics, inexplicable sensations, aches and pains, and tensions can have emotional sources that are rooted deep within our psyche. If we look at where, how, and when these things tend to occur, we may come to understand them on a deeper level and, in small or large ways, transform them or our relationship to them. One way to do this is to consider the chakras and their correspondences to see emotional and/or energetic patterns underlying physical symptoms, and perhaps begin unraveling the messages of the unconscious (see appendix A). Receiving a Polarity Therapy session or other forms of energy healing can be immensely helpful in this regard.

Exertion from physical exercise can sometimes have a way of making us more receptive to subtleties within our body, particularly if we allow ourselves to rest afterward. In that restful state after exertion, our muscles are still twinging; our blood is pulsing and flowing throughout our entire body, rejuvenated with the breath of spirit. Our cells and organs and bones have all been shaken out of their torpor and activated. It is during this state of heightened physical sensation, when we stop our activity, perhaps closing our eyes, that we become aware of our bodies, the abode of the unconscious. Of particular benefit are the yogic practices of hatha yoga, which help to balance and unify the opposing energies of the feminine and masculine within us, known as *ida* and *pingala*. Breathwork and meditation are also highly effective in stilling the thinking brain, balancing our energies, and creating space for the soul to reveal itself. One may also experiment with sensory deprivation or float tanks.

Simply paying attention to symbols that appear in the world around us, to correspondences, and to our emotional experience, are all ways that we invite the unconscious to make itself known. When we are too caught up in the world of ego and oriented entirely to the external world, we leave no room for the Soul to emerge. Like the oils contained in the body or a plant, Soul moves slowly, and so we must slow down to its rhythm, the frequency of the earthy body in which it resides. We must relinquish control for a time, soften ourselves into a passive, receptive, impressionable state. We move from judging, identifying, and categorizing to observing, contemplating, and receiving; from separation to integration; from external to internal; from control to release; from knowing to unknowing; from speaking to listening; from knowing to asking. There is a fountain of wisdom within us that longs to flow forth into our consciousness, but it is like a shy lover that must be coaxed out through attention, trust, and acceptance. For wisdom to emerge we must give it space; hence the cleansing of this work. Just as we might clean our house before inviting over a houseguest, we want to make a clean space for Soul to enter. If we want Soul to stay, then we make it comfortable with continual attention and nourishment, by creating an inviting space for it to inhabit.

The aim of the alchemist is the separation and reunion of the opposing principles within the Self. Thus it is necessary to allow oneself to drift away into the watery abyss for a time, but to always find the way back to solid ground where the treasures of the deep may be held up to the light of the Sun and integrated into the consciousness of the eternal Soul. For this work there is another alchemical process to which we may turn to *distill* the essence of what we have found in our journey thus far.

DISTILLATIO:
EXTRACTING THE ESSENCE OF THE IDEA

As fish who remain on dry land die, so do monks who linger
outside of the cell, or who pass time with people of the world,
slacken the tension of solitude. Therefore it is necessary—as
fish do to the sea—that we return to the cell, so as not to
forget, through dallying outside, our interior vigil.

—St. Anthony the Great, *Apophthegmata*

We introduce the process of *distillatio,* or distillation, here in the *albedo,* though it appears again in the subsequent phase of the *citrinitas* following the process of fermentation, when the spirit is distilled from the ferment. Here, however, distillation involves the application of fire to a mortified body (metal or plant) or solution (the result of the dissolution above) to release the pure, volatile essence or distillate. This is the unctuous, humid, and purified watery substance that represents the Soul (*anima/animus*) separated from the earth (*corpus*), or the "dead" body. As the Arabic alchemist Geber describes it, "Distillation is an Elevation of aqueous Vapours in their Vessel," the purpose of which is "the Purification of Liquid Matter from its turbulent Feces, and Conservation of it from Putrefaction."[34] The main purpose of distillation is purification and it is commonly performed using a retort, or else with an alembic—an apparatus invented by Geber—consisting of a *curcurbite,* or a lower vessel in which the substance to be distilled is placed, attached to another vessel called the *alembic* through which the liquid is cooled and condensed (see figure 7.5).

As we work with our internal alchemy, the heated "solution" releases vapors that rise to the top of our vessel as feelings, clarified and "en-lightened" by their transmutation into a gaseous state, resulting in a higher understanding of the painful insights perceived during the *nigredo.* These vaporous emotions rise in our awareness and co-mingle with our thoughts (Air element), allowing us to process them with clarity. Then we condense them once again into their liquid, emotional state in a more refined and purified form, collecting the essential drops of our internal pro-

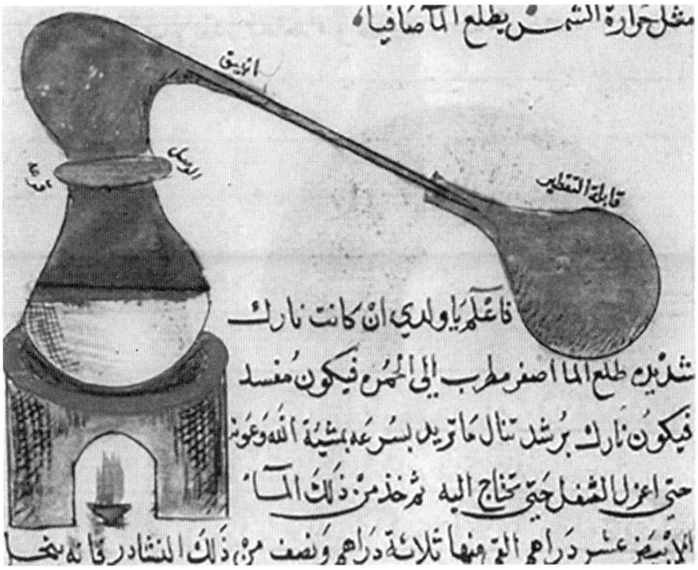

Fig. 7.5. Illustration of an alembic, by Jabir Ibn Hayyan, eighth century.
Courtesy of Wikipedia

cess as they slowly trickle into the receiving vessel—the conscious mind. Our soulful feelings, thus distilled, relate to the principle of *Eros,* and through their extraction and separation we begin to understand the essence of our personal desires, and what our soul purpose is in our creative work.

Essence is eternal; in the process of distillation, we are separating that eternal part of ourselves and communing with it, drinking in the memory of the One Soul of which we are each a unique expression. What has been internal and hidden within the body is now raised up, purified, and consolidated into a reservoir of wisdom that we can draw upon as we progress in the work, for circumstances will surely arise during this phase to challenge our nascent—and still superficial—spiritual awareness. This is what is meant in the *Emerald Tablet* when it says to "ascend with the greatest sagacity from the earth to heaven, and then again descend to earth, and unite together the powers of things superior and inferior. Thus you will obtain the glory of the whole world, and obscurity will fly away from you."[35] Through the analytical and separating powers of thought (*Logos*), correlated to the Air element, we are able to extract the ineffable images from the unconscious waters and make meaning from them. Without this perceptive quality of the mind, these aspects will sink back into the mystifying depths and remain elusive to further understanding.

Creatively, the fire of our awareness and intention is a gentle heat that refines and reveals the real essence of what we want to express. As Mallarmé puts it, "Our job is to learn the subtle dosages, deleterious or revitalizing, of the essences we call feelings."[36] Purging the lingering voices of the *nigredo* while distilling the finer qualities of the *albedo,* we come closer and closer to the central idea. For Mallarmé, the key to extracting the essence was to avoid directly naming an object and to evoke it with allusive words. How often in the attempt to name something, to define it, do we strip it of its ineffable qualities and rob it of its power? A vague remnant of a dream haunts us upon waking, and the more we grasp at it to solidify its memory, the more it slips away. We must release our attachment to the outcome and allow it to reveal itself, if it so pleases, while maintaining the fire of our attention and raising the unconscious images up into the heavens. Its essence is a thing unnameable, unquantifiable, and unseeable; we can dance around it in the open field of our psyche, but when we attempt to close in on it, we find it has suddenly disappeared. Distillation allows us to slowly, drop by drop, separate the subtle from the gross, with a gentle fire and patience, whereby the essence reveals itself by degrees.

Distillations can be repeated many times, like the ablutions of the *albedo,* to attain a more concentrated, highly purified, and increasingly subtle essence. Keeping the fire of our attention at a steady, consistent heat, distillation continues as we go about our lives. All of our interactions and experiences become part of the process. In creative alchemy we use a sevenfold circulation, repeating the process of distillation for each of the seven metals/chakras. Each distillation removes the corrosive passions and draws out the virtues of the metal. We can map the process through the body and understand the corresponding emotional and psychological aspects (see appendix A). Learning to think in terms of correspondence is key. The more we do this the more we learn that nothing in our life is unrelated to the process, and so every aspect of our reality becomes an opportunity for transmutation. Thus with lead we are purifying those issues pertaining to our physicality and sense of stability in the material world; with tin we

Liber de arte Distil

landi de Compositis.

Das büch der waren kunst zü distillieren die

Composita vñ simplicia/vnd dz Büch thesaurus pauperū/Ein schatz d armē ge=
nāt Micariū/die brōsamlin gefallen vō dē blichern d Artzny/vnd durch Experimēt
vō mir Jheronime brūschwick vff geclubt vñ geoffenbart zü trost denē die es begerē◆

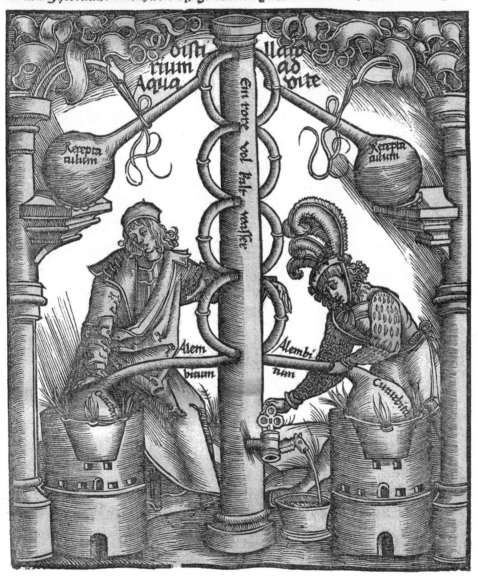

Fig. 7.6. An imaginative apparatus for distilling the aqua vitae, evoking the caduceus of
Hermes. From Hieronymus Brunschwig, *Grosses Destillierbuch,* 1512.
Courtesy of Wikimedia Commons

work upon the emotional body and our projections in relationship to others; with iron we address those things related to our aggression and actions, as well as our intense passions; with copper we consider the problems of the heart and our values; with mercury we purify our expression, communication, and hearing; with silver we work upon the mind and clarify the imagination; and with gold we deal with our relationship to our highest Self and with the cosmos. Planetary magic (see chapter 5) can be employed to help us draw down the positive qualities of the planets and release those qualities that are hindering our progress in the work.

Circular distillation—traditionally conducted with a vessel resembling a pelican piercing its breast, feeding its young with its own blood—represents a cyclical nourishment between the inner and the outer, the upper and the lower. With seven circulations for each of the metals that exist on the earthly plane and the planets in the heavens, the union between the above and below is facilitated and represented psychologically as a deep integration of their correspondence. In this process we are elevating our personal experience to the universal and bringing the universal down into our being—an experience of our own eternal nature, cyclically feeding itself from itself in endless transformations. It is a process of both individuating and assimilating into something greater than us. As we approach the creative process, we see that our passion is the lifeblood of creation, our imagination its source, and our creations are fed by our personal sacrifice to the greater spiraling cycles of life.

Distillation is assigned to Virgo (August 23–September 22), related to the ninth arcanum of the tarot, the Hermit, who holds the lamp of inner illumination as he navigates the solitary path of deep self-knowledge. This work helps us to lighten the heart before it is weighed upon the scales of Libra, the sign following Virgo. We look deep within by our internal light—not by the light of consciousness, but by stepping aside and allowing the unconscious to come forward. This is the idea behind automatism. In fact, Spare himself experienced the illumination of the Hermit's lamp: "The prophets and the seers were hermits. Because of circumstances I have lived for months a hermit's life. Poverty has made me live alone. It has been partly choice, partly compulsion. The result has been psychic development."[37] Spare believed that automatism could help to reveal the cause of our obsessions, by which he also presumably means neuroses, and we might extend that understanding to emotional, mental, and behavioral patterns that thwart our full creative potential and expression of life-force. Thereby we are literally drawing things out from the depths by averting our conscious gaze and allowing the inner, unconscious light to illuminate our consciousness through unintentional evocation. In effect, this is a form of purification of the unconscious mind and helps to reset our patterns, freeing our heart from the burden of unacknowledged wounds. By embodying the purity of the Virgin through our repeated washings and distillations, we attract the evasive unicorn into our lap, a creature symbolic of the process of sublimation.

SUBLIMATIO:
ASCENDING FROM EARTH TO HEAVEN

Enough of denying; one must affirm. Enough of trying to cure; one must sublimate! Enough of disintegration; one must integrate, integrate. Instead of automatism, style; instead of nihilism, technique; instead of skepticism, faith; instead of promiscuity, rigor; instead of collectivism and uniformization—individualism, differentiation, and hierarchization; instead of experimentation, tradition. Instead of Reaction or Revolution, RENAISSANCE!

—DALÍ, *THE SECRET LIFE*

At this point of the *opus alchymicum* we have had enough of death and putrefaction, enough of being dissolved and reduced—now we long to transcend our material limitations and rise through the mental realm to a new purified and sublime aspect of ourselves. In our creative process we are elevated by the remembrance of why we are creating in the first place, getting in touch with the Spirit of our Idea. After extracting the essence from our fist matter in the distillation, our idea is crystalizing into form within us. Now we want to purify this newly solidified concept and raise it up to the spirit, to contact our inner angel or guide and infuse our Idea with spiritual purpose. We've encountered the *anima* in the oily water, the *Eros* and the desire hidden within the depths of our being. Now we must rise and make contact with the *spiritus*, which descends to meet us in the heart of the air. Sublimation, or *sublimatio*, is a purifying process like distillation, though now we are working upon a solid substance rather than a liquid. Our Idea has come into form in our imagination, yet is hindered in its expression by the fixed concepts and beliefs—our story—that must be shed in order to fill the heart with the golden light of love. Indeed, this is a process of purifying the imagination, which according to the Dada artist Hugo Ball is to be initiated through language.[38] Likewise the poetry of Mallarmé may be viewed as an alchemical sublimation of words from their dense solidity into an exalted and rarified form, where they are released from their earthly bondage and made accessible in the world of ideas.

The term "sublimation" is rooted in the Latin *sublimis*, meaning "lofty, high, exalted; eminent, distinguished," and it is this lifting up or ascension that is the essential component of the process.[39] Sublimation is also related to *subliminal*, which means "below the threshold (of consciousness)." What is unknown is raised up from its slumber. Heat and pressure act upon our solid substance and turn it directly into a vaporous, gaseous state, and as it cools on the top of the retort it condenses upon the glass as a solid once again. This reformed and purified solid can be scraped off the retort and sublimated again to attain increasing levels of purification. As George Ripley describes it, to attain the sublime quality that we seek there are seven sublimations to be done, which we again relate to the seven metals and chakras. The purpose of sublimation is first to make the body spiritual; second to make the spirit corporeal so that it becomes fixed in the body; and third, to cleanse the body of its impurities.[40] On one level, sublimation is the internal process of transmuting a physical, or instinctual drive. As the drive is lifted from its physical expression and brought into the air, it no longer grips us and instead is transmuted into a more harmonious form through the creative process.

On another level, sublimation acts upon our most strongly fixed, hardened ideas and concepts about ourselves and the world, those things that are holding us down in the heaviness of earth that we confronted in the *nigredo,* and raises them up through a process of ascension into the cool clarity of the spiritual realm. These might also be ideas relating to the active aspects of our creative process, such as beliefs about how we ought to do things and in what order, or how much and how hard we ought to work to achieve results, or that we must suffer through the hours when our inner spirit is telling us otherwise. When we shed these stories and beliefs, we step into spiritual flow, our feet lifting off the ground as we fall in love with the eternal beloved, with no fixed direction but only moved by the holy breath. We realize, as Heraclitus observed so long ago, that "You could not step twice in the same river; for other and yet other waters are ever flowing on."[41] We rise to a lofty place high above the noise and the chatter, the blaring horns and sirens of our own mental metropolis, and we look into the cool blue eternity of the sky, and we listen. Our sprawling world of concepts and beliefs is viewed from the height of a golden eagle soaring in the Sun's radiance, and we ask Spirit how we may mold our world like a potter with clay.

Whereas dissolution submerses us in the lunar sea and distillation reveals and extracts the pure essence, sublimation acts upon our most earthly aspects to "volatilize the fixed." In turn, we fix the volatile as the vapors are cooled by objective thought. Having thus been purified by air, they can be reformed in a new spiritualized structure that serves our highest aims as creators. These fixed concepts also relate to our karma, the accumulation of energetic patterns that we carry with us, as well as to the Harmony of the Fate Spheres, discussed at length in *Hermetic Philosophy and Creative Alchemy.* Separated from the body in its ascent through the spheres, the Soul relinquishes the various energies that enveloped it during its initial descent. Therefore sublimation is not only a means of purifying the unconscious of negative patterns, but of liberating the Soul from astrological determinism. Thus it is written in the *Emerald Tablet,* "It ascends from the earth to the heaven and becomes ruler over that which is above and that which is below."[42] This is exemplified by the seventh sign of the zodiac to which sublimation is assigned, Libra (September 23–October 22), represented by the scales and the concepts of truth, balance, justice, and order, correlated in the Egyptian pantheon with the goddess Ma'at. In the Hall of Two Truths, the heart of the deceased is judged and weighed upon the scales against the ostrich feather of Ma'at. If the scales are balanced, the deceased is allowed to pass on to the Egyptian afterlife. If, however, the heart is too heavy with the sins of mortal existence it will be thrown to Ammit, a monstrous composite of crocodile, lioness, and hippopotamus, known as the Devourer. Sublimation helps us to lighten the heart, providing an opportunity to release karmic debt. This karma is both personal and collective, and the spiritual evolution of humanity is the process of transforming this karma and liberating its spiritual essence.

If we consider Jung's psychological concept of the libido as psychic energy, which is "not only creative and procreative, but possesses an intuitive faculty," then it is easy to understand that sublimation is a process of raising vibrations to purify the creations that are emerging through us.[43] In each of our psychic energy centers there are fixed patterns that may be elevated through sublimation, spiritualized, and reconfigured so that they are no longer obstructing our energy's free flow of expression. Bringing these fixed aspects into the spiritual realm allows them to be absolved by truth. In effect we are raising the libidinal impulses residing in the lower terrestrial chakras (root, sacral, solar, and heart) to the level of the throat chakra, *vishuddhi,* which functions like an energetic filter. This chakra is where we access the ætheric template, or that layer of the auric body where we can "edit" the blueprints of our psychic energy. Understanding matter as the structured form of thought, the Spirit imparts order (*Kosmos*) to creation. When we transcend the seven Rulers, or the seven planets, we become their ruler and learn to use the imagination consciously to create a life in alignment with Divine Will.

As Jung argues, "though the term 'libido,' introduced by Freud, is not without a sexual connotation, an exclusively sexual definition of this concept is one-sided and must therefore be rejected. Appetite and compulsion are the specific features of all impulses and automatisms."[44] He bases his concept of the term on the writings of Cicero, who considered libido "unbridled desire, which is found in all fools."[45] This brings us back to *Eros* and the *prima materia,* the primal life-force that is both devouring and generative. In its devouring aspect it expresses itself through the ravenous appetites of our desires and lust, which relate not only to sexuality, but also to the passions of gluttony, rage, control, arrogance, and cupidity, among others, expressed through the seven energy centers.

Freud's concept of sublimation is that we sublimate erotic and taboo sexual drives into higher forms of art and expression that are more acceptable to society and even of great benefit to the world. An example of this would be Shelley's Frankenstein, who sublimates his violent and passionate temperament, and sexuality, and channels them into his scientific quest. However, his repressed shadow expresses itself in a malformed and violent creation, underscoring the importance of purification in the process of sublimation. Jung rejected Freud's ideas about sublimation, and his disregard for the alchemical history of sublimation and the mysterious nature of the unconscious: "Freud invented the idea of sublimation to save us from the imaginary claws of the unconscious. But what is real, what actually exists, cannot be alchemically sublimated, and if anything is apparently sublimated it never was what a false interpretation took it to be."[46] Rather than the application of the will to forcibly channel unacceptable impulses into reasonable modes of expression, Jung argued for recognition of the mysterious alchemical transmutation, which we experience as grace, and for which the inner fire is quintessential.[47] In sublimation there is the will and the desire to rise above oneself and to reach new heights of experience and more profound levels of understanding, and there is the grace of divine aid that arrives to facilitate the process. As the will strives upward, grace descends to meet it in the heart where the above and the below are united. They are not opposed to one another, but one and the same.

On a spiritual and metaphysical level, sublimation is a quick release of energy, lifting us from the heavy constraints of the physical body and allowing us to experience the "light body," a truly transpersonal experience and the first step toward the art of astral projection and creating from the imaginal realm, which we will explore further in the final stage of the *opus.* Von Franz describes the psychological nature of sublimation as "a symbolic understanding of what one had considered before to be material reality."[48] Like the merging of dream and reality in the dissolution, we come to see interconnectedness between the inner and outer, and thus the unconscious begins to flow and inspire our creative relationship to life. We enter that place where, as the poet Jean Arp puts it, "both memory and dream flow into one another like powerful rivers." This, he writes, "is the real world . . . the blood relative of art, shaped on the edge of earthly reality."[49]

Here we encounter the unicorn in the alchemical process as a symbol for sublimation. The unicorn evades capture by those that seek it, but will run to the lap of the Virgin—Virgo, or the purified, feminine body of Mercurius. Virgo and Scorpio fall before and after Libra, standing on either side of the scales; the former leads to higher spiritual realization and liberation, while the latter descends back into matter through the processes of putrefaction and generation. By sublimating strong physical drives or emotions and transforming them directly into a volatile state, we attain the unicorn's horn, which will, by virtue of its purity and sanctifying power, repel negative energies and cut karmic cords. Channeling our vital sexual energy up to the top of the retort, it reforms with spiritual integrity, infusing our creative expression with divine purpose. Earthly love is sublimated and elevated to the love of the Divine, the One, the Universal Soul.

The self-protective impulse of the elusive unicorn relates to our level of self-respect, for as we become more comfortable in our own solitude and connection to the soul, we are better able to set boundaries around our sacred creative space, and in our lives in general. Our interactions are based on mutual integrity and authenticity, rather than obligation or compulsion. As artists we need to protect our process while also remaining open to the inspiration that love and connectivity bring to our work. Mars, our iron will, is in detriment in the sign of Libra and thus is weakened. The boundaries we create serve to protect the weakened Mars so that our willpower is maintained through the sublimation. It will likely feel like a natural impulse for solitude and sequestration, and may also require certain sacrifices that will allow us to focus on our creative and spiritual work. In his *50 Secrets of Magical Craftsmanship,* Dalí gives the following advice in relation to painting, but it can be applied to the creative process in any form:

Fig. 7.7. Painting of a unicorn, by Gustave Moreau, 1885.
Courtesy of Wikimedia Commons

Be as chaste as possible, and practice carnal abstinence during the periods when you are not materially launched on your work—that is to say during the inspiration and conception of your painting. For during this spiritual process it is most desirable that the accumulation of your libidinal impulses, unable to find outlet in an actual realization of desires, should nourish the process of your dreams and reveries, especially in the state of gestation which is, as Paracelsus said, above all a state of digestion, of transformation—of transubstantiation—and today that we know Freud we may add also and above all, of sublimation which, as we also know today, is the state which characterizes the constitutional basis of the artistic phenomenon.[50]

Sublimation is the opposite of repressing desire. It is about looking at our desires objectively and transmuting them into their highest potential through the creative act.

On the spectrum of sexual expression, the unicorn is balanced or opposed by the lion—the former being associated with chastity and the latter with passion. The lion is represented by the eleventh arcanum of the tarot, Lust, otherwise known as Strength. Sublimation separates the subtle from the gross to obtain the essence of lust, which is strength. In other words, we separate the spiritual power of sexuality's potent force from its material aspect. What one receives in this essence is the sulfuric impulse hidden within the libido, which longs to create. Before sublimation, this creative desire is dominated by the passions of the physical body and applied through multiplication of the species. After sublimation, this desire is applied through the imagination in the desire to create authentically from within the strength of our sovereignty and self-knowledge. As we purify the mind and transmute the inner voices, we can observe the positive effects this has on our life experience. We learn through this experience that we are creating continuously with every thought and feeling, leading us to further levels of mental and emotional refinement. By the same token, our art progresses through stages to become ever more refined, reflecting the unfolding authentic truth of our artistry.

NAVIGATING THE *ALBEDO*

People who live rashly and precipitately easily lose control over their impressions and are prey to unconscious emotions and motives. The activity of any art (painting, writing, composing) will do them good, provided that they do not pursue any purpose in their subjects, but follow the course of a free, unfettered imagination. The independent process of fantasy never fails to bring to light again those things that have crossed the threshold of consciousness without analysis. In an age like ours, when people are assaulted daily by the most monstrous things without being able to keep account of their impressions, in such an age aesthetic production becomes a prescribed course. But all living art will be irrational, primitive, and complex; it will speak a secret language and leave behind documents not of edification but of paradox.

—HUGO BALL, *DADA DIARY*

As we navigate the *albedo,* we may find ourselves confronting the welling up of old emotional patterns that threaten to pull us back into putrefaction. However, like the swan, we have been touched by grace and given the inner strength to transform even the most ferocious of crocodiles. As Hugo Ball asserts in the above quoted passage from his *Dada Diary,* when we allow ourselves to follow the intuitive movements of the unconscious in our art, we can begin the work of bringing the unconscious, hidden causes to light.[51] Through this cleansing process we bring the white stone to perfection, preparing it for the chemical wedding of the royal couple.

During this time, we undergo a merging of the two sides of our being in the first *coniunctio* to form the hermaphroditic lunar body. By this pairing of inner opposites, we have everything we need for the conception of the soul. This hermaphrodite is still weighed down with the Saturnian depression, however, and it takes time for the celestial dew falling from above to wash away corruption (see figure 7.8 on page 202). This

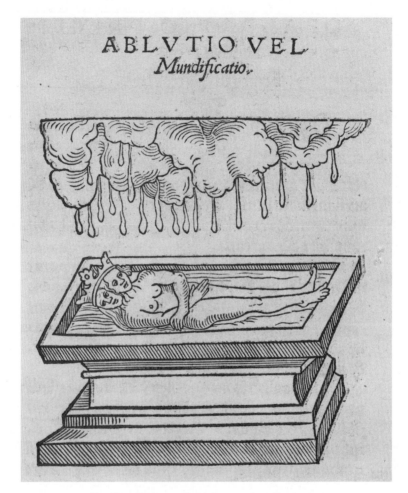

Fig. 7.8. Ablution of the hermaphroditic body.
From *Rosarium Philosophorum*, 1550.
Courtesy of Wellcome Collection

enlivening water brings the hermaphrodite back to life. The conception of the soul is the final result of the *albedo*. This is the *homunculus*, a divine child formed from the union of the *anima* and *spiritus* within the body and birthed within our vessel. This child will develop in the next stage of the *citrinitas*.

To create another life, it is necessary for the male and female to join, but it is impossible for the Soul to be born this way. The Soul is only born through Immaculate Conception, within the Androgynous body of the conjoined Mercury and Venus, the brother and sister, or the Spirit infused into the Body. As long as we are searching for another to complete us or to give us the answers, the purified body thus obtained will not be ready to receive the Spirit, and thus no Soul will be conceived. The purpose of the *ablutio* is to wash away impurities, but also to reveal the perfected Self, the microcosm of the universe containing everything within. The object of desire is recognized as a projection of our missing parts, and as a result, we realize we were never missing them in the first place.

The *albedo* is lunar work, so to deepen our process we can become like the Moon—continuously changing, dying and being reborn. Holding no story except the original story that unfolds spontaneously in each moment, the Moon rides in her chariot, swiftly drawn by white-winged steeds. Just when you think you have her pegged, she has changed into a new costume as she dances through the Circle of the Animals. In our magical practice this is a good time to communicate with the Moon and to ask for her guidance. Paying attention to the Moon's phases of waxing and waning as well as her transits through the signs, we can fine-tune our process to lunar rhythms.

8
Citrinitas
Solar Inspiration and Integration

*Gold is the ferment of the work without which nothing can be
brought to completion; it is as the ferment of the paste, or the
coagulation of the milk in the cheese, or the musk in a good
smell: by means of it is made the composition of the greater
elixir, for it lightens up and preserves from the scorching,
which is the sign of perfection.*

—HERMES, *ROSARIUM PHILOSOPHORUM*

After the *albedo's* purifying processes and dissolution of the body into the
mercurial waters, we enter *citrinitas,* the yellowing stage of solar illumination. The *citrinitas,* or yellowing, marks a transitional phase between
the white and red, a period of digestion, fermentation, and solidification,
like the time between the fading of the flower after its pollination and
the swelling of fertilized ovum into fully ripened fruit. *Citrinitas* represents seeding gold into the earth, a true inspiration from our transpersonal
consciousness—the masculine aspect of the Soul—that illuminates our
inner world and impregnates our imagination. This is a transition from
the encounter with the *anima* to an introduction of *animus* and *spiritus,*
from a passive process to an active one, as we begin consciously engaging
with the unconscious and integrating various parts of ourselves that were
broken open in the previous phases. The citrine or yellow color indicates
this active quality, and the transmutation of silver into gold. This stage is
often depicted with imagery of golden fertilizing rain, urine, gold coins
being sown into the earth, the winged hermaphrodite, birds ascending,
sunlight and the solar body, lions, and eagles. We see allusions to this third

phase in Breton's *Soluble Fish* in images of yellow: rain, rays, gauntlets, and a bridge, as well as the sign of Leo, verdigris, and an eagle.[1]

Like a storm, true inspiration can overwhelm and transform the psyche's internal landscape. Inspiration offers the mind an alternative path upon which to travel with curiosity and faith, and forms the antithesis of anxiety, in which the mind fixates upon uncertainties, spiraling downward with the weight of worry, doubt, and fear. Transforming this energy, as we do through processes like digestion and fermentation, requires acceptance of the unknown, as well as desire for understanding. Inspiration is neither earned by solar striving (Apollo) nor by mere lunar passivity (Artemis), but through balance of the two. This unification is the quintessence of the fourteenth arcanum of the tarot, Temperance, pictured as a winged angel holding a vessel in each hand, one red and one blue, between which flows a lateral stream of water. It is an impossible act according to the laws of gravity, the water flowing at an angle of about 45 degrees from one vase to another, and yet the angel accomplishes it with skill and grace. Having an existence devoted to contemplation of God and the heavens, the angel teaches us in the human realm how to balance polarities, and the *temperance* required to reach an integrated state of spiritual inspiration. The anonymous author of *Meditations on the Tarot* explains that inspiration is attained by marriage of the power of higher will (intuition) with the quiet receptivity of grace (vision), and that neither of these on their own produces true inspiration. Accordingly, they posit three principal modes of authentic spiritual experience: *vision, inspiration,* and *intuition.* It is *vision* that the lower self, or personality, receives as an imprint from above, the understanding of which is not necessarily implied. *Intuition,* on the other hand, results from surrendering the lower self to a point of complete passivity in the presence of the higher self, thereby tethering the personality completely and allowing the higher self to be solely active. This is precisely our concern within the *citrinitas.* True inspiration is active flow between the higher and lower selves, which, "being in contact, vibrate in unison, each with its own voice and in terms of its own language, and thus together [they] produce a concrete inspiration."[2]

The active principle forms the posing of a question or a mode of inquiry aimed like an arrow at the heavens, while the passive principle is an open heart ready to receive the return fire of divine intuitive understanding. It is not a matter of waiting, but of active participation—the *participation mystique,* where the universe becomes a living entity within the individual, rather than the individual experiencing itself within the externalized universe. In the Thoth deck of Crowley, arcanum fourteen is named Art, though it could just as well be titled Alchemy, for it represents the essential Hermetic axiom *solve et coagula,* a repeated process of dissolving and coagulating necessary in the great work. In Lady Frieda Harris's illustration a female alchemist mixes fire and water, or that which burns and that which melts, accompanied by a red (solar) eagle and a white (lunar) lion, the Sulfur and Mercury that are the fixed and changeable aspects of the psyche. She represents the alchymical union of the Lovers joined together in one androgynous figure. Behind her we see the words *visita interiora terra rectificando invenies occultum lapidem* (VITRIOL), advising us to journey inward, rectify, and find the hidden stone. Along the androgyne's central channel is an arrow aimed at heaven, piercing a rainbow arching on either side of her in spectral harmony. This is *spiritus* rising from the process of transformation taking place within her, *inspiration* born by the union of *vision* and *intuition.* As spirit rises it breaks into the rainbow light by which we can better see the accumulation of old patterns in order to let them go, illuminating new paths to embark on and new goals at which to aim our golden arrows.

To say *spiritus* rises from within is of course to say it descends from above, the world within being synonymous with heaven. As such when this *spiritus* descends, as a spiritual effluence of consciousness, we rise to meet it like bread that rises with the addition of a leaven. We are exalted by true inspiration, raised up in embodiment of our personal truth and highest aspirations, yet the work of receiving true inspiration is not without its difficulties and dangers. As the anonymous author of *Meditations* writes,

> Authentic inspiration always entails an inner upheaval. It *pierces* the soul like an arrow in wounding it and in making it experience that profound emotion which is a synthesis of sorrow and joy. The symbol of the Rose Cross—a cross from the centre of which a rose blossoms

out—renders the essence of the experience of inspiration in the best way that I know. The Rose Cross expresses the mystery of tears, i.e., that of inspiration, with force and clarity. It portrays the joy of sorrow and the sorrow of joy, which together comprise inspiration.[3]

With authentic inspiration comes responsibility and the necessity of inner reflection and integration. As the spirit enters our house, we must be accountable for all that lies therein, doing the work of rectifying what is no longer in alignment with our higher goal. Returning to Ernst's collage novel, *Une Semaine,* we can make a parallel between his third chapter and emotional processes catalyzed by the *citrinitas* and influx of spirit. In this chapter Ernst depicts male and female figures, primarily within closed rooms symbolic of the vessel. In one collage a flying man hovers in the air in a stairwell; in another a woman guides a winged, bird-headed figure into a parlor. Many appear in various states of emotional tension and union—the latter symbolized by several collages in which the male and female kiss joyfully—as they heat up in the conjunction. Several of the figures are crying or hunched over in anguish, while others struggle passionately. This volume is called "Mardi," or Tuesday, corresponding to the element Fire and "La Cour du Dragon," the court of the dragon (a district in Paris that is depicted in several of the collages). Dragons are sacred to Mars, the planetary ruler for Tuesday, typifying male aggression and fiery will. Yet dragons also stand for the primal matter, which must be beheaded, decayed, and purified of poisons. Hence these collages are filled with dragons, snakes, bats, smoke, and human figures with dragon wings symbolic of the volatile *spiritus.* After the separation of the primal pair and their purification in water, they are heated within the vessel to facilitate their red conjunction.

The alchemical processes of *digestio, fermentatio,* and *congelatio/coagulatio* are helpful in understanding the *citrinitas,* for they all have to do with development and processing of information and inspiration, in order that it becomes solidified as a physical knowing and brought into authentic expression as the philosopher's stone.

DIGESTIO:
UNCONSCIOUS ASSIMILATION

The Philosopher says Citrination is no other thing than completed digestion, for heat going into moisture, first engenders blackness, and going into dryness causes whiteness, because the fire if it transcends the agent in it changes it into a most pure citrineness.

—Rosarium Philosophorum

Digestion, which refers to applying gentle heat to a substance and allowing it to cook over an extended period of time, is such a central process to practical alchemy that it is nearly impossible to assign it to just one phase of the *opus*. Be that as it may, when looking at digestion from the lens of creative alchemy, we can understand it as part of the transitional stage of *citrinitas,* in which our creative process is maturing. Digestion corresponds to the sign of Leo (July 23–August 22), a fiery sign living in the bright light of consciousness, as opposed to the lunar depths of the unconscious to which the preceding sign of Cancer is assigned. In the northern hemisphere Leo is the time of the Sun's greatest intensity, and likewise digestion correlates with cultivation of a strong and controlled inner fire and harnessing of the will. It is a recognition of our inherent divinity and royal nature that lifts and empowers us to grow more fully into truth, just as the Sun's heat beckons fruit to emerge from a fertilized flower.

Digestive action takes place on the physical, mental, emotional, and spiritual planes and within the seven chakras, or metals. On a physical level alchemical digestion is mirrored by stomach acid that digests our food; on a mental level by processing of new ideas, inspirations, and information; on an emotional level by processing feelings; and on a spiritual level by breaking down and integrating symbols, insights, and unconscious material. Truly, healthy digestion is foundational to all levels of our well-being.

Creatively, *digestio* is a state of processing inspiration and unconscious contents received and encountered during *albedo,* and breaking them down into forms that we can assimilate and be nourished by. Thus we begin to integrate what we have learned, obtained, and experienced, submitting our matter to a gentle cooking process and refining it into a more subtle form. During this time it is important to cultivate patience in our creative process. Sometimes we need to put things aside for a while, letting them develop without our conscious involvement. We can rest and let things unfold, while remaining consciously present, awaiting inspiration as the unconscious nutrition transmutes into new creative energy. On the inner level digestion is akin to the "dynamics" phase of dreamwork as presented by Johnson, in which symbols presented in our dream are explored through free association and then related to our inner world.[4] The people and events of our dreams are understood as symbolic of things we are experiencing physically, emotionally, mentally, and spiritually in waking life. In recognizing and acknowledging them, we begin to understand and process what our dreams are communicating to us.

There is an inner fire at this stage driving us onward toward our goal. It is the fire of a gentle lion, burning steadily in our core, by which we assimilate the unconscious and form a new energetic body. Leo relates to eleventh arcanum (or eighth) in the tarot, called Strength (or Lust), denoting the inner strength required to master primal emotions and stand in one's sovereign power. The lion in this context symbolizes passions, like lust, that would run wild if it were not for the restraining hand of inner wisdom. However, these passions are vital to our creative process. We don't want to suppress them completely, but we can guide and give them healthy expression through our creativity. On another level this card represents the submission of the conscious solar lion to the will of the unconscious feminine powers. This correlates with the realization that while we return to a more conscious level of integration and understanding, we now understand the immense power of the unconscious. There is a strength in bowing to the unconscious as the lion submits to the woman; we do this when we pay attention to the unconscious, listen to its messages, and consciously acknowledge its validity.

In the esoteric anatomy of the body, Leo corresponds with the fire of the upper digestive organs and the solar plexus (*manipura*) chakra, which is the center of power, the will to act, and vitality. Hence we have risen from the sacral chakra (*svadhisthana*) and the watery processes of the *albedo* to reach the fire chakra, which connects us with the Mental Body, the third layer of the auric field. This is the center of inner solar fire, both physically and spiritually, as well as our sense of vision. Separating the subtle from the gross is a necessary part of expressing ourselves authentically, a process facilitated by the Divine Intellect by which we discern true knowledge and see things as they really are.

Digestion goes on within as a function of the autonomic nervous system; if it is progressing well, we likely won't notice it. This is the attitude of Leo, confident in the internal processes that are unfolding. The contents of our unconscious are placed in a sealed flask in the dark and left for the necessary time. An overactive mind, however, can wreak havoc on the digestive system. The parasympathetic nervous system is our "rest-and-digest" function. It tells our body everything is safe in our external environment, and it's ok to direct blood to the internal organs for digestion and away from the periphery. In a similar way alchemical digestion is a gentle and slow cooking process; we are not giving too much thought to the details and allow it to occur naturally, slowly, and in its own time. As we process and interpret information we want to refrain from overthinking, but we also want to give it the proper space to unfold, just as we wouldn't exert effort in digesting food, but we might breathe deeply and remain in a restful state so digestion is not inhibited. We may not have the answers yet and may feel a bit disconnected from the creative process at this point, perhaps listless, so patience is required until inspiration is assimilated and transformed into creative expression. Usually we will know when an unconscious symbol aligns with our experience, like a revelatory moment coming spontaneously and easily because we've been passively allowing digestion and assimilation to occur.

Dung is the end product of physical digestion, and yet alchemically it is sometimes the means of digestion. Reviled by most but esteemed by alchemists, dung represents on the one hand fertilization and on the other hand a source of heat. "The field is prepared for the grain," we are told in the "Gloria Mundi," when it is "well ploughed up, and manured with well rotted dung; for the earth consumes and assimilates the manure, as the body assimilates its food, and separates the subtle from the gross."[5] Geber is quoted in the *Rosarium* as saying, "The fire of dung is the agent cause in the work of the Digestion of our Stone," for sometimes digestion is accomplished by burying the vessel in moist horse manure, which provides a moderate and consistent fire of the second degree: "The fire of the horse dung, neither melts nor burns, but tames and increases the moistness."[6] Likewise our digestive fire shouldn't be so hot that we're experiencing something like calcination, but rather the moistness—the emotionality, the soul, *Eros*—needs to be retained. On another level, dung points to the fact that every creator, at some point, has to deal with the fact that they've essentially created shit. Yet the wise and persevering creators will see this excrement as being pure gold, for it provides a motivating fire to continue digesting life and moving forward with new creations. The same holds true for any of the "shit" we deal with in the world, which the alchemist does not turn away from, but rather sets to work in its transmutation into something divine and illuminating. We do this by placing ourselves firmly within it just as we would bury our flask in the dung.

The "Gloria Mundi" continues to say, "the earth separates . . . the good from the bad, and imparts it as nutriment to all growing things; for the destruction of one thing is the generation of another."[7] Putrefaction, digestion, and fermentation share similarities as processes that break things down and support generation of new life. Yet the truth is that sometimes we don't digest things as well as we'd like. Perhaps our inner fire is not burning hot enough, and unconscious material is not broken down but instead putrefies or ferments. When digestion turns to putrefaction, a depressive state results in which one has no alternative but to patiently await its completion, while the outcome remains unknown. Things are being broken down and separated, but it is a much more challenging experience. In this state the bright shining light of Leo is dimmed, as the dark watery processes of the unconscious take over and the artist turns their attention inward, into the discomfort, with little conscious understanding. Imagine what happens to undigested food in the gut as it begins to putrefy and ferment. It emits gasses that must be released somewhere—either externally or internally through the tissues, which causes shooting pains and headaches. Here we encounter the *aqua foetida,* the fetid or stinking water, the mercurial water,

Fig. 8.1. The lion and the aqua foetida. From Michael Maier, *Atalanta Fugiens,* Oppenheim, Germany: Johann-Theodor de Bry, 1618.

Courtesy of Science History Institute

and the water of the dragon that emits a sulfurous miasma, the stench of death.

The aqua foetida is associated with the green lion, a code name for green vitriol, the highly corrosive sulfuric acid, and represents the unconscious as it devours or dissolves our metals. So both the lion and the dragon share a mercurial nature that dissolves and devours. If the process is allowed to unfold in its own time, the lion (Sulfur) is overcome by the dragon (Mercury) and is devoured by him, and through digestive putrefaction a sweet fragrance issues forth as a stream from the lion's mouth. When the dragon consumes the lion's flesh, he fills to bursting and dies.[8] According to J. C. Cooper, "The lion and dragon devouring each other signifies union without loss of identity."[9] Both consciousness and unconsciousness have the power to overcome each other, but balance is maintained by mutual engulfment. In digestion we do not want to lose ourselves in unconscious subjectivity, nor do we want to subject our unconscious symbols to a harsh rational analysis. Rather, we aim for that middle ground where the unconscious and conscious merge, mutually supporting each other in the creative process. They appear together in their united state in the fifth plate of the *Splendor Solis* series (see figure 8.2 on page 214), as a green winged dragon with three leonine heads—one black, one white, and one red—representing the series of color changes of the Great Work. These color changes all take place within the vessel during alchemical digestion as the opposing principles come to union.

The lion is also described as being green and gold: "I am the true green and Golden Lion without cares, In me all the secrets of the Philosophers are hidden."[10] Greenness suggests the unripe state, and therefore the green and gold lion is a symbol of unripe gold on its way to perfection. Thus we see how the *citrinitas* is spiritual ripening brought forth by the heat of the Sun. The green and golden lion is "without cares" because it is resting in the heart and illuminated by consciousness, the golden ferment descending from above that will cause the soul to rise. As the material ripens and matures, the process of fermentation begins tingeing the matter with golden color.

Fig. 8.2. A king in golden raiments rides upon a solar chariot with the figure of Leo upon the wheel. Within the flask is a three-headed dragon painted in the three colors of the opus—black, white, and red. "Plate XV" from *Splendor Solis,* Germany, 1582.

British Library, Harley 3469, folio 26

FERMENTATIO:
AWAKENING THE TRUE IMAGINATION

Sow Your Gold in the white foliate Earth.

MICHAEL MAIER, *ATALANTA FUGIENS*

Fermentation relates to another form of putrefaction and spiritual activation of the successfully separated parts of the primal matter, which have been properly digested and purified. At this stage we are ready to receive the golden ferment of the Soul. For as we are advised in the *Rosarium,*

> The Philosophers have said, that our Stone is of a spirit, soul, and body, and they say the truth, for they have called the imperfect body—a body, ferment—the soul, and water—the spirit. And they have truly called them so, for the imperfect body by itself is a grievous body, weak and dead; water is the spirit purging the body, making it subtle and white; ferment is the soul which giveth life to the imperfect body, which life it had not before and bringeth it into a better form. The body is Venus and the woman; the Spirit is Mercury and the man; the soul is Sol and Luna. The Body must melt into his first matter which is Mercury.[11]

The white earth, according to Senior, is one of many names of the stone, along with "the holy thirsty earth . . . the earth of pearls, the starry earth and the snowy earth," and the "fountains of copper."[12] This latter name alludes to Venus, the planet associated with copper and the body. Venus also indicates the principle of *Eros,* which, according to von Franz, is the *prima materia* of the alchemists. Namely, it is the "erotic inner life of the human being" that catalyzes the mystical search for God.[13] This love must be sublimated and raised up from its earthly and ordinary state and exalted as the love for the Creator, and the inner identification with eternal perfection. In this process the white earth, in a passive state, is activated by the fermenting agent. Creatively it is acceptance of a necessary period of inactivity, or passivity, in preparation for receiving the activating authentic inspiration of the Soul. Yet this is the perfect time for active imagination, when we shine the light of solar consciousness into the lunar waters of the unconscious. We actively engage with forms and figures residing there, entering into conscious dialogue with them to receive wisdom, insights, and healing. What we learn through this process will inform the development of our creative work, and we will explore active imagination in more depth at the end of this section.

After the *albedo,* the white earth, which is pure but infertile, must be "foliated," as the dictum from *Atalanta Fugiens* advises to "Sow Your Gold in the white foliate Earth."[14] *Foliate* comes from the Latin *folium,* meaning "leaf," as the white earth is prepared and light, weighing no more than leaves. This foliated white earth, or *terra alba foliata,* is "ash of ashes" and the "crown of victory," according to Senior.[15] They derive from the intensity and suffering of the *nigredo* and the reduction to ashes, a primary rite of purification and reduction of ego, which prepares us to receive the golden inspiration that will bring us back to life.

While distillation extracts the oil (soul/Sulfur) of a substance, and calcination produces ashes (body/Salt), the product of alchemical fermentation is alcohol (spirit/Mercury), which involves another form of distillation. In this case a pure spirit is separated from the dead body—the "arid earth"—that has been moistened in its own water—the wisdom from within. The pure spirit, or Mercury, represents purification of thought, or Mind. To obtain this pure thought, it is necessary to "kill" the body in which the impure thoughts are stored, to let it putrefy and rot in order for the revivifying golden ferment to descend upon it from above and raise the "corpse" from the earth, imbuing it with new life. As Edward Kelly writes in "The Stone of the Philosophers," "As without the ferment there is no perfect tincture, as the Sages say, so without leaven there is no good bread. In our Stone the ferment is like the soul, which gives life to the dead body through the mediation of the spirit, or Mercury."[16]

Fabricius calls the *citrinitas* "'yellow' death and putrefaction," explaining that the treasures retrieved from the *albedo,* "achieved after so much toil and suffering," must be sacrificed as we step into the unknown, submitting our "white gold" to death and fermentation.[17] The difficult aspect of this stage is that the artist must relinquish through death "the mastery he has just gained in order to learn the finer details of his divine art."[18]

Fig. 8.3. The philosopher sowing the fermented gold into the "white foliate earth."
From Michael Maier, *Atalanta Fugiens,* Oppenheim, Germany:
Johann-Theodor de Bry, 1618.
Courtesy of Science History Institute

Creatively this may be experienced as disconnection from one's previous body of work, lack of new inspiration, and disappointment, for the clarity and the feelings of renewal, rebirth, and union experienced in the *albedo* are *in absentia*. It is as though the work done thus far has been for naught, but if one understands how to revitalize the white foliated earth—with the golden ferment of the soul—then we may open ourselves up to a rich experience.

Just as one would leave a ferment out at room temperature for a matter of days or weeks, the death of inspiration is grieved, and the transformation is given space to develop. Yet in fermentation everything must be sterilized to prevent contamination—the vessel in which fermentation takes place, or the body; the water, or the spirit and the mind; and the ferment itself, or the soul. Consider that when culturing something, an anaerobic fermentation is used to prevent contamination. Since air is the element of thought, this means we want to let this process happen without overanalyzing; otherwise it could become contaminated. This is then the purity required of our mind, which is an innocence of objectivity. We must be mentally involved in the process, but not obsessive, protecting the spirit from the harsh critical fire of the rational mind. In this way we fix the spirit in the body, through patient persuasion and detached but consistent attention. A successful fermentation will produce a pure spirit, yet this is also dependent on the purity of the body and the soul.

Fermentation is the process of Capricorn (December 22–January 19), an earth sign ruled by the heaviness of Saturn. Like the goat rising up the steep mountain and ascending from the material to the spiritual realms, or bread rising from a golden yeast, fermentation represents both a process of decay and an enrichment of the imagination. Rising toward the Sun, the white stone is tinged yellow as the lunar *albedo* transitions to the solar *rubedo*. The earthy quality of Saturn-ruled Capricorn relates to the body, which must be purged or purified through digestion and putrefaction in order for the spirit to be joined with it, as we read in the "Gloria Mundi":

> Spirits cannot join themselves to impure bodies; but when the body has been well purged, and digested by coction, the spirit becomes united to it, amidst a phenomenal exhibition of all the colours in the world, and the imperfect body is tinged with the indestructible colour of the ferment; this ferment is the soul, in and through which the spirit is joined to the body, and transmuted with the body into the colour of the ferment, whereupon all three become one thing.[19]

Fermentation, in this context, is a process of bringing the three principles of body, soul, and spirit to unity, which is not possible unless the body is pure. Within the body is where unconscious contents lie hidden, and these must be brought to light, or elevated into conscious awareness. Here the body and unconscious is spiritualized and we become receptive to its messages, little by little. This spiritualizing process develops over time as the spirit opens the drawers of the unconscious and removes that which lies hidden within, examines the contents, understands them with the light of consciousness, integrates what is useful, and discards what is not.

Just as important, if not more so, as the purity of the body is the purity of the soul, which is added to it as the leavening agent. There is an interesting essay entitled "Animus and Eros" in Barbara Hannah's book *The Animus* that pertains to the issue of contamination.[20] She interprets a passage written by the alchemist Eiraneus Philaletha (Philalethes), comparing it with a medieval case of a nun named Jeanne Fery who became possessed by demons and underwent an exorcism around the years 1584–1585. Hannah considers these demons to be negative *animus* figures that took possession of Fery when she was a child, giving her certain advantages while requiring her obedience to them. Later in life when Fery was possessed and submitted to an exorcism by the archbishop, Mary Magdalene appeared to her, an *Eros* figure and aspect of her transcendent Self. It took time for the demons to give way, but in the end it was this *Eros* function that eventually liberated Fery from negative *animus* figures, or demons.

The *animus* represents the masculine, or active and rational part of the soul. Correlated with *Logos,* it signifies the dissolving spirit that causes separation, while the *anima,* as a symbol of *Eros,* is the binding soul that seeks union.[21] Let us look at the related passage of Philalethes,* originally titled *Introitus Apertus* and otherwise known as *An Open Entrance to the Closed Palace of the King*:

> The arid earth must be irrigated, and its pores softened with water of its own kind, then this thief with all the workers of iniquity will be cast out, the water will be purged of its leprous stain by the addition of true Sulphur, and you will have the Spring whose waters are sacred to

---

*This passage is a different translation from the one quoted by Hannah.

the maiden Queen Diana. This thief is armed with all the malignity of arsenic, and is feared and eschewed by the winged youth. Though the Central Water be his Spouse, yet the youth cannot come to her, until Diana with the wings of her doves purges the poisonous air, and opens a passage to the bridal chamber. Then the youth enters easily through the pores, presently shaking the waters above, and stirring up a rude and ruddy cloud. Do thou, O Diana, bring in the water over him, even unto the brightness of the Moon! So the darkness on the face of the abyss will be dispersed by the spirit moving in the waters. Thus, at the bidding of God, light will appear on the Seventh Day, and then this sophic creating of Mercury shall be completed, from which time, until the revolution of the year, you may wait for the birth of the marvellous Child of the Sun, who will come to deliver his brethren from every stain.[22]

Hannah points out that the "arid earth" indicates "the lack of fantasy, the complete blank that overtakes so many people when they try, for example, to do active imagination."[23] We can extend this to creative inspiration in general, which has seemingly left us in this phase of the work. She goes on to provide a solution to this "arid lack of inspiration," saying that in her experience the means to overcome the block "is by concentrating on the unknown, by attempting to get some faint approach to that infinite even if one can only confess one's failure."[24] For this she suggests contemplation upon the infinite, for example where we were before birth, and where we might go after death.

Jung, in treating this text as dream analysis, advises that "if you will contemplate your lack of fantasy, of inspiration and inner aliveness, which you feel as sheer stagnation and a barren wilderness, and impregnate it with the interest born of alarm at your inner death, then something can take shape in you, for your inner emptiness conceals just as great a fulness if only you will allow it to penetrate into you."[25] Bringing attention to our mortality is a natural means to purify the mind, for hidden in the fear of death is the key to inner aliveness and inspiration. Contemplating the eternal, the self expands beyond the sterility of a life lived in a state of denial. We become present, inhabiting a larger energetic sphere in which our relationships, the environment around us, and circumstances of our lives are felt to be aspects of Self, rather than external to us. This is the meaning of receiving the golden ferment, for what is golden is everlasting, pure, and incorruptible. It is Sulfur—the Soul—which on account of having an active and dual nature of being both corrosive (as in sulfuric acid) and life-giving (our living Sulfur), must be likewise purified before it is taken into the white foliated earth—the prepared body of Mercury. This is then the "true Sulfur" that is a union of the red and white Sulfurs spoken of throughout alchemical texts. It is the Soul, *Eros,* or the true Self that "drives out and replaces the opinions of the animus," as Hannah puts it.[26] In Philalethes's text the negative *animus* is the thief "armed with all the malignity of arsenic" that is "feared and eschewed by the winged youth" who represents the positive *animus.* Jung equates this Sulfur with a "collective sickness" that takes us out of ourselves and into the desirousness of the "Everyman," "who has not yet discovered himself and stumbles through the world like a blind man leading the blind with somnambulistic certainty into the ditch."[27]

Sulfur that is contaminated emits the sulfurous odor reminiscent of hell, conjuring the Devil (fifteenth arcanum) of the tarot, the card of the major arcana to which Capricorn is attributed. The Devil card relates to the shadow, those parts of ourselves that we deny, suppress, and project outwardly upon others and the environment. As Hannah writes, "people who think they are just too marvelously good and thus deny their shadows altogether are as if possessed by devils."[28] Before learning to see our own shadow and come to terms with it, we will be unable to obtain the pure Sulfur necessary for proper fermentation, which will bring us the pure spirit, the positive *animus* or *Logos,* thus *inspiring* us and raising us from the dead by a true enrichment of the imagination. Hence we see why fermentation is yet another form of putrefaction and a continuation of the shadow work of the *nigredo.* This contamination is exemplified in Faust selling his soul to the Devil through his emissary, Mephistopheles, in exchange for magical powers, worldly knowledge, and pleasure and likewise in *The Picture of Dorian Gray,* written by Oscar Wilde, in which Dorian is corrupted by his friend Lord Henry to live a life of hedonism. In a magical transference between art and life, Dorian receives the gift of eternal youth while the corruption within his soul and his aging body is reflected in his portrait, which he hides away for fear that it will reveal to the world the truth of his inner depravity.

A similar bargain was made by Jeanne Fery and her demons, who gave her wit and charm and rich food so long as she obeyed their commands. According to Chevalier and Gheerbrandt, there is a German legend that says a person loses their shadow when they sell their soul to the Devil. "This may," they write, "symbolize the fact that the party to such a bargain has destroyed his or her own existence. The shadow would thus become the symbol of the lost soul in physical terms, since the soul now belongs to the world of darkness and can no longer show itself in the light of day. Lack of shadow is a sign of lack of light and substance."[29] Acknowledgment and integration of the shadow is quintessential to the expression of our solar creative light. In dealing with the principle of Sulfur it is essential that we rely on the true Sulfur, rather than the corrosive Sulfur. Otherwise, what we end up with are the distorted thoughts of a negative *animus* that slowly consume us like leprosy, rather than the living quintessence, a true source of eternal life and power that exists beyond the temporal nature of the body.

There are several expressions of the negative *animus,* according to Hannah: it interferes in our relationships with poisonous opinions that separate us from reality; it can be contaminated by collective unconscious figures that, becoming autonomous and destructive, wreak havoc on our lives, as in the case of Jeanne Fery; and it can separate us from our connection with the infinite by diverting our attention to superficial concerns.[30] This "thief" robs us of a relationship with the positive *animus,* the winged youth, and with the renewing waters of the unconscious. Thus Philalethes says that "though the Central Water be his Spouse, yet the youth cannot come to her, until Diana with the wings of her doves purges the poisonous air, and opens a passage to the bridal chamber."[31] The "Central Water" represents the inner source of emotional connection with the Self and with the unconscious. The positive *animus* is meant to be united with this inner *anima* in a unified expression of Soul. This is the authentic inspiration that is successfully wed to the imagination, giving birth to authentic creativity—"the marvelous Child of the Sun"—in every sphere of our lives.

Hence Philalethes states that "the darkness on the face of the abyss will be dispersed by the spirit moving in the waters,"[32] speaking to the process of Creation.

The bridal chamber is physiologically related to the hypothalamic region of the brain where the soul and spirit are united in the *hieros gamos.* Thus "the waters above" that the positive *animus,* or spirit, shakes into a "rude and ruddy cloud" correspond to the highly conductive cerebrospinal fluid that originates in the ventricles of the brain and circulates through the central nervous system, connecting the conscious and unconscious, or the above and below. The ruddy color is the reddening emerging with the final phase of the *magnum opus* and the conjunction of the opposites.

There is another passage of Philalethes in the *Introitus Apertus* that speaks to the necessity of pure Sulfur.[33] This is the true Sulfur that removes the impediments in the Mercury and with which "you will have the Spring whose waters are sacred to the maiden Queen Diana," or the fountain of inspiration and an ever-renewing source of connection with the unconscious, the waters of the Moon.[34] He begins by describing the quality of Mercury as it is found in the bowels of the earth. Though it was "intended to become a metal," Philalethes explains that the process was hindered by impurities that had tainted it, and that prevented alchemical digestion. Thus the spirit in the body is corrupted by its conditioning. The sages "found that that which should be active in the Mercury was passive; and that its infirmity could not be remedied by any means, except the introduction of some kindred principle from without." Here we are again shown that the means of activating the Mercury, the spirit and *Logos,* is something external, which is the metallic Sulfur, that could purify the Mercury and remove these impurities. He continues,

> In order that this sulphur might be effectual in purifying the Mercury, it was indispensable that it should itself be pure. All their efforts to purify it, however, were doomed to failure. At length they bethought them that it might possibly be found somewhere in Nature in a puri-fied condition—and their search was crowned with success. They sought active sulphur in a pure state, and found it cunningly concealed in the House of the Ram.[35]

To purify the sulfur, it is necessary to discover it in nature—our own nature. We find this in the "House of the Ram," sign of Aries, a cardinal fire sign and the traditional time to begin the *opus,* also corresponding with the anatomical head. Aries is attributed to the fourth arcanum in the tarot, the Emperor, who represents the authority within our mind. Hannah notes that the *animus* may be approached through dreams, where he often appears as an authority figure such as a priest, monk, teacher, ruler, father figure, brother, or romantic partner—essentially someone we see as having a certain authority over us.[36] Thus we are looking inward into the world of our thoughts and dreams, observing them in order to catch the thief: the inner authority that is not in alignment with our Divine Nature.

This thief has taken the place of the true authority, whose power is divinely ordained. Yet the true Sulfur and the true authority is that which has the power to catch this thief and expel him. Philalethes continues to say that the sages found that this pure Sulfur "mingled most eagerly with the offspring of Saturn, and the desired effect was speedily produced—after the malignant venom of the 'air' of Mercury had been tempered . . . by the Doves of Venus."[37] The "offspring of Saturn" is Mercury, from which the "malignant venom of the 'air'"—the poisoned thoughts—are tempered by the "Doves of Venus," the principle of *Eros. Eros,* personified in the figure of Mary Magdalene in the case of Jeanne Fery, is the eternal and incorruptible part of Soul that engenders gnosis, or "true knowing," what Jung called "absolute knowledge," an inner illumination of the unconscious through dreams, visions, intuitions, and synchronicity.[38] In *The Gospel of Mary Magdalene,* the teacher Yeshua says "If you are out of balance, take inspiration from manifestations of your true nature."[39] These manifestations of our true nature will appear to us as external figures or in certain environments through which a spiritual and holy presence—manifestations of our own indwelling Divine consciousness—may be felt. Or, in the case of the aspiring artist, these manifestations may be the masters of old or contemporary inspirations. This is perhaps what Philalethes means when he says that "the arid earth must be irrigated, and its pores softened with *water of its own kind,*" for it is in the recognition that these apparently external holy or masterful influences are sourced within us that we are reawakened and enlivened by the principle of *Eros*.

In recognizing the holy presence and inspiration as springing from within, we also come to balance the opposing principles within us of our active and passive natures:

> Then life was joined to life by means of the liquid; the dry was moistened; the passive was stirred into action by the active; the dead was revived by the living. The heavens were indeed temporarily clouded over, but after a copious downpour of rain, serenity was restored. Mercury emerged in a hermaphroditic state.[40]

Life is joined to life when we no longer adhere to the illusion of separation, and true wisdom is allowed to fall upon us like rain from our very own Crown. While we may derive solace from seeking wisdom from external sources, and this is a necessary part of the process, true serenity is found by recognizing our own inner, divine, creative authority, and living in the light of the eternally abiding truth within. Those parts of us that have been sealed up in fermentation begin to bubble and awaken from the addition of the ferment, our active consciousness, which awakens and enlivens the unconscious matter, shedding light upon it and revealing its hidden secrets. By the union of the active and passive sides of ourselves we emerge as the hermaphroditic Mercury, the divine child of inspiration, creative flow, and inner equilibrium. The hermaphrodite represents the initial union of opposites in one body.

Our fermentation takes its requisite time, just as a growing fetus receives its nourishment within the sealed vessel of the womb, existing in a unified fluid of imagination and possibility, before emerging into the world. We have come to understand the necessity of death in the process of creation, and how, once the body has been purified, we can step back and let the fermentation bring the body back to life, thriving with new inspiration and ready to create with a healthy ambition. This is the ambition of the Capricorn Sea Goat, imbued with life-force and purified of the personal ego. We ascend the mountain, rising with inspiration and awaiting the time when we are ready to share this medicine with the world. New life is stirring, the fruit is ripening, and we are glowing with the raw awareness that follows death. In the words of Rimbaud, "I am a spectator at the flowering of my thought: I watch it, I listen to it: I draw a bow across a string: a symphony stirs in the depths, or surges onto the stage."[41]

Capricorn is a sign that is firmly planted in reality, taking stock of the actual steps needed to progress in the direction of a vision. Saturn-ruled Capricorn thrives with structure, and hence we can see this as a time for building solid foundations and structures for our creative process to mature. If we have gotten off track in our "derangement of the senses," now we can pull in the reins and get focused in order to bring our work to its completion. As we await the upwelling energy of fermentation, we can ground into a routine and put in the time required of our work. Capricorn is serious and hard working; as any successful artist knows, discipline is absolutely essential in creative pursuits.

The Capricorn Sea Goat is a mythical creature that both attains the heights and descends to the depths, traversing both earth and water. As such it symbolizes the understanding that there is a time for getting lost in watery reverie and soaking up inspiration, and a time for engaging in the arduous work of ascending the mountain to the summit. It is also the balance between exploring the unconscious through active imagi-nation and staying grounded in physical reality and attending to our responsibilities in the material world. The Sea Goat falls into the water below so that it may confront the shadows lurking in the unconscious and be redeemed. In surrender to the darkness, the derangement of the dissolution, or the spirit of debauchery of the Saturnalia, it is reborn like the Sun on the winter solstice, rising like the fermented yeast into the heavens.

Active Imagination

We might think of fermentation as the solar active consciousness descend-ing into the lunar passive unconscious, illuminating and awakening it so that it becomes a living body once again. In much the same way, we can engage with the unconscious through active imagination, a technique developed by Jung involving an intentional, conscious use of the imagination to explore the internal realm of the psyche, facilitating insight, transformation, growth, and healing. "In this way," he writes, "conscious and unconscious are united, just as a waterfall connects above and below. A chain of fantasy ideas develops and gradually takes on a dramatic character: the passive process becomes an action."[42] Jung advises that conscious participation is crucial for this exercise to be of any benefit and for it to catalyze psychological progress. It will not suffice to passively observe the unfolding drama; rather we are called upon by these inner figures to make our presence known, to engage.

As we discussed in our discourse on fermentation, it is necessary that our Sulfur, the active principle of the conscious mind, is not corrupted but has been rightly purified. This means we must be psychologically sound to undergo this work, and that we must be able to remain objective, for in opening up the irrational unconscious mind we are vulnerable to the influence of dark forces within that may overwhelm us. Those who might have a difficult time returning from the inner world are advised to undergo active imagination with a trained Jungian analyst, rather than venture into these territories on their own.

It is the *imaginatio vera,* the true imagination, we wish to work with in active imagination, not the *imaginatio phantastica,* the fanciful world of fantasy that will sweep us away from the objective truth and inner wisdom we are seeking from the Soul. As Johnson explains in *Inner Work,*

> When we experience the images, *we also directly experience the inner parts of ourselves that are clothed in the images.* This is the power of symbolic experience in the human psyche when it is entered into consciously: Its intensity and its effect on us is often as concrete as a physical experience would be. Its power to realign our attitudes, teach us and change us at deep levels, is much greater than that of external events that we may pass through without noticing.[43]

We want to approach active imagination with an open mind and suspend our disbelief, accepting whatever appears on a symbolic level. Through active imagination we are contacting a divine wisdom within us that will guide us toward integration of all the many selves existent within us, and toward the unification of the opposing principles of Sol and Luna, of the conscious and unconscious.

Active imagination can be used to address a current "problem" that we are working out, a feeling, or a mood, and personify it, asking it to present itself to us in a form we can speak with. We can take a dream that we wish to understand on a deeper level and re-enter and continue the dream, which is particularly helpful if a dream is incomplete and lacks a conclusive resolution. We may also work with a memory, or we can simply allow a persona to arise spontaneously from the unconscious, without any preconceived notion, to see what our unconscious wants to communicate to us. The figure we encounter might take the form of a guide or psychopomp that brings us on a journey. A journey of this nature is described in *The Chemical Wedding by Christian Rosencreutz,* which provides an alchemical allegory of the great work, and there are many examples of active imagination at play in dialogues between alchemists and Hermes or Mercurius as the guide. Max Ernst's totemistic being named Loplop is an example of how a guide like this might present itself visually. In Ernst's collage series of "Loplop presents," this inner guide was, through the automatic collage process that allowed Ernst's unconscious to flow freely, presenting to him different aspects of his inner world.

Perhaps there is a part of the body where we are experiencing dis-ease, discomfort, tension, or pain that we want to understand. Every part of the body corresponds to different planetary archetypes through the chakras and the energies of the zodiac (see chapter 5 and appendices A and B). We can use active imagination to commune directly with a part of the body or with its associated planetary archetype. This is particularly powerful if we align our inner process with the days and hours of the planets, and integrate it with our daily planetary rituals. We may also choose a symbol or image from our studies in Hermeticism, alchemy, tarot, and other mystical pursuits to gain a deeper understanding.

Marie-Louise von Franz presents active imagination as a four-stage process:

1. Emptying the mind from ego-driven thoughts
2. Inviting the unconscious to enter

3. Expression of the fantasy

4. The ethical confrontation with the fantasy image and integrating the experience[44]

We can see how the stages of active imagination are mirrored in the four stages of the *magnum opus.* In the *nigredo,* we detach from the ego-mind; in the *albedo* we contact the unconscious; in the *citrinitas* we engage the unconscious in an active way; and in the final stage, which we have not yet reached, the *rubedo,* we integrate the conscious and unconscious, and come to a new realization and sense of wholeness. Let's look at the steps in more detail.

Step One: Inner Preparation

Before inviting the unconscious to enter, there must be a space for it to flow into. We must empty the mind of its continuous stream of ego-driven thoughts, essentially stilling the "monkey mind," which can be quite challenging if we are not accustomed to it. This is what the Eastern meditation techniques all help us to do—we are aiming for a state of physical relaxation while maintaining conscious alertness. You can use music, meditation, and slow rhythmic breathing to help you enter into this state. Have a ready means of recording the events that unfold—a pen and paper or a typewriter are sufficient, but you may use the other methods such as drawing or painting, dancing, sculpting, making music, or some sort of creative expression. Make sure that you are alone and won't be disturbed for the duration of the process. The duration of one's active imagination should be about 10–15 minutes.

Step Two: The Invitation

Set the intention that you would like to communicate with the unconscious part of yourself. Have your recording method at the ready, then relax and bring your awareness inward. Allow the unconscious into your awareness in the space of your imagination. Pay attention to whatever arises, however undeveloped the images may be. Perhaps they are just colors and morphing shapes. Focus on feelings that arise, and thoughts that seem to emerge spontaneously. These are all ways the unconscious is coming to the surface. The focus we bring to the image is directed, but unattached. When an image forms we must give it just the right amount of attention lest it become stagnant and unchanging or, on the other hand, too unruly, the images changing too rapidly and bringing us into a passive fantasy rather than an active imagination. Yet we want to bring clarity to them as much as we can through acknowledging them.

Step Three: Dialogue and Expression

Once we have perceived an unconscious image or form, allow a dialogue between your ego mind and the unconscious aspect to take place, allowing them to speak for themselves. The more reality we can bring to this, the greater the depth of understanding and meaning we will derive from the experience. Don't get caught up in asking yourself "Is this real?" or "am I just making this up?" Release any need for the inner images to make logical or linear sense. It is important to be fully involved and present in the experience, and to feel it on all levels: emotional, physical, mental, and spiritual. Johnson advises that we must feel like the experience is actually happening, to make it *real*.[45] This is how we make the unconscious conscious, through the medium of the feeling body.

Here we bring form to the fantasy through writing or one of the other methods mentioned above to solidify and make "real" the inner world. Von Franz warns against letting the aesthetic impulse overtake the process in this step and losing touch with the inner meaning. In active imagination we are not intending to create a work of art for others to see, and must not be overly concerned with the outcome. However we also must not rush through this step. We want to give it enough attention so that we are giving full expression to the inner world before embarking on any interpretation.

It is preferable to record the experience as it is unfolding, so that one captures the entirety of the experience and so it becomes fixed in our consciousness. As Jung puts it, "A running commentary is absolutely necessary in dealing with the shadow, because otherwise its actuality cannot be fixed."[46] If it feels too difficult following the inner experience while recording, then one may wait until the experience is complete. In this case it is helpful to keep the active imagination short, perhaps about five minutes, and to record immediately afterward while the memory is fresh. Another option is moving between the inner vision and the recording, closing our eyes to visualize and opening them to write, then re-entering the imaginal realm.

We can record the dialogue with abbreviations for who is speaking—yourself or your ego and the "other" with whom you are speaking. Johnson uses a typewriter to record his active imagination, typing his own words in lowercase and those of the "other" in all capitals.[47] If one is expressing the events in a form other than writing, such as painting or dancing, it should still be written down to clearly understand the experience on the conscious level. When one feels a sense of resolution and conclusion to the inner process and conversation, it can be helpful to develop a simple ritual in the imagination that will signify the return to consciousness.

Step Four: Ethics and Integration

Finally, we want to integrate the experience by taking action in the material world. Perhaps the unconscious has communicated some vital change that we need to make in our lives. If we make agreements with our unconscious to change a certain dynamic in our consciousness and in our life, it is vital that we follow through. Otherwise we risk further separating ourselves from the inner wellsprings of wisdom and figures of the unconscious, who will take note of our lack of sincerity and be less inclined to communicate with us in the future. This goes along with von Franz's ethical element and the importance of approaching the experience from our authentic ego and not the trickster part of ourselves that wants to evade responsibility. To integrate the experience in our everyday lives we may enact a simple ritual to acknowledge the experience, giving it tangible form and allowing the body to be engaged with the process.

Another important point made by Johnson is that we want to remember that these inner figures are parts of ourselves, and we should refrain from projecting them onto other actual people in our lives.[48] Our ritual can be quite simple and shouldn't be a literal expression of something experienced in active imagination, unless it is a personal ritual that brings no harm to others or ourselves. For example, I did an active imagination to explore a feeling of vulnerability within a newly budding relationship, during a period when things were quite uncertain. In my active imagination I encountered a mature woman wearing a blue veil who took me to a snowy mountain peak. She was helping me to remember the strength of my solitude, developed over years of working toward my own emotional sovereignty. There was much more to the journey that she took me on, however it was this part of it that I enacted a ritual around. I went out in the cold wearing a blue shawl over my head and climbed a high hill near my home. As I stood up there looking down at the world, with open sky all around me and the cold air awakening my senses, I recalled her words, encouraging me to rely on my inner strength and to not forget the part of myself that loves solitude. I felt the safety that I find in elevating myself to a place where I can get a greater perspective on life, and the peace of connecting with my inner sense of wholeness and well-being. The ritual enacted a part of the active imagination in a positive way in which I felt the message of the inner figure physically and emotionally.

At this point we may also evolve our inner experience into a piece of art to share with the world. However this should come after we have gone through the whole process and have understood it within our own sealed vessel. For example, perhaps I might paint a woman in a blue veil upon a lonely mountain peak. If you are taken on an epic journey through your imagination, this could form the basis for a story that you write. Transforming our inner experience into art not only deepens the integration, but it might also speak to others, helping them in their own process of self-discovery. We must not enter into active imagination with an agenda of making art, however. The purpose is to commune with our unconscious to discover hidden truths about our interior life and to grow from the experience. Having an attachment to a specific outcome for the sake of creating a piece of art will inhibit the process because it brings the focus outside of ourselves.

To understand the process of integration in a little more depth, let us now turn our attention to the alchemical process of coagulation.

CONGELATIO/COAGULATIO:
INTEGRATION OF THE UNCONSCIOUS

O Earth O Earth return!
Arise from out the dewy grass;
Night is worn,
And the morn
Rises from the slumberous mass.

—WILLIAM BLAKE, "SONGS OF EXPERIENCE"

Coagulation, from the Latin *co,* meaning "together," and *agere,* "to drive," is when a liquid is brought to a solid state, accomplished by heat or cold.[49] To congeal is to thicken liquid by a reduction in temperature, as in what happens when water turns to ice, or liquid wax hardens at room temperature. Hence *congelation* derives from the Latin *gelare,* or "to freeze."[50] It's a process by which a fluid inspiration is given a solid framework in which to be realized. In evaporation, exposure to air removes the volatile liquid, leaving behind a thickened residue or crystals, as in the formation of salts. This drying effect serves to extract the waters of personal ego and remaining impurities, revealing a crystalline framework suitable to house the Soul. However, as Paracelsus explains, cold coagulations are not fixed, meaning the solidification is not permanent, while coagulation by fire, "produced by the artificial and graduated fire of the alchemist," is "fixed and permanent."[51]

At this point we are integrating, or bringing together, the many parts of ourselves retrieved from our dreams and active imagination in order to reach a new state of inner solidity. This is where ritual can be employed to bring our inner experience into the physical experience. We must solidify our understanding by giving it physical representation, in the form of art, ritual, movement, and personal meaning. Leonora Carrington, when she created physical constructions of the various inner personalities that she encountered in her journey through mental illness, was conducting a ritual of integration, bringing herself back from a state of dissolution. Our ritual needn't be anything so extreme, but simply serves to acknowledge these inner parts and what it is they are asking of us in order to be integrated. Here we begin to feel the union of our conscious and unconscious selves, and how these can influence and affect one another in the process of making the philosopher's stone. We bring the nebulous and slippery aspects of the unconscious into our physical experience in a way that the body will understand in its own symbolic language.

Thus we see that coagulation is a process of solidification, but does not necessarily imply a final fixation, which we will discuss more in the next phase of the *opus*. Integration is a process and can't be rushed any more than digestion and fermentation. When one unconscious personality or symbol is integrated and understood, others will emerge from the depths to teach us something new. The *solve et coagula* formula can be repeated as many times as necessary to increase the purity and potency of the stone. We submit ourselves to dissolution and an immersion into the watery abyss of dreams, visions, and symbols, absorbing them into our psyche in order that they may be later distilled, refined, digested, fermented, and, subsequently, coagulated into form.

The process of coagulation is assigned to the sign of Taurus (April 20–May 20), ruled by Venus and composed of fixed earth, and represented by the Bull. This is the sign of the creative energy of spring and the bursting forth of new life beneath the rays of solar illumination. After the white earth has been sown with the golden ferment, and our spirit has been purified by the newly received inspiration, we are now growing into a new expression altogether. Here we are dealing again with the principle of *Eros,* represented by Venus, as the desire rising from the depths of the Soul for union with the Divine. We received the breath of the divine over the face of the waters, and now the waters are forming into earth—a stable ground from which we can sound our prayers to the heavens above. In connection with the *citrinitas,* the Taurus Bull imparts to us a libidinal force of life reanimating us after the purifying rights undergone in the *albedo,* where an air of chaste devotion surrounded the process. This idea recalls Mallarmé's "L'Ecclésiastique," in which he observes the springtime impulses that incite "an organism to actions which, in any other season, are alien to it," of an otherwise composed and devout ecclesiastic:

As the influence of the vernal breeze softly enlarged the immutable texts inscribed on his flesh, he too, emboldened by this disturbance that pleased his sterile thinking, had come to acknowledge the general well-being by an immediate, clean, violent, positive contact with Nature, stripped of all intellectual curiosity; and far from the obediences and constraints of his occupation, from canons and prohibitions and censures, he was rolling in the bliss of his innate simplicity, happier than a donkey.[52]

This passage correlates to a return to life after the black stone is whitened, and we are bringing it out into the daylight, perhaps with a playful, child-like, and innocent curiosity, seeking confirmation of the solidity of what has thus far been accomplished.

Looking at the fifth arcanum of the tarot, the Hierophant (or the Pope), to which Taurus is assigned, we see themes of the devout spiritual path. In Crowley's Thoth deck, this papal figure is joined by the birth of the child of the new Aeon, Horus, who represents a union of the microcosm and macrocosm. As illustrated by Lady Frieda Harris, this union is symbolized by the pentagram pattern emerging from the heart of the Hierophant and expanding around him, representing the microcosmic human and the star of Venus, as well as the alchemical *quintessence*. It is interlaced with the six-pointed star of the macrocosm. Venus appears standing before the Hierophant as the Scarlet Woman, armed with a sword and signifying her militant role in the new Aeon, in which Horus has supplanted the "dying god."[53] She is also representative of the goddess Isis in her familial role as wife to Osiris and mother of Horus—the Egyptian trinity, as suggested by the three interlaced circles on the Hierophant's scepter. According to Angeles Arrien in *The Tarot Handbook,*

> From a psychological perspective, the Hierophant connotes the inner family that is expressed outwardly in our own dynamics with family members or extended family. Archetypically, these figures represent different aspects of our nature which require faith: faith in exploring spiritual teachings of any kind (represented here by the papal figure);

faith in trusting our intuition (the feminine figure at the bottom of the card); and faith in following our child-like innocence and curiosity (the child in the star). Metaphorically, this symbol represents our capacity and need to learn how *to walk the mystical path with practical feet*. The Hierophant is that part of ourselves that knows how to directly apply the sacred, that is within all of us, into the outer world.[54]

Coagulation likewise represents a process of integrating our inner family, of standing firmly upon the earth and holding a deeply grounded faith in ourselves that unifies our spiritual and material aspirations. Like Mallarmé's ecclesiastic rolling around in the spring grass, our faith has gained a transcendent solidity and earthy joy. The devout faith of the papal figure is united with the nourishing moisture of the Earth Mother, a marriage of faith derived from trust in the internal and faith derived from lived experience in nature, and a realization that all wisdom is rooted within. The creative vigor of the male bull is coupled with the nurturing female cow as a symbol of the fecundity of Mother Earth.

Creatively, this is a formative time for new ideas to begin developing. It represents the feeling of renewal that comes with spring and the libidinal energy of Taurus, inspiring us into the initiatory steps of physical creation. It relates to the formation of the elements from out of the chaos; it's a coming together, the ordering principle of *kosmos,* as our ideas coalesce into tangible form. After a period of emotional release, coagulation brings a sense of calm and relief because the inner work is beginning to bear budding fruits in our waking life. Inspiration is flowing and inseminating the unconscious, which we actively engage with to integrate its contents. Spiritually, the sea of the unconscious yearnings thickens into a uniform substance, a solid awareness of our eternal divinity. Through this thickening process we come to realize the oneness of reality—the unconscious and the conscious acting as one, the inner and the outer being different expressions of the One Thing.

As we consider the relationship between the inner and the outer, and the above and below, let us refer to the words of Geber concerning the vessel and the heat to be employed in coagulation:

Argentvive is coagulated by the frequent *Precipitation* of it with violence by the forcible *Heat* of strong *Fire*. For the *Asperity* of *Fire* easily removes its *Aquosity*. And this work is best done by a *Vessel* of a great length, in the sides of which it may find place to cool and adhere, and (by reason of the length of the *Vessel*) to abide, and not flye, until it can be again precipitated to the *Fiery Bottom* of the same; which must always stand very hot, with great *Ignition*: and the same *Precipitation* be continued, till it be totally fixed. It is also coagulated with long and constant *Retention* in *Fire,* in a *Glass Vessel* with a very long *Neck* and round *Belly;* the *Orifice* of the *Neck* being kept open, that the *Humidity* may vanish thereby.[55]

Read symbolically, this passage touches upon an important point for an alchemical meditation upon coagulation. The vessel is the body, while the fire is the focus and attention of our energy. *Argentvive,* being our living, philosophical mercury of the mind and Spirit, is the accumulation of our thoughts, which before coagulation are still prone to volatility. Through *asperity,* or intensity, of attention, we remove the volatility of our thought process, slowing it down and bringing it into a stable place. The use of a vessel of great length implies the patience required of us in reaching coagulation, and the proper alignment of the spine in the meditative posture, which allows the breath of the spirit to move freely between the above and below. This creates space for these volatile aspects of the mind to circulate without escaping—which would mean that we are drawn away from our alchemical process and stimulated into some action that will prevent coagulation through the unnecessary expenditure of vital energy. Our thoughts run away, lusting with libidinal spring energy to satisfy the deep, undeniable desire for union in some external, animal form, a desire that at the core is desire for true union with our own eternally flowing and ever-changing river of creativity. Our thoughts run away, and we are no longer in the vessel. Conserving this vital, sexual energy is of utmost importance in coagulation, and thus we keep the fire at the base of our vessel—the root chakra—very hot, which keeps the coagulation going. This requires a level of groundedness, such as the bull embodies, to hold the intensity of the vernal libido as an actuating fire, rather than acting upon it to settle the flightiness of Mercury.

Next Geber advises that we may also use a vessel with a very long neck and round belly, keeping the neck open to allow for the humidity—those warming thoughts and feelings—to escape. In the body Taurus finds its home in the neck as the positive pole of Earth, and both the neck of the body and of the vessel signify a narrow passageway between the above and below. Imagine that your own neck is elongated and reaches down to your low belly, which is perfectly round and sitting in the flames of transformation—the *kundalini* resting at the base of the spine like a flaming dragon. This round belly is suggestive of deep belly breathing, the bellows to the fire, while the elongated neck, much like a giraffe, suggests a direct connection between the above and below, the upper waters and the lower waters of the womb, the domain of Venus-Taurus in the neck and the domain of Mercury-Virgo in the earthy bowels. Virgo's rulership over the bowels signifies the neutral pole of the Earth element in the body, balanced by Taurus as the positive pole and Capricorn in the knees and calves as the negative pole.

The ultimate goal of our repeated dissolutions and coagulations is *fixation,* which we will discuss in the next chapter. This is our ability to focus and fix our gaze inwardly and outwardly simultaneously. We can consider *solve et coagula* to be an alchemical meditation, moving back and forth between sense and nonsense, thoughts and feelings, rationality and irrationality, activity and passivity, expressing and imbibing the dew of inspiration, thinking and feeling, thinking and feeling, and allowing the volatile vapors to affix to the side of our vessel, which is not only our body but the vessel of our creativity. As we move between solution and solidity, wisdom is born from the union of opposites, expressing itself creatively in our lives in little bursts of insight and creative clarity. Back and forth, in and out, up and down, movement and rest, creating and experiencing, giving and receiving, being and nonbeing—until we reach the stillness that lies between them. Just when we think we might lose ourselves in the sea of the unconscious, we bring ourselves together again. In and out of the water, refining the dew that the Moon dribbled upon the ready earth while we were sleeping, the beauty of our thoughts congealing in the rising Sun.

To coagulate we must slow down while maintaining an intensity of attention to our process. The large-bodied Bull of Taurus is patient, practical, and stable, understanding the necessary time for the work to unfold, moving with a slow, purposeful determination, taking time to pay attention to the beauty surrounding it, and caring for the body. Roaming the open fields in the glow of a new day, the Bull symbolizes enduring fire and earth. Having a practice—whether physical or spiritual—that grounds you into your body is of great benefit at this time; it will allow you to fully receive the incoming energy of the *rubedo.*

Springtime is when we venture out into the fields where the ram and the bull graze, to collect the dewdrops upon albified canvas and wring them out into a ready vessel. We are gathering together the manna from heaven, the "seed of the morning air," the balsam of the air, "the spittle of the stars," the *prima materia,* the teardrops of the long night infused with the energy of the rising Sun, the *anima,* and the spiritualized elixir of the unconscious.[56] This dew is called *Ros* in Latin, also meaning "roses," which speaks to the redness of the dawn when it is collected, and to the rose of the heart, correlating to both Sol and Venus. It is also called the *prima materia* because it descends from the air above and stimulates growth on the earth below.[57] It is said there are two dews, one female and one male, derived from the spring and autumn dew, respectively. The May dew of spring is viewed as being feminine on account of being colder and closer to winter, and the September or autumn dew as masculine because it has been digested in the summer heat. Together these dews are named the "pearl of the chemists," the "emerald of the philosophers," or the "water of the equinoxes."[58] For this reason the dew is a symbol of the hermaphroditic Mercury, the combining of the spring and autumn dews being likened to the alchemical marriage. According to Chevalier and Gheerbrandt, "The importance of dew in so many rituals and magic spells arises from the fact that it resolves the confrontation between the upper and the lower, the heavenly and the terrestrial waters. Dew is pure water, precious water, pre-eminently primeval water, a distillation of the generative powers of the watery principle."[59] It is a projection of spirit into the motherly matrix of matter. Collecting the May dew speaks to the unifying *hieros gamos* of coagulation, just as the symbol for Taurus is the circle of the Sun surmounted by the horns of the Moon, and the Moon is exalted in Taurus. We see the lunar dew falling in the eighteenth arcanum of the tarot, the Moon, where it is also sometimes considered to be blood.

Thus we see that the regenerative dew is both male and female, relating to both Mercury and Venus. In terms of our coagulation, it is advised by Ascanius to "stir up war between copper and Mercury till they destroy each other and devour each other. Then the copper coagulates the quicksilver, the quicksilver congeals the copper, and both bodies become a powder by means of diligent imbibition and digestion. Join together the red man and the white woman till they become Ethelia, that is, quicksilver. Whoever changes them into a spirit by means of quicksilver, and then makes them red, can tinge every body."[60] Coagulation is a refinement of the creative impulse resulting in beautiful thoughts, a union of *Eros* and *Logos* (Venus + Mercury), *anima* and *animus,* preparing us for the sacred marriage, *hieros gamos*. These beautiful thoughts are a reflection of the love between the opposing principles, expressed in this passage from the *Rosarium*: "When we shall enter into the house of love, my body shall be coagulated and I shall be in my emptiness."[61]

NAVIGATING THE *CITRINITAS*

The *citrinitas* is a shift from lunar unconsciousness to solar consciousness, where we transition from just reflecting to actually projecting divine light—we are transmuting silver into gold. Our expressions become more authentic and we move from seeking to gnosis. This is an improvement on all levels—physical, emotional, mental, and spiritual. The *citrinitas* is a further purification and the fecundating energy of spirit (inspiration = spiritization), which activates new creative processes.

It may take some time for the processes of digestion, fermentation, and/or coagulation to unfold. With a steady fire, the intensity of the *magnum opus* slows down for a time, and our focus begins to shift from the limitations of the ego-centered mind to the freeflowing identification with our true unlimited consciousness. We are freed up to experience the stream of inspirations that take the form of a yellow elixir penetrating our thoughts. We receive a glimpse of enlightenment, igniting a new fire that brings us to the next and final phase of the work, the *rubedo,* where the last of the volatile aspects of our being (those residual emotions and attachments) are removed as we perfect our stone.

9

Rubedo
The Royal Marriage and the Philosopher's Stone

Yes, the artist, if he would gaze into the divine brightness of Absolute Beauty, must crystallize the immortal principle of his being. At once intuitive and sensitive, through the mysterious faculties which are the very condition of his creative life, he can then attain perfection, for which otherwise there exists but a vague and painful longing, and from which the external life, that depending on the senses alone, is far away.

—JEAN DELVILLE, *THE NEW MISSION*

In any creative endeavor, there comes a time when the work reaches its culmination, when the artist gazes upon their creation and sees nothing left undone. Yet first there are final refinements and special touches that bring it to its ultimate perfection. We arrive now at the heart of the Great Work, bringing opposing principles to union in the heart chakra. From here we continue to refine and augment our stone—our true imagination—and bring it to completion as we move up into the spiritual centers of the throat, third eye, and crown. With the consummation of the Red King and the White Queen comes the realization of cosmic consciousness, and the ability to create through the imaginal realm.

Creatively this inner union is a state of perpetual flow and continual creation in all aspects of life, a fluid dance of activity and receptivity. According to Samuel Taylor Coleridge, this is "not possible without an intermediate faculty, which is at once both active and passive," which he denominated the imagination.[1] Through imagination, refined into *imaginatio vera,* we unify and concentrate our creative power. This is described by Huelsenbeck as "the new man" who is "God of the moment, grandeur of blessed affects, phoenix of contradiction . . . neither for nor against, the pains of polarity are alien to him."[2] In essence, the "new man" is the hermaphrodite, or *rebis* (the double matter), having united the polarities in one body. Life itself becomes a work of art when the inner and the outer worlds are masterfully blended together in the perfection of each moment. The active and passive forms of the elements harmonize in a final conjunction that creates the *Ultima materia,* the final matter of our perfected stone.

The *rubedo,* or "reddening" of the stone, presents to us the greatest difficulty of the Great Work. Our stone was whitened in the *albedo,* and if submitted to no further cooking, is capable of transmuting base metals into silver. This is the ability to see life on the symbolic level, to understand the hidden unconscious aspects at play in the external world. It allows us to channel from the world of dreams and imagination without interference from the conscious mind, as one does in automatism. This is a crucial part of our creative awakening, but not the end goal. We must redden the stone in order to transmute base metals into gold, the art of bringing energy into its most divine and noble expression.

Red is an active color of passion, the vitality of blood, the ruby of self-realization, the rose of truth endlessly unfolding from the center, the carbuncle hiding beneath the unicorn's horn, the Red King and the solar eye. Breton captured the *rubedo* in *Soluble Fish* with images of red silk stockings and garments, brick chimneys, blood coral from the sea, and "a little red stream that nothing can dry up gliding capriciously over the stone." The conjunction of opposites is portrayed by Siamese twin sisters, a line reading, "my right eye the male flower, my left the female flower," and in a "burning metamorphosis."[3]

Light in the red spectrum brings plants to flowering and to the fruit-bearing stage, just as we bring our stone to its ultimate perfection, resulting in a flowering of consciousness and the fruit of our labor, the *filius philosophorum,* or red child. Red light has the longest wavelength of the visible light spectrum and a low frequency, relating to the dense physicality of matter. When the root chakra is activated, it vibrates red, indicating a state of spiritual fixation in the material world, providing a sense of safety, groundedness, confidence, and courage. Consciousness, like light flowing from the Sun and crown, becomes completely integrated with every cell of the body, thereby completing the circuit of energy and activating the root, infusing our entire awareness with a permanent divinity and self-knowledge. At the center of these two ends of the *sushumna nadi* lies the heart chakra, where our energy centers in pure love. Jodorowsky writes that the "universal solvent" is "a person who has developed divine love in his heart. Love is what dissolves all resistances."[4] Love is the antithesis of the constriction and limitation brought on by fear. Through the cosmic heart center we create wondrous miracles through the power of the One Thing. To reach this state we will go through four final processes: *fixatio, inceratio, multiplicatio,* and *proiectio.*

FIXATIO:
THE UNION OF SOL AND LUNA

> *The fourth degree of fire makes the matter red, and there appear divers colours.*
>
> —Paracelsus

Fixation, or *fixatio,* brings us from the *citrinitas* to the *rubedo* by purging the last volatile aspects from the stone and solidifying it into permanent unified perfection. For this, we must reach the greatest intensity of our fire and attention. The stone still expresses volatility when heated, just as the mind wants to fly away from the object of its meditation. Our inner fire reddens the stone, which, as Rulandus tells us, "is a sign of perfect fixation." It is called the "ligament" or "tie" of quicksilver, the fixation of Mercury and perfection of philosophical gold.[5] As the heat continues under our vessel, patterns arise in the vapors released from the body, patterns now perceived as the last remaining impurities. Watching them is an opportunity to transmute them into harmonious, stable patterns oriented toward our highest aspirations and the supreme guiding light of the Sun.

The task of fixing the volatile and volatilizing the fixed is the quintessential aim of both inner and outer alchemy. Maier describes this as "the machination or device of Universal Nature, always to raise heavy things by light, and to depress light ones by heavy."[6] The *coniunctio,* or conjunction of opposites, takes many different forms in alchemical imagery, including an eagle chained to a toad, where the spirit is inseparably linked to the *corpus* or body. It is also depicted as the winged and wingless eagles, the fixed aspect restraining the volatile and preventing its flight: "the one holds the other's Tail by its beak, that they cannot easily be separated."[7] This conjunction resolves the conflict between the active and passive states of mind, also represented by Lambspring's two birds, bound together and biting each other to death, so that "both are transmuted into white doves." In this way the "body is made white by the operation, but the Spirit red by the Art."[8] It's not that the polarities no longer exist within us; on the contrary, we are compelled even more so to pay heed to the "electric" and "magnetic" forces, as Franz Bardon calls them, or the impulse to expand and contract.[9] We are no longer subject to unconscious, polarized forces acting upon us, but the primal pair within are brought into balance. When these energies are stilled, the desire and will align, allowing soul and spirit to move freely together in the imagination.

The observations of the alchemist are of utmost importance in this stage. Honest self-reflection and personal responsibility are aspects of calcination and putrefaction we've become well familiar with. We dissolved in the philosophical water, breaking apart crystallized patterns held in the body and unconscious. With the *citrinitas* our lunar stone received inspiration from the Sun, and our thoughts began melding with this golden elixir; old thought patterns reorganized as we integrated unconscious parts of ourselves. Now the thinking mind begins to align with the crown chakra, solar divinity, higher consciousness, and eternal soul. With integration of the white and red stones, or the White Queen and the Red King, the *hieros gamos* engenders the winged solar hermaphrodite who wears the "crown of victory," otherwise known as the *lapis,* symbolic of the union and integration of the Sun and planets.[10] This is akin to the Double Crown uniting the red and white crowns of Lower and Upper Egypt. The hermaphrodite is Mercury who contains both natures in one; *herm* deriving from Hermes and *aphrodite* from the goddess Aphrodite, or Venus. Since Mercury is the spirit that dissolves and Venus is the impulse toward union, bringing them together in one form represents the quintessential axiom *solve et coagula,* the basis of the entire *opus.*

Fixation is assigned to Gemini (May 21–June 21), sign of the Twins

Fig. 9.1. The Rebis is the hermaphrodite, formed from Hermes (Mercury) and Venus. From Michael Maier, *Atalanta Fugiens,* Oppenheim, Germany: Johann-Theodor de Bry, 1618.

Courtesy of Science History Institute

that represent the Royal Pair, also correlating with the sixth arcanum of the tarot, the Lovers. Twins symbolize the essential duality of all things when represented as opposites: male and female, light and dark, good and evil, heaven and earth, spiritual and physical. We return to the issue of the double, this time in relation to autonomous complexes encountered in the depths of the unconscious during dissolution. These complexes can represent a conflict between opposing aspects of our personality. In the words of Antonin Artaud, our goal is "to resolve by conjunctions unimaginably strange to our waking minds, to resolve or even annihilate every conflict produced by the antagonism of matter and mind, idea and form, concrete and abstract, and to dissolve all appearances into one unique expression . . . the equivalent of spiritualized gold."[11] The dissolution merging dream and reality is followed by separation, and subsequently by union of the separated parts. These parts of ourselves, which have broken off to act independently of our immediate consciousness, are then "fixed," and put back together, or integrated, into a cohesive and unanimous whole. According to Jung, this union is facilitated by the symbolic unified wholeness of the mandala in its simplest form of a circle, which is then divided in its most basic components through the cross.[12] This creates the symbol for earth (⊕): the unbroken circle of consciousness, of eternity, and of the Sun, divided into the four quadrants of the elements, and united into one harmonious form. Sacred geometry, with its use of symmetry and harmonious shapes and angles, is another way of symbolizing this union. In Carrington's painting depicting the red conjunction discussed earlier, *The Burning of Giordano Bruno* (1964), she incorporates variations of the "flower of life" geometry of interlacing circles, mandalas that symbolize the interconnectedness of all life and the process of creation. Through harmonious art, particularly symmetry, the artist can facilitate a successful fixation. Symmetry is often employed in alchemical diagrams signifying the consummation of the *magnum opus* (see figures 9.2–9.4 and 9.12), as are circular diagrams portraying the spherical ordering of the cosmos, often organized into the four quarters.

In some cases the double aspect of the personality is not so easily integrated, as the two natures battle against one another for dominance. In his

Fig. 9.2. The symbol for Mercury rests as the unifying central point
between heaven and earth and between the dual natures of the alchemist-magician.
From Johann Daniel Mylius, *Medico Chymicum,* 1618. In *Musaeum Hermeticum
Reformatum Et Amplificatum,* Frankfurt, 1678.
Courtesy of Science History Institute

autobiography, Dalí recounts a personal experience that bears a remarkable semblance to the doppelgänger, or double, in Gérard de Nerval's "The
King of Bedlam." This is a story of the multiple personalities of Raoul
Spifame, who, bearing an uncanny similitude to King Henry II, develops a dangerous conflation with the king. After an increasingly intense
nightly affirmation of this in his dreams, he "directed his gaze deep into
the monarch's eyes and there suddenly acquired consciousness of a second
personality."[13] Like Spifame, Dalí experiences identification with King
Alfonso XIII, who makes a visit to the Academy of Art in Madrid, where

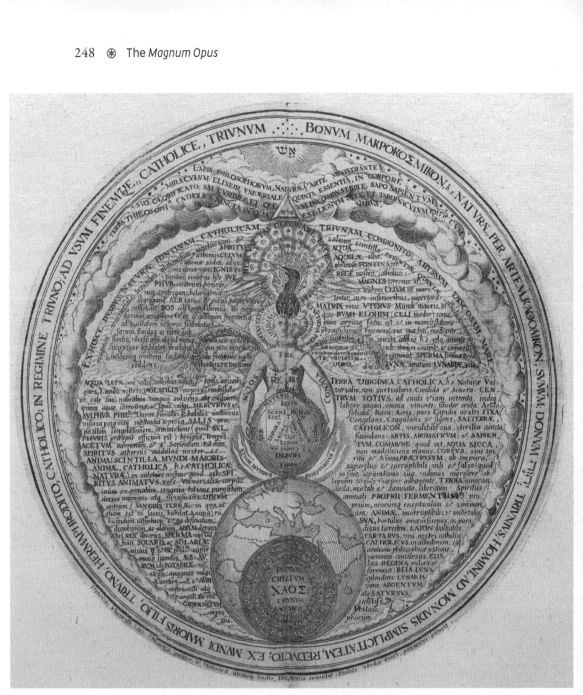

Fig. 9.3. The alchemical hermaphrodite lies along the central column within a unifying mandala. From Heinrich Khunrath, *Amphitheatrum Sapientiae Aeternae Solius Verae*, Hanau, Germany: Wilhelm Antonius, 1609.

Courtesy of Science History Institute

Dalí is a student. He feels the king has singled him out from all the other students, recognizing him to be a king as well. As he explains, "The King's presence revived in my mind the King I bore within my skin! . . . I had this

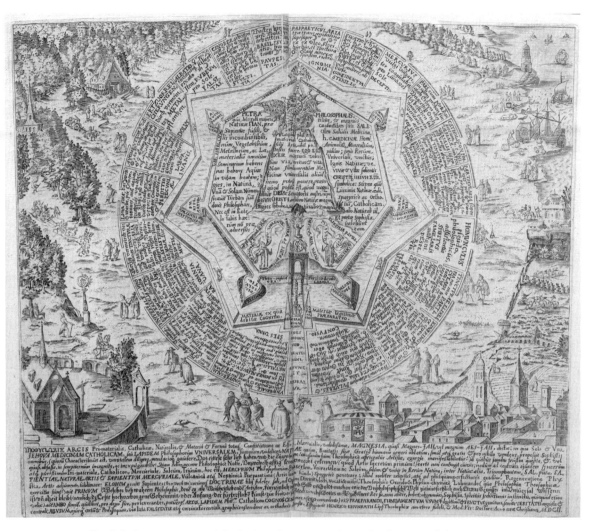

Fig. 9.4. A septagon mandala depicts the many paths to the fortress of the stone, but the only entrance lies between the pyramidal pillars of the Sun and Moon. From Heinrich Khunrath, *Amphitheatrum Sapientiae Aeternae Solius Verae,* Hanau, Germany: Wilhelm Antonius, 1609.

Courtesy of Science History Institute

impression . . . that the two of us were uniquely and continually isolated from all the rest."[14] One thing that troubles Dalí, however, is his complicity with the school's desire to fool the king by erecting a facade of organization and success. This weighed with such gravity upon Dalí's conscience that his unconscious had to release the floodgates, resulting in a dream in which he causes a river of plaster to cascade down a stairwell in the school.

He then brings this dream to reality, repeating the white flood by pouring white paint over two aborted figure paintings. This encounter awakens in him "violent royal feelings" from his childhood and a hermaphroditic desire to transform into the opposite sex. Dalí's "autocratic desires," centered on authority and power, are revealed to him and purified by the white paint and plaster—the flood of the dissolution, a milky *ablutio*.

Both Spifame and Dalí approached these royal doubles through dreams and visions, dissolving duality and becoming completely identified with their double. Yet Dalí managed to regain conscious fixation and integrate his kingly authority, dissolving the dualism by overcoming the "false king" within himself, and returning to his own inner authority as the true king. Spifame, on the other hand, becomes enveloped by his complex.

With Gemini, the alchemical process of fixation requires that we return to reality, learning to integrate and reconcile the opposites. For Dalí, such was the purifying effect of the flood, which descended from above and spread over everything below. Gemini's ruler Mercury is also the psychopomp that guides us into the underworld, as well as the hermaphroditic magician that has mastered the art of walking in two worlds; with his lemniscate hat, he wears upon his crown the continual flux and flow between between dream and reality, not becoming identified with either but understanding the continual need for dissolving and coagulating, losing oneself in the abysmal depths and resurfacing to integrate the symbols, visions, and messages received from the other side.

There is a passage in the twelfth key of Basil Valentine that speaks to this issue of the double Mercury, and the union of the fixed and volatile in one body:

> Seek for that Stone which has no fleshly nature, but out of which a volatile fire is extracted, whence also this stone is made, being composed of white and red. It is a stone, and no stone; therein Nature alone operates. A fountain flows from it. The fixed part submerges its father, absorbing it, body and life, until the soul is returned to it. And the volatile mother like to him, is produced in her own kingdom; and he by his virtue and power receives greater strength. The volatile mother

when prepared surpasses the sun in summer. . . . Bind together the fixed and the volatile; they are two, and three, and yet one only. If you do not understand you will attain nothing. . . .There is nothing, says the Philosopher, save a double mercury; I say that no other matter has been named; blessed is he who understands it. Seek therein, and be not weary; the result justifies the labour.[15]

To say that "it is a stone, and no stone" points to the inherent paradoxical nature of describing something that is beyond our ability to truly grasp, or as Jung puts it, "paradox is the natural medium for expressing transconscious facts."[16] The fountain flowing from the stone is the mercurial spirit, the water of the unconscious that submerges the father, or consciousness, thereby bringing back the feminine unconscious soul. Awakening the inner world bestows strength to the conscious mind because it is no longer fighting against the contradictions arising from the volatile nature of the unconscious. When this volatility is fixed, it becomes a transcendent quality of the imagination, surpassing even the bright consciousness of summer sun. The double Mercury is the hermaphrodite, the *rebis*, containing both natures in one body with two heads. "Give Fire to fire, Mercury to Mercury, and you have enough,"[17] advises Maier. He explains that there is an external and internal fire, and likewise an external and internal Mercury, and that our task is to bring these together; hence the unification of the inner and outer worlds, the fire of the soul and the water of the spirit. We too are double, containing within us an astral double that is not bound by the constraints of the body, but may be liberated through binding the fixed and volatile aspects within to enter the imaginal world. This requires us to dissolve by water of the unconscious and coagulate by fire of consciousness.

Regarding the doubles of Spifame and Dalí, the difference is a matter of integration. Spifame allowed his idealized version of himself to split off into a full identification. On a positive level, the king awakened in him his sovereign and royal potential, the perfection of gold, but without integrating this with the original personality, Spifame lost his footing in reality. Spifame sought more and more control, issuing edicts never to reach his imagined subjects, all the while descending further

Fig. 9.5. The projection of the double Mercurius. From Michael Maier, *Atalanta Fugiens*,
Oppenheim, Germany: Johann-Theodor de Bry, 1618.
Courtesy of Science History Institute

into madness and the splitting of his personality—a point to which we
will return when we discuss alchemical projection. Dalí, on the other
hand, relinquished control. In a symbolic ritual of purification in which
dream and reality were merged through art, Dalí reconciled the opposites
within himself. In this way the creative process can facilitate fixation.

When twins are identical, they represent the clarity of consciousness that pierces through the veil of duality and perceives the oneness of
all things. The planet Mercury, whose corresponding metal is necessary
for the successful conjunction by which nondualistic awareness is real-

ized, rules Gemini. Indeed, as Jung asserts, Mercury "*is* this marriage on account of his androgynous form."[18] The union of Spirit and Soul is that of Diana and Apollo, Mercury and Sulfur, the unicorn and stag, white and red lions, winged and wingless eagles, light and shadow, moist and dry, east and west, left and right, *yin* and *yang, ida* and *pingala,* and all opposites. Through its ascent the Mercurial spirit acts as the unifying agent, facilitating nondual awareness. The seven rulers, and chakras, thus "de-energized" as described in the *Corpus Hermeticum,* come to balance, allowing for the freeflow of life energy through the subtle body.

Mercury rules the throat chakra, the center of purification between the lower, terrestrial chakras and the upper, celestial chakras of Sol (crown) and Luna (third eye). At this point we have opened the bodies of the earthly metals of lead (root/earth), tin (sacral/water), iron (solar/fire), and copper (heart/air). Our life energy has ascended to the fifth center, correlated with the fifth element, or *quintessence,* the subtle field containing all four elements within it. Through the throat chakra we express our creative will and hear the voice of Spirit. When it is open we are authentically inspired and able to translate this inspiration into material form. Jung writes that "fixation in the Mercurius of the wise would then correspond to the traditional Hermetic knowledge, since Mercurius symbolizes the Nous; through this knowledge the self, as a content of the unconscious, is made conscious and 'fixed' in the mind."[19] With the *hieros gamos* of the primal pair we experience true love within ourselves, a state of marital bliss and fixation upon the infinite possibilities of the imagination. Our thoughts have been purified and liberated of the volatility that leads us to run away with unconscious fantasies that scatter our energy in aimless directions; that inhibit our creative capacities and stifle our true imagination. In this way we become focused on the one goal, masters of the flames of transformation.

Aleister Crowley says of Gemini that it is "perfected by active thoughts, aimed and tinged by spiritual intention."[20] This perfection is completed when the spiritual intention of the Red King overtakes the volatility of the White Queen in the *coniunctio,* the solidification of the stone. As it is described in the *Rosarium,* "Here ends the life of Luna, And the spirit subtly ascends on high."[21] Removing this volatility can be completed by a cyclical rotation between dissolution (Cancer) and coagulation (Taurus). In the heavens Gemini lies between Cancer and Taurus, just as fixation represents the still point between dissolution and coagulation, resulting in full integration and the indestructibility of the stone. The alchemists likened this enduring quality to the salamander. "Its blood is more precious than all trea-

Fig. 9.6. The Stone lives in the fire as the Salamander of the philosophers.
From Michael Maier, *Atalanta Fugiens,* Oppenheim, Germany:
Johann-Theodor de Bry, 1618.
Courtesy of Science History Institute

sures, and has power to render fertile six trees . . . and to make their fruit sweeter than honey," writes Sendivogius.[22] Thus the stone, Maier advises, "is by Fixation to be reduced to the Nature of the Salamander, that is to the greatest Fixednesse which neither declines nor refuses Fire. For it is no Salamander till it has learnt to endure Fire with the utmost patience, which must of necessitye be effected in long processe of time."[23] As a fire elemental, the salamander is nourished by the flames and lives amidst the blazing heat. Likewise, the stone is made impervious to fire.

The laboratory process of making the philosopher's stone involves a purification of Mercury, elevating it from its vulgar form into its "philosophic" state. Similarly the Mind is purified and prepared for the work of perfecting the indestructible awareness of the artist. The purified Mercury is "reanimated" by the addition of purified gold.[24] These are digested together and integrated as the male gold, like a seed, inseminates the female Mercury. In our work, we purify our thoughts and take time to allow divine consciousness to animate the unconscious and bring it to life within us, infusing the mind with the noble essence of gold and the joy of creation.

Mercury is both the unifying agent of the Sun and Moon, and the red child born of their union. Synonymous with the rebis, the double matter, the royal child contains the essence of each parent and yet eclipses them with its radiant perfection. For the artist, this represents a return to a state of creative innocence and childlike wonder. It is a rebirth and return to the paradisal state that preceded the original split of the opposites, a state beautifully captured by Wordsworth in *The Prelude,* where he writes:

> *Our childhood sits,*
> *Our simple childhood, sits upon a throne*
> *That hath more power than all the elements.*[25]

It has more power because the elements have been brought to harmony, and thus the philosophical child is the *quintessence*. This is also the principle behind the Magus who wields the cup, sword, wand, and disk as magical weapons corresponding to the elements. With these forces at our command, we are, as Wordsworth continues, in league with those

> *Who make our wish, our power, our thought a deed,*
> *An empire, a possession,—ye whom time*
> *And seasons serve; all Faculties to whom*
> *Earth crouches, the elements are potter's clay,*
> *Space like a heaven filled up with northern lights,*
> *Here, nowhere, there, and everywhere at once.*[26]

Through the unlimited power of childlike imagination, born from the successful union of Sol and Luna, the elements become "potter's clay," and all creative potentials are opened to us.

As described by Warlick, Ernst depicted the red child in his painting *Dada Gauguin* (1920, see figure 9.7), a work exemplifying Ernst's use of Freudian and alchemical symbolism.[27] In the foreground is a red figure, while two more figures appear in the background, one red and the other a light flesh-color. Though these characters have no facial features, we can surmise their alchemical relationship based on the other elements of the painting. Enclosing the red body is a green vessel resembling an artichoke adorned with phallic appendages, suggesting a masculine energy aligned with the red solar principle. A white, womb-like vessel encompasses the lighter figure, evoking the feminine quality of the white lunar principle. The central figure, like the red child born from the union of Sol and Luna, stands with right hand touching a tall white phallic wand, combining the qualities of the parental forms and their vessels. In another painting, titled *Birds also Birds, Fish Snake and Scarecrow* (ca. 1921, see figure 9.8 on page 258), Ernst portrays a double-headed bird creature, like the rebis, standing next to a red shirt of a smaller stature, again suggesting the red child. They stand within a green boat, or vessel, before which is the mercurial serpent of transmutation. For the red child, or the red stone, to be born within the vessel, the primal pair must be brought to union and mutually transmuted through the power of love.

The red child, or *filius philosophorum,* unlocks the secrets of reality and awakens our eternal "I-Am-ness," the equivalent of the Taoist con-

Fig. 9.7. *Dada Gauguin* (1920), by Max Ernst.
Public Domain, courtesy of WikiArt

cept of the diamond body, or an adamantine awareness that can navigate with nondualist perception. It is a state of complete interconnectedness between matter and spirit, subject and object, resulting from all the preceding processes of breaking down and dissolving the ego and reuniting the separated parts of the psyche. When the two primal aspects of our being have been completely integrated, the dual-bodied hermaphrodite transforms into the Divine Androgyne, the peaceful Consciousness that transcends the active polarized Mind of Gemini. We experience the realization of divine unity and wholeness that we glimpsed throughout the precursory work—in our submersion in the seas of the unconscious, in the distilled essence, in the coagulating dew of spring—now coming to fruition. However, fixation does not necessarily occur on the first attempt and that is why the alchemists emphasized the necessity of "often iteration," repetition of the process until our matter is "made ashes of perpetual enduring, and that the whole remain in the fire."[28]

Up until now we have been focused primarily on inner work. Now

Fig. 9.8. *Birds also Birds, Fish Snake and Scarecrow*, by Max Ernst, ca. 1921.
Public Domain, courtesy of WikiArt

we begin the outer work, where our stone can create changes in the outer world. At this point we truly step into our role as creators; from a place of *fixation* upon the One Thing, our entire life becomes art. On this point I will share a quote by poet and writer Henry Miller:

> The mastery of any form of expression should lead inevitably to the final expression—mastery of life. In this realm one is absolutely alone, face to face with the very elements of creation. It is an experiment whose outcome nobody can predict. If it be successful the whole world is affected and in a way never known before.[29]

With a successful fixation the consciousness of the adept becomes anchored and firmly established in its eternal, abiding, stable, unanimous being. An unwavering, childlike trust in and devotion to the Divine permeates every aspect of the adept's life. Once this is established, the real magic can begin. In the processes to follow, we will see how the stone becomes a powerful means of affecting the outer world. As it is written in *The Book of Lambspring,* "the Body is made white by the operation, but the Spirit red by Art. The End of the work tends to perfection, and thus is prepared the Stone of the Philosophers."[30]

INCERATIO:
FINAL CRISIS AND CREATIVE MALLEABILITY

The work is not brought to perfection except it be incerated and made fusible like wax.

—PARACELSUS, "PHILOSOPHICAL CANNONS"

The stone is hardened by fixation, and then softened by *inceratio.* Inceration, or ceration, is a process that pulls something in on itself, transforming it so that the old form ceases to exist altogether. Another word for it is *ingress,* from the Latin verb *ingredi,* which means "to step into, enter." This refers to the stone's ability after inceration to enter into metallic bodies and transmute them into gold. In the *Rosarium* we are told that ceration, or the melting of the stone, is accomplished "by a philosophical solution which is done by water."[31] Our water is the philosophical Mercury, the solvent that has been infused or "animated" with gold and then added to the stone as an imbibition, or a slow, drop by drop absorption. This, according to Paracelsus, gives "being to the Stone."[32] In another passage of the *Rosarium* we are advised to use oil, or air, rather than water; then we are told that "water, air and oil are all one, that is Spirit of mineral Mercury."[33] As the stone takes in the spirit of Mercury, it expands into a waxlike substance, a malleable and yet solid state that liquefies in the fire, but is not consumed by it. To animate Mercury with gold is to infuse the unconscious with conscious awareness, bringing life and being to the stone, the true imagination. Inceration combines aspects of both fixation and sublimation, for by "inceration the spirit is fixed and the body is sublimed."[34]

Inceration is assigned to the fiery sign of Sagittarius (November 22–December 21), a sign that is also commonly related to sublimation. Corresponding to the thighs, where fire energy propels the body into movement and action, Sagittarius is represented by the powerful Centaur. This mythical creature inhabits two worlds, as half-man and half-horse. With bow and arrow aimed to the stars and four hooves grounded upon the earth, the Centaur symbolizes a spiritual tension and desire to sublimate earthly, animal compulsions into their divine, heavenly expressions. Sagittarius, a mutable sign, is ruled by the greater benefic, Jupiter, ruler of the heavens. This sign epitomizes the need for balance between the instinctual nature and spiritual enlightenment, between the ego and supraconscious. Jupiter's lightning bolt illuminates the inner vision, revealing a world of higher potential. Like inceration, Sagittarius represents the body's sublimation by the fixation of spiritual awareness. Yet this sign also presents the danger of an ego inflated by spiritual superiority, and thus inceration is a necessary humbling process.

Though we have completed our stone and attained the red color, we encounter a final creative crisis. If faced with courage and integrity, our stone is brought to life with the immutable and fluid power of true imagination. It is often at the end of a creative endeavor that the greatest challenges present themselves, yet we must maintain our resolve to carry on in the face of adversity. This can also be experienced as a healing crisis in which it is necessary for the old negative patterns to be purged by fire, resulting in a phoenix-like resurrection from the ashes. Hence inceration is often closely associated with *incineration,* as elucidated by Fabricius: "The calcining fire initiates the crucial process of incineration where the hermaphrodite's body, already reduced to a skeleton of white bones, is further reduced by being pulverized and turned to ashes. As a result of this act of ultimate sublimation, the alchemist aims at the creation of a subtle body capable of sheltering the soul and spirit at their hoped-for return from heaven."[35] This pulverizing or pounding action, with the slow addition of our water, is what results in the softening of

Fig. 9.9. Submit the hermaphrodite to the flame and thereby attain the tincture. From Michael Maier, *Atalanta Fugiens,* Oppenheim, Germany: Johann-Theodor de Bry, 1618.
Courtesy of Science History Institute

the stone and its transformation into a waxlike substance. In effect this final crisis works upon us, grinding us down as we relinquish the last remaining attachments of ego. While at the same time, we continue to drink from the waters of our inner wisdom, softening into a deep and abiding awareness of our subtle body.

With all great work comes a sacrifice, a revolutionary shift within the psyche, a shedding of the skin to be transfigured and reborn, an observable change in thought and form. The dragons that previously assailed the mind are slain by the arrows of truth, and with them a part of us must die. As a result, our eternal consciousness is not only fixed within us, but becomes like a fluid, adaptable awareness and creative malleability. We begin to breathe in rhythm with the universe, knowing when to act and when to rest, moving with a conscious, intuitive, knowing liquidity—like wax, able to take solid form but easily softened and reshapable, at the whim of creative impulses. Such an ideal is captured by Hermann Hesse in *Magister Ludi* (*The Glass Bead Game*), in which he writes that "the kind of person we want to develop, the kind of person we aim to become, would at any time be able to exchange his discipline or art for any other. . . . That is how we ought to be. We should be so constituted that we can at any time be placed in a different position without offering resistance or losing our heads."[36] As a result of our alignment with the cosmic creator within us, we follow the flow of inspiration wherever it may lead.

MULTIPLICATIO:
AUGMENTING TRUE IMAGINATION

Those are rare who have the courage to sacrifice their artistic egoism on the altar of art to resume it in the hey-day of success. Mediocre artists, like the vulgar, instinctively avoid great art because they find that it needs too much unselfishness. They are afraid of it—as a fool is afraid in the presence of a man of genius.

—Jean Delville, *The New Mission of Art*

The philosopher's stone, once fixed and incerated, is further refined by the process of multiplication, which increases the potency of the stone's tingeing powers 10-, 100-, 1,000-, 10,000-, and 100,000-fold. Multiplication prepares us for the next phase of projection in which the stone is capable of transmuting base metals into gold, just as great art transmutes the souls of others, as the inner self-realization and purified consciousness of the artist is projected outward through their vision. As the quote from Delville, above, asserts, great art requires a sacrifice of the artistic ego.

At this point in our journey upward through the chakras, we reach the third eye (*ajna*), ruled by the Moon. Our inner vision becomes unified, aiming toward the highest spiritual ideals to be expressed and multiplied by the generative power of the Moon through our creations. Like the Moon's gravitational pull upon the waters of Earth, the third eye draws the waters of the unconscious upward through the *sushumna nadi*. Purified by Mercury in the throat chakra, the waters rise into the bridal chamber, where the union of conscious and unconscious is consummated. Hence Luna, in the final part of the *Rosarium,* "multiplies and brings forth infinite Children."[37]

Multiplication is depicted in Valentine's eleventh key by two male lions in the process of devouring one another (see figure 9.10 on page 265). Upon their backs sit two twin sisters, each raising a heart in their hand that sprouts the Sun and Moon. Meanwhile Mars, raising his sword, prepares to harvest the fruit. Valentine explicates the augmentation of the stone through a parable seemingly unrelated to the image:

There lived in the East a gilded knight, named Orpheus, who was possessed of immense wealth, and had everything that heart can wish. He had taken to wife his own sister, Euridice, who did not, however, bear him any children. This he regarded as the punishment of his sin in having wedded his own sister, and was instant in prayer to God both by day and by night, that the curse might be taken from him.

One night, when he was buried in a deep sleep, there came to him a certain winged messenger, named Phœbus, who touched his feet, which were very hot, and said: "Thou noble knight, since thou hast wandered through many cities and kingdoms, and suffered many things at sea, in battle, and in the lists, the heavenly Father has bidden me make known to thee the following means of obtaining thy prayer: Take blood from thy right side, and from the left side of thy spouse. For this blood is the heart's blood of your parents, and though it may seem to be of two kinds, yet, in reality, it is only one. Mix the two kinds of blood, and keep the mixture tightly enclosed in the globe of the seven wise Masters. There that which is generated will be nourished with its own flesh and blood, and will complete its course of development when the Moon has changed for the eighth time. If thou repeat this process again and again, thou shalt see children's children, and the offspring of thy body shall fill the world."

When Phœbus had thus spoken, he winged his flight heavenward. In the morning the knight arose and did the bidding of the celestial messenger, and God gave to him and to his wife many children, who inherited their father's glory, wealth, and knightly honours from generation to generation.[38]

Like the fighting lions who shed their blood in figure 9.10, Orpheus and Euridice must mix their blood in order to produce the red tincture. Before multiplication, the gilded knight is wed to his sister in the *hieros gamos,* yet they have been unsuccessful in producing any offspring. Only by mixing their two original natures, the blood of their parents that is to be extracted from his right side and her left, can the secret of multiplication be understood. Like the pelican sacrificing its own blood to feed its young, we must give of ourselves to conceive the red tincture.

Blood is the element assigned to Ernst's fourth chapter of *Une Semaine,* Wednesday.[39] Looking at the collages, it becomes evident that blood corresponds to air, symbolized as bird-headed figures, nests, and balloons. Air is associated with Wednesday's traditional ruler Mercury, correlating with Mercury's importance in the completion of the stone. Air is also the element of the heart chakra, the center of love through which the *magnum opus* is realized. Like the blood in Valentine's allegory, which "may seem to be of two kinds, yet, in reality, it is only one," Ernst uses the example of "Oedipus" for this chapter, alluding to the incestual relationship of the primal pair. Several of the images contain cages and prison bars, suggesting the vessel and reminiscent of the parable in Silberer's *Hidden Symbolism,* in which the incestual couple are punished and shut up together in a prison. Equivalent with the philosophical egg, the prison is where the main part of the work takes place.[40] This relates to Valentine's statement that the mixture of the two bloods must be kept "tightly enclosed" in the globe. When the initiate begins to warm the chamber, the pair embraces in the conjunction of opposites.[41]

Blood represents the intensity of our passion and desire to reach the

Fig. 9.10. The multiplication of the lions proceeds from the mixing of two bloods.
Basil Valentine, "Clavis XI." In *Musaeum Hermeticum Reformatum Et Amplificatum,*
Frankfurt am Main, Germany: Apud Hermannum a Sande, 1678.
Courtesy of Science History Institute

end of the work; it is also a name of the *prima materia,* linking us with
our progenitors and the original sacrifice of the archetypal mother-father
pair from which all things are generated. As such, the artist sacrifices
their personal ego to the original primal parents working *through* them.
This primal blood mixture, placed within the "globe of the seven wise
Masters"—the seven planetary archetypes, metals, and chakras found
within the vessel of Self—is digested for a period equal to the nine
months of gestation. Through the perfection of the primal blood, it
becomes the Royal Blood of the fully realized King and Queen within,
de-energizing the seven spheres. Repeating the process will result in the

exponential generative powers of the stone in its powers of projection.

The reiteration of the *opus* occurs in abbreviated form. There is another period of blackening and putrefaction; a period of whitening and dissolution into dreams; a phase of transition and yellowing development through integration; and finally a return to the redness of unification and completion. Ernst appears to have recognized this, for his fifth chapter, Thursday, is assigned to the element "blackness," evoking a return to the first phase of the work. Ernst gives two examples: "the Laugh of the Cock" and "Easter Island." The cock, or rooster, is sometimes used as a name for the *prima materia* (see figure 4.3, page 86).[42] Stone-headed figures in the collages resemble those of Easter Island, intimating the appearance of the stone and perhaps a return to primitive, unified consciousness. Easter might additionally refer to the resurrection of the renewed body of the hermaphrodite.[43] Jupiter, ruler of Thursday, reminds us of the stone emerging from the blackness of Saturn— his stomach—and Jupiter's victory over his father. Interestingly, the first collage of this chapter depicts a skull, emblematic of Saturn, at the top of an egg-shaped space; within the space a man hunches over an intestinal tract. Intestines, according to Cirlot, are "connected with the labyrinth and with death (the return to the interior of the earth = mother, along the 'curved way' = Saturn's scythe)," and likewise denote the alchemical vessel.[44]

To the next chapter, Friday, Ernst assigns the element "sight," exemplified by "the Interior of Sight." This section is composed of three "visible poems." Venus, the planet of love and union, rules Friday. Fittingly, the collages in the first poem merge flowers, bones, and other anatomical and organic imagery, suggestive of the creative powers of Venus and the body. The second poem begins with a quote by Breton: "A man and a woman absolutely white." One collage from this poem features two shadowy stonelike figures—one with a sea creature and the other with a bird, suggestive of the fixed and volatile aspects of the soul. In the third "visible poem" the unifying powers of Venus are represented by an image of seven pairs of joined hands receding into the distance. Another collage depicts two parallel rows of human eyes on pedestals facing each other; three on the left (body, mind, soul) and seven (metals/planets) on the right, equaling ten altogether. These images evoke the multiplication of the stone, while the eyes suggest its final projection.

With each reiteration of the stages, the power of our stone is multiplied by a factor of ten, a number of great spiritual significance. The one and zero are found in the symbol for the Sun and gold: a point (one) within a circle (zero), representing eternal unified consciousness, the ceaseless emanations of the One, and the first cause. Thus the number ten signifies a return to unity and is symbolic of the completion of a cycle and spiritual realization. It is the number of perfection, in which the active and passive principles, life and death, end and beginning, are brought together in unity.

Once completed, the *magnum opus* results in the perfection of the stone, the birth of the red child. We may still encounter new phases of putrefaction, purification, and refinement, but once we have the stone the process becomes not only faster, but easier and more efficient because we have attained the indestructible awareness of our eternal and true nature. This becomes an inextricable part of us, the equivalent of Hermetic gnosis, god-realization, or enlightenment. As we go through cyclical reiterations of the *opus,* our inner strength, creative expression, and power to positively affect the world becomes more potent.

Multiplication was first encountered in the *citrinitas* with its fertilizing solar rain that impregnated our stone with inspiration. The seeds that took to earth are sprouting and multiplying in the permanent rose garden (see figure 9.11 on page 268) that we have opened with a skeleton key—the death encountered in the *nigredo.* Our stone has been augmented; its potency has increased, and it now can regenerate any imperfect body and bring it to perfection. This skeleton key is a gift of Saturn, traditional ruler of Aquarius (January 20–February 18), the eleventh sign of the zodiac and that of multiplication. It is the *lead* that lies at the beginning of the work, the heaviness of earth and the root chakra, *muladhara,* transmuted from its black primal matter to the white stone, and then the red. Aquarius is the Water Bearer who connects above and below by means of the airy water that streams from his chalice, the water of the spirit. In the body, Aquarius is housed in the ankles, whereas the feet are submerged in the mutable water of Pisces, the Two Fish, and the calves rise like the mountains of Capricorn above the water's surface. Aquarius occupies the boundary between consensus reality and the world of dreams.

Aquarius is a fixed air sign, and with Saturn relates to the structuring

Fig. 9.11. The philosopher arrives at the permanent rose garden of
multiplication and projection. Michael Maier, *Atalanta Fugiens*,
Oppenheim, Germany: Johann-Theodor de Bry, 1618.
Courtesy of Science History Institute

of the mental world of ideas within the artist. Idealism, rebelliousness,
open-mindedness, independence, creativity, innovation, an active intellect,
and a concern for the collective are qualities of this sign. In a continuous
stream of imaginative possibility, the Water Bearer dissolves and unifies
the celestial and earthly waters, pouring them back and forth between
their vessels, connecting the ideal forms of the heavens with their material
manifestations upon earth in a continuous stream of creativity. Through

the gateway of Aquarius we access our biggest, most fantastic dreams, particularly those aligned with divine wisdom, truth, and an altruistic aim. In essence, as we augment the power of our stone, repeating the four stages, we get closer and closer to the creative ideal. Our focus shifts from our own liberation to the liberation of the whole as the expression of the ideal multiplies through the collective. The revolutionary energy of Aquarius calls us to make a big shift in our orientation to the world, ultimately liberating our imagination and energy for a greater calling. As Delville asks us, "Is it not rather by employing ideal themes raised above inferior and commonplace contingencies that artists will exert a much wider influence on the moral life of the people?"[45] By increasing our sphere of influence, we create more positive transformation within and without. As Delville differentiates, "The dream is the unconscious and instinctive feeling of confused aspirations; the ideal is the ordered aspiration of the harmonious will."[46] We must take the confused, volatile aspirations of the unconscious and fix them into their ideal, conscious expression.

In the final engraving of Stephan Michelspacher's *Cabala,* named *The End: Multiplication* (see figure 9.12 on page 270), we see the five base metals ascended to a mountaintop, representing the triumph over unconscious drives and ascension through the spheres. Sol and Luna kneel before the King and his fountain of blood. Like the resurrected Christ and the pelican, he offers his blood to his glorified children. Above the Red King the planets make another appearance in their exalted form upon the integrated, balanced fountain flowing with eternal consciousness, with Mercury at the crown. With the concentration of vital creative energy now available, the power of true imagination is multiplied through our creations, like ripples in the sea.

Apollinaire elucidates a clear example of such an ideal in an influential lecture he gave in 1917. This manifesto of creativity, called "The New Spirit and the Poets," invokes the powers of innovation within the poet or creator, and their responsibility to the greater good. The new spirit, he argues, is antiformulaic and inherently opposed to aestheticism, and seeks to reestablish the equality of the inner world with that of science. Recognizing that "poetry and creation are one and the same," he declares that "poets will be charged finally with giving by means of lyric teleologies and arch-lyric

Fig. 9.12. The King's blood flows and the fruit multiplies at the end of the work. Stephan Michelspacher, *Cabala, Speigel der Kunst und Natur in Alchymia*, 1654.
Courtesy of Wellcome Collection

alchemies a constantly purer meaning to the idea of divinity, which is so alive within us, which is perpetual rental of ourselves, that eternal creation, that endless rebirth by which we live."[47] The new spirit is in alignment with Huelsenbeck's *Neue Mensch* and the liberated imagination of the artist, freed not only from conventions of tradition but freed from the restricting and confusing, impure directives of an unassimilated unconscious.

Multiplication, as we have seen, reiterates the entire *opus* and can be repeated as often as necessary, but requires the addition of purified Mercury, or in other words, the purified contents of the unconscious. As we are advised in *An Open Entrance to the Closed Palace of the King,* the purified Mercury is added to the stone in a tightly sealed vessel and gently cooked for seven days, passing quickly and easily "through all the Reigns." This increases the tingeing power of the stone a thousandfold, and with each repetition the process is faster, the concentrated medicine becoming "most marvelous."[48] The "Reigns" that the stone's digestion passes through over seven days are the spheres of the bodily vessel. This is a process of refinement reiterating all of our previous work, now occurring at a faster rate and with less difficulty because we have discovered our true imagination, the philosopher's stone, the red tincture. We now move into the culmination and most powerful process of the *opus,* the *proiectio.*

PROIECTIO:
THE RED TINCTURE OF IMAGINAL CREATION

> *For body's sleep became the soul's awakening, and closing of the eyes true vision, pregnant with Good my silence, and the utterance of my word (logos) begetting of good things.*
>
> —*Corpus Hermeticum,* from G. R. S. Mead

Ernst completes his week of kindness with the chapter for Saturday, assigned the "unknown" element and example, "The Key to Songs."[49] Yet Saturday's ruler, Saturn, signifies the beginning of the work. Ernst's transposition of the Sun, symbol of gold and completion, and Saturn, symbol of impure lead, exemplifies the occultation of the work while simultaneously intimating its cyclical nature. Like the tail in the mouth of the ouroboros, the end lies in the beginning. The "unknown" element likewise reveals the impenetrable mystery of creation where birth and death are indistinguishable. The collages in this section are filled with women (from Charcot's studies of hysteria) suspended in dark masses of fabric or abysmal space, like the liberated *anima* and the shadowy, unfathomable unconscious.[50] Luna has been liberated to fly through the astral realm. The third collage features a boy, which brings to mind the philosophical child or the philosopher's stone, and the return to innocence that comes with the completion of the work. A stone upon a flight of stairs in the final collage suggests completion of the work. Perhaps Ernst chose the "unknown" element because in completing the work, we inevitably come to realize how little we truly know, and that this is a marvelous place to be. As Jung asserts, "what the union of opposites really 'means' transcends human imagination."[51] We regain our childlike wonder and step into the unknown, the realm of true imagination and infinite possibility.

The Green Lion and the Demonstration of Perfection

The final part of the *Rosarium* is titled "The Demonstration of Perfection" as the transmuting powers of the stone are proven through their projection onto molten metals. Here we find the image of the green lion devouring the Sun, which we encountered in the process of digestion. Now this image provides a message about the humility necessary to hold the powerful responsibility of the true tincture. The lion shares the same nature as gold, the Sun, and Sulfur. Yet as we discussed previously, the *green* lion denotes an unripe gold that has not yet reached the red state of complete integration. In his commentary on the *Rosarium,* Adam McLean describes the green lion as the dissolving powers of the unconscious that must be allowed to devour the solar consciousness in a final egoic death, resulting in resurrection.[52] This aligns with the green lion's conflation with the solvent Mercury, or the alkahest. As it consumes/dissolves the Sun and integrates its nature, solar blood gushes from its jaws, producing the red tincture, or pure gold. Hence Paracelsus calls the green lion an all-healing balsam, a tincture that is further perfected into the "true, clear Green Lion," which is "the Tincture, transparent gold."[53] As a goal of the *opus,* the balsam, a universal medicine and elixir of life, is that unifying and strengthening effect of inner truth and wholeness, the quintessence arrived at through the trials of the work. It is a living stone, everlasting and indestructible.[54] Jodorowsky describes the elixir as "a person who accepts life and lives everything as it is without self-annihilation."[55] Jung equated it with a union between the self and the *unus mundus,* the "one world" or the "potential world."[56] The elixir is able to amalgamate other substances to its own likeness.[57]

An example of the green lion can be seen in Ernst's painting *Dada Gauguin* (see figure 9.7), which Warlick compares to Silberer's alchemical exegesis. Pointing to the yellow hairs and flowery crown around the artichoke vessel, she cites a passage from Silberer in which he quotes Maier's *Septimana Philosophica*: "The green lion [a usual symbol for the material at the beginning] encloses the raw seeds, yellow hairs adorn his head . . . i.e., when the projection on the metals takes place, they turn yellow, golden."[58] On this Silberer notes, "Green is the color of hope, of growth. Previously only the head of the lion is gold, his future. Later he becomes a red lion, the philosopher's stone, the king in robe of purple. At any rate he must first be killed."[59] Warlick equates the green lion and the green artichoke of Ernst's painting with the *prima materia,* which must be opened, or killed, to be transmuted into the red lion.

There are far too many interpretations of the green lion to cover here; for our purposes it is a reminder to continually dissolve the ego, preventing our inner realizations from producing an inflation. The true, clear green lion represents the transparent state of consciousness necessary for the Divine solar light to be projected into our creations. Projection is the unlimited tingeing power of the tincture, also described as a red powder. Spiritually, it is the ability to take any situation, no matter how corrupt, and transmute it into a noble opportunity for growth. The true perception of the artist pierces through falsity, comprehending the inherent perfection in all things, drawing forth their inner beauty and radiance through the perfected powers and projection of true imagination. Red tincture flows through the body, bringing the unconscious into union with cosmic consciousness, as the artist multiplies the stone through the projection of their fully realized essence. Like the pelican, truth overflows from the heart in an act of sacrificial love, tingeing all it touches.

Energetically, fixation stabilizes the volatile aspects of the conscious and unconscious, entraining the heartbeat with the breath. These two rhythms, for the most part occurring automatically, are brought under conscious control through attention and focus, stabilizing the mind. This is fundamental to projecting divine ideals through our creations, and to creating in the imaginal realm. In Hermetic philosophy this would be considered the eighth sphere of Creation that exists above the Harmony of

Fate. With the purifications of our stone, the imagination is freed from corrupting factors that limit and impinge upon innovation, and we enter the realm of ultimate creative potential. All the powers of the spheres/chakras are at our command, and we direct our energies with the perfect alignment of desire (heart, Venus) and divine will (throat, Mercury). As Paracelsus elucidates:

> The Will is a dissolving power, which enables the body to become impregnated by the "tincture" of the imagination. He who wants to know how a man can unite his power of imagination with the power of the imagination of Heaven, must know by what process this may be done. A man comes into possession of creative power by uniting his own mind with the Universal Mind, and he who succeeds in doing so will be in possession of the highest possible wisdom; the lower realm of Nature will be subject to him, and the powers of Heaven will aid him, because Heaven is the servant of wisdom.[60]

Will, the dissolving spirit, is the master and the alkahest in its highest form.[61] Imagination, directed by the Will, is the spiritized tincture inseminating and impregnating the body—the unconscious and plastic material.[62] Sendivogius describes this in terms of Nature: "[T]he four elements by their continual action project a constant supply of seed to the centre of the earth, where it is digested, and whence it proceeds again in generative motions. Now the centre of the earth is a certain void place wherein nothing is at rest; and upon the margin or circumference of this centre the four elements project their qualities."[63] This "void place" is like the *prima materia* within the body, the undifferentiated field of potential from which creation is generated through separation and reorganization of the four elements.

There are three essential ways we can understand projection: (1) transmitting divinized consciousness through art; (2) creating from the imaginal realm; and (3) traveling through the astral plane. The first we've already discussed with multiplication and the expression of the ideal; the third we will introduce the essential basis of. However, as this book pertains to the creative process, we will devote our greatest attention to creating through the imaginal realm. All of these methods rest on aligning true imagination with the Universal Mind, where the desires of the individual and collective good align. This is the *demonstration of perfection,* realized by our awakened inner fire, which, as Sendivogius writes, "attracts to itself all the pure elements, which are thus separated from the impure, and form the nucleus of a far purer form of life."[64]

Pisces and the Dream of Life

The completion of the *opus* coincides with winter's end and the start of a new cycle, as we come to the twelfth and final sign, Pisces (February 19–March 20). Assigned to projection, Pisces is a mutable water sign represented by two fish swimming in opposite directions, the Soul and Spirit (see figure 9.13 on page 276). They are "two, and nevertheless one," joined together in one Body, the sea of the unconscious.[65] Our work has been to extract the Soul and Spirit from their undifferentiated state in the *prima materia,* raise them to the spiritual realm above, purify them with divine ideals, and bring them back down to earth where they are reunited in the Body.

Anatomically, Pisces resides in the feet, where the oldest patterns are held in our energetic framework. As we ascend through the chakras/spheres, we simultaneously descend through the *corpus,* unifying above and below in the energetic field—an integration of past, present, and future. Within the feet we find a microcosm of the entire body; each part of the foot reflexes to specific organs and anatomical regions, reminding us of the whole contained within the parts and the infinite complexity of the universe existing within.

Pisces is a dreamy sign ruled by the gaseous giant and ruler of the heavens, Jupiter, wielder of the lightning bolt, the creative spark of life. He is a beneficent king that facilitates projection through his heavenly vision, projecting his royal eagles outward in search of inner truth: "Two Eagles come together: One from the East, and the other from the West."[66] The Soul and Spirit separate, flying in opposite directions and meeting at the *omphalos:* center of the world, the true Self. Like a dream, our waking experience is shaped by unconscious factors until we awaken the creative spark within us, realizing it to be the formative cause of our reality. When the conscious and unconscious merge, waking life becomes a malleable dream, experienced as a projection of the inner

Fig. 9.13. The two fishes of the Soul and Spirit swimming in the sea of the Body.
The Alchemical Book of Lambspring, in the *Musaeum Hermeticum*
Reformatum Et Amplificatum, 1678.
Courtesy of Science History Institute

world. Imagine becoming lucid in a dream in which you gain a certain
level of control over events and outcomes. We can likewise become lucid
or "awakened" in the world of consensus reality, interpreting life like a
dream and opening a whole world of possibilities. Lucidity gives a cer-

tain level of creative control and prevents a complete dissolution by the unconscious. With a clear will and true imagination, we can influence the circumstances of our lives. Lucidity also creates a neutral objectivity in which one is no longer identified with the previously unquestioned reality of the dream; the same principle applies in waking life. The work of the previous stages of breaking down our rigid conceptions of reality has prepared us for this creative involvement with reality, in which we are no longer limited by preconceived notions of who we are, and how the world is supposed to work. We are open to possibility and actively engaging the imagination.

That which we experience internally as feeling is seeded into the unconscious and brought to realization in the physical world—"as within, so without." "Its father is the Sun and its mother the Moon," as the *Emerald Tablet* tells us; "The Earth carried it in her belly, and the Wind nourished it in her belly . . . as Earth which shall become Fire."[67] The primal opposites of the conscious and unconscious are the progenitors of the creative idea— a feeling held in the body, projected as an idea and carried in the ætheric vessel, taking on a subtle ætheric template. When we "feed the Earth from that which is subtle, with the greatest power," we draw upon the immense powers of the subtle body, the astral body, to feed the world of forms with our own creative volition. And, as Lévi states, "The form is proportional to the idea."[68] Everything you see is *you* projected externally; the work of the *magnum opus* helps us to transmute this from the lesser personality and ego to the transpersonal Soul. In the words of Paracelsus,

> Man is mind; he is what he thinks. If he thinks fire, he is on fire; if he thinks war, then will he cause war; it all depends merely on that the whole of his imagination becomes an entire sun; i.e., that he wholly imagines that which he wills.[69]

It is necessary that we purify the inner world so the outer projection is in alignment with the Soul's purpose, unobstructed by impurities acquired through lifetimes of conditioned responses and patterns of thought and behavior. Imagine projecting a movie on a screen, but the lens is covered in dust and grime; the projected image is likewise unclear. Our chakras must be open for a clear projection, from the root planted in physical reality to the crown reaching toward Source. Lévi advises that "the imagination of the adept is diaphanous, whilst that of the crowd is opaque; the light of truth traverses the one as ordinary light passes through clear glass, and is refracted by the other, as when ordinary light impinges upon a vitreous block, full of scoriae and foreign matter."[70] The processes of alchemy give us the means to become clear vessels through which the light of truth can shine unobstructed.

In the *nigredo* we recognized and reclaimed our false projections—those inner irreconcilable drives and urges, things of which the ego is unaware, that are projected externally, manifesting through a variety of external reflections, neuroses, and bodily afflictions. Jung's alchemical concept of projection was fairly limited to the unconscious projection on the part of the alchemists externalizing inner processes in their retorts. This sort of projection is of a different nature altogether from the power of the stone to transmute metals. It lacks conscious intention, faith, and will. Transmuting metals into gold symbolizes a projection of consciousness to affect matter. It is intentional and grounded in the truth of the soul and its eternal nature.

Energetic Dynamics of Projecting the Astral Body

Each of the chakras functions in a triad of electromagnetic energy: positive, neutral, and negative or, in other words, projection, rest, and attraction. We project through the imagination, rest and let go of any attachment to the outcome, and thereby attract the object of our desire. The two primary forces of attraction and projection correspond to the *Emerald Tablet*'s precept: "It ascends from the earth to the heaven and becomes ruler over that which is above and that which is below."[71] The way Lévi explains it, we become like the Sun, "at once attracting and repelling all the planets of its system," which is "to have accomplished the Great Work and to be master of the world. Armed with such a force you may make yourself adored: the crowd will believe that you are God."[72]

Projection is accomplished by the union of the Sun and Moon within the bridal chamber, the "heart of the brain" or the hypothalamic region. Here the pineal and pituitary glands work synergistically in the projection of consciousness, via the imagination, to not only traverse the astral plane, but to create therefrom. In a mystical sense projection is akin to the flight of the soul. This requires a unification between the brain and heart, between our thinking mind and our feeling mind.

According to Paracelsus, the Sun corresponds to the heart and the Moon to the brain. This does not conflict with our conception of the Sun residing in the crown and Venus in the heart. Rather, it is an expression of the state of consciousness of the adept who draws down the powers of the above, the celestial emanations transmitted through the Sun's rays, into the heart. Paracelsus believed that the volatile spirit rises continuously up from the heart to the brain.[73] Spirit, or *pneuma,* is equivalent to Air, the element of the heart chakra. As the heart shares such an intimate relationship to the lungs, it is through the breath that we unify the heart and brain. Becoming aware of our breath and breathing in a slow, controlled manner from the diaphragm slows down the volatile spirit that causes anxiety and restlessness, giving us the focus required for successful projection. "Man is not body, but the heart is man," writes Paracelsus, "and the heart is an entire star out of which it is built up. If, therefore, a man is perfect in his heart, nothing in the whole light of Nature is hidden from him."[74] Further, we must fix the volatile desires and fears of the lower chakras, which if not properly channeled will inhibit the flight of the soul. Lévi included the brain, heart, and genital organs in what he called the "centres of fluidic attraction and projection," which relate to the crown/third eye, heart, and root chakras.[75] These are "the seat of a triple magnetic operation," which when aligned by a lucid consciousness can be directed like a "Magic Wand."[76]

Our astral body is our celestial star body, the ætheric double of the physical body that we access through the heart star. It is a body of light, what Lévi calls the "Astral light," known in the yogic and tantric traditions as the subtle body, or *linga sharira* (Sanskrit). The double is identified with the Egyptian *ka,* the spiritual likeness of a person that can move independently of the body while still alive, and that may be sustained after the physical body dies if properly nourished. Paracelsus used the alchemical term *Azoth,* also *Azoc(h),* which is also the philosophic Mercury, the stone, the universal medicine, or elixir. It is called the "Astral

Quintessence, Flying Slave, Animated Spirit," flying freely in service to consciousness with the power to affect the greatest transmutations in the physical world.[77] The human being is the astral quintessence of the macrocosm, "a little world" existing as "an extract" of all the stars, planets, and the earth. We are the *quint*-essence, or fifth element, containing the four elements within and existing as their extracted "nucleus."[78] We can experience the astral body while still embodied in the flesh by the withdrawal of the physical senses, partaking in the infinite knowledge and wisdom of the macrocosm through our soul's sympathy with it.[79] Paracelsus calls this the spiritual breath, which may be sent out to great distances, traveling "fast as the wind" to accomplish one's will.[80]

Recall that Paracelsus referred to the astral body as the "invisible man," as well as the "sidereal," "celestial," or "sacramental" body. This is differentiated from the "terrestrial" or "elemental" body, the physical body known in the Hindu tradition as the *sthula sharira*.[81] The astral body is the "shadow (æthereal counterpart) of the body," resembling the physical body yet existing somewhere between the material and immaterial world.[82] It partakes of the nature of both. Paracelsus writes that these two bodies are separated in death, when the sidereal body "soars on high, like an eagle" and the terrestrial body "sinks down to the earth, like lead."[83] We are reminded of the image mentioned previously of the eagle chained to a toad. Yet according to Paracelsus, the astral body is not necessarily immortal. While the astral form, which carries the imprint of the individual personality, may be more enduring than the physical body, it will eventually dissolve into its æthereal elements unless the personality is sufficiently developed and spiritualized, or enlightened. The astral body then becomes the vehicle, the resurrection body, for the retention of self-awareness and our memories and experiences. Thus immortality can be understood as the retention of the personality, or self-consciousness, through the cycles of death and rebirth. This is affected by spiritual development, identification with the Divine Self, or the inner realization of the eternal life while experiencing physical existence. The *ka* of the Egyptians was likewise said to hover close to the body upon death, and would dissipate unless given offerings or sustained by the paintings upon the wall of the tomb or given a body in the form of a statue. On the other hand, the *ba,* which is like the soul, comes into being upon death of the body. The *ka* and the *ba* may be joined in union, a marriage resulting in the *akh,* a transfigured and powerful spirit. Hence the Egyptian funerary rites and the emphasis on the deceased employing magic and reciting protective spells to pass through all the trials that await one upon death, in order to be granted eternal life.

Developing a relationship to the astral body and learning to navigate the astral plane helps us to strengthen our identification with the eternal, immutable aspect of our being. The work we have done cultivating a non-dual awareness has prepared us to journey in the astral plane, the macro-cosm of the celestial spheres and the other world inhabited by the spirits of all things: elementaries, intelligences, angels, and demons. It is part of the eternal, everlasting, all-encompassing field of energy that permeates the universe and gives life to every living thing; variously called Æther, *prana, chi, akasha,* or pneuma. We connect to the astral body via the heart chakra, the bridge between the spiritual and physical planes. Astral pro-jection requires fixation in the lower vessel—the heart of truth—and a perfect balance between above and below. Then the third eye (Moon) and crown (Sun), working in unison, facilitate projection of the astral body to traverse the astral plane and interact with spirits, guides, teachers, and people from all places and times. An example of this is given by Apollonius of Tyana, who learned the Brahma-vidya and wisdom of the Indian sages, as well as how to converse with them on the astral plane: "by sharing with me your wisdom ye have given me power to travel through heaven . . . I will hold converse with you as though ye were present."[84]

Travel and creation through the astral realm both require a strong will and true imagination to induce a waking dream state. This also entails a complete unification between the subject and object, and an unshake-able faith. Paracelsus advises, "Faith renders the spirit strong; doubt is the destroyer."[85] Yet it is not blind faith that is required, but faith grounded in gnosis, from having faced one's own spiritual death and experienced resurrection. Astral projection should be active and intentional. It may be passively experienced without conscious direction, like what happens in hypnagogia in which one is simply watching a cascade of visual stimulus.

Active astral projection, on the other hand, is a controlled use of imagination. The level of refinement of our stone, which could take many years to acquire, determines the degree of control.

According to Paracelsus, there are six primary states of mind that corrupt our imaginative power: fear, terror, passion, desire, joy, and envy.[86] We must separate and release these powerful mental states to liberate the astral body. Obviously fear, terror, and envy are negative states we want to rid ourselves of for a successful projection. However, what about passion, desire, and joy? Can these not be employed positively in the imaginal realm to increase the potency of that which we are creating? Desire is the source from which imagination is birthed; however, desire can be both pure and corrupt, and we must be able to tell the difference.[87] Feelings of joy and fulfillment are indispensable to successful projection, as we will see, however we must take heed that our passions not get the better of us and carry us away into unconscious fantasy. The same thing happens in a lucid dream when the excitement takes over and we slip back into unconsciousness. It is important to stay balanced, allowing ourselves to feel the joy of imaginal creation, like the ecstatic joy and passion of conception, while not losing conscious focus.

Our intention with alchemical projection is to transmute our reality or to create something—to manifest an experience, to expand and grow in new ways, to cultivate a quality we wish to develop, or to manifest an object of our true, authentic, and purified desire. We choose the scenario from a vast sea of potential. Once it gets going, our projection takes on a life of its own according to our conscious intent, becoming a spontaneous outflowing of positive and affirming imagery, words, and events that fill us to the brim with feelings of harmony, peace, and gratitude as our authentic desires are fulfilled. We invite the unconscious to play along with us through persuasion; if we are convincing enough, it will jump on board to aid us in the realization of our vision. If, however, we have ignored the inner world and failed to acknowledge its needs, then the unconscious may very well refuse to play along, throwing doubts into our mind, or taking over the vision and pulling us into unconscious fantasy. Like a wounded lover, it can derail our best intentions. We may still succeed in manifesting, but whatever manifests will be tainted by these unacknowledged aspects, offering us another opportunity for integration. If we go about our projection while ignoring these deep inner needs, we also run the risk of fragmentation, as we saw in the case of Nerval's character Spifame, who was unable to integrate the various aspects of his personality into a cohesive unity. This is the importance of active imagination, coagulation, and fixation. It is vital that we first learn to listen to the unconscious before we approach it consciously as the imaginal realm of creation.

One way we can foster integration is to combine the techniques of active imagination and projection. When we are in the imaginal world of our projection, we can address our unconscious to see if there are any objections to our imagined scenario. This could appear as a figure encountered in active imagination, or perhaps someone new. Talk with them, ask them why they object, and address their concerns. Make a case for yourself, and make deals with them if necessary, so long as it is mutually beneficial and results in the highest good for both your ego and this unconscious aspect. The figure may transform before your eyes to reflect the inner change that you have catalyzed through your imagination.

Projection rests upon the Law of Attraction, namely that we attract things to the self through our sympathetic resonance with them. For instance, the idea that if we hold the vibration or frequency of love, then love will be magnetized to us. It is akin to the idea of sympathetic magic, whereby the magician draws down influences of the planetary archetypes with plants, stones, incense, incantations, and the like. However, in this case, we embody the qualities we wish to draw forth through the depth and intensity of feeling. This was clearly elucidated by Neville Goddard, who lectured and wrote extensively on the technique of creating through the imagination. He asserts, "Feeling is the one and only medium through which ideas are conveyed to the subconscious."[88] Yet like Paracelsus, he cautions, "the man who does not control his feeling may easily impress the subconscious with undesirable states."[89] Goddard compares the imagination to the Mind of the Hermetic texts. His concept of "The Law" posits that the world is the objectification of humanity's conditioned consciousness; male and female divisions of the conscious and subconscious work together in the generation of form. "The conscious generates ideas and impresses these ideas on the subconscious," says Goddard, "the subconscious receives ideas and gives form and expression to them."[90] Compare this with the words of Paracelsus: "The imagination of man becomes pregnant through desire, and gives birth to deeds."[91] We read this same sentiment in the Gospel of Thomas, a collection of secret teachings of Jesus: "If two make peace with each other in a single house, they will say to the mountain, 'Move from here,' and it will move."[92] Through controlling one's ideas and feelings, one can create through the imagination to experience the miracles of the One Thing. As we are advised by Hermes in the *Corpus Hermeticum* (10.2), "Man is separated into soul and body, and only when the two sides of his sense agree together, does utterance of its thought conceived by mind take place."[93]

Projection requires full engagement, as though the experience were really happening—emotionally, physically, mentally, and spiritually. While guided imagery can certainly help us to do this, in projection we are not following a script that someone else has laid out for us. We are tapping into our own true imagination, in harmony with the Ideal. We consciously decide what we want to feel, be, do, and experience. This is not merely wish fulfillment, but a creative engagement with one's deepest truth and authenticity. Through purification of the inner world and controlled feeling, we remove obstructions to our full self-realization, to co-create a life that is in alignment with our deepest and most profound truth—which we truly feel we deserve, of mutual benefit to Self and Other.

In addition to imaginal creation, we can also simply embody the feeling we want to generate, while holding affirming consubstantial thoughts. This entails purifying the internal dialogue, relating back to the purification of Mercury. If one has a negative, anxious, worried thought, it can be overwritten by another more powerful thought and concomitant feeling that prevails over it. According to Goddard it is the feeling that wins out when it comes to impressing the unconscious, determining what will be brought forth into being. The more we ruminate on something, the more likely it is that we will bring it into reality. That is not to say that every negative thought we have is going to manifest. We are referring to obsessive patterns of thought and mental conversations, lingered upon and returned to repeatedly, which we give power to with our emotional energy.

If we listen closely to our inner conversations, we will likely notice that some of the voices we hear are not even our own, and thus we must separate what is truly ours versus what we have been conditioned to by our family, friends, and society.

Opening the Doors to the Imaginal Realm

The red tincture is a medicine that has a clarifying effect on consciousness, just as the Sun dispels shadows and brightens the world. This is what Blake implies when he says that "if the doors of perception were cleansed every thing would appear to man as it is: infinite."[94] Or as it is stated in the *Chaldæan Oracles,* "Let the immortal depths of thy soul be opened, and open all thy eyes at once to the Above."[95] Perhaps John Keats perceived this when in the poem "Endymion" he wrote of a "fellowship divine" that causes us to shine, "full alchemized, and free of space:"

> *Feel we these things?—that moment have we stept*
> *Into a sort of oneness, and our state*
> *Is like a floating spirit's. But there are*
> *Richer entanglements, enthralments far*
> *More self-destroying, leading, by degrees,*
> *To the chief intensity: the crown of these*
> *Is made of love and friendship, and sits high*
> *Upon the forehead of humanity.*[96]

Upon the forehead we find the third eye, center of the Moon, which when energetically aligned with the crown and Sun through divine love is the gateway to oneness and flight of the spirit. Thought (*yang*) and emotion (*yin*), when brought together in the *hieros gamos,* is a mystical union. "And so we become a part of it," writes Keats, "nurtured like a pelican brood,"[97] just as we are nurtured by the red tincture.[98] Senior describes this ultimate consummation: "When we shall enter into the house of love, my body shall be coagulated and I shall be in my emptiness."[99] What is emptiness, but the state of energetic peace? In the yogic tradition this is the *sattvic* principle that brings the two serpents of the caduceus, *ida* and *pingala,* into perfect balance.

Imaginal creation requires that we enter a state of energetic balance as the body becomes heavy and completely relaxed. Hermes advises his son Tat in the *Corpus Hermeticum* (8.6–7), "Withdraw into thyself, and it will come; will, and it comes to pass; throw out of work the body's senses, and thy Divinity shall come to birth; purge from thyself the brutish torments—things of matter."[100] We purge ourselves of the passions rooted in ignorance, withdrawing from the senses of the body and engaging our Divine Will. Goddard echoes this wisdom when he advises that "denying the evidence of the senses and appropriating the feeling of the wish fulfilled is the way to the realization of your desire."[101]

It is worth repeating some of the lines of Wordsworth's "Tintern Abbey," previously quoted, that speak to this state of suspension by which the soul is liberated, and from which the true sight is birthed:

> *Almost suspended, we are laid asleep*
> *In body, and become a living soul:*
> *While with an eye made quiet by the power*
> *Of harmony, and the deep power of joy,*
> *We see into the life of things.*[102]

This suspension is much like what happens when we fall asleep. Keats's poem "Endymion" draws upon the Greek myth of the titular figure, a beautiful shepherd greatly loved by Selene, immortal goddess of the Moon. In order for Selene to consummate her love with the mortal Endymion, she asks Zeus to put him into a state of perpetual sleep in which he never grows old or dies. Endymion is given the elixir of immortality, and his eternal sleep is induced with poppies, red flowers evoking the *rubedo* and symbolic of peace, sleep, and death. In Keats's poem, red poppies produce visions and a dream-filled slumber. Like Endymion, it is through sleep that we unite with our lunar unconscious, drinking deep from the Moon's chalice of immortality.

Sleep is a gateway that can be approached to facilitate the union of the conscious and unconscious. Remaining conscious as we stand upon the brink of sleep is the key to accessing the astral body, as well as incubating our dreams and planting our conscious desires into the unconscious. "Your conception of yourself as you fall asleep," writes Goddard, "is the seed you drop into the ground of the subconscious. Dropping off to sleep feeling satisfied and happy compels conditions and events to appear in your world which confirm these attitudes of mind."[103] By releasing our worries and entering sleep while holding the feelings we want to generate, we inseminate the unconscious with our truest aspirations, which the Moon will faithfully bring to materialization. Such is the secret promise of sleep, as Keats captures in the following lines:

> *O magic sleep! O comfortable bird,*
> *That broodest o'er the troubled sea of the mind*[104]

Sleep is the state of union where the opposites within become one, our personal experience of the love between Endymion and Selene. The energy dynamics discussed previously come into play here: projection, rest, attraction. Before we fall asleep, we *project* our desires in the imaginal realm, then we drift off into sleep and *rest,* and thereby *attract* through resonance that which we wish to manifest.

According to Goddard, prayer is another gateway to the unconscious. Rather than asking or pleading for what we want, we can pray by projecting, through our imagination, the objective of our authentic and purified desires as though they have already come to pass. "Prayer is the art of assuming the feeling of being and having that which you want," asserts Goddard.[105] In prayer we still the mind and enter the imaginal world, aligning our feeling with our wish, and allowing doubt to pass away. Essentially, we *become* that which we *desire* to be, with utmost faith. "Thus the work is concluded and perfected," writes Paracelsus, "that which imagination conceives is brought into operation."[106]

It is possible to reach a state where one needn't exert any effort in the imaginative powers; all fugitive thoughts and fleeting desires having been driven away from a focused and steady mind, centered within, while the body holds the resonant vibration of pure joy, aligned with the Good, for the creative powers of the One Thing to work through one's very existence. The "Riddle of Hermes Concerning the Red Tincture" in the *Rosarium* speaks to this creative joy: "I am crowned, and decked with a precious crown and adorned with princely garments, for that I cause joy to enter into bodies."[107] Such joy is the effect of the red tincture, a product of the *rubedo* and the crucial ingredient in successful projection, for we must be able to feel the joy and the love of our imaginal creation for it to properly inseminate the unconscious.

As we begin to experience success in the power of projection to manifest our experience, we must hold the green lion in our heart and remember that we are not the sole creator of the universe. This is a co-creative process; we can direct the flow of universal forces, but the outcome is not completely in our control. The best we can do is purify our intentions and underlying belief structures to allow for the expansion of possibilities to unfold within us. If we are trying to imagine great amounts of wealth coming to us, and yet hold a core belief that wealth is contradictory to virtue, or some other negative belief about wealth, then we are unconsciously blocking this manifestation. That is why the preliminary stages are so important for projection to work in a way that aligns with our desire. We must know what our true desire is, which is often the most difficult part. Perhaps we don't actually care about wealth, but are more concerned with right livelihood and mutual integrity in our work. Success rests on our ability to persuade the unconscious to work with us. The more we can clarify our intention and bring it into fellowship with universal truth, the greater our creative power becomes.

Ways to Use Projection

- Journeying to the planetary spheres, the sphere of the fixed stars, elemental journeys to invoke their qualities within us
- Conversing with spirits, guides, and teachers
- Seeing the completion of a creative project in our imagination and feeling the joy, the satisfaction, of the work being completed and presented to the world; seeing it being received with great acclaim and being of service to others
- Transmuting challenging aspects of our reality into ennobled expressions that support us in our authenticity and highest truth
- Manifesting authentic desires in the physical world: experiences,

material objects, or feelings we want to cultivate such as joy, health, wealth, success, or love

Tips for Projection

- ◆ Projection is typically visual, but can also be developed through the other subtle sensations, experienced independent of the physical body but felt to be real: touch, sounds, tastes. Those who have trouble visualizing should simply focus on the feeling of the experience.
- ◆ Don't concern yourself with how your imaginal creation will come to be. Simply rest in the feeling of your objective being realized.

Creating in the Imaginal Realm

Before you begin, spend some time throughout your day just reflecting on what it is that you want to transmute or create in your life.

1. PROJECTION

When you go to bed, make yourself comfortable, lying on your back with your neck and body aligned, and eyes closed.

Place your right hand over your low belly, halfway between your navel and pubic bone, and your left hand on your heart. Breathe rhythmically and slowly. Allow your body to relax completely and lie perfectly still. As you relax more deeply, you should feel as though you're about to fall asleep, while maintaining your conscious awareness.

Focus on your third eye in the center of your forehead (your projector). Begin visualizing your desire, and create a scene in your mind's eye capturing what it would look and feel like if this desire were fully realized. Focus on the end result, and not the steps to get there.

Make it as real as you can, and visualize everything from the first person and as though it were happening right now. What would you do and how would you behave if this desire were manifested? What would you say? What would it feel like physically? Emotionally? Really allow it to become tangible, feeling the emotions of joy, relief, satisfaction, and gratitude, focusing on a few key details. Imagine a few different scenarios of things you would do if this were true. Remain conscious and focused throughout, lest you drift off into unconscious fantasy.

2. REST

Repeat the words "Thank you" to yourself, and from here you can drift off to sleep, resting in the love and joy in your heart and carrying it into your dreams.

3. ATTRACTION

During your waking hours, allow those feelings of love and gratitude to return to you. You can repeat your projection as many times as you desire. It may take some time for the unconscious mind to bring it into your conscious experience. Trust, and do not fret over the details or try to make it happen. Have faith and remain open and receptive in a state of confident, magnetic attraction.

If doubt arises, simply acknowledge it and then brush it aside, bring your attention to your heart and trust that if this desire is truly in alignment with your highest good, it will come to pass, because it has already been created through your powers of projection.

Do what you love and feel passionate about, and let the joy of the red tincture flow through your entire being. As they present themselves be open to opportunities that will guide you toward your goal.

NAVIGATING THE RUBEDO

The *rubedo* is a time of integration and structuring of ideas to bring them to perfection in the material world. The fruit is ripe, taking on the crystalline structures that allow it to hold that golden nectar of life within its framework, ready to be transmitted to the world. The possibilities for what this expression will look like are entirely up to the seed, and the health of the soil in which it is planted. But the work does not end with the fruit. Instead the fruit—which is Mastery of one's own art—carries the seed of a new world altogether.

On one level, the consummation of the *magnum opus* relates to the completion of a creative endeavor. At its deepest level it is the complete integration of heaven and earth within, a new relationship to reality and transfiguration of Self. It is nothing less than Self-realization, nothing more than the perception of what has always been there, a fructification whose beginnings lay in putrefaction. The fusion of solar and lunar illumination allows the artist to see with full clarity on all levels of being, conscious and unconscious, understanding their oneness with life and transmuting personal motivations toward the collective good. Divine truth is fully realized and emanates through their work, multiplying with greater influence in the outer world. With this comes the true wealth of life, found not in external forms, but in the quintessence of life itself.

While the creative process is inherently based on desire—the desire to express, reveal, discover, share, reflect, beautify, or otherwise contribute to the world or ideas, forms, and experiences—the Great Work purifies this desire and brings it into alignment with a higher order of creation, beyond egoic striving for recognition and glory to the desire for all sentient life to discover its inherent divinity. When this is the foundation of our work, there is nothing that can impede our desire, because everything that we do, great or small, arises from an authentic desire to be of service. With humility we recognize that sometimes we must relinquish control to forces beyond our control; this is balanced by gentle and persistent dedication to our goals and faith in our creative agency. We develop trust in the inherent value of our heart's deepest desire, the divine seed that must be nourished by the philosophical water until it sprouts into the material world. There is nothing selfish about true desire; it is transpersonal, existing within us as an æthereal blueprint for cosmic evolution. Our personal story is intimately connected to and reflected in the collective drama unfolding.

With this final stage, we have passed through the last of the twelve gates of the circle of animals—Aquarius and Pisces. A red dawn spreads over the horizon as we are resurrected from the flames like the phoenix, born anew as the crowned hermaphrodite, self-realized through the profound opening and purification of the first matter. Master of our own fate and no longer bound by time, our soul unfettered and imagination liberated, we are complete within ourselves, able to create from the interplay of opposing principles as they dance around the neutral field of our expansive, unlimited I-Am-Ness. No longer separate from the cosmos, we breathe with it, realizing the interpenetrating levels of reality coalescing within our bodies, forever fixed in the heart of the Sun.

CONCLUSION

Creatio Continua

Let us not mince words: the marvelous is always beautiful, anything marvelous is beautiful, in fact only the marvelous is beautiful.

—André Breton, *Manifesto of Surrealism* (1924)

The alchemists understood the union of the inner and outer worlds in a way that was lost to modern chemistry. With the Hermetic foundation beneath their laboratories they were involved not only in understanding the nature of metals and their transmutations, but the nature of consciousness itself. No amount of scientific inquiry can substitute for the personal experience of the Divine, for gnosis. This is not a regression to some lost archaic paradise, but a revelation and realization of what has always been true—namely, the coexistence of the real and imaginary, rational and irrational, masculine and feminine, above and below, inner and outer, science and art. We stand at the confluence of two mighty rivers converging in the human mind; our great work is to reunite them in a unified river of continual creativity in alignment with our highest spiritual ideals. Understanding the nature of our creative abilities and true power of the imagination is quintessential to integrating our collective shadow and co-creating a world of equality, abundance, sustainability, and imaginative freedom. This begins with understanding through personal experience the nature of the Self and the critical role that our thoughts, feelings, and unconscious desires play in shaping our lives.

Throughout this book I have attempted to reveal how the royal marriage of art and alchemy—creative alchemy—provides a path toward inner and outer reconciliation; how the union of conscious and unconscious within the creative process can lead to the discovery of the philosopher's stone, the true imagination, and marvelous powers of the One Thing. From the Romantic era through Surrealism and into the present, artists have recognized the pivotal role that art plays in the evolution of consciousness. In a sense the Romantic movement had the same quality as the beginning of the alchemical work, liberating the inner world from its fetters of austerity and assumed manners. It was a reaction against the collective suppression of the shadow for the sake of social cohesion, and the recognition that the inner passions must be given expression. Despite their subjugation, these irrational forces will find their way to the surface, and, if not properly understood and channeled, lead to social fragmentation and war. In the evolution of art through the nineteenth century, this process went deeper into a state of dissolution with the Symbolists, who went beyond the release of the irrational to a full immersion into the symbolic world. The step away from direct representation and reliance on thickly veiled meanings set the stage for the decomposition of meaning that emerged with Dada. While the Symbolists applied effort toward concealment, they were still heavily attached to aesthetic concerns; Dada relinquished control to the element of chance and threw out aestheticism in favor of absurdity. It was only with the Surrealists that the true union was sought between sense and nonsense, morality and personal freedom, conscious rationality and unconscious wisdom.

Within every individual there lies a vast storehouse of creative potential, waiting to be accessed. This energy, however, is too often tied up and misspent, or otherwise obscured from the Self by the deposition of familial and social conditioning. Time will do its work to erode the accrued sediment, eventually liberating the core, which remains solid and everlasting. Or we can take it upon ourselves to liberate that indestructible core of creative power, joining forces with time and quickening our own evolution. Creativity is our most potent gift, especially when integrated with spiritual awareness and brought into alignment with the creative impulse of the universe.

Great art is a union of both personal and universal truth, which together transmit the divine seed of consciousness. If the personal is lacking, art can feel detached and inauthentic; without the universal, it is insular and out of reach. Authentic expression, rooted in one's own personal gnosis, is developed through our willingness to delve into the unknown parts of ourselves. When approached creatively, the *magnum opus* facilitates the transmutation of the artist and their art, and in turn transforms the world. Art should, above all, have this transformative quality, along with being healing, revelatory, multivalent in its interpretation, subjective and objective, intuitive, inventive, surprising, and unashamed. However, it is not for the creation of art alone that we must concern ourselves with the royal marriage, for if it does not penetrate all levels of our being, then the union has not been fully consummated. Further, we are not simply initiating an enantiodromia of the conscious and unconscious, though this is part of the process; rather, we are merging the two together. Sometimes we are dissolving in the unknown, and sometimes we are pulling ourselves together—coagulating—into an integral state of being.

There is a part of us that is only accessible by allowing the conscious and unconscious minds to work in harmony, like lovers, two bodies and one experience, moving with the rhythms of breath, beating hearts, and *kundalini*. This is what happens inside us when we enter trance states; our actions become spontaneous and unexpected, as our unconscious awakens and speaks. Our body becomes an open channel for the birth of something new, surprising, and marvelous. The dance of the serpent draws us into the trance state—the mercurial, undulating movement between the opposing principles within us, a meandering river, the ouroboros whose end lies in its beginning, the dragon of the *prima materia* whose fiery breath engulfs us in the flames of transformation. Submersing ourselves in the Bacchanalian visions, we embark upon a temporary journey into divine madness, and emerge upon the unknown shore.

Through the fire and putrefaction that reduces our ego, through the dissolution and derangement of all the senses, we are humbled and opened up for a greater purpose. When one has a truly transformative experience, the natural result is a sense of humility, respect for the suffering of all life, and the deep abiding desire to be of service to others. Life has a way of leading us to the abyss when we are ready for it, though it is never easy. All we can do is recognize it and approach it with curiosity, using the gift of our creative powers to transmute the darkness into light. This work has taught me how to reach into the depths of my being and extract the raw ores, corrupted by the experiences of youth and inherited trauma, and bring them into the light of consciousness through the creative process. The work that I share with you is based on years of studying and experimenting in my own creative laboratory to understand the physiological mechanisms behind spiritual awakening, and how to transmute toxic energy through the creative process.

This book and the one before, *Hermetic Philosophy and Creative Alchemy,* were born from my own journey through the *magnum opus,* and integration of everything that I learned and experienced along the way. I endured a long dark night of the soul—the *nigredo*—and painful confrontation with my own shadow that left me shattered and fragile. After several years of putrefaction, light appeared on the horizon—the *albedo*— and I entered a period of dissolution into dreams, symbols, and myths, during which I dove deep into experimentation with automatic painting and writing, grounding into a practice of planetary magic. I gave the unconscious free reign to express itself in the alchemical laboratory of my studio, and I was surprised and fascinated by what emerged. The work digested, fermented, and coagulated over many years—the *citrinitas*—as I processed the unconscious material, illuminated the dark waters with conscious curiosity, and integrated what I found through personal ritual and major life changes. Through purifying and refining my own metals, I developed inner strength and resilience, and a deep abiding faith in the powers of the imagination. The completion of these books has been my *rubedo*. Through the process I've gone through all of the stages of transmutation many times as I integrated years of experience and translated it into material form, slowly refining and bringing the books to their final perfection. I learned how to project my consciousness outward to create in the imaginal realm. The completion of these books required the full intensity of my inner fire of attention and periods of Hermetic sequestration from the world. With their consummation, they have the potential to multiply in the outer world. My sincere desire is that whatever wisdom I may have attained in this process is projected through these pages, contributing in some small way to the collective good.

Though I can make this comparison of my creative process to the Great Work, it is not my intention to say that I have by any means reached the end. The *magnum opus* is a lifelong process, bringing us simultaneously deeper into the mysteries of the self and ever upward toward our highest spiritual realization. Yet once we've had a true initiation through all the stages and felt the power of true imagination, the philosopher's stone, we acquire an indissoluble strength and inner resilience to the fires of life. As we are all unique individuals, this work will be different for everyone and won't necessarily follow a linear trajectory. I encourage the reader not to take my word for it, but to trust your own process and experience it for yourself. Continue learning and studying. Reflect on your own elemental balance, and form your own personal relationship to the planets, metals, and energies of the chakras. Experiment with dreamwork, automatism, active imagination, and projecting from the imaginal realm. Read alchemical texts and make your own meaning. Step into the river of continual creation, the *creatio continua,* and allow these transformative processes to penetrate you in body, mind, and soul, giving them form and life through your creative expression.

APPENDIX A

Chakra Correspondence Charts

OVERVIEW OF PLANETARY AND ENERGETIC CORRESPONDENCES

PLANET	GLYPH	METAL	CHAKRA	COLOR	GLAND	ATTRIBUTE	ACTION	ELEMENT
Sun	☉	Gold	Crown *Sahasrara*	Purple	Pineal*	Consciousness	I know	N/A
Moon	☽	Silver	Third Eye *Ajna*	Indigo	Pituitary*	Perception	I see	N/A
Mercury	☿	Quicksilver	Throat *Vishuddhi*	Blue	Thyroid	Communication	I speak	Æther
Venus	♀	Copper	Heart *Anahata*	Green	Thymus	Compassion	I love	Air
Mars	♂	Iron	Solar Plexus *Manipura*	Yellow	Pancreas	Will	I will	Fire
Jupiter	♃	Tin	Sacral *Svadhisthana*	Orange	Ovaries/ Testes	Creation	I feel	Water
Saturn	♄	Lead	Root *Muladhara*	Red	Adrenal Glands	Survival	I have	Earth

*Sometimes the glands assigned to the Crown and Third Eye chakras are reversed, such that the pineal is assigned to the Third Eye and the pituitary to the Crown. Since it is the union of the Sun and Moon that we are concerned with in alchemy, we understand that both of these glands relate to both of these chakras in different ways.

INDIVIDUAL CHAKRA CHARTS

ROOT CHAKRA

Element	Earth
Planet	Saturn
Name & Meaning	Muladhara: "root," "foundation"
Location	Base of Spine / Perineum (between genitals and anus)
Sense	Smell
Color	Red
Symbol	Square with inverted triangle in the center, in a circle with four petals
Emotions/Qualities	Courage, Trust, Safety, Groundedness, Power, Belonging, Discipline, Determination, Healthy Boundaries, Timeliness, Resilience, Confidence
Signs of Imbalance	Fear, Insecure, Unstable, Materialistic, Survival Mode, "Anal Retentive," Rigid, Serious, Dull, Stubborn, Stress, Panic, Anxiety, Financial Issues, Tension, Dissociation, Ungrounded/Spacey, Insomnia
Body Parts	Skeletal System, Sexual Organs, Excretory System, Coccyx
Glands	Adrenal Glands
Energetic Function	Physical Manifestation, Grounding, Stability
Physical Function	Survival, Elimination (of solid waste)
Physical Issues	IBS, Celiac, Diarrhea, Constipation, Gas, Fibroids, Tumors, STDs, Vaginal Infections, Prostate Problems, Over/Underweight, Rectal Issues, Nervous System Disorders, Skin Issues, Leaky Gut, Hereditary Illnesses, Sexual Trauma, Adrenal Fatigue, Sciatica, Burnout, Knee Problems, Bone Disorders
Goals	Security, Groundedness, Physical Well-Being, Right Livelihood, Stability, Healthy Boundaries
Right	"I have"
Art	Sculpture
Metal	Lead

ROOT CHAKRA (*continued*)

Alchemy	*Nigredo:* Shadow Work, Underworld Journey; Salt; Putrefaction; Coagulation (earth); *Prima Materia*
Stones	Garnet, Red Carnelian, Red Jasper, Red Calcite, Bloodstone, Red Coral, Hematite, Lodestone, Onyx, Jet, Black Kyanite, Black Tourmaline, Shungite
Animals	Earth Animals: Bull/Bison, Elephant, Tortoise, Ox, Hippo, Rhino, Mole, Earthworms, Snake; Saturnian Animals: Wolf, Raven, Dragon, Crocodile
Archetypes	Earth Deities, Saturnian Deities, Death
Astrology (Earth Triad)	Taurus (+): neck Virgo (Ø): bowels Capricorn (-): knees and calves
Polarity	*Yang:* Active
Auric Layer	Ætheric Body

SACRAL CHAKRA

Element	Water
Planet	Jupiter
Name & Meaning	*Svadhisthana:* "one's own abode"
Location	Low belly, about three finger-widths below navel
Sense	Taste
Color	Orange
Symbol	Crescent moon in a circle with six petals
Emotions/Qualities	Pleasure, Joy, Expansiveness, Gratitude, Self-Acceptance, Healthy Relationships, Openness
Signs of Imbalance	Depressed, Addictions, Negative, Guilt, Possessive, Lazy, Lust, Unconscious/Repressed Emotions, Joyless, No Boundaries, Creative Blocks, Toxic/Addictive/Codependent Relationships, Antisocial, Avoidant, People-Pleasing, Mania, Mood Lability, Hedonism, OCD

SACRAL CHAKRA (*continued*)

Body Parts	Reproductive Organs, Urinary System, Bodily Fluids (blood, tears, semen, lymph, tears, craniosacral fluid), Sacrum, Lumbar Vertebrae
Glands	Ovaries, Prostate
Energetic Functions	Creativity, Attraction of Opposites
Physical Functions	Elimination, Lymphatic Flow, Detoxification, Reproduction
Physical Issues	Sexual Dysfunction, Lower-Back Pain, Ovarian Cysts, PMS, UTIs or Incontinence, Reproductive Issues, Pelvic Issues, Edema, Dehydration
Goals	Creative Flow, Pleasure, Healthy Relationships and Connection
Right	"I feel"
Art	Writing
Metal	Tin
Alchemy	*Albedo:* Purification and Connection to the Feminine, Dreams, Unconscious Dissolution (Cancer), Putrefaction/Separation (Scorpio), Projection (Pisces)
Stones	Orange Carnelian, Orange Calcite, Moonstone, Aragonite, Goldstone, Red Coral, Beryl, Aquamarine, Quartz, Gold Calcite
Animals	Water Animals: Fish, Crustaceans, Whale, Dolphin, Shark; Swan, Snakes, Turtles, Scorpion, Dove, Heron, Eagle; Jupiterian Animals: Swan, Cuckoo, Unicorn, Lion, Bull, Wolf, Woodpecker, Eagle, Quail, Elephant, Whale, Rhinoceros
Archetypes	Water Deities, Jupiterian Deities, Creator Gods and Goddesses, the Moon
Astrology (Water Triad)	Cancer (+): breast Scorpio (Ø): reproductive organs Pisces (-): feet
Polarity	*Yin:* Receptive
Auric Layer	Emotional Body (lower)

SOLAR PLEXUS

Element	Fire
Planet	Mars
Name & Meaning	*Manipura:* "lustrous gem"
Location	Diaphragm, about three finger-widths above navel
Sense	Sight
Color	Yellow
Symbol	Downward-facing triangle in circle with ten petals
Emotions/Qualities	Passion, Assertiveness, Ambition, Laughter, Joy, Warmth, Vitality, Energy, Focus, Activity, Clear Thinking
Signs of Imbalance	Anger, Rage, Aggression, Control/Power Issues, Arrogance, Resentment, Blame, Narcissism, Stimulant Use, Depressed, Apathy, Fatigue, Cloudy Thinking, Lack of Focus, Timidity, Submissiveness
Body Parts	Upper Digestive Organs (stomach, gallbladder, liver), Muscular System, Blood/Circulation
Glands	Pancreas, Spleen
Energetic Functions	Transformation, Processing Energy, Willpower, Personal Empowerment, Protection
Physical Functions	Digestion, Mental Acuity, Vision, Stamina, Metabolism, Circulation, Vitality
Physical Issues	Inflammation, Digestive Disorders, Ulcers, GERD, Liver Disease, Pancreatic Disorders, Gallbladder Congestion, Gallstones, Anemia, ADHD, Hypochlorhydria
Goals	Strength, Personal Will, Sovereignty, Independence, Responsibility, Self-Confidence, Self-Esteem, Self-Worth, Discrimination, Masculinity, Purpose, Drive, Aligning Personal Will with Divine Will
Right	"I will"
Art	Visual Arts
Metal	Iron
Alchemy	*Citrinitas:* Activated Imagination, Calcination, Separation (Putrefaction), Digestion, Fermentation, Coagulation

SOLAR PLEXUS (*continued*)

Stones	Yellow Calcite, Topaz, Amber, Jasper, Citrine, Yellow Sapphire, Tiger's Eye, Ruby, Fire Opal, Diamonds, any yellow or red stones
Animals	Fire Animals: Phoenix, Salamander, Lion, Stork, Dragon; Mars Animals: Horse, Wolf, Bear, Boar, Ram, Scorpion, Jaguar, Lion, Hawk, Sparrow, Cock, Magpie, Woodpecker
Archetypes	Warrior, Fire Deities
Astrology (Fire Triad)	Aries (+): head Leo (Ø): solar plexus Sagittarius (-): thighs
Polarity	*Yang*: Active
Auric Layer	Third layer, Mental Body (lower)

HEART CHAKRA

Element	Air
Planet	Venus
Name & Meaning	*Anahata*: "unstruck, unbeaten"
Location	Center of chest
Sense	Touch
Color	Green
Symbol	Interlaced triangles—six-pointed star—in a circle with twelve petals
Emotions/Qualities	Compassion, Unconditional Love, Tranquility, Trust, Self-Worth, Forgiveness, Contentment, Joy, Harmony, Balance
Signs of Imbalance	Jealousy, Greed, Anxiety, Nervousness, Lacking Empathy, Narcissism, Selfishness, Fear of Touch, Joyless, Boredom, Lack of Trust, Keeping Others at Arm's Length, Isolation, Melancholy, Overwhelm, Sentimental, Feeling Burdened
Body Parts	Heart, Lungs, Chest, Ribs, Breasts, Shoulders, Arms, Hands, Circulatory System, Bronchial Tubes, Thymus Gland, Thoracic Vertebrae
Glands	Thymus

HEART CHAKRA (continued)

Energetic Functions	Circulation of *Prana/Spirit/Chi*; Bodily Rhythms
Physical Functions	Heartbeat, Circulation, Breath
Physical Issues	Heart Trouble, Poor Circulation, Blood Pressure Issues, Asthma, Lung Disorders, Bronchitis, Pneumonia, Anemia
Goals	Prosperity, Abundance, Sensuality, Love (as state of being), Physicality, Embodiment, Openness, Sovereign Heart, Self-Acceptance
Right	"I love"
Art	Dance
Metal	Copper
Alchemy	*Rubedo:* Union of opposites and realization of divine love, Fixation, Coagulation, Conjunction
Stones	Aventurine, Emerald, Turquoise, Chrysoprase, Green Calcite, Jade, Zoisite with Ruby, Rose Quartz, Malachite, Rhodochrosite, Pink Kyanite, Pink Calcite, Chalcedony, Topaz, Kunzite, Green Tourmaline, Peridot
Animals	Dove, Peacock, Eagle, Raven, Hawk, Owl, Swan, Sparrow, Kite, Turtledove, Nightingale, Pheasant, Goat, Sow, Antelope
Archetypes	The Lovers, Love Deities, Air/Wind Deities
Astrology (Air Triad)	Gemini (+): shoulders Libra (Ø): kidneys Aquarius (-): ankles
Polarity	*Yin:* Receptive
Auric Layer	Fourth Layer, Astral Body

THROAT CHAKRA

Element	Æther/Quintessence
Planet	Mercury
Name & Meaning	*Vishuddhi:* "purity"
Location	Throat, Larynx
Sense	Sound/Hearing
Color	Bright blue

THROAT CHAKRA (*continued*)

Symbol	Downward-facing triangle with a circle within it, seated within a circle with sixteen petals
Emotions/Qualities	Bliss, Self-Confidence, Clear Communication, Peace
Signs of Imbalance	Grief, Longing, Self-Righteousness, Difficulty Communicating, Arrogance, Self-Pity, Low Self-Esteem, Anxiety, Impulsivity, Restlessness, Ambivalence/Indecisiveness, Not Having a Voice
Body Parts	Neck, Throat, Vocal Cords, Ears, Mouth, Cerebrospinal Fluid (CSF), Cervical Vertebrae, Nervous System
Glands	Thyroid
Energetic Functions	Filtering Psychic Energies between Above and Below, Psychic Communication, Mediumism, Channeling, Automatism
Physical Functions	Hearing, Speaking, Breath, Balance, CSF Flow, Nerve Transmission
Physical Issues	Throat Congestion, Neck and Shoulder Pain/ Tension, TMJ, Thyroid Disorders, Tonsillitis, Tinnitus, Vertigo
Goals	Authenticity, Inspiration, Communication, Stillness, Ability to Listen and Receive, Wisdom, Truth, Alignment with Divine Will, Creative Expression, Spiritual Connection
Right	"I speak"
Art	Music
Metal	Mercury/Quicksilver
Alchemy	*Rubedo*: Fixation, Distillation
Stones	Sapphire, Aquamarine, Larimar, Angel Stone, Chalcedony, Turquoise, Celestite, Cavansite, Blue Kunzite, Opal, Blue Lace Agate
Animals	Snake, Elephant, Bull, Ape, Wolf, Ibis, Dragon
Archetypes	Magician and Messenger Deities, Tricksters, the Virgin
Astrology	Gemini (+) and Virgo (-) (Ruled by Mercury)
Polarity	*Yang* and *Yin*: Active and Receptive
Auric Layer	Fifth Layer, Ætheric Template (physical aspect)

THIRD EYE

Element	N/A
Planet	Moon
Name & Meaning	*Ajna:* "command," "perceive"
Location	Center of forehead
Sense	Sixth Sense, Mind
Color	Indigo (also White, Silver)
Symbol	Downward-facing triangle in circle with two petals
Emotions/Qualities	Peace of Mind, Tranquility, Clairvoyance, Imagination, Intuition, Wisdom, Idealism
Signs of Imbalance	Unconscious Emotions, Hallucinations, Lunacy, Unconscious Projections, Lack of Vision/ Inspiration, Nightmares
Body Parts	Brain, Endocrine System, Nervous System, Sinuses
Glands	Pituitary
Energetic Functions	Psychic Vision, Projection of Inner Vision, Psychic and Energetic Discernment, Intuition, Enlightenment
Physical Functions	Regulating Hormonal and Endocrine Function, Homeostasis
Physical Issues	Glandular and Endocrine Disorders, Hormonal Imbalance, Headaches, Vision Problems
Goals	Liberated Imagination, Dreams, Manifesting Dreams into Reality, Transcendent Vision, Nonduality
Right	"I see"
Art	Trance, Visionary Art
Metal	Silver
Alchemy	*Albedo* (Moon): Conjunction, *Hieros Gamos,* Lunar Hermaphrodite, the White Stone, Projection
Stones	Azurite, Calcite, Moonstone, Lapis Lazuli, Sodalite, Ulexite, Quartz, Pearl, Chalcedony, Howlite, Labradorite, Blue Apatite
Animals	Rabbit, Toad, Unicorn, Owl, Cat, Dog, Wolf, Butterfly, Moth, Camel, Frog, Baboon, Crab, Bat, Otter, Sow
Archetypes	The Hermit, Lunar Deities, Mother Goddesses

THIRD EYE (*continued*)

Astrology	Cancer (Ruled by the Moon)
Polarity	*Yang* and *Yin*: Union
Auric Layer	Sixth Layer, Celestial Body (Emotional)

CROWN CHAKRA

Element	N/A
Planet	Sun
Name & Meaning	*Sahasrara*: "thousand-petaled," "infinite"
Location	Top of head
Sense	Higher knowing
Color	Violet, White (all colors)
Symbol	Thousand-petaled lotus
Emotions/Qualities	Unity, Consciousness, Integration, Gratitude, Perfection, Divine Wisdom, Truth, Enlightenment, Bliss, Acceptance, Selflessness, Presence
Signs of Imbalance	Disconnected, Alienated, Depressed, Learning Disabilities, Confusion, Dissociation, Lack of Purpose or Meaning, Lack of Understanding, Inability to Focus, Schizophrenic, Fear of Death, Joyless, Suicidal, Materialistic, Neurosis/Psychosis
Body Parts	Pineal Gland, Cerebral Cortex, Central Nervous System
Glands	Pineal
Energetic Functions	Connection with Source, God-Knowing
Physical Functions	Production of Melatonin, Circadian Rhythm, Vision, Hormonal Balance, Homeostasis
Physical issues	Nervous System Disorders, Cancer, Bone Disorders, Autoimmune Disease, Hormone Imbalances, Low Vitality, Brain Disorders, Immune System Disorders, Calcification of the Pineal Gland, Mental Disorders, Headaches, Dizziness
Goals	Liberation, Enlightenment, Gnosis, Unity, Cosmic Consciousness

CROWN CHAKRA (*continued*)

Right	"I know"
Art	Co-creating with the Universe
Metal	Gold
Alchemy	*Rubedo:* Generation of the Philosopher's Stone, Completion of the Great Work, Multiplication and Projection, Crowned Hermaphrodite
Stones	Goldstone, Clear Quartz, Amethyst, Lepidolite, Alexandrite, Diamond, Selenite
Animals	Lion, Eagle, Elephant, Ox, Bull
Archetypes	The Universe, Buddha, Father, Sun Deities, Dying and Rising Gods
Astrology	Leo (Ruled by the Sun)
Polarity	*Yang* and *Yin*: Union
Auric Layer	Seventh Layer, Ketheric Body (higher mental aspect)

APPENDIX B

Planetary Correspondences

METALS AND MINERALS

PLANETS	METALS AND MINERALS
Sun	Gold; Carbuncle, Chrysolite, Goldstone, Pyrite, Sunstone, Tiger's Eye
Moon	Silver; Chalcedony, Crystal, Labradorite, Moonstone, Pearl, Selenite, Ulexite
Mercury	Mercury/Quicksilver; Agate, Alexandrite, Aquamarine, Cavansite, Celestite, Fluorite, Labradorite, Larimar, Opal
Venus	Copper; Aventurine, Chrysocolla, Emerald, Jade, Malachite, Moldavite, Pearl, Peridot, Rose Quartz, Ruby with Zoisite, Green Tourmaline, Turquoise
Mars	Iron; Aragonite, Bloodstone, Coral, Diamond, Fire Opal, Garnet, Red Carnelian, Red Jasper, Lodestone, Magnetite, Ruby
Jupiter	Tin; Amethyst, Diamond, Lapis Lazuli, Sapphire, Sodalite
Saturn	Lead; Black Kyanite, Black Tourmaline, Bloodstone, Hematite, Jet, Lodestone, Obsidian, Onyx, Shungite

PLANTS

PLANETS	PLANTS
Sun	Angelica, Balsam, Barley, Buttercup, Cabbage, Calamus, Cardamom, Cedar, Celandine, Chamomile, Chrysanthemum, Cinnamon, Clove, Corn, Gentian, Elecampane, Eyebright, Frankincense, Heliotrope, Juniper, Laurel, Lavender, Lemon Balm, Lotus, Marigold, Marjoram, Orange, Palm, Passionflower, Peony, Plantain, Rosemary, Rue, Saffron, Sandalwood, Sage, St. John's Wort, Sundew, Sunflower, Tansy, Thyme, Walnut
Moon	Acanthus, Adder's Tongue, Camphor, Chickweed, Clary Sage, Cleavers, Crabapple, Cucumber, Daisy, Hazel, Hyssop, Iris, Lettuce, Linden Tree, Mandrake, Melon, Moonwort, Mugwort, Mushrooms, Myrtle, Nutmeg, Opium Poppy, Pumpkin, Purslane, Reed, Sassafras, Tamaris, Turmeric, Watercress, Waterlily, Wallflower, White Lily, Willow
Mercury	Acacia, Aniseed, Beet, Bryony, Carrot, Caraway, Celery, Chamomile, Chicory, Cinquefoil, Clover, Dill, Elder, Elecampane, Endive, Fenugreek, Flax, Foxglove, Hazelnut, Honeysuckle, Horehound, Juniper, Lavender, Lily, Licorice, Marjoram, Mercury, Millet, Myrtle, Oats, Oregano, Palm, Parsley, Parsnip, Savory, Sarsaparilla, Sorrel, Valerian, Vervain, Wormwood, Yarrow
Venus	Almond, Birch, Blackberry, Boneset, Buckthorn, Burdock, Cassia, Catnip, Celandine, Clover, Columbine, Coltsfoot, Daisy, Elder, Eringo, Feverfew, Figwort, Forget-me-not, Foxglove, Goldenrod, Hawthorn, Honeysuckle, Hyacinth, Lemon, Lily, Marshmallow, Medlar, Mint, Motherwort, Mugwort, Myrtle, Pansy, Pennyroyal, Plantain, Periwinkle, Poppy, Purslane, Primrose, Rose, Strawberry, Verbena, Yarrow
Mars	Agaric, All-heal, Aloe, Artichoke, Asparagus, Barberry, Basil, Bean, Belladonna, Burdock, Catnip, Cayenne, Garlic, Gentian, Hawthorn, Hemp, Hops, Horseradish, Mint, Mustard, Nettle, Onion, Pepper, Radish, Rhubarb, Rue, Thistle, Tobacco, Wormwood
Jupiter	Agrimony, Aloe, Amaranth, Arnica, Ash, Bay Laurel, Bilberry, Borage, Cedar, Chervil, Cherry, Cinquefoil, Comfrey, Daisy, Dandelion, Dock, Endive, Fig, Flax, Jasmine, Jimsonweed, Juniper, Houseleek, Hyssop, Lemon Balm, Melilot, Melissa, Mistletoe, Mulberry, Myrrh, Oak, Oats, Olive, Oregano, Plum, Poplar, Quince, Rose, Sage, Sesame, Strawberry, Violet, Wood Betony, Yellow Dock
Saturn	Amaranth, Angelica, Ash, Barley, Beet, Black Elder, Black Fig, Blackthorn, Box, Buckthorn, Cactus, Cocoa, Comfrey, Corn, Cornflower, Cumin, Cypress, Datura, Elm, Fennel, Fenugreek, Fern (male), Flax, Hellebore, Hemlock, Hemp, Holly, Horsetail, Ivy, Lichen, Lungwort, Mandrake, Moss, Mullein, Nightshade, Opium Poppy, Parietary, Quince, Rue, Saxifrage, Serpentine, Shepherd's Purse, Soapwort, Solomon's Seal, Spurge, Tobacco, Weeping Willow, Wintergreen, Woad, Yew

ANIMALS

PLANETS	ANIMALS
Sun	Lion, Cock, Eagle, Falcon, Phoenix, Salamander, Sparrowhawk, Swan, Tiger, Wolf
Moon	Rabbit, Toad, Dog, Wolf, Cat, Unicorn, Bat, Owl, Goose, Cow, Camel, Crab, Bull
Mercury	Ibis, Ape, Coyote, Dog, Dragon, Fish, Fox, Jackal, Mullet, Weasel, Snake, Stork
Venus	Dove, Peacock, Swan, Sparrow, Fish, Goat, Kite, Turtledove, Nightingale, Pheasant, Dolphin
Mars	Boar, Dragon, Cock, Bear, Horse, Jaguar, Hawk, Ram, Scorpion, Magpie, Woodpecker, Phoenix, Pike, Salamander
Jupiter	Swan, Cuckoo, Eagle, Bull, Dolphin, Goose, Unicorn, Lion, Elephant, Rhinoceros, Fox, Cock
Saturn	Bat, Crane, Crocodile, Alligator, Crow, Cuttlefish, Goat, Goose, Lapwing, Mole, Owl, Oyster, Raven, Reptiles, Snake, Toad, Vulture, Wolf

PERFUMES AND INCENSE

PLANETS	PERFUMES / INCENSE
Sun	Amber, Cinnamon, Golden Copal, Frankincense, Lavender, Olibanum
Moon	Aloes, Camphor, Black Copal, Jasmine, Myrrh
Mercury	Frankincense, Mace, Mastic, Myrrh, Nutmeg, Clary Sage, Storax, White Sandal
Venus	Myrtle, Musk, Oak Moss, Patchouli, Rose, Sandalwood
Mars	Cape Aloes, Dragon's Blood, Pepper, Red Sandal
Jupiter	Ammonicacum, Ash, Balm of Gilead, Cedar, Golden Copal, Mace, Saffron
Saturn	Assafoetida, Indigo, Opium, Scammony, Styrax, Sulfur

TREE OF LIFE

PLANETS	TREE OF LIFE
Sun	Tiphareth: "Beauty"
Moon	Yesod: "Foundation"
Mercury	Hod: "Splendor"
Venus	Netzach: "Victory"
Mars	Geburah: "Strength"
Jupiter	Chesed: "Mercy"
Saturn	Binah: "Understanding"

TAROT

PLANETS	TAROT
Sun	XIX, The Sun; 4 of Disks (Power), 8 of Disks (Prudence), 10 of Swords (Ruin), 6 of Cups (Pleasure), 6 of Wands (Victory)
Moon	II, The High Priestess; 6 of Disks (Success), 2 of Swords (Peace), 7 of Swords (Futility), 4 of Cups (Luxury), 9 of Wands (Strength)
Mercury	I, The Magus; 5 of Disks (Worry), 10 of Disks (Wealth), 6 of Swords (Science), 3 of Cups (Abundance), 8 of Wands (Swiftness)
Venus	III, The Empress; 9 of Disks (Gain), 5 of Swords (Defeat), 2 of Cups (Love), 7 of Cups (Debauch), 4 of Wands (Completion)
Mars	XVI, The Tower; 3 of Disks (Work), 9 of Swords (Cruelty), 5 of Cups (Disappointment), 10 of Cups (Satiety), 2 of Wands (Dominion), 7 of Wands (Valour)
Jupiter	X, Wheel of Fortune; 2 of Disks (Change), 4 of Swords (Truce), 8 of Swords (Interference), 9 of Cups (Happiness), 6 of Wands (Victory)
Saturn	XXI, The Universe; 7 of Disks (Failure), 3 of Swords (Sorrow), 8 of Cups (Indolence), 5 of Wands (Strife), 10 of Wands (Oppression)

MAGICAL WEAPONS

PLANETS	MAGICAL WEAPONS
Sun	Bow and Arrow, Lamen
Moon	Bow and Arrow
Mercury	Wand or Caduceus, Lamp
Venus	Girdle
Mars	Sword, Dagger
Jupiter	Scepter, Lightning Bolt
Saturn	Sickle

DEITIES

PLANETS	A SELECTION OF DEITIES
Sun	Sol, Helios, Apollo, Aurora, Dionysus, Ra, Khepri, Atum, Aten, Osiris, Sekhmet, Shamash, Surya, Buddha
Moon	Luna, Selene/Endymion, Artemis, Diana, Hecate, Thoth, Osiris, Khonsu, Isis, Hathor, Bast, Iah, Sin/Nanna, Loki, Soma/Chandra
Mercury	Mercury, Hermes, Thoth, Odin, Enki, Hanuman, Sarasvati, Maya, Vishnu
Venus	Venus, Aphrodite, Ishtar, Inanna, Freyja, Anuket, Hathor, Quan Yin
Mars	Mars, Ares, Vulcan, Adonis, Prometheus, Horus, Maahes, Set, Reshpu, Nergal, Freyja, Kartikeya, Agni, Angaraka, Lohit
Jupiter	Jupiter, Zeus, Amun, Marduk, Bel, Ea/Enki, Enlil, Indra, Dagda, Thor, Sabaoth
Saturn	Saturn, Kronos, Cronus, Typhon, Set, Sebek, Apophis, Ninurta, Yaldabaoth

COLORS

PLANET	COLORS
Sun	Gold, Yellow, Violet, White
Moon	Silver, White, Indigo
Mercury	Blue, Purple, Orange, Multicolor
Venus	Green, Pink, Red, White
Mars	Yellow, Red
Jupiter	Orange, Royal Blue, Purple
Saturn	Black, Red, Brown

APPENDIX C
Elemental Meditation

Sit in a relaxed position and breathe slowly and rhythmically. Turn your attention inward and imagine that you are descending deep into the earth, into a cavernous darkness. In this place nothing is distinguishable in the darkness, but you can feel there is something here. This is your prima materia, *the primal matter, the first Mother and Source of all creative potential.*

Now imagine that you are gathering this prima materia *together in your hands. You place it into an alchemical vessel and seal the top of the vessel tightly so that nothing can escape.*

Place the vessel over a gentle flame, and slowly observe as the elements begin to emerge from the mass of undifferentiated dark matter. You begin to see them separate into Earth, Water, Fire, and Air.

Observe each of these and take note of their compositions.

Observe the Earth element. What is its general composition as it appears in your imagination? Is it hard or soft? Flexible or rigid? Dry or muddy?

Consider your physical body, your daily routines, your material possessions, your home, sense of stability and groundedness, fears, anxieties, environment, and physical boundaries.

Observe the Water element. What is its general composition? Is it flowing or contained? Deep or shallow? Clear or turbid? Frozen or liquid or gas?

Consider your emotional well-being, relationships, attachments, addictions, creativity, sexuality, dreams, emotional boundaries, fluidity of your experience, hydration, and connection to your unconscious.

Observe the Fire element. What is its general composition? Is it a bright conflagration, a focused candle flame, or just a smoldering ember? What is feeding your fire?

Consider your relationship to power, willpower, confidence level, expression of emotions, digestive health, activity/energy levels, ability to process information and emotions, circulation and heat in the body, vision, motivation, self-image, imagination, inspirations, and intuition.

Observe the Air element. What is its general composition? Is it stagnant or free flowing? Is it clear or cloudy?

Consider your thoughts—are they racing and troubled, or clear and calm? Consider your breath, the relationship between your thoughts and emotions, your ability to sit still, sense of calm or distress, lightness of the body vs. heaviness, ungrounded tendencies, spaciness, clarity, compassion, issues of the heart, and desires.

Choose one of these elements that you feel needs balancing. Keeping the fire of attention upon your vessel, you begin to see the elements separating. Everything except your chosen element dissipates. This is now the element that you will hold within your vessel, keeping it in your awareness as you go about your day.

Whatever is out of balance in this element is now the object of your meditation. Think of it when you wake, and when you go to sleep. Let the fire of your attention remain upon it with a gentle, consistent heat. In everything that you do, ask yourself how this element is expressing itself and in what ways you might help it to find its more ennobled, balanced expression. Explore this element through your creative process.

Spend at least a week with one element, and journal about your experience and insights. Make changes in your life that reflect your new understanding of this element.

Repeat the meditation and choose another element to work with. Come back to this exercise anytime you feel that your elements need attention and balancing.

Notes

INTRODUCTION: *IMAGINATIO VERA*

1. Arp, *Arp on Arp,* 387.
2. Hermes Trismegistus, "The Emerald Tablet of Hermes," available at Sacred-Texts (website), accessed August 27, 2022.
3. Rulandus, *Lexicon,* s.v. "Imaginatio."
4. Waite, *Writings of Paracelsus,* 1:116.
5. Waite, *Writings of Paracelsus,* 1:122–23, 1:173–74, 2:120–21.
6. Pagel, *Paracelsus,* 121.
7. Waite, *Writings of Paracelsus,* 2:7.
8. Paracelsus, *Archidoxes,* 60–63.
9. Lévi, *Dogma et Rituel,* 1:6.
10. Lao Tzu, *Tao Te Ching,* 94.
11. Goddard, "Order: Then Wait," 1.
12. Goddard, "Order: Then Wait," 3.
13. Lewis, *The Problem of Pain,* 90.
14. Mallasz, *Talking with Angels,* 25.
15. Mallasz, *Talking with Angels,* 36.
16. Sendivogius, "The New Chemical," 142.
17. Hartmann, *Life of Philippus,* 232.
18. Waite, *Hermetic Museum,* 1:9.
19. Hermes Trismegistus, "The Emerald Tablet of Hermes," available at Sacred-Texts (website), accessed August 27, 2022.
20. Morienus, *Book of Morienus.*
21. Jung, *Aion,* 164, 169.
22. Jung, *Aion,* 169.
23. von Franz, *Corpus Alchemicum,* 16.
24. Bargh and Morsella, "The Unconscious Mind."
25. Bargh and Morsella, "The Unconscious Mind."

26. Spare, *Automatic Drawing,* 19.

27. von Franz, *Corpus Alchemicum,* 16; Jung, "Confrontation," 170–99; Jung, *Psychology and Alchemy;* von Franz, *Alchemical Active Imagination.*

28. Copenhaver, *Hermetica* (V.1), 18.

29. Pagel, *Paracelsus,* 113.

30. Delville, *New Mission,* 32–33.

31. Marcel Duchamp, interview by George Heard Hamilton, *Third Programme,* BBC Radio, January 19, 1959. Available at The Art Newspaper (website), January 31, 1992. Accessed August 28, 2022.

I. ROMANTICISM: IRRATIONAL FREEDOM

1. Baudelaire, *Mirror of Art,* 43.

2. Baudelaire, *Mirror of Art,* 44.

3. Honour, *Romanticism,* 245.

4. Russell, *A History,* 681.

5. Honour, *Romanticism,* 12.

6. Keats, *Complete Poetical Works,* 16.

7. Twitchell, "Romanticism," 292.

8. Wordsworth, *The Poems,* 449.

9. Twitchell, "Romanticism," 306.

10. Twitchell, "Romanticism," 290.

11. Wordsworth, *The Poems,* 160.

12. Sendivogius, "New Chemical Light," 105–6.

13. Waite, *Writings of Paracelsus,* 1:289.

14. Waite, *Writings of Paracelsus,* 1:289.

15. Hartmann, *Life of Philippus,* 51.

16. Percy Shelley, *Complete Poetical Works,* 16–17.

17. Kathryn Calley Galitz, "Romanticism," *Heilbrunn Timeline of Art History,* Metropolitan Museum of Art (website), October 2004. Accessed August 29, 2022.

18. Delacroix, *Journal,* 39.

19. Mary Shelley, *Frankenstein.*

20. Mary Shelley, *Frankenstein,* 183.

21. Choucha, *Surrealism,* 8.

22. Stephenson, "Introduction," 19.

23. Noelle Paulson, "Henry Fuseli, *The Nightmare,*" Smarthistory (website), August 9, 2015.

24. Baudelaire, *Mirror of Art,* xiii.

25. Delacroix, *Journal,* xx.

26. Delacroix, *Journal,* 6.

27. Baudelaire, *Mirror of Art,* 234–37.

28. Baudelaire, *Mirror of Art,* 234–37.

29. Hanegraaff, "Romanticism," 259.

30. Keats, *Complete Poetical Works,* 277.

31. Blake, *The Portable Blake,* 179.

32. Blake, *Complete Poetry and Prose,* 132.

33. Honour, *Romanticism,* 17–18.

34. Wilson, *Axel's Castle,* 5–6.

35. Baudelaire, *Mirror of Art,* 198.

36. Choucha, *Surrealism,* 8.

37. Goodrick-Clarke, *Western Esoteric,* 173–91.

38. Goodrick-Clarke, *Western Esoteric,* 169.

39. Swedenborg, *Heaven and Its Wonders and Hell,* 72.

40. Swedenborg, *Secrets of Heaven,* 2:188.

41. Blake, *Portable Blake,* 49; Lepetit, *Esoteric Secrets of Surrealism,* 353–54.

42. Blake, *Complete Poetry and Prose,* 42–43.

43. Balakian, *The Symbolist Movement,* 12.

44. Coleridge, *Biographia,* 172.

45. Coleridge, *Biographia,* 97, 180.

46. Nerval, *Selected Writings,* 374.

47. Wilson, *Axel's Castle,* 11–12.

2. SYMBOLISM: DARK DREAMS
AND IDEALS OF THE OTHER WORLD

1. Baudelaire, *Mirror of Art,* 195; Baudelaire, "Correspondances."

2. Balakian, *The Symbolist Movement,* 36.

3. Baudelaire, *Prose and Poetry,* 211.

4. Balakian, *The Symbolist Movement,* 37.

5. Balakian, *The Symbolist Movement,* 27–28.

6. Gibson, *Symbolism,* 20–21.

7. Wilson, *Axel's Castle,* 6–7.

8. Gibson, *Symbolism,* 20.

9. Rimbaud, *Complete Works,* 102, 104.

10. Gascoyne, *A Short Survey,* 7.

11. Choucha, *Surrealism,* 11.

12. Balakian, *The Symbolist Movement,* 54–71.

13. Balakian, *The Symbolist Movement,* 67.

14. Verlaine, *Selected Poems.*

15. Wilson, *Axel's Castle,* 20.

16. Chisholm, "Mallarmé and the Act of Creation," 111.

17. Mallarmé, "Magie," in *Divagations,* 264.

18. Chisholm, *Mallarmé's Grand Œuvre,* 2.

19. Mallarmé, "Magic," in *Divagations,* 264.

20. Raymond, *From Baudelaire,* 38.

21. Chisholm, "Mallarmé and the Act of Creation," 113–14.

22. Huysmans, *Against Nature,* 27.

23. Mallarmé, "Crisis of Verse," in *Divagations,* 201.

24. Mallarmé, "Crisis of Verse," in *Divagations,* 208.

25. Mallarmé, *Collected Poems,* 53–55.

26. Huysmans, *Against Nature,* 63.

27. Huysmans, *Against Nature,* 74.

28. Huysmans, *Against Nature,* 69.

29. Huysmans, *Against Nature,* 58.

30. Lévi, *Dogma et Rituel,* 1:6.

31. Baudelaire, *Mirror of Art,* 234–35.

32. Baudelaire, *Mirror of Art,* 198.

33. Huysmans, *Against Nature,* 35–36.

34. Schuré, *The Great Initiates,* 45–46.

35. Schuré, *The Great Initiates,* 46.

36. Lahelma, "The Symbolist Aesthetic," 38.

37. Delacroix, *Journal,* 34–35.

38. Baudelaire, "Alchimie de la douleur."

39. Rimbaud, *Complete Works,* 204.

40. Rimbaud, *Complete Works,* 204.

41. Balakian, *The Symbolist Movement,* 167.

42. Quoted in Gibson, *Symbolism,* 144.

43. Mallarmé, *Collected Poems,* 161–81.

44. Mallarmé, *Collected Poems,* 168.

45. Gascoyne, *A Short Survey,* 10.

46. Lautréamont, *Maldoror,* 37.

47. Rudwin, "Satanism of Huysmans."

48. Rudwin, "Satanism of Huysmans," 243.

49. Rudwin, "Satanism of Huysmans," 244.

50. Baudelaire, "Au Lecteur."

51. Huysmans, *Là-Bas,* 82.

52. Huysmans, *Là-Bas,* 83.

53. Rudwin, "Satanism of Huysmans," 242.

54. Lahelma, "The Symbolist Aesthetic," 31–47.

55. Lahelma, "The Symbolist Aesthetic," 36–37.

56. Nicole Myers, "Symbolism," *Heilbrunn Timeline of Art History,* Metropolitan Museum of Art (website), August 2007. Accessed August 28, 2022.

57. Jean Moréas, *The Manifesto of Symbolism,* 5, translated by A. S. Kline, 2019 (originally published 1886), Poetry in Translation (website). Accessed August 28, 2022.

58. Gibson, *Symbolism,* 28–31.

59. Gibson, *Symbolism,* 35.

60. Delville, *New Mission,* 45–46.

61. Delville, *New Mission,* 61.

62. Delville, *New Mission,* 69–70.

63. Cole, "Jean Delville," 138.

64. Delville, *New Mission,* 176, 177.

65. Delville, *New Mission,* 84.

66. Delville, *New Mission,* 36.

67. Gibson, *Symbolism,* 27.

3. DADA:
CUTTING TO THE CHANCE

1. Huelsenbeck, *Memoirs,* xiv.

2. Huelsenbeck, *Memoirs,* xiv.

3. Gascoyne, *A Short Survey,* 23.

4. Hugo Ball, *Dada Manifesto,* read at the first public Dada soirée, Zurich, July 14, 1916, available at Wikisource (website), last edited October 14, 2021. Accessed August 28, 2022.

5. Ball, *Dada Manifesto.*

6. Ball, *Dada Manifesto.*

7. Ball, afterword, *Flight,* 250.

8. Ball, *Flight,* 68.

9. Ball, *Flight,* 68.

10. Ball, *Flight,* 96, 99.

11. Ball, *Flight,* 104, 109.

12. Bru, "Schliesslich."

13. Huelsenbeck, "Dada Manifesto."

14. Huelsenbeck, *Memoirs,* xxxviii.

15. Ball, *Flight,* xxxv.

16. Tzara, "Manifeste Dada."

17. Tristan Tzara, "To Make a Poem," Tristan Tzara 1896–1963, Dadart.com (website). Accessed August 14, 2022.

18. Huelsenbeck, *Memoirs,* 15.

19. Arp, *Arp on Arp,* 216.

20. Arp, *Arp on Arp,* 215.

21. Karen Barber, "Hannah Höch, *Cut with the Kitchen Knife Dada through the Last Weimar Beer Belly Cultural Epoch of Germany,*" Smarthistory (website), August 18, 2020. Accessed August 28, 2022.

22. Makela and Boswell, *The Photomontages,* 25.

23. Barber, "Hannah Höch."

24. Peter Boswell, "Hannah Höch: Through the Looking Glass," in Makela and Boswell, *The Photomontages,* 8.

25. Höch, "A Few Words on Photomontage," 119.

26. Boswell, "Hannah Höch," 7–8.

27. Duchamp, "The Great Trouble with Art."

28. Burnham, "Bride Stripped Bare," part 1, 28.

29. Burnham, "Bride Stripped Bare," part 2, 44.

30. Duchamp, "Great Trouble with Art."

31. Duchamp, "Great Trouble with Art."

32. Duchamp, "Great Trouble with Art."

33. Gascoyne, *A Short Survey,* 28.

34. Choucha, *Surrealism,* 44.

35. Art Institute Chicago, "Broken and Restored Multiplication." Available online at Artic.edu. Accessed January 2, 2023.

36. Camfield, *Max Ernst,* 11.

37. Buffet-Picabia, "Memories of Pre-Dada," 261.

38. Camfield, *Max Ernst,* 11.

39. Waldman, *Max Ernst,* 21.

40. Gascoyne, *A Short Survey,* 37.

41. Waldman, *Max Ernst,* 22.

42. Gascoyne, *A Short Survey,* 45.

43. Gascoyne, *A Short Survey,* 45.

4. SURREALISM:
THE AUTOMATIC SOLUTION

1. Lautréamont, *Maldoror,* 263.

2. Waldberg, *Surrealism,* 22.

3. Choucha, *Surrealism,* 52; Waldberg, *Surrealism,* 41; Warlick, *Max Ernst,* 35.

4. Waldberg, *Surrealism,* 43; Warlick, "Max Ernst's Alchemical Novel," 61.

5. Warlick, "Max Ernst's Alchemical Novel," 62.

6. Fulcanelli, *Le Mystère;* Warlick, "Max Ernst's Alchemical Novel," 62.

7. Breton, *Manifestoes,* 23–47, 178.

8. Waldberg, *Surrealism,* 27.

9. Grillot de Givry, *Le musée;* Warlick, "Max Ernst's Alchemical Novel," 62.

10. Waldberg, *Surrealism,* 44.

11. Gascoyne, *A Short Survey,* 45.

12. Warlick, *Max Ernst,* 40.

13. Aragon, "Une Vague de rêves."

14. Aragon, "Une Vague."

15. Artaud, *The Theater,* 66.

16. Aragon, "Une Vague."

17. Breton, *Manifestoes,* 32.

18. Aragon, "Une Vague."

19. Breton, "The Automatic Message," 25.

20. Choucha, *Surrealism,* 56.

21. Spare, *Automatic Drawing,* 13–15.

22. Spare, *Book of Pleasure.*

23. Spare, *Automatic Drawing,* 32.

24. Spare, *Automatic Drawing,* 33.

25. Spare, *Automatic Drawing,* 28.

26. Spare, *Automatic Drawing,* 9–10.

27. Breton, *Manifestoes,* 22–23.

28. Choucha, *Surrealism,* 52.

29. Ellenberger, *Discovery of the Unconscious,* 359–60.

30. Breton, *Manifestoes,* 23.

31. Breton, *Manifestoes,* 24–25.

32. Breton, *Manifestoes,* 26.

33. Breton, *Manifestoes,* 26–27.

34. Breton, *Manifestoes,* 27.

35. André Masson, quoted in Martin, *Essential Surrealists,* 84.

36. André Masson, quoted in Martin, *Essential Surrealists,* 86.

37. Martin, *Essential Surrealists,* 9.

38. Martin, *Essential Surrealists,* 124.

39. Martin, *Essential Surrealists,* 126.

40. Choucha, *Surrealism,* 58.

41. Camfield, *Max Ernst,* 33.

42. Ernst, *Beyond Painting,* 21.

43. Ernst, *Beyond Painting,* 22–23.

44. Breton, "The Automatic Message," 27–30.

45. Breton, "Surrealism and Painting," 84.

46. Breton, "Surrealism and Painting," 85.

47. Waldberg, *Surrealism,* 7.

48. Dalí, "Conquest of the Irrational," 92.

49. Choucha, *Surrealism,* 91.

50. Breton, "The Automatic Message," 32.

51. Breton, *Manifestoes,* 39–40.

52. Breton, *Manifestoes,* 31–32.

53. Breton, *Manifestoes,* 181.

54. Breton, *Manifestoes,* 203.

55. Breton, *Manifestoes,* 300–301.

56. Éluard, "Beyond Painting," 89.

57. Artaud, "Letter to the Buddhist Schools."

58. Jung, *Memories,* 150.

59. Balakian, *Surrealism,* 130–33.

60. Breton, *Manifestoes,* 241.

61. Breton, *Manifestoes,* 11.

62. Breton, *Manifestoes,* 12, 13.

63. Breton, *Manifestoes,* 186.

64. Choucha, *Surrealism,* 2–3.

65. Breton, "The Automatic Message," 26.

66. Breton, *Manifestoes,* 10.

67. Breton, *Manifestoes,* ix.

68. Breton, *Manifestoes,* 14.

69. Breton, *Manifestoes,* 123–24.

70. Breton, *Manifestoes,* 174–75.

71. Breton, *Manifestoes,* 40.

72. Artaud, *The Theater,* 49.

73. Artaud, *The Theater,* 49.

74. Breton, *Manifestoes,* 9

75. Breton, *Manifestoes,* 49–109.

76. Breton, Manifestoes, 49–109.

77. Breton, Manifestoes, 49–109.

78. Warlick, *Max Ernst,* 43–44.

79. Ernst, *Une Semaine de Bonté.*

80. Ernst, *Une Semaine.*

81. Warlick, "Max Ernst's Alchemical Novel," 64–71.

82. Waldman, *Max Ernst,* 16; Camfield, *Max Ernst,* 33.

83. Ernst, "Beyond Painting," 99; Choucha, *Surrealism,* 114.

84. Ernst, *The Hundred Headless Woman.*

85. Moorhead, *The Surreal Life,* 161.

86. Choucha, *Surrealism,* 116; Moorhead, *The Surreal Life,* 162.

87. Moorhead, *The Surreal Life,* 42–50.

88. Moorhead, *The Surreal Life,* 39.
89. Carrington, "Down Below."
90. Carrington, "Down Below," 72.
91. Carrington, "Down Below," 81.
92. Carrington, "Down Below," 74–84.
93. Lepetit, *Esoteric Secrets,* 232–33.
94. Dalí, *The Unspeakable Confessions of Salvador Dalí,* 150, 162–63.
95. Dalí, *The Unspeakable,* 166.
96. Dalí, *The Unspeakable,* 162.
97. Dalí, *The Unspeakable,* 164.
98. Breton, *Manifestoes,* 14.
99. Breton, *Manifestoes,* 186–87.
100. Warlick, *Max Ernst,* 72.

5. CREATIVE ALCHEMY:
ESSENTIALS OF THE GREAT WORK

1. Balakian, *The Symbolist Movement,* 16.
2. Delville, *New Mission,* xxxiii.
3. Nicolas Flamel, *The Summary of Philosophy,* transcribed by Antonio Balestra, available online at The Alchemy Website on Levity.com. Accessed August 29, 2022.
4. Breton, "The Automatic Message," 32.
5. Cole, "Jean Delville," 138.
6. *Rosarium Philosophorum,* available online at The Alchemy Website on Levity.com.
7. *Rosarium Philosophorum,* available online at The Alchemy Website on Levity.com.
8. Morienus, *Book of Morienus.*
9. Jung, *Aion,* 162.
10. Delville, *New Mission,* 66.
11. Taylor, *The Mystical Hymns of Orpheus;* Greer and Warnock, *The Illustrated Picatrix.*
12. *Rosarium Philosophorum,* available online at The Alchemy Website on Levity.com.
13. Mead, *Thrice-Greatest Hermes,* 3:11–12 (excerpt by Stobaeus 1.16–17).
14. Delacroix, *Journal,* 27.
15. Schuré, *The Great Initiates,* 139.
16. Valentinus, "The 'Practica,' with Twelve Keys," 316.

6. *NIGREDO*: PUTREFACTION AND THE GENERATION OF THE IDEA

1. *Rosarium Philosophorum,* available online at The Alchemy Website on Levity.com.

2. Jung, *Aion,* 8.

3. Jung, *Memories,* 335.

4. Ernst, *Une Semaine.*

5. Sanchuniathon et al., *Phoenician History,* 1–2; West, *Orphic Poems,* 178.

6. Silberer, *Hidden Symbolism,* 7.

7. Silberer, *Hidden Symbolism,* 98.

8. Fabricius, *Alchemy,* 24.

9. Smith, *Alchemical Book of Lambspring,* 17.

10. Hesiod, *Theogony,* 9.

11. Lawrence, *Birds, Beasts, & Flowers,* 12.

12. Breton, *Manifestoes,* 49–109.

13. Sendivogius, "New Chemical Light," 105–6.

14. Valentinus, "The 'Practica,' with Twelve Keys," 331.

15. Huelsenbeck, *Memoirs,* xxxi.

16. Silberer, *Hidden Symbolism,* 123.

17. Ball, *Flight,* 29.

18. Mallarmé, *Collected Poems,* 175.

19. Silberer, *Hidden Symbolism,* 310.

20. Percy Shelley, *Complete Poetical Works,* 21.

21. Morienus, *Book of Morienus.*

22. Valentinus, "The 'Practica,' with Twelve Keys," 341–42.

23. Atchity, *Classical Greek Reader,* 113.

24. Mead, *Apollonius,* 149–50.

25. Plato, *Phaedo,* 17.

26. Plato, *Phaedo,* 8, 31.

27. Breton, *Manifestoes,* 32.

28. Atchity, *Classical Greek Reader,* 116.

29. Krishnamurti, *Freedom from the Known,* available online at Holybooks .com. Accessed August 29, 2022.

30. Lévi, *Dogma et Rituel,* 1:4.

31. Swedenborg, *Secrets of Heaven,* 2:408.

32. Swedenborg, *Secrets of Heaven,* 2:16.

33. Jung, *Mysterium Coniunctionis,* xv.

34. Jung, *Mysterium Coniunctionis,* xvii.

35. Silberer, *Hidden Symbolism,* 26–27.

36. Jung, *Mysterium Coniunctionis,* 9.

37. Delacroix, *Journal,* 34–35.

38. Mallarmé, *Collected Poems,* 170–71.

39. Vaughan, *Coelum Terrae.*

40. Panofsky, *Albrecht Dürer,* 157.

41. Liddell and Scott, *Greek-English Lexicon,* s.v., "μέλας;" "χολή."

42. Panofsky, *Albrecht Dürer,* 158.

43. Panofsky, *Albrecht Dürer,* 166.

44. Pinkus, *Alchemical Mercury,* 142–43.

45. Panofsky, *Albrecht Dürer,* 168–69.

46. Agrippa, *Three Books,* chapter 60.

47. Mary Shelley, *Frankenstein.*

48. Kaske & Clark, *Introduction,* 19–22.

49. Panofsky, *Albrecht Dürer,* 165; Kristeller, *The Philosophy,* 212.

50. Aristotle, *Problemata* 30.1.953–55.

51. Aristotle, *Problemata* 30.1.953–54.

52. Aristotle, *Problemata* 30.1.955.

53. Ficino, *Three Books,* 115.

54. Ficino, *Three Books,* 115.

55. Ficino, *Three Books,* 115.

56. Panofsky, *Albrecht Dürer,* 165.

57. Ficino, *Letters,* 1:40.

58. Delacroix, *Journal,* 29.

59. Valentinus, "The 'Practica,' with Twelve Keys," 344.

60. Cirlot, *Symbols,* 278.

61. Cirlot, *Symbols,* 278–79.

62. Panofsky, *Albrecht Dürer,* 164.

63. Panofsky, *Albrecht Dürer,* 164.

64. Panofsky, *Albrecht Dürer,* 157.

65. Nerval, *Selected Writings,* 268.

66. Jung, *On Psychological and Visionary Art,* 55.

67. Mallasz, *Talking with Angels,* 36.

68. Mallasz, *Talking with Angels,* 36.

69. Nerval, *Selected Writings,* 363.

70. Ficino, *Letters,* 42.

71. Ficino, *Letters,* 43.

72. Chevalier and Gheerbrandt, *Symbols,* 528–29.

73. *Rosarium Philosophorum,* available online at The Alchemy Website on Levity.com.

74. Lewis and Short, *Latin Dictionary,* s.v. "Ops."

75. Valentinus, "The 'Practica,' with Twelve Keys," 355.

76. Vaughan, *Coelum Terrae.*
77. Hermes Trismegistus, "The Emerald Tablet of Hermes," available at Sacred-Texts (website), accessed August 27, 2022.
78. Muraven and Baumeister, "Self-Regulation."
79. Muraven and Baumeister, "Self-Regulation," 254–55.
80. Delacroix, *Journal,* 28.
81. Breton, *Manifestoes,* 32.

7. *ALBEDO:* PURIFICATION AND THE LUNAR STONE

1. Ficino, "Liber de Arte."
2. Breton, *Manifestoes,* 49–109.
3. von Franz, *Alchemy,* 220–21.
4. Ernst, *Une Semaine.*
5. Warlick, "Alchemical Novel," 66.
6. Mallarmé, *Collected Poems,* 113–19.
7. Silberer, *Hidden Symbolism,* 98.
8. Carrington, "Down Below," 70–72.
9. Mallarmé, *Collected Poems,* 161–81.
10. Mary Shelley, *Frankenstein,* 141–42.
11. *Rosarium Philosophorum,* available online at The Alchemy Website on Levity.com.
12. *Rosarium Philosophorum,* available online at The Alchemy Website on Levity.com.
13. Nerval, *Selected Writings,* 269.
14. Rimbaud, *Complete Works,* 102.
15. Nerval, *Selected Writings,* 270.
16. von Franz, *Corpus Alchemicum,* 149.
17. Nerval, *Selected Writings,* 273.
18. Carrington, "Down Below," 74.
19. Nerval, *Selected Writings,* 274.
20. Jung, *Psychological and Visionary Art,* 68.
21. Nerval, *Selected Writings,* 285–86.
22. Rimbaud, *Complete Works,* 100.
23. Nerval, *Selected Writings,* 286.
24. Nerval, *Selected Writings,* 290.
25. Jung, *Psychological and Visionary Art,* 78.
26. Nerval, *Selected Writings,* 316.
27. Twitchell, "Romanticism."

28. Miller, *Big Sur,* 29.

29. Jodorowsky, *Psychomagic,* 79.

30. Hartmann, *Life of Phillipus,* 135–36.

31. Johnson, *Inner Work,* 43–134.

32. Johnson, *Inner Work,* 43–134.

33. von Franz and Boa, *Way of the Dream,* 43–47.

34. Holmyard and Russell, *The Works of Geber,* 96.

35. Hermes Trismegistus, "The Emerald Tablet of Hermes," available at Sacred-Texts (website), accessed August 27, 2022.

36. Mallarmé, *Divigations,* 264.

37. Spare, *Automatic Drawing,* 10.

38. Ball, *Flight,* 76.

39. Douglas Harper, Online Etymology Dictionary, s.v. "Sublimation," available at Etymonline.com (website).

40. Ashmole, *Theatrum Chemicum Britannicum,* 171–73.

41. Atchity, *Classical Greek Reader,* 113.

42. Hermes Trismegistus, "The Emerald Tablet of Hermes," available at Sacred-Texts (website), accessed August 27, 2022.

43. Jung, *Symbols,* 125.

44. Jung, *Symbols,* 128–30.

45. Jung, *Symbols,* 130.

46. Jung, *Dreams,* 100.

47. Jung, *Memories,* 335.

48. von Franz, *Corpus Alchemicum,* 106.

49. Arp, *Arp on Arp,* 216.

50. Dalí, *50 Secrets,* 68.

51. Ball, *Flight,* 49.

8. *CITRINITAS:* SOLAR INSPIRATION AND INTEGRATION

1. Breton, *Manifestoes,* 49–109.

2. Anonymous, *Meditations,* 391.

3. Anonymous, *Meditations,* 389.

4. Johnson, *Inner Work,* 65–86.

5. Waite, *Hermetic Museum,* 1:193.

6. *Rosarium Philosophorum,* available online at The Alchemy Website on Levity.com.

7. Waite, *Hermetic Museum,* 1:193.

8. Maier, *Atalanta,* Discourse 37.

9. Cooper, *Traditional Symbols,* 98.

10. *Rosarium Philosophorum,* available online at The Alchemy Website on Levity.com.

11. *Rosarium Philosophorum,* available online at The Alchemy Website on Levity.com.

12. von Franz, *Corpus Alchemicum,* 61.

13. von Franz, *Corpus Alchemicum,* 64.

14. Maier, *Atalanta,* Emblem 6.

15. von Franz, *Corpus Alchemicum,* 65–66.

16. Kelly, "The Stone."

17. Fabricius, *Alchemy,* 140, 143.

18. Fabricius, *Alchemy,* 143.

19. Waite, *Hermetic Museum,* 1:232.

20. Hannah, *The Animus,* 59–96.

21. Hannah, *The Animus,* 18.

22. Waite, *Hermetic Museum,* 2:168–69.

23. Hannah, *The Animus,* 64.

24. Hannah, *The Animus,* 64.

25. Jung, *Mysterium Coniunctionis,* 160–61.

26. Hannah, *The Animus,* 79.

27. Jung, *Mysterium Coniunctionis,* 162.

28. Hannah, *The Animus,* 9.

29. Chevalier and Gheerbrandt, *Symbols,* 898.

30. Hannah, *The Animus,* 65–66.

31. Waite, *Hermetic Museum,* 2:169.

32. Waite, *Hermetic Museum,* 2:169.

33. Waite, *Hermetic Museum,* 2:172–74.

34. Waite, *Hermetic Museum,* 2:168–69.

35. Waite, *Hermetic Museum,* 2:173.

36. Hannah, *The Animus,* 17.

37. Waite, *Hermetic Museum,* 2:173.

38. Hannah, *The Animus,* 69.

39. Leloup, *Gospel of Mary,* 27.

40. Waite, *Hermetic Museum,* 2:173.

41. Rimbaud, *Complete Works,* 102.

42. Jung, *Mysterium Coniunctionis,* 495–96.

43. Johnson, *Inner Work,* 25.

44. von Franz, "On Active Imagination."

45. Johnson, *Inner Work,* 181.

46. Jung, *Mysterium Coniunctionis,* 496.

47. Johnson, *Inner Work,* 161–62.

48. Johnson, *Inner Work,* 196–99.

49. Stratford, *Dictionary,* 20.

50. Stratford, *Dictionary,* 21.

51. Waite, *Writings of Paracelsus,* 1:154.

52. Mallarmé, *Collected Poems,* 119–21.

53. Crowley, *Book of Thoth,* 78–79.

54. Arrien, *Tarot Handbook,* 41–42.

55. Holmyard and Russell, *Works of Geber,* 114.

56. Rulandus, *Lexicon,* s.v. "Margarita," and Chevalier and Gheerbrandt, *Symbols,* 289.

57. Rulandus, *Lexicon,* s.v. "Prima Materia," 10.

58. Rulandus, *Lexicon.*

59. Chevalier and Gheerbrandt, *Symbols,* 290.

60. Kelly, "The Stone."

61. *Rosarium Philosophorum,* available online at The Alchemy Website on Levity.com.

9. *RUBEDO:* THE ROYAL MARRIAGE AND THE PHILOSOPHER'S STONE

1. Coleridge, *Biographia,* 78.

2. Huelsenbeck, *Memoirs,* xxxii.

3. Breton, *Manifestoes,* 49–109.

4. Jodorowsky, *Psychomagic,* 192.

5. Rulandus, *Lexicon.*

6. Maier, *Atalanta,* Discourse 7.

7. Maier, *Atalanta,* Discourse 7.

8. Smith, *Alchemical Book of Lambspring,* 24–25.

9. Bardon, *Initiation,* 27–28.

10. Jung, *Mysterium Coniunctionis,* 17.

11. Artaud, *The Theater,* 52.

12. Jung, *Memories,* 335–36.

13. Nerval, *Selected Writings,* 9.

14. Dalí, *The Secret Life,* 173.

15. Valentinus, "The 'Practica,' with Twelve Keys," 351–52.

16. Jung, *Mysterium Coniunctionis,* 82.

17. Maier, *Atalanta,* Epigram 10.

18. Jung, *Mysterium Coniunctionis,* 17.

19. Jung, *Aion,* 169.

20. Crowley, *777*, 76.

21. *Rosarium Philosophorum,* available online at The Alchemy Website on Levity.com.

22. Sendivogius, "New Chemical Light," 113.

23. Maier, *Atalanta,* Discourse 29.

24. Bartlett, *Real Alchemy,* 157–67.

25. Wordsworth, *The Poems,* 472.

26. Wordsworth, *The Poems,* 472–73.

27. Warlick, *Max Ernst,* 89.

28. *Rosarium Philosophorum,* available online at The Alchemy Website on Levity.com.

29. Miller, *The Colossus,* 206–7.

30. Smith, *Alchemical Book of Lambspring,* 25.

31. *Rosarium Philosophorum,* available online at The Alchemy Website on Levity.com.

32. Paracelsus, "Philosophical Cannons."

33. *Rosarium Philosophorum,* available online at The Alchemy Website on Levity.com.

34. *Rosarium Philosophorum,* available online at The Alchemy Website on Levity.com.

35. Fabricius, *Alchemy,* 120.

36. Hesse, *Magister Ludi,* 68–69.

37. *Rosarium Philosophorum,* available online at The Alchemy Website on Levity.com.

38. Valentinus, "The 'Practica,' with Twelve Keys," 348–49.

39. Ernst, *Une Semaine.*

40. Silberer, *Hidden Symbolism,* 103.

41. Silberer, *Hidden Symbolism,* 12–13.

42. Rulandus, *Lexicon,* s.v. "Materia Prima et Hujus Vocabula."

43. Silberer, *Hidden Symbolism,* 126.

44. Cirlot, *Symbols,* 158.

45. Delville, *New Mission,* 132.

46. Delville, *New Mission,* 65.

47. Apollinaire, "New Spirit," 234–35.

48. Waite, *Hermetic Museum,* 2:197.

49. Ernst, *Une Semaine.*

50. Warlick, "Alchemical Novel," 71.

51. Jung, *Mysterium Coniunctionis,* 167.

52. McLean, "Commentary."

53. Waite, *Writings of Paracelsus,* 1:38.

54. Jung, *Mysterium Coniunctionis,* 539.

55. Jodorowsky, *Psychomagic,* 192.

56. Jung, *Mysterium Coniunctionis,* 534.

57. Rulandus, *Lexicon,* s.v. "Elixir."

58. Warlick, *Max Ernst,* 50–53; Silberer, *Hidden Symbolism,* 99.

59. Silberer, *Hidden Symbolism,* 99.

60. Hartmann, *Life of Phillipus,* 141.

61. Hartmann, *Life of Phillipus,* 30, 140.

62. Hartmann, *Life of Phillipus,* 140–41.

63. Sendivogius, "New Chemical Light," 88.

64. Sendivogius, "New Chemical Light," 142.

65. Smith, *Alchemical Book of Lambspring,* 10.

66. Maier, *Atalanta,* Emblem 46.

67. Hermes Trismegistus, "The Emerald Tablet of Hermes," available at Sacred-Texts (website), accessed August 27, 2022.

68. Lévi, *Dogma et Rituel,* 1:6.

69. Hartmann, *Life of Phillipus,* 138.

70. Lévi, *Dogma et Rituel,* 1:24.

71. Hermes Trismegistus, "The Emerald Tablet of Hermes," available at Sacred-Texts (website), accessed August 27, 2022.

72. Lévi, *Dogma et Rituel,* 1:19.

73. Pagel, *Paracelsus,* 120.

74. Waite, *Writings of Paracelsus,* 2:308.

75. Lévi, *Dogma et Rituel,* 1:29.

76. Lévi, *Dogma et Rituel,* 1:29–30.

77. Waite, *Writings of Paracelsus,* 2:355–56.

78. Waite, *Writings of Paracelsus,* 2:289.

79. Hartmann, *Life of Phillipus,* 82–83.

80. Hartmann, *Life of Phillipus,* 82–83.

81. Waite, *Writings of Paracelsus,* 1:161.

82. Hartmann, *Life of Phillipus,* 82–83.

83. Waite, *Writings of Paracelsus,* 1:161.

84. Mead, *Apollonius,* 88.

85. Hartmann, *Life of Phillipus,* 143.

86. Hartmann, *Life of Phillipus,* 140–41.

87. Hartmann, *Life of Phillipus,* 137.

88. Goddard, *Feeling.*

89. Goddard, *Feeling.*

90. Goddard, *Feeling.*

91. Hartmann, *Life of Phillipus,* 140–41.

92. Meyer, "Gospel of Thomas," 145.
93. Mead, *Thrice Greatest Hermes,* 2:130.
94. Blake, *Complete Poetry and Prose,* 39.
95. Mead, "Chaldæan Oracles," 2:50.
96. Keats, *Complete Poetical Works,* 60.
97. Keats, *Complete Poetical Works,* 60.
98. Silberer, *Hidden Symbolism,* 98.
99. *Rosarium Philosophorum,* available online at The Alchemy Website on Levity.com.
100. Mead, *Thrice-Greatest Hermes,* 2:223.
101. Goddard, "Feeling."
102. Wordsworth, *The Poems,* 160.
103. Goddard, *Feeling.*
104. Keats, *Complete Poetical Works,* 55.
105. Goddard, *Feeling.*
106. Waite, *Writings of Paracelsus,* 2:307.
107. *Rosarium Philosophorum,* available online at The Alchemy Website on Levity.com.

Bibliography

Agrippa, Henry Cornelius. *Three Books of Occult Philosophy.* Translated by J. F. London: R. W. for Gregory Moule, 1651. Available at Internet Archive (website) at Archive.org.

Anonymous. *Meditations on the Tarot.* Translated by Robert Powell. New York: Tarcher/Penguin, 1985.

Apollinaire, Guillaume. "The New Spirit and the Poets." In *Selected Writings of Guillaume Apollinaire,* translated and edited by Roger Shattuck, 227–37. New York: New Directions, 1971.

Aragon, Louis. "Une Vague de rêves." *Commerce,* 1924. Translated as "A Wave of Dreams," by Adam Cornford, Surrealism-Plays (website). Accessed August 28, 2022.

Aristotle. *The Works of Aristotle.* Vol. 7, *Problemata.* Translated and edited by E. S. Forster and W. D. Ross. Oxford: Clarendon Press, 1927. Available at Internet Archive (website) at Archive.org.

Arp, Jean. *Arp on Arp: Poems, Essays, Memories.* Edited by Marcel Jean and translated by Joachim Neugroschel. New York: Viking Press, 1972.

Arrien, Angeles. *The Tarot Handbook: Practical Applications of Ancient Visual Symbols.* New York: Jeremy P. Tarcher/Putnam, 1997.

Artaud, Antonin. "Letter to the Buddhist Schools." *La Révolution Surréaliste,* no. 3 (1925). Reprinted in Waldberg, *Surrealism,* 60.

———. *The Theater and Its Double.* Translated by Mary Caroline Richards. New York: Grove Press, 1958.

Ashmole, Elias. *Theatrum Chemicum Britannicum: Containing Several Poeticall Pieces of our Famous English Philosophers, who have written the Hermetique Mysteries in their owne Ancient Language.* Seattle, Wash.: Ouroboros Press, 2011.

Atchity, Kenneth, ed. *The Classical Greek Reader.* New York: Oxford University Press, 1996.

Balakian, Anna. *Surrealism: The Road to the Absolute.* New York: Dutton, 1970.

———. *The Symbolist Movement: A Critical Appraisal.* New York: New York University Press, 1977.

Ball, Hugo. *Flight Out of Time: A Dada Diary (Die Flucht aus der Zeit).* Edited by John Elderfield and translated by Ann Raimes. Berkeley: University of California Press, 1996.

Bardon, Franz. *Initiation into Hermetics: The Path of the True Adept.* Salt Lake City, Utah: Merkur, 2009. Originally published in Germany, 1956.

Bargh, John A., and Ezequiel Morsella. "The Unconscious Mind." *Perspectives on Psychological Science* 3, no. 1 (2008): 73–79.

Bartlett, Robert Allen. *Real Alchemy: A Primer of Practical Alchemy.* Lake Worth, Fla.: Ibis Press, 2009.

Baudelaire, Charles. "Alchimie de la douleur." Translation in *Flowers of Evil,* by William Aggeler, The Flowers of Evil, Fresno, CA: Academy Library Guild, 1954. Available at fleursdumal.org (website).

———. "Au Lecteur." Translation in *Flowers of Evil,* by Jacques LeClercq. Mount Vernon, N.Y.: Peter Pauper Press, 1958.

———. *Baudelaire: His Prose and Poetry.* Edited by Thomas Robert Smith. New York: Boni and Liveright, 1919. Available online as Project Gutenberg ebook. Accessed August 29, 2022.

———. "Correspondances." Translation in *Flowers of Evil,* by Wallace Fowlie, New York: Dover Publications, 1964. Available at fleursdumal.org (website).

———. *The Flowers of Evil.* Translated by Cyril Scott. London: E. Mathews, 1909. Available at Internet Archive (website) at Archive.org.

———. *The Mirror of Art: Critical Studies by Charles Baudelaire.* Edited and translated by Jonathan Mayne. Garden City, N.Y.: Doubleday, 1956. Available at Internet Archive (website) at Archive.org.

Blake, William. *The Complete Poetry and Prose of William Blake.* Rev. ed. Edited by David V. Erdman. New York: Anchor Books, 1988.

———. *The Portable Blake.* Edited by Alfred Kazin. New York: Viking Press, 1946.

Bremner, Marlene Seven. *Hermetic Philosophy and Creative Alchemy: The Emerald Tablet, the Corpus Hermeticum, and the Journey through the Seven Spheres.* Rochester, Vt.: Inner Traditions, 2022.

Breton, André. "The Automatic Message." Translated by Antony Melville. In *The Automatic Message, The Magnetic Fields, The Immaculate Conception,* by André Breton, Paul Eluard, and Philippe Soupault. London: Atlas Press, 1997.

———. *Manifestoes of Surrealism.* Translated by Richard Seaver and Helen R. Lane. Ann Arbor: University of Michigan Press, 1972.

———. "Surrealism and Painting." In Waldberg, *Surrealism*, 81–88. Originally published in *Le Surréalisme et la Peinture,* Paris, 1927.

Bru, Sascha. "Schliesslich . . . Don't Forget. Richard Huelsenbeck, Cultural Memory, and the Genericity of (Dada) Historiography." *Revue belge de Philologie et d'Histoire* 83, no. 4 (2005): 1319–31. Available online at Persee.fr. Accessed August 28, 2022.

Buffet-Picabia, Gabrielle. "Some Memories of Pre-Dada: Picabia and Duchamp (1949)." In *The Dada Painters and Poets: An Anthology,* 2nd ed., edited by Robert Motherwell, 253–67. Cambridge, Mass.: Belknap Press of Harvard University Press, 1979.

Burnham, Jack. "Duchamp's Bride Stripped Bare: The Meaning of the Large Glass." Pts.1 and 2. *Art Magazine,* March 1972, 28–32; April 1972, 41–45.

Camfield, William A. *Max Ernst: Dada and the Dawn of Surrealism.* Munich, Germany: Prestel-Verlag, 1993.

Carrington, Leonora. "Down Below." *VVV* 4 (February 1944): 70–86. Beinecke Rare Book and Manuscript Library, Yale University, New Haven, Conn.

Chevalier, Jean, and Alain Gheerbrant. *The Penguin Dictionary of Symbols.* Translated by John Buchanan-Brown. London: Penguin, 1994.

Chisholm, A. R. "Mallarmé and the Act of Creation." *L'Esprit Créateur* 1, no. 3 (1961): 111–16.

———. *Mallarmé's Grand Œuvre.* Manchester, UK: University Press, 1962.

Choucha, Nadia. *Surrealism and the Occult: Shamanism, Magic, Alchemy, and the Birth of an Artistic Movement.* Rochester, Vt.: Destiny Books, 1991.

Cirlot, J. E. *A Dictionary of Symbols.* 2nd ed. Translated by Jack Sage. London: Routledge & Kegan, 1971.

Cole, Brendan. "Jean Delville and the Belgian Avant-Garde." In *Symbolism, Its Origins and Its Consequences,* edited by Rosina Neginsky, 129–46. Newcastle upon Tyne, UK: Cambridge Scholars Publishing, 2010.

Coleridge, Samuel Taylor. *Biographia Literaria; Or, Biographical Sketches of my Literary Life and Opinions.* New York: Leavitt, Lord & Co., 1834. Available at Internet Archive (website) at Archive.org. Accessed October 17, 2022.

Cooper, J. C. *An Illustrated Encyclopaedia of Traditional Symbols.* London: Thames and Hudson, 1978.

Copenhaver, Brian P. *Hermetica: The Greek Corpus Hermeticum and the Latin Asclepius in a New English Translation with Notes and Introduction.* Cambridge, UK: Cambridge University Press, 1992.

Cotnoir, Brian. *The Weiser Concise Guide to Alchemy.* Edited by James Wasserman. San Francisco: Red Wheel/Weiser, 2006.

Crowley, Aleister. *777 and Other Qabalistic Writings of Aleister Crowley*. Edited by Israel Regardie. San Francisco: Weiser Books, 1912.

———. *The Book of Thoth: A Short Essay on the Tarot of the Egyptians*. Boston: Weiser Books, 1986.

Dalí, Salvador. *50 Secrets of Magic Craftsmanship*. Translated by Haakon M. Chevalier. New York: Dover Publications, 1992.

———. "Conquest of the Irrational." In Waldberg, *Surrealism*, 91–92.

———. *The Secret Life of Salvador Dalí*. Translated by Haakon M. Chevalier. New York: Dial Press, 1942.

———. *The Unspeakable Confessions of Salvador Dalí, as told to André Parinaud*. Translated by Harold J. Salemson. London: Quartet Books, 1977.

Delacroix, Eugene. *The Journal of Eugene Delacroix*. 3rd ed. Edited by Hubert Wellington and translated by Lucy Norton. London: Phaidon Press, 1995.

Delville, Jean. *The New Mission of Art: A Study of Idealism in Art*. Translated by Francis Colmer. London: F. Griffiths, 1910. Available at Internet Archive (website) at Archive.org.

Duchamp, Marcel. "The Great Trouble with Art," an Interview with James Johnson Sweeney. *Bulletin of the Museum of Modern Art* 13, no. 4–5 (1946): 19–21.

Ellenberger, Henri Frédéric. *The Discovery of the Unconscious: The History and Evolution of Dynamic Psychiatry*. New York: Basic Books, 1970.

Éluard, Paul. "Beyond Painting." In Waldberg, *Surrealism,* 89–90.

Ernst, Max. "Beyond Painting (*Au delà de la peinture*)." In Max Ernst et al., *Beyond Painting*. Washington, D.C.: Solar Books, 2009. First published in *Max Ernst: Oeuvres de 1919 à 1936, Cahiers d'Art,* Special Ernst Issue, 1937.

———. *The Hundred Headless Woman (La Femme 100 Têtes)*. Translated by Dorothea Tanning. New York: George Braziller, 1981.

———. *Une Semaine de Bonté: A Surrealistic Novel in Collage*. New York: Dover Publications, 1976. Originally published 1933–1934 in 5 volumes by Éditions Jeanne Bucher, Paris. Available online at MOMA.org as "Max Ernst: Une Semaine de bonté ou les sept éléments capitaux (A Week of Kindness or the Seven Deadly Elements)."

Fabricius, Johannes. *Alchemy: The Medieval Alchemists and Their Royal Art*. London: Diamond Books, 1994.

Ficino, Marsilio. *The Letters of Marsilio Ficino*. Vol. 1. Translated by members of the Language Department of the School of Economic Science, London. London: Shepheard-Walwyn, 1975. Available at Internet Archive (website) at Archive.org. Accessed August 29, 2022.

———. "Liber de Arte Chemica." Transcribed by Justin von Budjoss. In *Theatrum*

Chemicum. Vol. 2, pp. 172–83. Geneva, 1702. Item 7, MS Sloane 3638, British Library. Available online at Levity.com. Accessed August 29, 2022.

———. *Three Books on Life: A Critical Edition and Translation with Introduction and Notes by Carol V. Kaske and John R. Clark.* Tempe, Arizona: Medieval & Renaissance Texts & Studies in conjunction with The Renaissance Society of America, 1998. Available at Internet Archive (website) at Archive.org. Accessed October 15, 2022.

Freud, Sigmund. "Mourning and Melancholia." In *Collected Papers,* vol. 4, translated by Joan Riviere, 152–70. New York: Basic Books, 1959. Available at Internet Archive (website) at Archive.org.

Fulcanelli. *Le Mystère des Cathédrales: Esoteric Interpretation of the Hermetic Symbols of the Great Work.* Translated by Mary Sworder. Albuquerque, N.Mex.: Brotherhood of Life, 1984.

Gascoyne, David. *A Short Survey of Surrealism.* San Francisco: City Light Books, 1935.

Gibson, Michael. *Symbolism.* Köln, Germany: Taschen, 1995.

Goddard, Neville. *Feeling Is the Secret.* Los Angeles: G. & J. Publishing, 1944. In *Neville Goddard Workbooks,* available online at Internet Archive at Archive.org.

———. "Order: Then Wait." Lecture, April 16, 1970. Available at online at ainWorld.com.

Goodrick-Clarke, Nicholas. *The Western Esoteric Traditions: A Historical Introduction.* New York: Oxford University Press, 2008.

Greer, John Michael, and Christopher Warnock, trans. *The Illustrated Picatrix.* Morrisville, N.C.: Lulu, 2015.

Grillot de Givry, Émile-Jules E. A. *Le musée des sorciers, mages et alchimistes.* Paris: Librairie de France, 1929.

Hanegraaff, Wouter J. "Romanticism and the Esoteric Connection." In *Gnosis and Hermeticism from Antiquity to Modern Times,* edited by Roelof van den Broek and Wouter J. Hanegraaff, 237–68. Albany: State University of New York Press, 1998.

Hannah, Barbara. *The Animus: The Spirit of Inner Truth in Women.* Vol. 1. Wilmette, Ill.: Chiron Publications, 2011.

Hartmann, Franz. *The Life of Philippus Theophrastus Bombast of Hohenheim Known by the Name of Paracelsus and the Substance of His Teachings.* 2nd ed. London: Kegan Paul, Trench, Trubner, 1896. Available at Internet Archive (website) at Archive.org. Accessed August 27, 2022.

Hesiod. *Theogony and Works and Days.* Translated by M. L. West. Oxford: Oxford University Press, 1988.

Hesse, Hermann. *Magister Ludi (The Glass Bead Game).* Translated by Richard and Clara Winston. New York: Bantam Books, 1970.

Höch, Hannah. "A Few Words on Photomontage." 1934. In *Photomontage Between the Wars (1918–1939)*, 118–19. Ottawa, Canada: Carleton University Art Gallery, 2012. Exhibition catalog.

Holmyard, E. J., and Richard Russell, eds. *The Works of Geber*. London: J. M. Dent and Sons, 1928. Reprint by Kessinger Publishing, 2010.

Honour, Hugh. *Romanticism*. New York: Westview Press, 1979.

Huelsenbeck, Richard. "Dada Manifesto." In *German Expressionism, Documents from the End of the Wilhelmine Empire to the Rise of National Socialism*, edited and translated by Rose-Carol Washton Long, 267–69. Berkeley: University of California Press, 1993.

———. *Memoirs of a Dada Drummer*. Edited by Hans J. Kleinschmidt and translated by Joachim Neugroschel. New York: Viking Press, 1974.

Huysmans, Joris-Karl. *Against Nature*. Translated by Robert Baldick. Baltimore, M.D: Penguin Books, 1959. Originally published in 1884 as *À Rebours*.

———. *Là-Bas*. Translated by Keene Wallace. New York: Dover Publications, 1972.

Jodorowsky, Alejandro. *Psychomagic: The Transformative Power of Shamanic Psychotherapy*. Translated by Rachael LeValley. Rochester, Vt.: Inner Traditions, 2010.

Johnson, Robert A. *Inner Work: Using Dreams and Active Imagination for Personal Growth*. New York: HarperOne, 1989.

Jung, Carl Gustav. *Aion: Researches into the Phenomenology of the Self*. 2nd ed. Bollingen Series. Translated by R. F. C. Hull. Princeton, N.J.: Princeton University Press, 1969.

———. "Confrontation with the Unconscious." In *Memories, Dreams, Reflections*, 170–99.

———. *Dreams*. Bollingen Series. Translated by R. F. C. Hull. Princeton, N.J.: Princeton University Press, 1974.

———. *Memories, Dreams, Reflections*. New York: Vintage Books, 1989.

———. *Mysterium Coniunctionis: An Inquiry into the Separation and Synthesis of Psychic Opposites in Alchemy*. 2nd ed. Bollingen Series. Princeton, N.J.: Princeton University Press, 1977.

———. *On Psychological and Visionary Art: Notes from C. G. Jung's Lecture on Gérard de Nerval's Aurélia*. Edited by Craig E. Stephenson. Princeton, N.J.: Princeton University Press, 2015.

———. *Psychology and Alchemy*. 2nd ed. Bollingen Series. Princeton, N.J.: Princeton University Press, 1968.

———. *Symbols of Transformation*. 2nd ed. Bollingen Series. Translated by R. F. C. Hull. Princeton, N.J.: Princeton University Press, 1967.

Kaske, Carol V., and John R. Clark. *Introduction* to *Three Books on Life* by

Marsilio Ficino, 3–90. Tempe, Ariz.: Medieval & Renaissance Texts & Studies In conjunction with The Renaissance Society of America, 1998. Available at Internet Archive (website) at Archive.org. Accessed October 15, 2022.

Keats, John. *The Complete Poetical Works and Letters of John Keats.* Boston: Houghton, Mifflin, 1899.

Kelly, Edward. "The Stone of the Philosophers." In *Tractatus duo egregii, de Lapide Philosophorum, una cum Theatro astronomi terrestri, cum Figuris, in gratiam filiorum Hermetis nunc primum in lucem editi, curante J. L.M.C.* [Johanne Lange Medicin Candidato]. Hamburg, 1676. A version transcribed by L. Roberts is available online at The Alchemy Website at Levity. com. Accessed August 29, 2022.

Kristeller, Paul Oskar. *The Philosophy of Marsilio Ficino.* Translated by Virginia Conant. Gloucester, Mass.: Peter Smith, 1964.

Lahelma, Marja. "The Symbolist Aesthetic and the Impact of Occult and Esoteric Ideologies on Modern Art." *Approaching Religion* 8, no. 1 (April 2018): 31–47.

Lao Tzu. *Tao Te Ching.* Translated by D. C. Lao. New York: Penguin Books, 1963.

Lautréamont, Comte de. *Maldoror: Les Chants de Maldoror.* Translated by Guy Wernham. New York: New Directions, 1965.

Lawrence, D. H. *Birds, Beasts, & Flowers.* Jaffrey, N.H.: Black Sparrow Books, 2008.

Leloup, Jean-Yves. *The Gospel of Mary Magdalene.* Rochester, Vt.: Inner Traditions, 2002.

Lepetit, Patrick. *The Esoteric Secrets of Surrealism: Origins, Magic, and Secret Societies.* Translated by Jon E. Graham. Rochester, Vt.: Inner Traditions, 2012.

Lévi, Eliphas. *Dogma et Rituel de la Haute Magie.* Vol. 1, *The Doctrine of Transcendental Magic.* Translated by Arthur Edward Waite. England: Rider, 1896. Transcribed and converted to Adobe Acrobat format by Benjamin Rowe, June 2001. Available online at Holybooks.com.

———. *Dogma et Rituel de la Haute Magie.* Vol. 2, *The Ritual of Transcendental Magic.* Translated by Arthur Edward Waite. England: Rider, 1896. Transcribed and converted to Adobe Acrobat format by Benjamin Rowe, January 2002. Available online at Holybooks.com.

Lewis, Charlton T., and Charles Short. *A Latin Dictionary.* Oxford: Clarendon Press, 1879. Available online at Perseus Digital Library.

Lewis, Clive Staples. *The Problem of Pain.* New York: MacMillan, 1947.

Liddell, Henry George, and Robert Scott. *A Greek-English Lexicon.* New York: American Book Company, 1901. Available at Internet Archive (website) at Archive.org. Accessed August 29, 2022.

Maier, Michael. *Atalanta Fugiens, or New Chymical Emblems of the Secrets of Nature*. Oppenheim, Germany: Johann Theodor de Bry, 1617. Available online at The Alchemy Website on Levity.com. Accessed October 30, 2021.

Makela, Maria, and Peter Boswell. *The Photomontages of Hannah Höch*. Minneapolis, Minn.: Walker Art Center, 1996.

Mallarmé, Stéphane. *Collected Poems and Other Verse, with Parallel French Text*. Translated by E. H. Blackmore and A. M. Blackmore. New York: Oxford University Press, 2008.

———. *Divagations*. Translated by Barbara Johnson. Cambridge, Mass.: Belknap Press of Harvard University Press, 2007.

Mallasz, Gitta. *Talking with Angels: A Document from Hungary Transcribed by Gitta Mallasz*. Translated by Robert Hinshaw and assisted by Gitta Mallasz and Lela Fischli. Einsiedeln, Switzerland: Daimon Verlag, 1998.

Martin, Tim. *Essential Surrealists*. Bath, UK: Parragon Publishing, 2000.

McLean, Adam. "A Commentary on the Rosarium Philosophorum." Originally published in the Magnum Opus Hermetic Sourceworks series, vol. 6, *The Rosary of the Philosophers*. Edinburgh, 1980. Available online at The Alchemy Website on Levity.com. Accessed August 29, 2022.

Mead, G. R. S. *Apollonius of Tyana: The Philosopher-Reformer of the First Century A.D.* New York: University Books, 1966.

———, trans. "The Chaldæan Oracles." 2 vols. In *Echoes from the Gnosis,* vol. 8. London: Theosophical Publishing Society, 1908.

———. *Thrice-Greatest Hermes: Studies in Hellenistic Philosophies and Gnosis*. 3 vols. London: Theosophical Publishing Society, 1906.

Meyer, Marvin, trans. "The Gospel of Thomas with the Greek Gospel of Thomas." In *The Nag Hammadi Scriptures,* edited by Marvin Meyer, 133–56. New York: HarperCollins, 2007.

Miller, Henry. *Big Sur and the Oranges of Hieronymus Bosch*. New York: New Directions, 1957.

———. *The Colossus of Maroussi*. New York: New Directions Paperbook, 1958. First published in 1941.

Moorhead, Joanna. *The Surreal Life of Leonora Carrington*. Great Britain: Vertigo, 2019.

Morienus. *The Book of Morienus*. Translated and edited by Lee Stavenhagen. Published as *A Testament of Alchemy*. Hanover, N.H.: University Press of New England, 1974.

Muraven, Mark, and Roy F. Baumeister. "Self-Regulation and Depletion of Limited Resources: Does Self-Control Resemble a Muscle?" *Psychological Bulletin* 126, no. 2 (2000): 247–59.

Nerval, Gérard de. *Selected Writings*. Translated by Richard Sieburth. New York: Penguin Books, 1999.

Pagel, Walter. *Paracelsus: An Introduction to Philosophical Medicine in the Era of the Renaissance*. 2nd Rev. ed. Basel, Switzerland: Karger, 1982.

Panofsky, Erwin. *The Life and Art of Albrecht Dürer*. Princeton, N.J.: Princeton University Press, 1955.

Paracelsus. *The Archidoxes of Magic*. Berwick, Maine: Ibis Press, 2004. Originally published London, 1656.

———. "The Philosophical Cannons of Paracelsus." Transcribed by Adam McLean from the seventeenth-century MS Sloane 3506, folio 37–41, British Library. Available online at the Alchemy Website on Levity.com. Accessed August 29, 2022.

Pinkus, Karen. *Alchemical Mercury: A Theory of Ambivalence*. Stanford, Calif.: Stanford University Press, 2010.

Plato. *Plato's Phaedo*. Translated by F. J. Church. New York: Liberal Arts Press, 1951.

Raymond, Marcel. *From Baudelaire to Surrealism (Du Baudelaire au Surrealisme)*. Translated from the French. London: Methuen, 1970.

Rimbaud, Arthur. *Complete Works*. Translated by Paul Schmidt. New York: Harper & Row, 1975.

Rudwin, Maximillian J. "The Satanism of Huysmans." *Open Court: A Monthly Magazine* 34, no.4 (1920): 240–51.

Rulandus, Martin. *A Lexicon of Alchemy*. Translated by A. E. Waite. London: John M. Watkins, 1964.

Russell, Bertrand. *A History of Western Philosophy*. New York: Touchstone, 2007.

Sanchuniathon, Eusebius of Caesarea, Eratosthenes, and Philo of Byblos. *Sanchoniatho's Phoenician History: Translated from the first book of Eusebius De praeparatione evangelica*. Translated by Richard Cumberland. London: W. B. for R. Wilkin, 1720. Available at Library of Congress (website). Accessed August 29, 2022.

Schuré, Edward. *The Great Initiates: A Study of the Secret History of Religions*. (1889). Translated by Gloria Rasberry. N.p.: Rudolf Steiner Publications, 1961.

Sendivogius, Michael. "The New Chemical Light." In Waite, *The Hermetic Museum,* vol. 2, 79–158. Available at Sacred-Texts (website). Accessed October 13, 2021.

Shelley, Mary Wollstonecraft. *Frankenstein: Or the Modern Prometheus*. London: George Routledge and Sons, 1888. Available at Internet Archive (website) at Archive.org.

Shelley, Percy Bysshe. *The Complete Poetical Works of Percy Bysshe Shelley*. Edited by Thomas Hutchinson. London: Humphrey Milford, Oxford University Press, 1914. Available at Internet Archive (website) at Archive.org.

Silberer, Herbert. *Hidden Symbolism of Alchemy and the Occult Arts*. Translated by Smith Ely Jelliffe. New York: Dover Publications, 1971. Published in 1917 as *Problems of Mysticism and Its Symbolism* by Moffat, Yard (New York).

Smith, Patrick J., trans. *The Alchemical Book of Lambspring Concerning the Philosopher's Stone*. Sequim, Wash.: Holmes Publishing Group, 2007.

Spare, Austin Osman. *The Book of Automatic Drawing*. Facsimile ed. N.p.: I-H-O Books, 2005.

———. *The Book of Pleasure (Self-Love): The Psychology of Ecstasy*. London: Printed by the author, 1909–1913. Available at Internet Archive (website) at Archive.org.

Stephenson, Craig E. "Introduction." In Jung, *On Psychological and Visionary Art: Notes from C. G. Jung's Lecture on Gérard de Nerval's Aurélia*, 1–48.

Stratford, Jordan. *A Dictionary of Western Alchemy*. Wheaton, Ill.: Theosophical Publishing House, 2011.

Swedenborg, Emanuel. *Heaven and Its Wonders and Hell: From Things Heard and Seen*. Translated by John C. Ager. West Chester, Pa.: Swedenborg Foundation, 2009. Available at Swedenborg.com. Accessed August 28, 2022.

———. *Secrets of Heaven: The Portable New Century Edition*. Vol. 1. Translated by Lisa Hyatt Cooper. Westchester, Pa.: Swedenborg Foundation, 2010. Available at Swedenborg.com. Accessed August 28, 2022.

———. *Secrets of Heaven: The Portable New Century Edition*. Vol. 2. Translated by Lisa Hyatt Cooper. Westchester, Pa.: Swedenborg Foundation, 2012.

Taylor, Thomas, trans. *The Mystical Hymns of Orpheus*. London: Bertram Dobell, 1896.

Twitchell, James B. "Romanticism and Cosmic Consciousness." *Centennial Review* 19, no. 4 (1975): 287–307.

Tzara, Tristan. "Manifeste Dada." *Dada* 3 (December 1918). English translation of the University of Pennsylvania is available on SmartHistory (website). Accessed August 28, 2022.

Valentinus, Basilius. "The 'Practica,' with Twelve Keys, and an Appendix Thereto, Concerning the Great Stone of the Ancient Sages." In Waite, *The Hermetic Museum, Restored and Enlarged*, vol. 1, 312–57. Available at sacred-texts.com (website).

Vaughan, Thomas [Eugenius Philalethes, pseud.]. *Coelum Terrae, Or the Magician's Heavenly Chaos*. Originally published as *Magia Adamica: Or the antiquitie of magic, and the descent thereof from Adam downwards, proved. Whereunto is added a . . . full discoverie of the true coelum terræ . . . By*

Eugenius Philalethes. London: T. W. for H. B, 1650. Available online at Levity.com (based on A. E. Waite translation). Accessed August 29, 2022.

———. *Lumen de Lumine: Or a New Magicall Light Discovered, and Communicated to the World*. London: Printed for H. Blunden, 1651. Available online at the WellcomeCollection.org. Accessed August 29, 2022.

Verlaine, Paul. *Selected Poems in Translation*. Translated by A. S. Kline. London: Poetry in Translation, 2010.

von Franz, Marie-Louise. *Alchemical Active Imagination*. Rev. ed. Boston: Shambhala, 1997.

———. *Alchemy: An Introduction to the Symbolism and the Psychology*. Toronto: Inner City Books, 1980.

———. *Corpus Alchemicum Arabicum: Book of the Explanation of the Symbols, Kitāb, Ḥall ar-Rumūz, by Muḥammad ibn Umail*. Edited by Theodor Abt. Zurich: Living Human Heritage Publications, 2006.

———. "On Active Imagination." In *Methods of Treatment in Analytical Psychology,* edited by Ian F. Baker, 88–89. Stuttgart: Verlag Adolf Bonz, 1980.

von Franz, Marie-Louise, and Fraser Boa. *The Way of the Dream*. Toronto: Fraser Boa, 1988.

Waite, Arthur Edward, ed. *The Hermetic and Alchemical Writings of Paracelsus*. 2 vols. Mansfield Center, Conn.: Martino, 2009.

———, trans. *The Hermetic Museum, Restored and Enlarged*. 2 vols. London: J. Elliot, 1893. Available at Sacred-Texts (website). Accessed August 29, 2022.

———. *The Holy Kabbalah: A study of the secret tradition in Israel as unfolded by sons of the doctrine for the benefit and consolation of the elect dispersed through the lands and ages of the greater exile*. Secaucus, N.J.: University Books, 1960. Available at Internet Archive (website) at Archive.org.

Waldberg, Patrick. *Surrealism*. London: Thames and Hudson, 1997.

Waldman, Diane, ed. *Max Ernst: A Retrospective*. New York: Solomon R. Guggenheim Foundation, 1975.

Warlick, M. E. *Max Ernst and Alchemy: A Magician in Search of Myth*. Austin: University of Texas Press, 2001.

———. "Max Ernst's Alchemical Novel: *Une Semaine de bonté.*" *Art Journal* 46, no. 1 (1987): 61–73.

West, M. L. *The Orphic Poems*. Oxford: Oxford University Press, 1983.

Wilson, Edmund. *Axel's Castle: A Study in the Imaginative Literature of 1870–1930*. New York: Charles Scribner's Sons, 1959. Originally published 1931. Available at Internet Archive (website) at Archive.org. Accessed August 28, 2022.

Wordsworth, William. *The Poems of William Wordsworth*. London: Edward Moxon, 1858. Available at Internet Archive (website) at Archive.org. Accessed August 28, 2022.

Index

Phœnix